MW00529225

Birds
of the Greater South West

SIMON J NEVILL

Birds of the Greater South West

Simon Nevill Publications
Published by Simon Nevill Publications, Perth, Western Australia
Email: snpub@bigpond.net.au

ISBN 978-0-9803481-2-5

Cover photograph: Red-winged Fairy-wren
Above photograph: Crested Shrike-tit
Back cover photograph: Southern Boobook

CONTENTS

INTRODUCTION

The book attempts to cover the needs of both those beginning birdwatching and those who have a more extensive knowledge of birding. In the first section the emphasis is on assisting the novice birdwatcher with general background information on birds. The main section contains photographs of most land and shore birds seen in this region and should assist both the novice and the advanced birdwatcher.

The area covered by this publication extends from Carnarvon in the north across to Kalgoorlie and Esperance in the south east of Western Australia. In vegetation terms, the true South West is a region known as the 'South West Botanical Province'; within this region lies one of the richest flora areas in the world. It certainly is not the richest birding area in the world or in fact in Australia, however some fascinating species occur in the Greater South West including fourteen species endemic to Western Australia. There are also several near endemic species and many subspecies.

The guidebook takes us past the South West Botanical Province into what is known as the 'Mulga Region', part of a far greater botanical area botanists refer to as the 'Eremaean Province' which covers most of the semi-arid and arid regions of Australia. By doing so, it includes many species not found in the South West, including some mangrove species.

Pelagic birds have not been included as many are rare or vagrant to the south west seas and most people rarely see them unless venturing out past the south west ocean shelf. Pelagic birding is a very specialised hobby, requiring intense skills in identifying the many similar species that occur on the high seas such as the petrels, shearwaters and albatrosses.

Numerous birding books have been published throughout the world, no more so than in Australia. However, the objective of this book is to give more local detailed information pertaining to those species that can be found in the Greater South West Region and where to find them. Photographs have been used rather than paintings to illustrate the birds. There are advantages to both forms of presentation. Photographs are simply what one sees, the true bird as seen by the observer in its natural environment. The majority of photographs were taken by the author and only a few show birds near the nest. There are several reasons for this but the primary one is that too much disturbance at the site may attract predators and jeopardise the survival of the young and, if there are eggs, disturbance will certainly increase the chance of the adult birds deserting the nest.

The author has not only attempted to write in a direct factual manner but also to add a slight personal aspect to the guidebook, hopefully to add some interest to the reader as much of the information is founded on nearly forty years of birding in Australia.

Birdwatching is a very rewarding hobby that requires little capital expenditure unless you are one of those who choose to travel the world looking for new species to add to your world list. Here in Western Australia, we are blessed with some wonderful parks and reserves that contain a great variety of bird species; it's a wonderful hobby and whether you're a visitor or just simply enjoy observing the beauty of birds and nature in general, hopefully this publication will be of some use to you.

THE GREATER SOUTH WEST REGION

Choosing the geographic parameters for this book has been an arbitrary decision not based on the limits of a type of vegetation but rather to assist people living in the more highly populated parts of Western Australia and help them find birds in their region.

The map on page 8 is schematic only and does not totally adhere to formal vegetation maps. It is based on the general terms used within the text that describe where a bird can be found; for example, it may say that a species is common in the 'Wheatbelt Region' and yet that region contains a variety of vegetation types including Mallee Woodland, Kwongan Heath, Salmon Gum Woodland and Salt Lake systems. However, the general areas shown on the map do bear some relationship with the fundamental vegetation zones of this state.

The term 'Greater South West' (abbreviated from here on as GSW) has been used loosely to describe an area that extends well past the South West Region and into the semi-arid and arid regions of Western Australia, from Carnarvon in the north to Esperance in the south east. It supports populations of many birds that do not occur or rarely occur in the South West Region.

The term 'South West Region' is used extensively in the book and describes the area that generally receives a higher rainfall than areas outside its limit. It is described as an area within the confines of the Greater South West primarily due to the fact that many bird species only occur in this region, either as sedentary birds or as birds that mainly migrate to it during the spring and summer months.

The major habitat or regional zones shown on the maps within the Greater South West Region

The Swan Coastal Plain: Describes the lands that run as a lateral belt from just north of Perth to the Busselton area in the south and are flanked by the Indian Ocean on the west and the Darling Range on the east. It consists primarily of limestone and alluvial sands with many permanent wetlands being important area for waterbirds.

The Jarrah Forest: Describes the dominant eucalypt that grows on laterite soils mainly on the Darling Range, although in vegetation terms it should truly be classed as the Jarrah-Marri Forest with Marri the equally dominant eucalypt. It is not rich in bird species but nevertheless is a very important forest belt that contains the highest numbers of certain species found in the state.

Karri-Tingle Forest: Describes the forest area of the tall Karri and Tingle trees combined with a dense understorey of acacia and Karri Sheoak.

The Southern Coastal Belt: Describes all lands within ten to thirty kilometres of the southern coast and is a region that not only has many seabirds and shore birds but is also home to some of our rarest passerines that occur in the coastal heaths and wetter vegetation gullies. The area loosely described covers a narrow belt from Cape Naturaliste in the west to Cape Arid in the east.

The Wheatbelt Region: Describes lands within the farming region. Although much of the natural vegetation has been cleared, the region supports a higher number of bird species than the thick Jarrah Forest. The whole area is interspersed with fragmented remnant reserves; some are extremely flora species rich and accordingly have a greater variety of birds. Within this region there are several macro habitat types including granite outcrops, salt lakes and samphire systems, breakaway country, Mallee Woodland, Salmon Gum Woodland and Kwongan Heath.

Transitional Eucalypt Woodland: Describes the eucalypt belt that is the natural transition zone between the cleared lands of the Wheatbelt and the semi-arid lands of the Mulga Region. It contains many species of eucalypt, particularly between Hyden and Norseman and in the Kalgoorlie region. It supports many species of birds that no longer exist in those areas of the Wheatbelt that have been cleared. It is also an important area for the nesting sites of several members of the parrot family.

The Mulga Region: Describes a vast region that extends well past the area covered in this publication. Its primary vegetation type is the acacia family, which is the largest plant genus in Australia with well over two thousand plant species. One of the dominant acacias is Acacia aneura simply known as 'mulga', a collective term loosely applied to describe most of the acacias in the semi-arid and arid regions although the true mulga *(Acacia aneura)* only touches the coast near Carnarvon and north at Karratha. It is home to a wealth of bird species some of them very uncommon or even rare.

Maps on the following pages are a guide only and official maps should referred to for travel, and more concise detail.

THE GREATER SOUTH WEST REGION

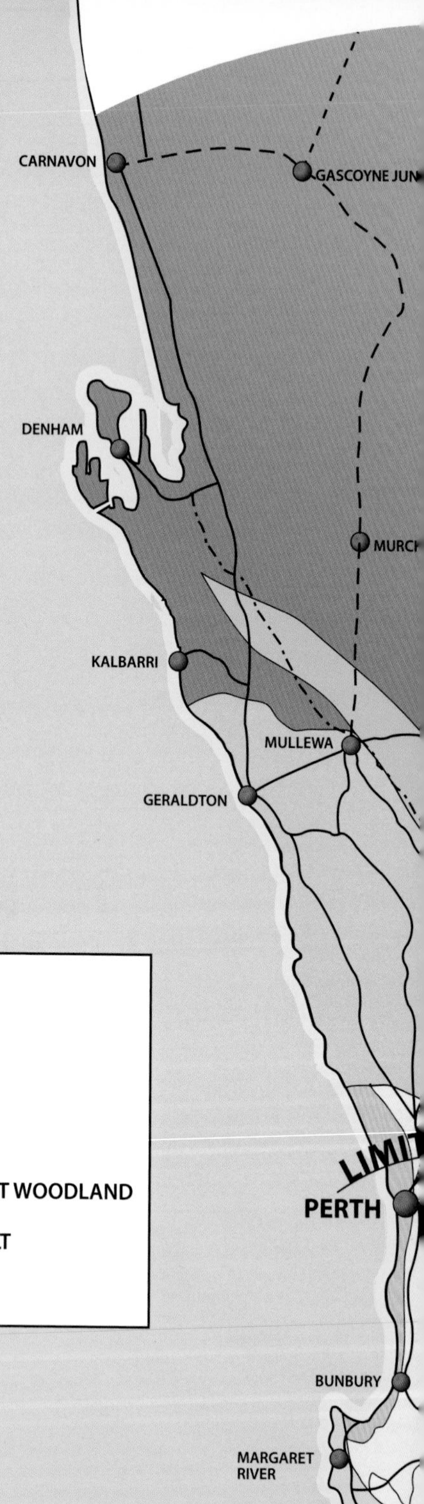

- KARRI-TINGLE FOREST
- JARRAH FOREST
- SWAN COASTAL PLAIN
- WHEATBELT
- TRANSITIONAL EUCALYPT WOODLAND
- SOUTHERN COASTAL BELT
- MULGA REGION

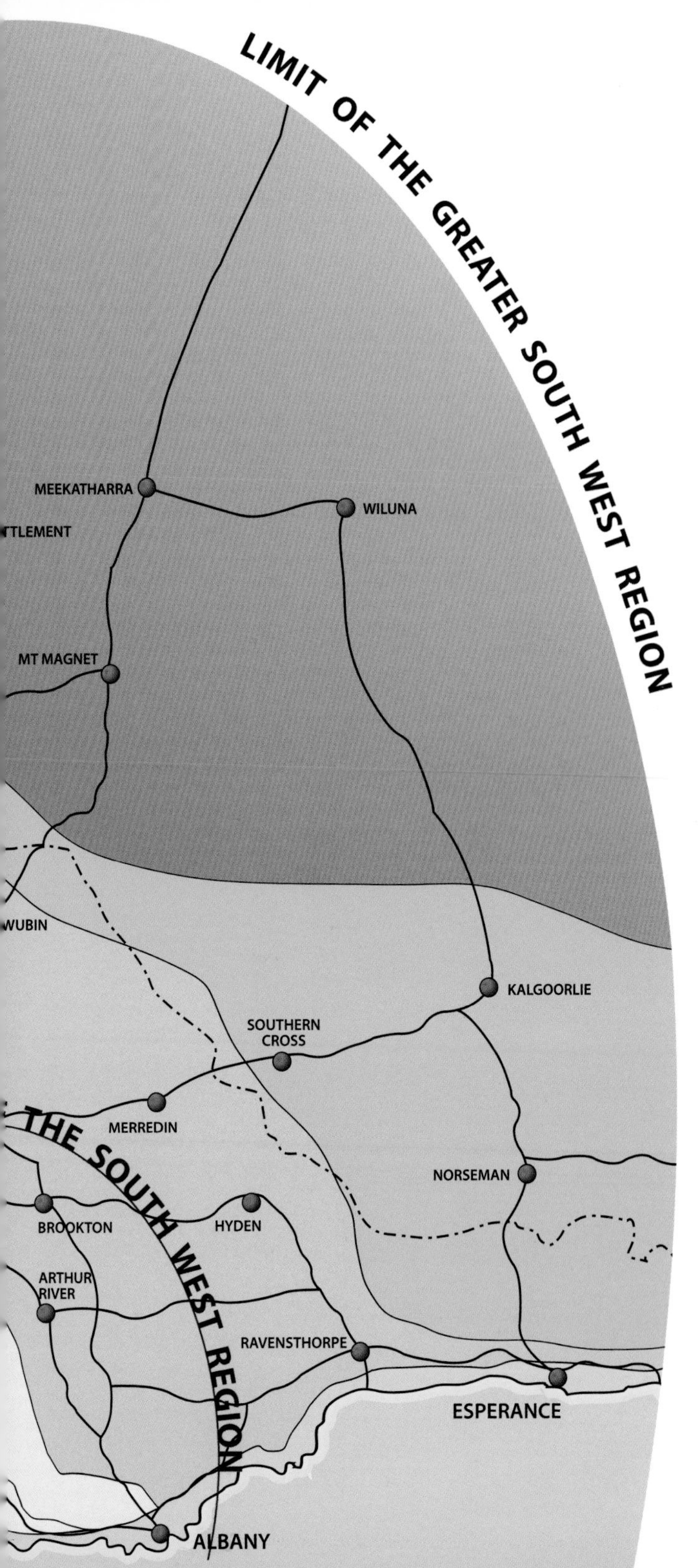
LIMIT OF THE GREATER SOUTH WEST REGION
MEEKATHARRA
WILUNA
TTLEMENT
MT MAGNET
WUBIN
KALGOORLIE
SOUTHERN CROSS
MERREDIN
THE SOUTH WEST REGION
NORSEMAN
BROOKTON
HYDEN
ARTHUR RIVER
RAVENSTHORPE
ESPERANCE
ALBANY

PERTH REGION

1. ERIC SINGLETON SANCTUARY
2. HERRISSON ISLAND
3. KINGS PARK
4. LAKE MONGER
5. HERDSMAN LAKE
6. BOLD PARK
7. FLOREAT BEACH RES.
8. LAKE GWELUP
9. BIG CARINE SWAMP RES.
10. STAR SWAMP RES.
11. WHITEMAN PARK
12. GNANGARRA
13. LAKE GOOLLELAL
14. LAKE JANDABUP
15. LAKE JOONDALUP
16. JOHN FORREST NP
17. GOOSBERRY HILL
18. KALAMUNDA NP
19. MUNDARING WEIR
20. BICKLEY BROOK
21. ELLIS BROOK
22. VICTORIA RESERVOIR
23. BUNGENDORE RES.
24. WUNGONG BROOK
25. JANDAKOT RP
26. FORRESTDALE LAKE
27. THOMSONS LAKE
28. KOGALUP LAKE
29. YANGEBUP LAKE
30. BIBRA LAKE
31. MANNING LAKE
32. WOODMANS POINT
33. NORTH MOLE
34. BOORAGOON LAKE
35. BLUE GUM LAKE
36. ALFRED COVE
37. POINT WALTER
38. ROTTNEST ISLAND

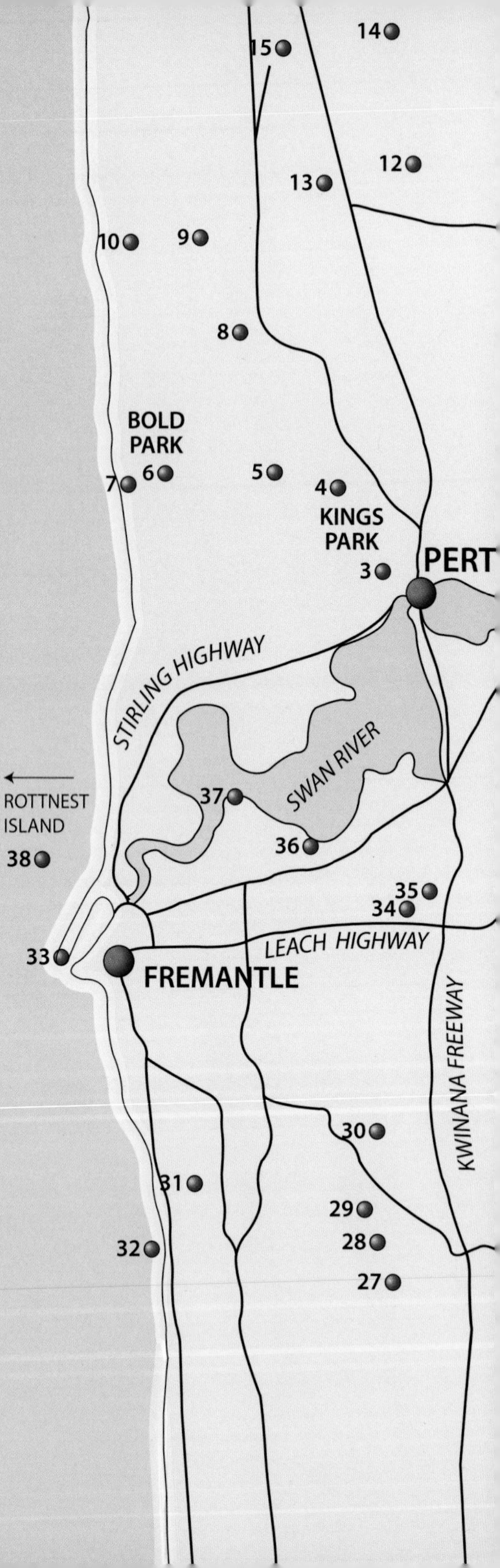

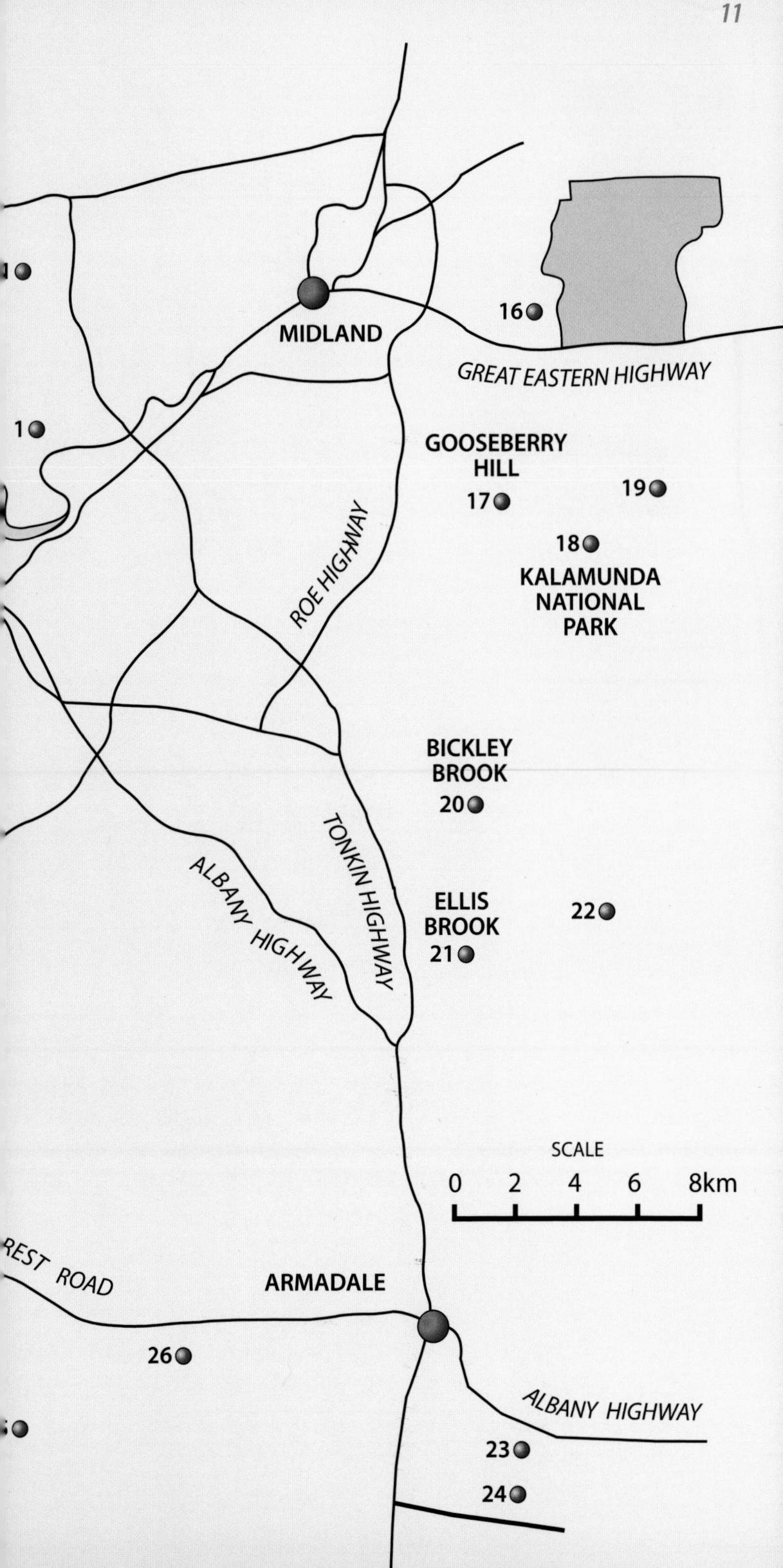
MIDLAND
16
GREAT EASTERN HIGHWAY
1
GOOSEBERRY
HILL
17
19
18
KALAMUNDA
NATIONAL
PARK
ROE HIGHWAY
BICKLEY
BROOK
20
TONKIN HIGHWAY
ALBANY HIGHWAY
ELLIS
BROOK
21
22
SCALE
0 2 4 6 8km
REST ROAD
ARMADALE
26
ALBANY HIGHWAY
23
24

SOUTH WEST REGION

1. BOYAGIN ROCK NR
2. DRYANDRA WOODLAND NR
3. TUTANNING NR
4. DONGOLOCKING NR
5. TARIN ROCK NR
6. NORTH TARIN ROCK NR
7. CORNEECUP NR
8. COYRECUP NR
9. JINGALUP NR
10. NARLINGUP NR
11. CHINOCUP NR
12. DUMBLEYUNG LAKE
13. COBLININE NR
14. TOOLIBIN NR
15. NORTH YILLIMINNING NR
16. EAST YORNANING NR
17. CORRIGIN WATER RES.
18. JILIKIN ROCK
19. BENDERING NR
20. NORTH KARLGARIN NR
21. LUPTON CON. RES.
23. BOOLANOOLING NR
24. NANGEEN NR
25. CHARLES GARDENER RES.
26. STIRLING RANGE NP
27. CAMEL LAKE NR
28. UNICUP LAKE NR
29. KULUNILUP LAKE NR
30. LAKE MUIR NR
31. PORONGURUP NP
32. TORNDIRRUP NP
33. TWO PEOPLES BAY NR
34. WAYCHINICUP NR
35. LAKE PLEASANT VIEW NR
36. WEST CAPE HOWE NP
37. WILLIAM BAY NP
38. WALPOLE-NORNALUP NP
39. MT FRANKLAND NP
40. D'ENTRECASTEAUX NP
41. SCOTT NP
42. LEEUWIN-NATURALISTE NP
43. TUART FOREST NP
44. LESCHENAULT PENINSULA CP
45. YALGORUP NP
46. LANE POOLE RES.
47. LAKE Mc CLARTY NR
48. PEEL INLET

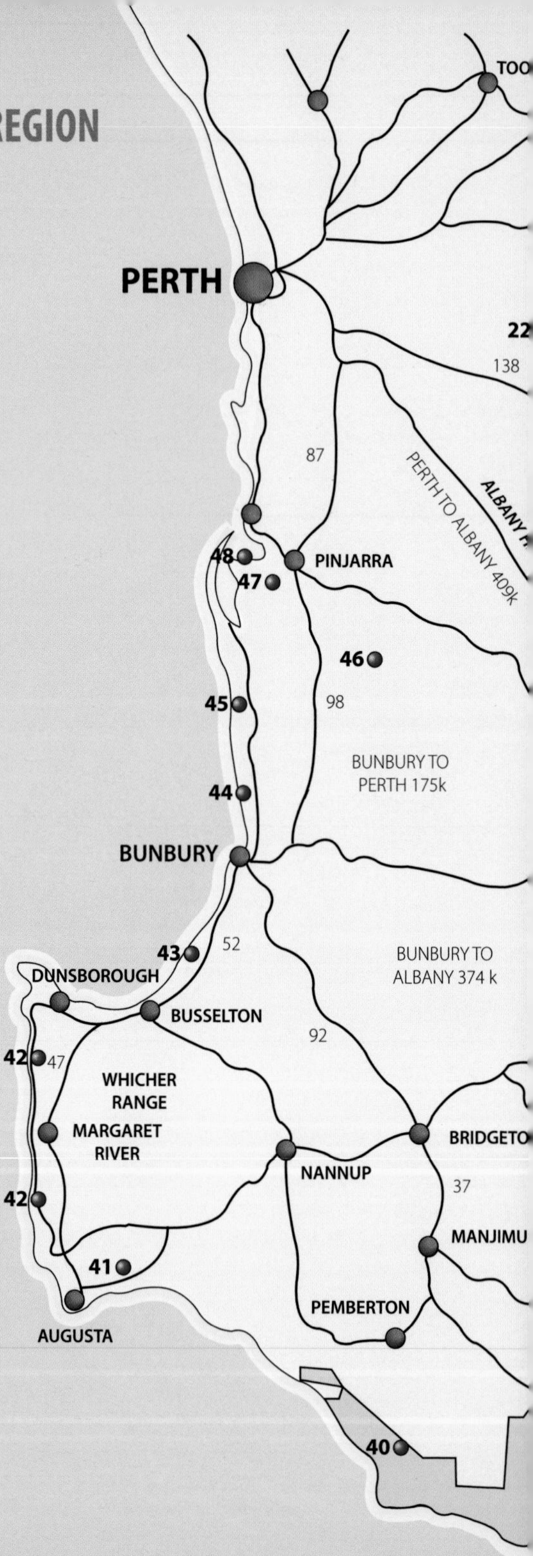

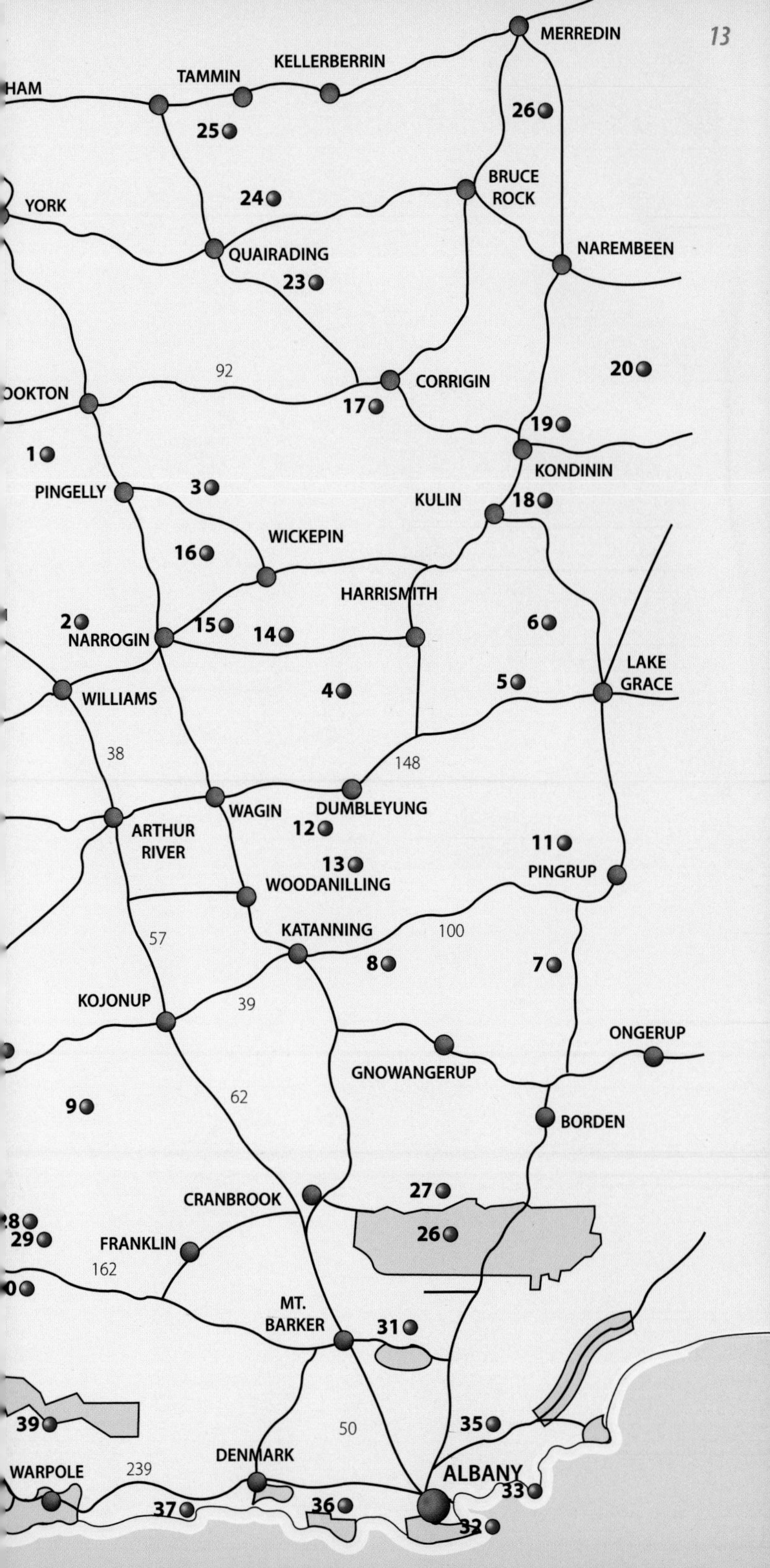

MERREDIN
HAM
TAMMIN
KELLERBERRIN
26
25
BRUCE ROCK
24
YORK
QUAIRADING
NAREMBEEN
23
20
92
OOKTON
CORRIGIN
17
19
1
KONDININ
PINGELLY
3
KULIN
18
WICKEPIN
16
HARRISMITH
2
15
14
6
NARROGIN
LAKE GRACE
5
WILLIAMS
4
38
148
WAGIN
DUMBLEYUNG
ARTHUR RIVER
12
11
13
PINGRUP
WOODANILLING
KATANNING
100
57
8
7
KOJONUP
39
ONGERUP
GNOWANGERUP
9
62
BORDEN
27
CRANBROOK
28
26
29
FRANKLIN
162
0
MT. BARKER
31
39
50
35
DENMARK
WARPOLE
239
ALBANY
33
37
36
32

PERTH ESPERANCE REGION

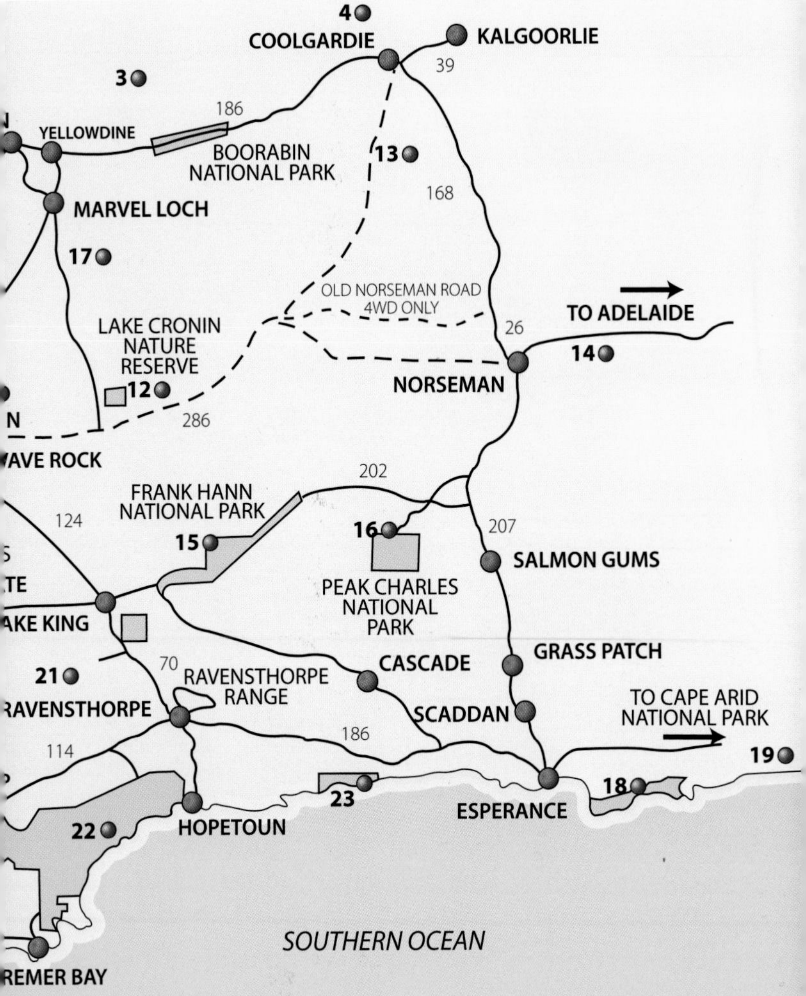

1. CHIDDARCOOPING NR
2. WALYAMONING NR
3. JAURDI NR
4. ROWLES LAGOON
5. SANDFORD ROCKS NR
6. LAKE CAMPION NR
7. DUROKOPIN NR
8. CHARLES GARDNER RES.
9. MAUGHAN NR
10. DRAGON ROCKS
11. THE HUMPS NR
12. LAKE CRONIN NR
13. VICTORIA ROCK
14. DUNDAS NR
15. FRANK HANN NR
16. PEAK CHARLES NR
17. JILBADJI NR
18. CAPE LE GRAND NP
19. CAPE ARID NP
20. LAKE MAGENTA NR
21. DUNN ROCK
22. FITZGERALD RIVER NP
23. STOKES NP
24. LAKE GOUNTER NR

NORTHERN REGION

1. BUNTINE RES.
2. JIBBERDING NR
3. WHITE WELLS NOW CHARLES DARWIN NR
4. GOODLANDS NR
5. PETRUDER ROCKS
6. EAST NUGADONG
7. L HINDS
8. MANMANNING NR
9. BOONARING NR
10. MOORE RIVER NP
11. NAMBURG NP
12. BADGINGARRA NP
13. WATHEROO NP
14. LESUEUR NP
15. HILL RIVER
16. ALEXANDER MORRISEN
17. TATHRA NP
18. COALSEAM NR
19. ELLENDALE POOL
20. WANDANA NR
21. KALBARRI NP
22. TOOLONGA NR
23. FRANCOIS PERON NP
24. DIRK HARTOG ISLAND
25. ROCKY POOL

The stations are listed as guides to localities but most do not have tourist facilities although several sheep stations have accommodation for travellers.
Check with the various tourist centres.

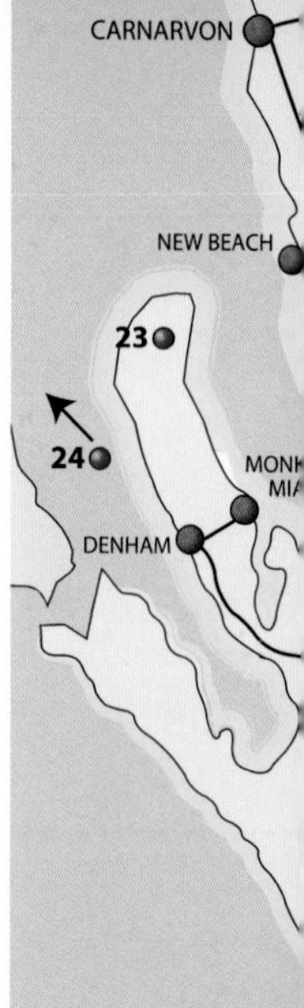

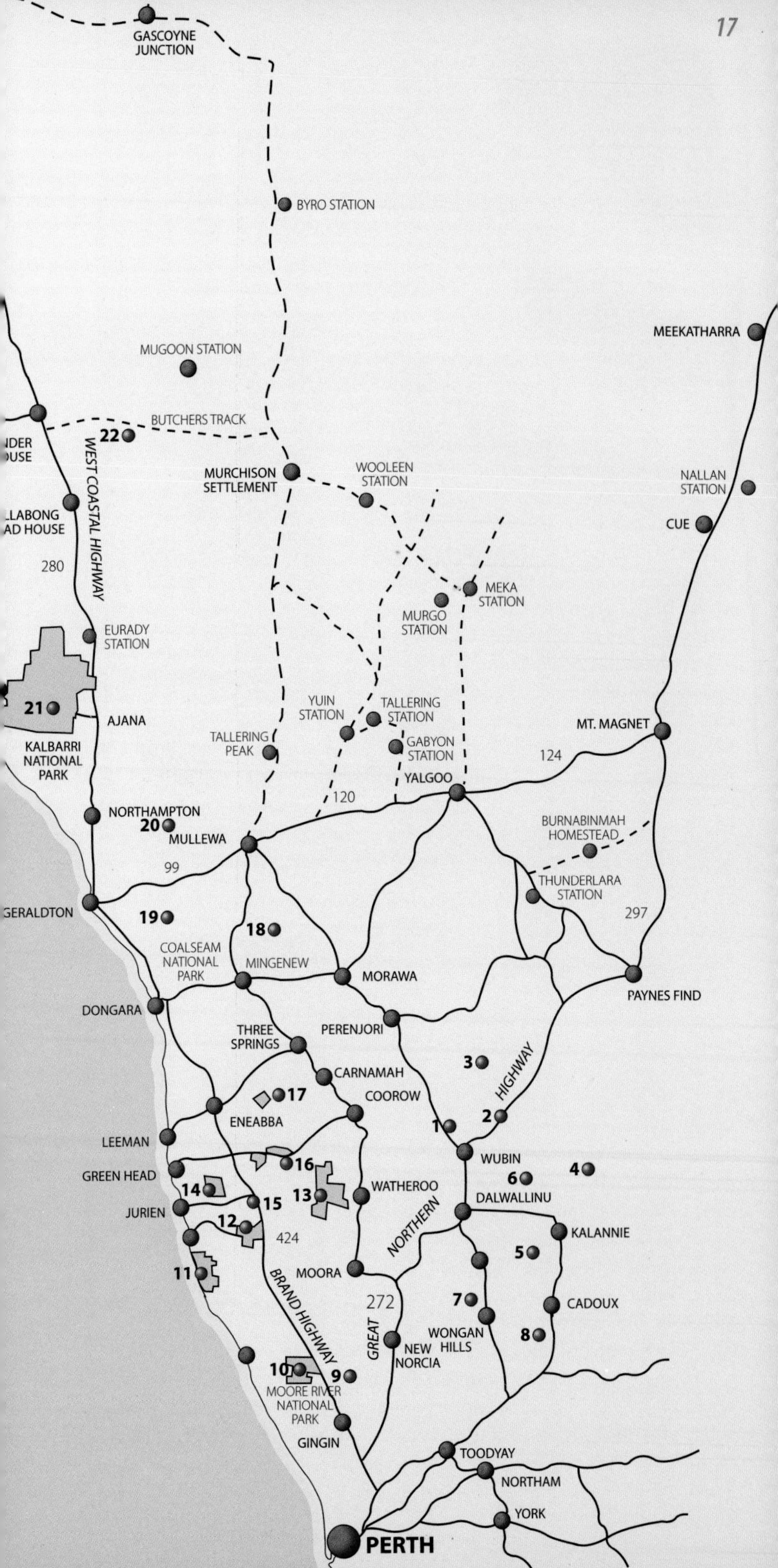

GASCOYNE JUNCTION
BYRO STATION
MEEKATHARRA
MUGOON STATION
BUTCHERS TRACK
22
NDER
OUSE
WEST COASTAL HIGHWAY
MURCHISON SETTLEMENT
WOOLEEN STATION
NALLAN STATION
LLABONG
AD HOUSE
CUE
280
MEKA STATION
MURGO STATION
EURADY STATION
YUIN STATION
TALLERING STATION
21
AJANA
MT. MAGNET
KALBARRI NATIONAL PARK
TALLERING PEAK
GABYON STATION
124
YALGOO
120
NORTHAMPTON
20
MULLEWA
BURNABINMAH HOMESTEAD
99
THUNDERLARA STATION
GERALDTON
19
18
297
COALSEAM NATIONAL PARK
MINGENEW
MORAWA
PAYNES FIND
DONGARA
THREE SPRINGS
PERENJORI
3
HIGHWAY
CARNAMAH
17
COOROW
ENEABBA
2
1
LEEMAN
WUBIN
16
4
GREEN HEAD
6
14
13
WATHEROO
15
NORTHERN
DALWALLINU
JURIEN
12
KALANNIE
424
5
11
MOORA
BRAND HIGHWAY
272
7
CADOUX
GREAT
WONGAN HILLS
8
NEW NORCIA
10
9
MOORE RIVER NATIONAL PARK
GINGIN
TOODYAY
NORTHAM
YORK
PERTH

HABITAT TYPES

Habitat types that occur in the Greater South West Region and some of the birds that can be found in them.

The type of vegetation habitat is the primary factor that influences where a certain species will reside. To aid the visitor and also the resident birdwatchers of this State, some of the species found in certain habitat areas are given below. Obviously, many of the birds listed can be sighted in a variety of habitats but those listed are typical of that habitat.

Karri Forest

In the deep South West and along part of the southern coastline lies an extensive belt of tall Karri trees (*E. diversicolor*). Right, these massive trees grows a thick understorey of Karri Hazel (*Trymaliun florabundum*) with its distinctive smell, which always reminds one of the Karri Forest.

This is one area where the two vegetation stratum have you either straining your neck to see birds in the canopy or looking through the lower bushes for ground frequenting birds.

Birds to be found: Long-billed Black Cockatoo. Western Rosella. White-breasted Robin. Red-winged Fairy-wren. Red-eared Firetail. White-naped Honeyeater. New Holland Honeyeater. Tree Martin. Splendid Fairy-wren. Scarlet Robin. White-browed Scrubwren. Rufous Treecreeper. Purple-crowned Lorikeet. Crested Shrike-tit (the uncommon western subspecie *leucogaster*). Grey Currawong. Red-tailed Black Cockatoo. Inland Thornbill. Golden Whistler. Dusky Woodswallow. Grey Fantail. Shining Bronze-Cuckoo. Fantail Cuckoo. and the majority of deep South West raptors particularly the Peregrine Falcon, Square-tailed Kite and Collared Sparrowhawk.

Jarrah Forest

Even though the Jarrah Forest is far more extensive than both the Karri Forest and Wandoo Woodland, it does not carry quite the variety of species that particularly the Wandoo Woodland holds. However it has the greatest number of Western Thornbills, not a rare bird but surprisingly missed by some visiting birdwatchers on short trips to the state.

It is also the primary habitat for the subspecies of the Red-tailed Black Cockatoo *naso* that feeds on the large Marri and smaller Jarrah fruits. The largest population of Long-billed Black Cockatoos also occurs here as well as the few Masked Owls in the deeper South West Jarrah Forest.

Birds to be found: Western Rosella. Weebill. Long-billed and Short-billed Black Cockatoo (in this region more so the Long-billed). Common Bronzewing. Varied Sittella. Australian Ringneck. Red-capped Parrot. Inland Thornbill. Western Gerygone. Grey Shrike-thrush. Splendid Fairy-wren. Western Spinebill. Scarlet Robin. Grey Butcherbird. Grey Currawong. In the northern Jarrah Forest and around the Perth region if you wish to see three of the endemics, Red-eared Firetail, White-breasted Robin and Red-winged Wren, it is best to walk along the riverine habitats that hug the streams on the Darling scarp. Be aware when looking for the Red-eared Firetail that the introduced east coast species the Red-browed Finch also occurs in a few isolated gullies adjacent to Perth.

Wandoo Woodland

Wandoo Woodland carries a greater variety of habitat within its range than most other vegetation zones and including the flora species rich Kwongan Heath.

Birds to be found in one of the few remnant Wheatbelt reserves, namely Dryandra Woodland Nature Reserve: Common Bronzewing. Brush Bronzewing. Yellow-plumed Honeyeater. White naped Honeyeater. Brown-headed Honeyeater. White-cheeked Honeyeater. New Holland Honeyeater. Tawny-crowned Honeyeater. White-eared Honeyeater and Brown Honeyeater. Western Spinebill. Splendid Fairy-wren. Western Yellow Robin. Red-capped Robin. Scarlet Robin. Golden Whistler. Rufous Whistler. Western Gerygone. Western Thornbill. Weebill. Inland Thornbill. White-browed Scrubwren. Striated Pardolote. Spotted Pardalote. Dusky Wood Swallow. Welcome Swallow. Tree Martin. Rainbow Bee-eater. Grey Shrike-thrush. Black-faced Cuckoo-shrike. Grey Currawong. Restless Flycatcher. Shining Bronze-Cuckoo. Fantail Cuckoo. Pallid Cuckoo. White-winged Triller. Sacred Kingfisher. Collared Sparrowhawk. Wedge-tailed Eagle. Little Eagle. Whistling Kite. Peregrine Falcon. Australian Hobby. Western Rosella. Australian Ringneck. Elegant Parrot. Purple-crowned Lorikeet. Short-billed Black Cockatoo. Varied Sittella. Jacky Winter. Rufous Songlark (not every season). Tawny Frogmouth. Boobook Owl. Barn Owl. Owlet Nightjar.

Birds for listers: Blue-breasted Fairy-wren. Hooded Robin (getting scarce here). Crested Shrike-tit. Mallee Fowl. Bush Stone-curlew. Short-billed Black Cockatoo. Regent Parrot. Square-tailed Kite. Painted Button-quail. The author has seen Black Honeyeater several times (rare in the south-west Wheatbelt), Horsfield's Bronze Cuckoo. Sadly the last remaining Crested Bellbird has now gone. This list is obviously not a complete list for Dryandra

Mallee Woodland

A vegetation type that stretches from the west just east of the Stirling Range as a narrow band along the southern coast to the southern edge of much of the Nullarbor and across to eastern Australia. Mallee can sometimes be very extensive as illustrated. Much of the Mallee belt has been cleared to make way for the Wheatbelt farms and only remnant patches remain. It is well known that this is the prime habitat for Mallee Fowl, which still survive in several inner Wheatbelt reserves.

Birds to be found in the southern Mallee: Spotted Pardalote (Yellow-rumped form *xanthopygus*). Shy Heathwren. Spotted Nightjar. Painted Button-quail. Mallee Fowl. Purple-gaped Honeyeater. White-eared Honeyeater. Common Bronzewing. Brush Bronzewing. Blue-breasted Wren. Striated Pardalote. Southern Scrub-robin. Blue-breasted Wren. Yellow-rumped Thornbill. White-browed Babbler.

South West beaches

Many wonderful beaches border this vast coastline of Western Australia. The remoter beaches are by far the best locations to see the less common species as human disturbance certainly affects the number of bird species one can see.

Birds to be found: Besides the common species like Silver Gull. Pacific Gull. Crested Tern. Red-capped Plover. Pied Oystercatcher, less common species occur, namely Hooded Plover. Rock Parrot. White-bellied Sea Eagle. Sanderling. Sooty Oystercatcher. Fairy Tern. Off shore; Australian Gannet. Yellow-nosed Albatross. Black-browed Albatross. Occasionally Shy Albatross and Wandering Albatross. Wedge-tailed Shearwater (mostly on the west coast). Fleshy-footed Shearwater (common off the south coast, less so off the west). Occasionally Short-tailed Shearwater and Great-winged Petrel. If you wish to find Rock Parrots don't just walk along the beach but climb up over the sand dunes as they often feed in the swales of the sand dunes on the fruits and seeds of the salt tolerant succulent plants.

Coastal Heath

The flora rich belt of heath that abuts the coastal belt of the Greater South West Region.

Birds to be found: In the habitat shown here at Waychinicup, three uncommon birds occur: Noisy Scrub-bird. Western Whipbird (a near endemic) and Western Bristlebird (opposite). Also many of the other endemics are here including White-breasted Robin. Red-eared Firetail. Red-winged Fairy-wren. Western Rosella. Red-capped Parrot. Western Wattlebird and Western Spinebill.

The low heath in the foreground shown in the picture below is the territory of the Western Bristlebird. The vegetation is often no higher than 60-80 cm. On the hill side in the far distance resides the Western Whipbird in the taller mallee trees known as Tallerack (*Eucalyptus pleurocarpa*) with their glaucous leaves. In the damp vegetation shown on the opposite page lives the elusive Noisy Scrub-bird. The author maintains this is one of the hardest Australian species to see and as a comparison finds it much easier to sight the east coast Rufous Scrub-bird. Although people at Cheynes Beach often get good sightings and some birdwatchers get lucky and see all three quickly, I can assure you that is not the norm. This area is also ideal country to see Southern Emu-wren. Brush Bronzewing. White-breasted Robin. White-cheeked Honeyeater and Swamp Harrier.

Noisy Scrub-bird habitat

Western Bristlebird

Female Noisy Scrub-bird

Photo Graeme Chapman

Western Whipbird

Transitional Woodland

This tall eucalypt belt runs as a narrow band from north of the Murchison River at Kalbarri in a south-east direction all the way to east of Hyden and down to the southern coast. In the north and middle of this band grows the dominant eucalypt York Gum (*E. loxophleba* subsp *loxophleba*). When you leave the northern and eastern Wheatbelt you will enter this woodland. It is an important region for the parrot family with Major Mitchell's Cockatoo or Pink Cockatoo. Red-tailed Black Cockatoo (the arid subsp *samueli*). Regent Parrot. Western Corella. Little Corella and Galah.

Birds to be found: Rufous Treecreeper. Red-capped Robin. Weebill. Rufous Whistler. White-browed Babbler. Redthroat. Chestnut-rumped Thornbill. Splendid Wren.

At the very northern part of the Transitional Woodland, the author has seen Black-breasted Buzzard, uncommon that far south although he has had an even more southerly sighting just before Johnston Lakes east from Hyden, a long way out of its normal range. In the Transitional Woodland east of Hyden illustrated below, you will come across woodland dominated by Salmon Gum (*E. salmonophloia*) with an understorey of low trees called Goldfields Teatree (*Melaleuca pauperiflora*) and Bluebush (*Mareana sedifolia*). This is the ideal habitat for Gilbert's Whistler and Chestnut Quail-thrush.

Birds to be found: Western Yellow Robin. Regent Parrot. Dusky Woodswallow. Spiny-cheeked Honeyeater. White-fronted Honeyeater. White-eared Honeyeater. Restless Flycatcher. Jacky Winter. Crested Bellbird. Purple-crowned Lorikeet. Western Rosella (drier region subsp. *xanthogenys* red-backed form). Rufous Treecreeper. Grey Currawong.

The author has seen flocks of Masked Woodswallows on the Hyden-Norseman road. The southern Transitional Woodland is also an important habitat for nesting Square-tailed Kite, maybe more so on the western side of this southern band of eucalypts adjacent to where extensive heaths occur 60–100 km east of Hyden.

Kwongan Heath

Kwongan is one of the few Aboriginal names to be used for a type of vegetation habitat that occurs in the Greater South West Region. It is one the richest flora regions in the world and occurs in many areas mostly in the Wheatbelt Region. The photograph shows a typical small patch of Kwongan Heath in Dryandra Woodland Reserve. The varying flowering species attract several honeyeaters including White-cheeked Honeyeater. Brown Honeyeater. New Holland Honeyeater. White-eared Honeyeater. Brown-headed Honeyeater. Red Wattlebird and Little Wattlebird and Western Spinebill. Also the following occur in the heath: White-browed Scrubwren. Blue-breasted Fairy-wren. Splendid Fairy-wren and Silvereye.

Mulga Woodland

In recent years much of the Mulga Region has experienced a prolonged drought. Some of the author's station friends have not had decent rains from 2001 -2002 . Obviously birds still survive in bad times even in the arid mulga. However when good rains fall the countryside can become a blaze of colour as illustrated below with many everlasting species, and bird activity and the number of species increases greatly. At Wooleen Station in 2006, the author found a particularly active breeding area, in about a 300 square metre block where he set up hides. The following species were found breeding in that one small area: Red-capped Robin. Southern Whiteface. White-browed Treecreeper (not common throughout the mulga). Crimson Chats (four nests). Bourke's Parrot. Hooded Robin. Pied Honeyeater (three nests). Zebra Finch. Rufous Songlark. Chestnut-rumped Thornbill. Spiny-cheeked Honeyeater and not too far away the uncommon Ground Cuckoo-shrike.

Birds to be found: All the above as well as Orange Chat. Masked Woodswallow. Little Woodswallow particularly near granite outcrops. Crested Bellbird. White-browed Babbler with Grey-crowned overlapping north of Murchison Settlement. White-winged Triller. White-plumed Honeyeater. Singing Honeyeater. Grey-fronted Honeyeater. Black Honeyeater. Rufous Whistler. Little Button-quail (mainly in the northern mulga grasslands and into the deserts). Spotted Harrier. Little Eagle. Wedge-tailed Eagle. Whistling Kite. Brown Falcon. Australian Bustard. Banded Lapwing. Bush Stone-curlew. Common Bronzewing. Crested Pigeon. Australian Ringneck (the drier region subsp. *zonarius* with the yellow instead of green underbelly, also markedly smaller than in the northern regions). Mulga Parrot. Budgerigar. Cockatiel. Little Corella. Pallid Cuckoo. Horsefield's Bronze-Cuckoo. Black-eared Cuckoo. Brown Songlark. Variegated Fairy-wren. Red-backed Kingfisher. Sacred Kingfisher. Western Bowerbird. Western Gerygone. Inland Thornbill. Mistletoe Bird. Pied Butcherbird. Little Crow.

Birds for listers: Chestnut-breasted Quail-thrush. Banded Whiteface (mostly north and north-east of this books range). Inland Dotterel. Black-breasted Buzzard Grey Honeyeater. Slaty-backed Thornbill. Samphire Thornbill. Remote possibility of Black Falcon and Grey Falcon. The author has seen Black Falcon flying over Lake Anneen just at the northern limit of this book, also a few White-browed Woodswallow with flocks of Masked Woodswallow.

Granite outcrops

The South West Region is one of the few areas in the world that has remained fairly stable during the geological and topographical changes that have occurred throughout the planet's evolution. One of the larger geological areas in this region is known as the Yilgarn Craton that stretches from the Darling Range in the west to east of Kalgoorlie. The Wheatbelt Region covers a greater part of the Yilgarn Craton and throughout the region there are numerous intrusions of the ancient underlying bedrock that consists of granite and gneisses, the second oldest rocks in the world. Often they form huge domed features in the landscape as in Boyagin Rock Nature Reserve.

With the additional water runoff from these outcrops, thicker vegetation often occurs at their base and they are good areas to birdwatch. In the Transitional Woodland zone at the base of these rock outcrops there are often Purple-gaped Honeyeaters in the eastern Wheatbelt. In the northern Wheatbelt Redthroat are often seen near the outcrops and further into the Mulga, Little Woodswallows frequent some of them. A few specialised mistletoes parasitise certain acacias at the base of the rocks and when in bloom attract Spiny-cheeked Honeyeater, White-fronted Honeyeater, Mistletoebird and even Grey Honeyeater.

Stony plains

In many areas in the Mulga Region one can come across areas of open stony plains. In eastern Australia they are called gibber plains and are often quite extensive, particularly in northern Southern Australia and south-east Queensland. Here in Western Australia, the Arabic term 'hamada' plain is given to these sparse stony areas, although they are rarely devoid of some form of plant life unlike their counterpart in eastern Australia. Where the photograph was taken (opposite top) the author decided to camp in a very exposed area of stony country. The following morning, scanning for Banded Whiteface and possibly Inland Dotterel, I sighted a bird that I knew was in the region but thought this particular location was far too exposed for them, but from under one of the low bushes in the middle of the photograph walked out a Chestnut-breasted Quail-thrush with its characteristic jerky head movement, uttering the typical high pitched Quail-thrush call. It demonstrated that you could never know everything about what bird will reside where. The country is typical of that required by Inland Dotterel and Banded Whiteface, although Banded Whiteface exist in a variety of areas but the one common factor is that it is generally very open country, unless one is in the desert regions where they often are found in the swales of sand dunes. Open stony country is also favoured by Ground Cuckoo-shrike and Banded Plover.

Breakaway country

In the picture taken in the Tallering Peak area north of Mullewa are stony flat tops which support populations of Chestnut-breasted Quail-thrush. Nesting on the cliff face are a resident pair of Peregrine Falcon. The male thinks nothing of taking Ringneck Parrots in the valley below. Little Woodswallows nest on the small rock crevices. The mulga in the valleys supports numerous other birds.

WETLANDS

Perth wetlands

Before European settlement, the Swan Coastal Plain had an extensive wetland system. Many of the water bodies particularly the smaller ephemeral wetlands have been filled in, which has made the feeding areas for uncommon birds like Long-toed Stint even more difficult to find. In the authors own lifetime here, areas that he would visit to see this species are now gone. Luckily a few lakes still remain. The majority of all the *Anatidae* family, which includes ducks, swans and geese, can be found in Perth including Hardhead. Black Duck. Grey Teal. Australasian Shoveler. Pink-eared Duck. Australian Shelduck. Blue-billed Duck. Australian Wood Duck. Musk Duck and occasionally Chestnut Teal and less so our rare duck, the Freckled Duck. Other wetland birds to be found in Perth include Little Pied Cormorant. Little Black Cormorant and Great Black Cormorant. Yellow-billed Spoonbill. Occasionally Royal Spoonbill. Australasian Grebe. Hoary-headed Grebe. Great Crested Grebe. White-necked Heron. Nankeen Night-Heron. Great Egret and to a lesser degree Intermediate Egret. Straw-necked Ibis. Glossy Ibis. Australian White Ibis. In the reed beds can be found Baillon's Crake. Spotless Crake. Australian Spotted Crake. Buff-banded Rail. Three Bitterns are threatened in the South West. Two have occurred in the Perth region, Little Bittern and Australasian Bittern. As they are very cryptic and elusive this makes them very hard to see. In the mid 1980s they were in greater numbers than we know they are now. Swamp Harriers still frequent some of our larger wetlands particularly Herdsman Lake. On the muddy shorelines of lakes like Thomsons Lake. Forrestdale Lake and Joondalup Lake. Red-kneed Dotterel. Black-fronted Dotteral. Red-capped Plover. Marsh Sandpiper and Sharp-tailed Sandpiper may be found. In late spring, early summer Thomsons Lake can still get Long-toed Stints and the occasional Pectoral Sandpiper and rarely Ruff.

Paperbark swamps

For those willing to wade or use a small canoe, some of our dense paperbark swamps support the occasional Freckled Duck. Also if there are reed beds crakes will allow closer viewing if you are actually in the water rather than approaching by land, a trick that a fellow birdwatcher told the author many years back. Many duck species breed in paperbark swamps including Grey Teal. Black Duck. Hardhead. Wood Duck as well as cormorants, egrets, spoonbills and herons that make their rookeries in them.

South West wetlands

Wetlands like the Vasse-Wonnerup Estuary illustrated, support huge numbers of waterbirds far more than the wetlands in Perth. In one count in January 1986, 33,000 birds were counted comprising 60 species and ducks and swans accounted for 12,500 of that number. These are very large numbers and show how important the South West wetlands are but there is immense pressure to develop some of the foreshores of these wetlands, which would greatly affect the number of species visiting this region.

Inland river systems

The country that abuts the inland rivers and creeks, often with tall stands of River Red Gum (*E. camaldulensis*) supporting a higher density of birds than the surrounding open country, particularly raptors, parrots and nocturnal birds, as tall trees supply good nesting sites.

Birds to be found: White-plumed Honeyeater. Spiny-cheeked Honeyeater. Striated Pardalote. Red-browed Pardalote (southern limit). Rufous Songlark. Owlet Nightjar. Boobook Owl. White-browed Babbler. Grey-crowned Babbler. Blue-winged Kookaburra (southern limit). Red-backed Kingfisher. Mulga Parrot. Budgerigar. Little Eagle. Black-breasted Buzzard. Whistling Kite. Grey Falcon (rare). Australian Hobby.

Ephemeral lakes

These inland freshwater lakes can, as the name implies, be short lived but like the salt lakes discussed above they can attract many species of waterbirds including Freckled Duck. The author camped at one such lake (see photograph below) on the Gary Highway called Lake Cohen (agreed, out of this book's region). Several species of parrot took advantage of the additional water to nest nearbye (parrots have to drink regularly) including Mulga Parrots, Pink Cockatoos (Major Mitchell's Cockatoo) and Budgerigars. Also many species of waterbirds were there including many Black-tailed Native-hen. Several species of duck were nesting there. If you check the rainfall on the Internet regularly, you get to know where certain areas will receive greater rains, which create thes ephemeral lakes.

Inland salt lake systems and surrounding samphire flats

After heavy rains, these inland playa lakes systems can fill often for several kilometres in some locations. When they do, literally thousands of birds will take advantage of these newly created wetlands. One does not always associate Black Swans with inland areas but Lake Anneen south of Meekatharra below had many hundreds of Black Swans and Pelicans. The surrounding samphire flats are the nesting locations for two specialised birds, the Samphire Thornbill and Orange Chat, as well as White-winged Wren and Brown Songlark. To see Orange Chats, just sit patiently with binoculars and scan the tops of the samphire. Soon enough, one will pop up on top of the samphire showing its bright orange plumage.

Reed swamps

In the South West, particularly close to the south coast are many wetland areas with extensive reed beds like the one illustrated. These swamps are almost permanently waterlogged. The swamp illustrated top right opposite is typical of the dense reed beds that the Australian Bittern requires. Also the low heath that abuts the swamp has been the territory of one of our rarest land birds, the Western Australian subspecies of the Ground Parrot, whose population in Western Australia is threatened.

Mangroves

Mangroves stretch from as far south as Bunbury and then at various locations all the way to the Northern Territory border. Only a few mangrove species occur in the Greater South West around the Carnarvon and Shark Bay area, namely White-breasted Whistler. The endemic Dusky Gerygone. Mangrove Fantail and Yellow White-eye. All can be found along the coast south of Carnarvon to Long Point. (Please note the mangrove species illustrated are different from those found around the Carnarvon region.)

Offshore islands

Western Australia is blessed with numerous islands stretching from the Recherche Archipelago in the south east, to the Kimberley and Northern Territory border in the north. There are in fact over 200 islands larger than 30 hectares. On the south coast, some of the islands can be visited by tourists. One such island is Woody Island, just off the coast of Esperance. On a boat trip you can normally see Black-faced Cormorant, uncommon in Western Australia. The island is a good place to see Rock Parrot. Red-eared Firetail. . Brush Bronzewing. Spotted Pardalote. Brown Quail and Sea Eagle. In winter and early spring Shy Albatross, Black-browed Albatross and Yellow-nosed Albatross can be sighted; the tourist boats do not always go out in the winter months, so do check. Closer to Perth is Rottnest Island. Here, besides the numerous small sandy bays that occur, there are several saline lakes that can be very productive for birds, particularly Government House, Lake. Lake Herschell and Lake Serpentine. Several migratory birds visit in late spring mostly common species like Ruddy Turnstone. Grey Plover. Red-necked Stint. Curlew Sandpiper. Grey Plover. Sanderling. One bird that is rare in Australia but has been seen over many years is the Red-necked Phalarope with its distinct high raised neck, its body twisting and turning as it takes insects from the surface of the water. It is also a very good place to see non-breeding Banded Stilt both in summer and winter, although numbers in winter are far lower and most are immature birds, the adults having left to nest in some far inland salt lake where rains have fallen. Often Red-necked Avocet are on the lakes and a small number occasionally nest on the island. Both the avocet and stilt feed on the brine shrimps in the lakes. There are a few pairs of resident Osprey that nest on the offshore limestone stacks. A few Reef Egrets, a species not common in the Perth region. Bridled Tern, Crested Tern and Fairy Tern have nested on the island. It's a good place to look for Rock Parrot, Red-capped Robin and White-fronted Chat. The Houtman Abrolhos archipelago off the Geraldton coast is one of the gems of Western Australia. Here the only breeding population of Lesser Noddies breed (although they have been found on Ashmore Reef). The other subspecies nest thousands of miles away on the Seychelles and Maldives Islands in the Indian Ocean. There are some relatively large islands in the Abrolhos group, including Woody, North Island, East and West Wallabi and Pelsaert Island. The author has visited East Wallabi, Beacon and Long Island but has concentrated most visits on the long island of Pelsaert, out of the main breeding season in April but mostly in the breeding season in November, when there are thousands of breeding Common Noddy and Lesser Noddy. The Common Noddy nests in the samphire and saltbush. The Lesser Noddy requires mangroves. To see thousands of birds that do not fear man is a real joy and privilege in these hectic times. On the island there are several other species to be seen including Roseate Terns. Bridled Tern. Caspian Tern. Crested Tern. Fairy Tern. Sooty Tern. The Roseate Terns nest on a small islet at the northern end of Pelsaert. Other birds seen include Red-tailed Tropicbird. Pacific Gull. Osprey. White-breasted Sea-Eagle. Pied Cormorant. Buff-banded Rail. Curlew Sandpiper. Grey-tailed Tattler. Ruddy Turnstone. Greater Sand Plover. Pied Oystercatcher.

The most northerly large island within the range of this book is Dirk Hartog Island in the Shark Bay region. Accommodation is available at the station and you can visit the island from the township of Denham. On the island are two small passerines that are very interesting. The black and white form of the White-winged Wren subsp. *leucopteris* which is truly black; the other specie of interest is the remnant population of Southern Emu-wren subspecies *hartogi*. This species is nearly 600 km north of the nominate race

MACRO HABITATS

Over the previous pages, larger general habitats have been discussed but what is of interest to some birdwatchers is that within a general vegetation zone, such as the Wandoo Woodland Region, there are differing macro habitats. The picture shows the typical dominant habitat of open Wandoo Woodland in Dryandra Woodland Reserve with the Sandplain Poison (*Gastrolobium microcarpum*) in the foreground and Wandoo trees (*E. wandoo*).

Leaving the open Wandoo one may come across a dense concentration of young Wandoo trees. This is often a favoured habitat for the Western Yellow Robin that loves to cling to the sides of the sapling in typical robin fashion, looking for moving insects on the ground.

Further on one will come into a very dense stand of sheoak growing on the shallow soils that surround granite outcrops. You rarely get Western Yellow Robin in sheoak thickets but you are more likely to get Red-capped Robin along with Grey Fantail, and on the edge of the sheoak is a favourite location for roosting Tawny Frogmouth. You will not find a great variety of bird life in here although you will see a good variety of orchids which love the acidic soil.

Leaving the sheoak you may come to the long fence line that stops abruptly where the cleared country occurs. At first glance you may think there is nothing on the edge but it's a favoured area for the Jacky Winter, Red-capped Robin and Yellow-rumped Thornbill, all taking advantage of the open space but having the added benefit and safety of the sheoak and Wandoo to return to. At night Barn Owls and Tawny Frogmouth use the fence posts as launching points to catch prey.

If you leave open Wandoo Woodland in a reserve like Dongolocking Nature Reserve south east of Narrogin, you will come to a lower stratum of closed shrub-heath with a few interspersed mallees as in the photograph. The experienced birdwatcher knows that possibly Southern Scrub Robin and Shy Heathwren may occur here and they certainly do.

Walking only 30-40 metres from the previous location, one looks over a large area of low heath as illustrated in the photograph. Besides several honeyeaters visiting the area like Tawny-crowned Honeyeater, White-cheeked Honeyeater, Western Spinebill and on the perimeter White-eared Honeyeater, there is another elusive ground dwelling bird very similar to the Shy Heathwren, namely the Rufous Fieldwren. For many it is a real joy to know that such birds still survive within the Wheatbelt with all the environmental pressures of fire, fox and cat predation and loss of habitat by clearing.

The point of all the above brief accounts of the macro habitats is to highlight the importance of knowing a little about what birds reside where and what habitat they require, as this will help you find the birds you know as well as the birds that you may not have seen.

One of the joys of birdwatching is to see a bird species you have never seen before. However when you first start seriously looking at birds you may find that what you thought was a Weebill was in fact a Western Thornbill, or the Scarlet Robin was a Red-capped Robin, or the White-napped Honeyeater was a Brown-headed Honeyeater, but you will soon learn to pick up the small features that differentiate one bird from another.

Then you reach another level of difficulty. Was the wren a Blue-breasted Fairy-wren or Variegated Fairy-wren, or was the bird you just got a glimpse of a Western Gerygone or the uncommon Grey Honeyeater? It really does not matter as long as you keep learning and building on your own knowledge base.

What do I need to start successful birdwatching? Equipment:

Firstly, it is essential to purchase a pair of binoculars and there is a good reason for this. Birds have a tolerance distance beyond which they will allow people or other animals to get near them. What is meant by that, is that birds will go about their business relaxed and unperturbed even when you are walking towards them, but suddenly they become alert and nervous when you get too close. The reason is that you are now a potential threat and they will either walk away or fly off. Here lies the problem for you. What was the colour of their throat or tail? Did they have markings on the wing? You couldn't answer these questions, as they were too far away to see such detail. Binoculars are the answer to this problem but what size to get is the real question. Binoculars come in various sizes and types. Modern binoculars have internal roof prisms, which makes them lighter and slimmer and easier to handle. They come in various sizes e.g. 7 x 30, 8 x 35, 8 x 40 or 10 x 40. The first smaller number is the magnification, the second and larger number is the field of vision. Generally speaking the 7 x 30s are good for backpacking and just general identification where it is not vital if you miss birds; they are better than nothing, similar to those that you would take to a theatre. The minimum magnification is ideally 8 but the field of vision is very important. If you select say 8 x 30s you may have trouble getting onto a bird as you literally don't have much area to look at and it can be like looking through a keyhole rather than a small window.

So what is the ideal size ? Well this depends on a few things. Some people will always have problems getting onto a bird with binoculars, as the author knows from years of guiding.

If this is the case, it is better to cut down on the magnification to 8 but retain a good field of vision namely 40. The author uses 10 x 40.

How much do I have to pay? Well you can get cheap binoculars, but there is one thing you cannot do with them and that is to drop them or knock them as the prisms inside will almost certainly go out of alignment, although surprisingly your eyes will in fact try and adapt to this misalignment if it is not too great but it certainly is not good for your eyesight. Agreed, even the best binoculars will be damaged if you drop them but generally if they are top quality they will take reasonably rough wear and tear. Obviously when you are first starting, don't waste money on the best equipment as you may not enjoy the hobby. Serious birdwatchers spend up Aud$1500–Aud$2000 but that may be the only major purchase they ever have to make to enjoy this wonderful hobby.

A brief word on telescopes

Telescopes are used mostly by serious birdwatchers who are often particularly interested in wader and waterbirdwatching, although people also use them in rainforest birding or take them on field trips to aid viewing some distant bird. The telescope will more than triple the magnification of most binoculars, sometimes as much as five times.

If you do buy a scope, the author finds a 45-degree eyepiece far better than the horizontal type. This makes viewing up into tree tops much easier and also even for level viewing, say for waders, as you don't have to lean down straining your back. It takes a while to get used to them, but once mastered it is less tiring on the neck and back.

There is also the additional possibly of having a zoom eyepiece, say 20 to 40 times magnification. This can be useful if the birds are so far away that you need every possible magnification you can get, although there is sometimes a degree of loss in sharpness and the light entering gets progressively duller at the larger magnification end of the zoom.

Clothing

We know birds can see colour, in fact studies have shown that some species can actually see into the ultraviolet part of the spectrum; that is to say they can see some colours that many mammals cannot see, including man. Colour aids identification of other birds not only for us but for them. A Red-capped Robin can see at a glance that the head of a Scarlet Robin has a white dot not red, immediately warning him of the presence of that bird; the Red-capped Robin will normally make a hasty retreat as the Scarlet Robin dominates when territories overlap which is not often but does happen. Colour has aided that recognition.

If we wear bright colours like red or yellow shirts, we are bound to be seen sooner than if we wear sombre colours that match the bush, i.e. browns and greens. The clothes will not win you adulation on a catwalk, but will certainly help you blend into the background and allow you a much closer approach to many birds.

How to identify birds

Birding can become a daunting affair; for example even in this small publication there are well over 300 species illustrated, but have faith, with perseverance you will slowly build up your knowledge and species list and, for many, the challenge is very rewarding building on that life list. However, before you start travelling, it pays to read as much as possible and check the birds in your guidebook to build up pre-knowledge.

There are some basic important things to do when you first sight a bird you don't know.

1. First and foremost, get the colouring of the bird sorted out quickly. Where are the colours, What is the upperbody colour? What is the head colour? What is the underbody colour? Then look for colour features, i.e. red on the throat or a white neckband. Are there markings on the wing? Often birds have wing bars called 'chevrons'.
2. What is the size of the bird? Sounds obvious but it eliminates the bulk of other birds if you gauge the size. 'How do I guage the size'? When you first start looking at birds in your garden, you may notice that a Singing Honeyeater is smaller than a Red Wattlebird but is larger than a Brown Honeyeater. You see, you have already established the foundation of comparative size. So from your humble garden, you start the long process of establishing comparative sizes for all birds you see.
3. What is the shape of a bird? This is very important. Pigeons in general are thick bodied. All Fairy-wrens have small rounded bodies and long tails. Most Honeyeaters have a similar shape (not all).

When raptors are in flight, it is predominantly the shape that tells the experienced birdwatcher what species it is, particularly if it is flying against the light showing no colour or flying extremely fast.

When you see a bird very quickly flying by, you don't have time to get all the colour features and when you are starting you may not be able to identify the bird; that's fine but with experience and further sightings, and maybe the next time when the bird is flying longer and closer, you may say 'that was the bird I saw the other day', confirming what you have seen. For experienced birdwatchers, shape is vital and often the term 'jizz' is used. It actually should be written 'gis' as it comes from the abbreviation for the words 'general identifying shape' which is a phrase used by fighter pilots who have been trained to identify the type of plane flying at them by its shape, and so be aware of its capabilities. So too knowing the shape of the bird will aid you with your identification.

The author recalls driving at speed in a convoy on the Birdsville Track when a very sharp-eyed bird guide from the UK cried 'There's a raptor on the right flying fast'. The author only had seconds to see it. It was an uncommon raptor, a Black Falcon chasing an Inland Dotterel, and the speed at which both birds flew past our vehicle allowed little time to identify them but knowing the flight silhouettes and the jizz of both species made it easier to do so. Developing a memory for what a bird looks like, particularly in flight, will help you go a long way to identifying species especially the difficult birds.

4. What is the bird doing? How is it behaving? Is it climbing up a trunk like a treecreeper? Is it running along the ground not taking flight like a quail? This will help you when checking the guidebook.
5. What is the beak shape and how is it using it? If it is fine and curved it will most probably be a honeyeater. You may see a beautiful uncommon bird with a thick wide beak, prising bark off a Wandoo tree. The colouring is similar to the lovely Golden Whistler that you have become familiar with but this bird has a thick bill. What is it? Turning to the book will show you it is a Crested Shrike-tit and it was the beak that helped confirm what you had seen.
6. What is the length of the legs? This helps with all the plovers and waders. It is basic information but it lays the foundation for your early sightings.

All this sounds a lot to take in at the first sighting of a new bird but we know how fast the brain works. Alas we also know how quickly it forgets what we saw, particularly remembering a myriad of facts. Some birdwatchers recommend taking a notepad and sketching and noting the detail. The author prefers to use a mini tape recorder so he can still look at the bird, not lose sight of it, and can record on a tape in seconds what would take minutes by hand. However, he will never have the lovely art piece of a notepad that becomes the record for some good birdwatchers.

The tape is mainly used while driving, obviously in remoter country where it is safe to do so with one hand firmly on the wheel. It is used when recording birds in certain habit locations but not wishing to stop. It is also used to describe locations or features that the author wishes to revisit. At the end of the day, the diary is brought out and the daily notes are transcribed. It has been a wonderful aid for over thirty years.

Although you may have developed a reasonable degree of bird knowledge, your partner or friend may not have the same knowledge level. When you have identified a bird, say in a tree, and wish to show it to your friend, it can be frustrating if they can't even see it, let alone know what it is.

Time is critical in this situation as the bird may fly off. Having led large groups for years, the author finds by far the best way to get people to see a bird is to be specific and positive. If you just say 'It's in that tree over there', they may ask 'What tree'? The best way is to give quick instructions: 'See the broken off white dead tree ahead, go to the first tree on the right, go in about one metre from ten o'clock of the tree and there is a small gap, the bird is sitting on a branch in that gap'. So rather than refer just to a tree, as there may be many, it's best to use some feature which stands out from everything else. It may be a large rock or a dead white tree trunk, which is surrounded by lots of green trees. This immediately locates the distance and area of view and it's then easy to go to one of the trees near it. The face of a clock is used by many tour group leaders to describe the location of a bird within the profile of a tree. Giving the time location, and then distance in, helps tremendously, particularly if the tree is big and close. All this sounds so basic but the author has seen and witnessed people trying to direct others to a bird and the bird has flown off because they were not clear with their directions. If you are close to a skulking bird in low bushes and helping people, make sure they are still and silent and not throwing hands everywhere, then lower your voice and describe where a bird is. Just slowly point with a clear description and normally they will get it. Silence is so important when birding as sound is vital to birds and they may hear you before sighting you.

How to approach birds and where to find them

Try not to walk straight towards birds if you are in an open area but walk on an angle as birds find this less threatening. If there are trees or bushes to block your view make your way towards the bird by using them as a hide or cover.

One of the best methods to see birds is actually just to sit quietly somewhere and it is surprising how close birds will come if you are not moving and blending in with the scenery.

Most birds must come to drink somewhere particularly in warmer weather. If you sit near any small body of water you will increase your chances of getting birds. Visiting a lake system will normally guarantee you some waterbirds. If you are really keen, you can walk with boots into areas of reed beds and you will be amazed how accepting of your presence birds will be; many of the waterbirds will become quite tame, particularly the crakes and rails.

Checking weather on the Internet before you plan a trip to the inland or drier regions will let you know where the heavier rains have fallen and, in the appropriate season, birds will breed in profusion and make a trip most rewarding. If you don't have Internet connection try and find out where the rains have fallen in the previous months.

Try to know the seasons when birds breed as this will increase your chances of seeing more species, and also the birds are far more active and will often allow a closer approach as they are so intent on defending territory and being involved in the breeding process. In the deep South West the majority of birds will breed from mid August right through to December but in the mid west they will normally breed earlier from end of July through to October. However in the drier regions birds may breed in the middle of winter or even in summer after heavy cyclonic storms turn the brown spinifex green and the insect life multiplies even though the temperatures will be high.

Early morning is by far the best time to go birdwatching and the first 3 hours or so will often give you twice to three times the number of species as in the mid afternoon particularly in hotter weather.

Bird songs as a means to identification

If the author has any special skills in birdwatching at all, it may be possibly his knowledge of bird calls. This has proved invaluable throughout Australia. All birds sing or make calls of some kind, it is their way of communicating and if you can build up knowledge of their calls over time, it is of great benefit. Where it really helps is when you hear a call you're not sure of and that will often lead you to a species you may not have seen, particularly a rare or uncommon bird. The author remembers driving in rainforest in Cape York when the calls of about eleven species were well programmed in the brain from listening to tapes; when he suddenly heard a call, the car was brought to a halt fast and everyone leapt out. There above in a large tree were at least eight Palm Cockatoos, a wonderful new bird for all to see.

Identifying waders

This may not be the first group of birds that you will start to view, mainly because getting close to waders is not easy and those that watch waders seriously tend to purchase telescopes, which is not an essential purchase until you really start to enjoy this hobby. However when you do start, the identification of waders is still not easy, particularly as most of our waders are seen in their non-breeding plumage and at best in their eclipse plumage. Also there are subtle changes in moult. A first year non-breeding bird retains its juvenile wing feathers before it develops full adult plumage. So in simple terms most of them end up being dull grey-brown in overall appearance making the task even more difficult. Waders test even the most experienced birdwatchers but there are some points that may assist with identification. When there are a group of waders all together don't get daunted. It's actually better that way as you can compare sizes and shape.

It is best to take it in stages. First select the larger or more obvious waders like curlew or the godwits. This gives you a base from which to start. Size is the first important factor. How does it compare say with a godwit?. There may be very small waders in the group, most probably Red-necked Stints, but there are some dumpy birds much larger than the stint but smaller than the godwit. They could be Knot. It's not important when you start for the first time whether the godwits were Bar-tailed or Black-tailed or that the knot was a Red or Great Knot. You are already recognising the genus to which the birds belong.

Now it is time to look at the guidebook. There are two godwits together but one has a slightly upturned bill (not its best diagnostic feature although easy to see) but more importantly one has a darker duller upperbody with less white on the margins of the wing feathers (coverts and scapulars). It's not clear but it is just showing solid black whereas the other is showing barring on the rump. Ah, the duller plumaged bird has just stretched its wings showing clearly a white rump and black to the end of the tail. That confirms it, that is the Black-tailed Godwit but what of the dumpy birds alongside; there seem to be two sizes but it's not as easy as the godwits. After looking at the book you decide they are Knots but which one is which. One is slightly larger and the bill is one and half times the length of its head (nape to forehead) whereas the other is certainly smaller and the bill is the same length as the head, so the smaller one must be the Red Knot.

You have now started the skilful process of identification, comparing one bird to another. It is much better to start with a group of waders first than a single bird. Also the more you view waders the easier it becomes. Sometimes the author has not looked at waders for a long period; even though he has been viewing waders for many years, it takes a while getting back into it and recalling all the important features one knows.

To summarise, these are the important features to look out for. What is the size? What is the size and length of bill? What is the length of the legs? What is the typical standing posture? How is it feeding? Take note of the eye stripe (supercilium). Yes, this is a technical point but knowing its length and position over the eye can be an important in identification.

How best to view waders

Most importantly try to view waders with the sunlight falling on them and from behind you, and the lower the angle of light the better the view you will get.

Regarding tides, waders will disperse at very low tide but tend to congregate at high tide. Waders feed most on the receding tide soon after high tide.

Waders can be nervous birds with people getting too close. If you possess a light stool/chair take it with you and sit yourself down not too far from the water's edge and you will be amazed how accepting they can become. Sitting is always less threatening to both shore and land birds.

To summarise, take birdwatching slowly and build on your knowledge in stages. It all sounds so easy forty years on from the author's first birds but with perseverance your knowledge will increase ten fold.

BUSH SAFETY AND AWARENESS

Many areas mentioned in this book, particularly in the Mulga Region, are fairly remote and one must be extremely careful to avoid getting lost or disorientated. It is tempting when seeing a bird briefly while driving, to suddenly stop and quickly get out of the car and start following it into the bush. It is at this point that you may get into trouble. However tempting it is, you must first take bearings of where you are and where you intend to go.

A few pointers

We live in the southern hemisphere, so familiarise yourself by knowing that the mid day sun will be in the north. In winter it is easier to relate to north as the angle is lower but in the summer the angle is higher and it is not so easy. Knowing where north is will certainly help with knowing where you are. However it's meaningless if you have not registered where you entered the bush. Did you enter an area walking south or north east or west?

However experienced you are, it is essential to take along a compass. Even though I have been walking in the bush for nearly 40 years, I still check a few facts before setting off in remoter country. Get out your compass and check in what direction the road you are on runs. Take a bearing on the road, to make it easier to assess where you are. If it runs east–west you will either walk north of the road or south. If the road is running in a north-south direction register if you will walk east of the road or west. You then can set off in a much more relaxed manner knowing that you can keep walking even in the thickest of woodland, but remember that when it is time to return just check your compass and then head back. A word of warning, it's easy to be too relaxed and you can forget - did I enter the mulga woodland from the east or the west? If the sun is out it helps but it still does not help if you forgot what direction you walked in. Some of us are lucky and have a built-in memory map of all the main tracks and where they lead to, but not everyone has this. I carry a GPS which of course makes it so easy to return to your original starting point. I rarely use it to guide me back, more often for registering the location of a bird, but it certainly helps when the direction you walked in is not a simple north-south or east-west but say north-north-east which makes working out where you travelled a little harder.

Even if you possess a GPS, always carry a compass and a couple of batteries as a back up just in case the batteries fail.

A simple word about walking at night in the bush: sure if the sky is clear and you're one of those few who know the stars and where they are at anytime of the year, then it may be all right; but if you're not and it is an overcast night, be careful. Most of you would never walk in the bush in the dark anyway. It is a problem, and it has happened to people particularly if they don't have a good sense of direction, when you leave a tent to go to the toilet in the night. With no full moon or an overcast sky, even with a torch it's easy to get disorientated, so be very careful when it's pitch black and ideally leave a spare light somewhere near the tent.

All the above may be obvious but many people still walk in remote areas without adequate knowledge or directional aids to assist them. Do take note of where you walk and do inform people of your proposed travels particularly if venturing into remoter areas; also let them know when you will be returning home, it's only fair to other people.

A BRIEF 'WHERE TO WATCH BIRDS' IN THE GREATER SOUTH WEST REGION

Having run bird tours for twenty plus years, one certainly gets to know where most of the best locations to view birds occur. The author is sometimes reluctant to mention them all as people have differing needs or likes but some of the better areas are described here in general terms only.

Looking for the endemics

Perth to Dryandra Woodland Nature Reserve and the Stirling Range

If you are a visitor to the state and your time is limited and your primary objective is to see most of the endemic birds of the WA, then you must travel down to the south coast east of Albany. A typical seven day journey from Perth could take you via Dryandra Woodland Reserve located between the towns of Williams and Narrogin. There is basic accommodation in the old foresters' houses within the reserve itself. For more upmarket facilities one would have to stay overnight in Narrogin. There are some farmstays adjacent to the reserve as well. Several endemic birds and near endemic birds can be found, as well as a multitude of other species. The endemics include Western Thornbill. Western Spinebill. Short-billed Black-Cockatoo. Western Rosella; the near endemics include, like the Blue-breasted Fairy-wren and Western Yellow Robin and the uncommon subspecies of the Crested Shrike-tit *leucogaster*. The next area to visit on your way south could be the Stirling Range, where a very good camping and accommodation facility is located, namely the Stirling Range Retreat. The staff are most accommodating and know where many of the bird species occur. In birding terms it is a reasonable area and many occur within the camping and accommodation grounds. Floristically this region is one of the flora hot spots of the whole of Australia, being incredibly rich particularly in regards to the quantity of terrestrial orchids. Possible birds to see include: Elegant Parrot. Rufous Treecreeper. Varied Sittela. Square-tailed Kite. Little Eagle. Western Whipbird. Southern Emu-wren. Peregrine Falcon. Crested Shrike-tit. Western Rosella. Regent Parrot and Owlet Nightjar.

Stirling Range to Cheyne Beach and Albany

Not far from the Stirling Range is the Porongurup Range with a totally different suite of flora including some impressive Karri trees in one of the most eastern populations of this tall tree. There is more bird species accustomed to the wetter South West forests here. You may go on to Cheyne Beach or decide to stay here. There are camping and accommodation facilities and tearooms in the Porongorups. From Porongurups or the Stirling Range you can travel down to Cheyne Beach where there is camping and basic accommodation in the form of self contained chalets. Here several of the rare endemics are located, including Western Bristlebird and Noisy Scrub-bird; also other endemics: Red-eared Firetail. White-breasted Robin. Red-winged Fairy-wren and the near endemic Western Whipbird. Sadly, we think that the Ground Parrot subspecies *flaviventris* has gone from the Waychinicup area near Cheyne Beach but it still may remain in some localities nearby.

Not far from the beach township of Cheyne Beach is the large town of Albany; near here is Two Peoples Bay and it has all of the birds listed for the Cheyne Beach and Waychinicup area. Albany itself has some good birdwatching localities, particularly some wader watching areas such as at Emu Point. The walk along Middelton Beach to Emu Point is a good site for Southern Emu-wren and Rock Parrots. Not far from here is Lake Seppings, which is a very good place for Red-winged Fairy-wren, Western Rosella and White-breasted Robin. The author has had a species of snipe here, most probably Latham's Snipe. Except in the Kimberleys, snipe are very uncommon in Western Australia, unlike the eastern states. Musk and Blue-billed Duck occur on the lake.

Hyden and beyond

If your time in the state is short, then you will have to return to Perth hopefully after getting most of the endemics; but if you have more time, you can combine what you have just done over the last few days and, instead of returning to Perth, you can travel to Hyden, either along the coast via the magnificent Fitzgerald River National Park with its 1800 plus species of plant life or head directly north east, wandering through the Wheatbelt Region to Hyden where there are camping areas, chalets and also motel facilities. Due east of Hyden past the Vermin Fence are some interesting habitat zones. The open heath has Blue-breasted Fairy-wren. Rufous Fieldwren. Tawny-crowned Honeyeater and occasionally Black Honeyeater. In the sand pits White-backed Swallow. Further into the Salmon Gum Woodland and melaleuca understorey are Chestnut Quailthrush and Gilbert Whistler. In the denser vegetation, Shy Heathwren and Southern Scrub-robin. Other birds include Regent Parrot, Purple-crowned Lorikeet and Square-tailed Kite (spring–early summer). None of these birds are rare but the habitat is more pristine than the Wheatbelt although, sadly, mining is moving into many more areas in a big way now and it is losing that remote feel and new tracks are being laid.

The Kalgoorlie region particularly north to Goongarrie Nature Reserve has lots to offer; you are now entering the marginal areas that abut the true desert regions. Goongarrie Nature Reserve is a good place to see White-browed Treecreepers. In the samphire after good rains Orange Chats can be seen. It is not uncommon to start seeing Budgerigars and Cockatiels here. Keep a look out for Scarlet-chested Parrots they have been sighted in this part of the far eastern Goldfields. Heading north to Laverton and the deserts takes you to wonderful country but this is out of the range of this book. North-west of Coolgardie is the nature reserve of Rowles Lagoon. It is a good place to see many inland species of duck and it is one of the few wetlands where our rarest duck is seen regularly, the Freckled Duck. The eucalypts of the Goldfields region are exceptional and more species of eucalypt can be found around the Kalgoorlie area than anywhere else in Australia. Both south and north of the Great Eastern Highway near Boorabbin, many areas have Gilbert's Whistler and Chestnut Quail-thrush, Purple-crowned Lorikeet and Regent Parrots.

South of Kalgoorlie via Norseman is the Esperance region with its stunning beaches and rich flora heath. There are some very good wetlands namely Lake Wheatfield, Lake Warden and Lake Windabout. Some of the greatest numbers of Hooded Dotterel in the state and in fact Australia are found here, particularly at Lake Warden. Near the car park at Lake Wheatfield there are often many Western Wattlebirds feeding on the Showy Banksia (*B. speciosa*). Cape Barren Goose can be found on the well watered grasslands on the small farmlets on the edge of town as well as the Esperance Golf Course. The islands off the township of Esperance have several species of birds including: Sooty Oystercatcher. Cape Barren Goose. Black-faced Cormorant. Rock Parrot. White-breasted Sea-Eagle, even Red-eared Firetails and Brush Bronzewing on some islands such as Woody Island.

Hyden to Wubin

If you choose not to venture far east of Hyden, you can head due north-west making tracks to any of the lower mid west towns such as Wongan Hills or Dalwallinu. There are several reserves in this region and Western Corella subspecies *derbyi* is found here. Some of the populations of Redthroat closest to Perth can be found in the Wongan Hills area. Floristically, it is very rich even though the land is predominately cleared. The roadside verges just north of Wubin travelling to Perenjori have some of the highest species rich flora in Australia; they are best seen in late August to early October. The New Norcia area is not only worth visiting for historical reasons but it also has a population of Western Corella mostly active just south of the township; so too has Moora where they nest just north of the town.

Wubin northeast along the inland highway

From the mid west area you can leave the Wheatbelt Region and pass through the Transitional Woodland area north east of Wubin on the Great Northern Highway that eventually goes all the way to Newman and then to Port Hedland via the inland route.

Approximately 40 km from Wubin you pass through patches of Transitional Woodland and also thick melaleuca heath in between each open woodland. In the woodland off the main road several species of parrot occur including Regent Parrot, Red-tailed Black Cockatoo (subspecies *samueli*). Purple-crowned Lorikeet, and best of all, Pink Cockatoo, always a stunning sight (but not common here). Leaving the Transitional Woodland just north of the Ningham Station turn-off, you enter the vast region of the Mulga Woodland; obviously the region is not restricted to the core vegetation type of mulga trees but has a diverse habitat including breakaway country, salt lake systems with samphire as well as open stony plains.

In this region, a wealth of bird life awaits you. Common birds like Chestnut-rumped, Yellow-rumped and Inland Thornbill. Weebill. Western Gerygone. Crested Bellbird. Spiny-cheeked Honeyeater. White-plumed Honeyeater. Bourke's Parrot. Budgerigar. Mulga Parrot. Torresian and Little Crow. Then less common birds such as Redthroat. Slaty-backed Thornbill (more common in some areas than people think). Spotted Bowerbird. The further north one travels, other species become more common such as Diamond Dove. Cockatiel. Chiming Wedgebill. Less common species: Banded Whiteface. Inland Dotterel. Grey Honeyeater and White-browed Treecreeper. The raptors may become more plentiful with Whistling Kite, Little Eagle, Brown Falcon, Kestrel and Wedge-tailed Eagle being some of the more common and then Black-breasted Buzzard and Spotted Harrier less so. When the Mulga is ablaze with colour from the everlastings: Crimson Chat. Pied Honeyeater. Black Honeyeater breed in profusion. Budgerigars often fly everywhere and the cuckoos such as Pallid Cuckoo, Black-eared Cuckoo and Horsfield's Bronze-Cuckoo centre on these areas to parasitise many of the passerine species.

Many of the stations in this region offer basic facilities and the author would far rather share an evening meal any day with a station owner, than be stuck in a five star plastic hotel in a city. The bonus of staying on a station is that they will sometimes (mostly) allow you to visit some of the interesting areas on their property such as granite outcrops or wetlands (often rare in this region) which you would otherwise never have been able to see or visit. Obviously be 'bush wise' about where you are, as station owners have one major fear and that is you getting lost in the often featureless sea of mulga woodland; so do register the tracks indicated and most station owners will give you a small printed map of their station. One such station is Nallan Station just north of Cue where the people are very friendly and the mulga bird life is very good. It is almost at the southern limit of Banded Whiteface. Also it is a good location for Grey Honeyeaters and Slaty-backed Thornbill. Around the homestead, Western Bowerbird is common and some of the nearby water tanks have Bourke's Parrots coming to the troughs just after sunset.

Wubin to Mullewa

If you have chosen not to travel this time on the inland highway, you may have decided to go north on the Dalwallinu, Wubin, Perenjori, Morawa and Mullewa road or the New Norcia, Moora. Three Springs road. As mentioned before, the road between Wubin and Morawa is one of the richest flora drives, with many small towns that one can stay in. From Mullewa due east is the small town of Yalgoo. In the station country here is a good place for Grey Honeyeater and Slaty-backed Thornbill. On the samphire flats south east of the townsite, Orange Chat and Brown Songlark can be found when the season is good; and occasionally the uncommon Samphire Thornbill has been sighted here although the author has not seen it in this particular locality. There are a few sheep stations north of the Mullewa-Yalgoo road that have tourist accommodation on their property.

Mullewa to Murchison Settlement and Gascoyne Junction

Another wonderful drive takes you through the small Murchison Settlement on the road to Gascoyne Junction. In the winter months, although cold at times particularly at night, the weather can be glorious during the day with clear skies and temperatures in the low twenties. The best time to visit is mid August (still cool) through to the second week of October. The main breeding season occurs from July to October. Areas like Tallering Peak have Chestnut-breasted Quail-thrush, Peregrine Falcon and Little Woodswallow.

The Quail-thrush becomes quite common in the area around the turn-off where the Butchers Track commences to go to the Coastal Highway. Wooleen Station has very good accommodation facilities in the form of quality rammed earth chalets. Wooleen is perhaps one of the finest birding areas in the mid west, as it has such a diverse range of habitat, not least a wonderful wetland, Wooleen Lake with its beautiful white barked Coolibah trees *(E. victrix)*. Most years there is some permanent water there and the adjacent samphire has populations of Orange Chat and lots of Brown Songlark. All the inland duck species have been recorded here. The Mulga Woodland in a good season is wonderful and White-browed Treecreepers and Ground Cuckoo-shrikes breed here.

Perth to Geraldton

On this route, there are countless areas you can visit and some of the major reserves have been located on the northern map. On the coastal belt just north of Perth, around the Mt Lesueur area there is a cross over region for Blue-breasted Fairy-wren and Variegated Fairy-wren so be careful of too hasty an identification. In the small wetter vegetated gullies around Hill River there still occur small populations of White-breasted Robin. The area has also several populations of Western Corella near Mt Lesueur. You may combine your birding with viewing the Pinnacles in Nambung National Park. On the coastal dunes Southern Emu-wren and Rufous Fieldwren occur. White-backed Swallows can be found in some of the sandpit areas on the road to Jurien. Fairy Terns and Rock Parrots occur all the way from Lancelin up to Leeman on some of the beaches.

Ellendale Pool about 30 km south-west (gets a little overcrowded so try midweek) has Peregrine Falcon and Variegated Fairy-wren. A pleasanter and less frequented area is Coalseam Gorge about 27 km north east of Mingenew. Peregrine Falcon is resident there as well; it's a lovely place to camp and in early spring it is an oasis for everlastings in the centre of a cleared farming region and several mulga frequenting species of bird manage to survive here.

Out of Geraldton is the wonderful Abrolhos Islands and if you contact the tourist centre in Geraldton, they may be able to put you on to a charter boat are going out to one of the islands, but do this well ahead of your travels as they are not visited regularly. It is a wonderful set of islands but too much people pressure has to be avoided, so going with a legitimate authorised charter group or tour is the only way to visit these wonderful islands.

Kalbarri to Denham

North of Geraldton is Kalbarri National Park and the township of Kalbarri with lots of tourist facilities and a tourist centre. The park has one of the richest floras in Western Australia and tends to have vibrant colours longer than many other areas, as the banksias and some of the verticordias are in bloom right up till Christmas and beyond, although the temperatures will be very warm then. The park has lots of Rufous Fieldwren. On the top of the gorge face of the Murchison River at many of the lookouts, there is a surprising array of birds at times, more so than in the heath itself; birds like Black Honeyeaters, Southern Scrub-robin, Redthroat and Black-eared Cuckoo and Horsfield's Bronze-Cuckoo have been seen by the author close to the top of the gorge.

Leaving Kalbarri National Park and only14 km along the North West Highway, one crosses over the Murchison River. It's not a favoured area of the author's as there can be a lot of overnight stayers there, but it is worth a stop for a while as there is almost always some permanent water in the pools just upstream from the bridge. This is a major attraction for birds in the semi-arid region and even Grey Falcon has been sighted here, one of the most southerly sightings for this species. You may also see your first Diamond Dove or Peaceful Dove here on your journey travelling north.

Further north, you pass through some very rich flora heath with lots of Ashby's Banksia

(Banksia ashbyi). Here in spring occasionally lots of White-cheeked Honeyeaters can be found, at their very northern limit; however a more interesting zone will soon be reached, just 40 km from the bridge near the turn-off to Eurady Station. This is part of the narrow northern band of the Transitional Woodland that extends all the way south east to Norseman and beyond. It is home to a large population of Red-tailed Black Cockatoos subspecies *samueli*. You can stay on Eurady station run by the Bush Heritage Council of Australia, either camping or staying in basic accommodation; the grounds are a little exposed but it's a base and your payment goes towards a good cause – the Bush Heritage Council. It is a good base from where you can visit parts of the Transitional Woodland; lots of semi-arid species can be found here but the big flocks of Red-tails are the real bonus.

Further north starting south of Billabong Roadhouse and past Overlander Roadhouse opposite the turn-off to Shark Bay, is one of the most spectacular regions to see everlastings when in full bloom but it has to be a season when reasonable to good winter rains have fallen. In recent years this has not always been a regular occurrence. When it is, if you park well off the highway (do refer to the section on bush safety) or turn off the highway on the Butchers Track for a few kilometres, you will find a wealth of Mulga Region birds particularly Pied Honeyeater. Crimson Chat. Rufous Songlark. Splendid Fairy-wren. Chiming Wedgebill. Crested Bellbird and several of the Thornbills but less so Slaty-backed.

If you turn off to travel to the township of Denham in Shark Bay you begin to pass through some different habitat; firstly there will be a few kilometres of more open Mulga, often with large clumps of one of the mistletoes that parasitise the acacias and this is always an attraction for a variety of honeyeaters including Spiny-cheeked Honeyeater. Pied Honeyeater and Black Honeyeater. Soon you come to an expanse of samphire at the base of Hamelin Pool. If the samphire is lush after reasonable rains, Orange Chats may be here. If Monkey Mia is your destination, then you will be aware that this is the territory of Thick-billed Grasswren and around the car park and in the dunes you should have little trouble finding these little birds as well as Variegated Fairy-wren, White-winged Fairy-wren and Chiming Wedgebill.

At the northern part of Peron Peninsula in the larger areas of samphire, Slender-billed Thornbill do occur but be careful as these tracks are for four wheel drive and are particularly sandy in many areas and even tricky for experienced four wheel drivers.

Denham to Carnarvon

Back on the North West Highway heading north, closer to Carnarvon, you come to a turn off to New Beach and Bush Bay. Only 6–7 km down this dirt graded track you find a band of low mangroves running north and south. There is only one species of mangrove here, *Avicennia marina*, a low mangrove at most 4 metres high. Unlike the larger mangroves further north and in the Kimberley, like *Avicennia eucalyptifolia* and *Rhizophora mucronata* that hold a larger diversity of mangrove bird species, these mangroves have only four species specialising in feeding in mangroves: White-breasted Whistler. Mangrove Grey Fantail. Dusky Gerygone and Yellow White-eye. Getting the White-breasted is not always easy here. Slender-billed Thornbill have been sighted in the samphire flats behind the mangroves, although in the last few years the author has not managed to see them here but obviously it depends on the seasons as they do move.

Back on the highway, it's a short distance to Carnarvon and here one is truly aware that you have entered the more tropical regions of Australia and the bird life can mirror that. It is one of the most southerly towns that occasionally can get some of the rarer vagrant waders and uncommon waders like Little Curlew and Broad-billed Sandpiper which come to this area. Also vagrants like Yellow Wagtail come as far south as Carnarvon. Carnarvon is one of the southern limits of White-breasted Woodswallow, Lesser Crested Tern and Brahminy Kite.

Carnarvon to Gascoyne Junction

Driving east from Carnarvon to Gascoyne Junction the road runs parallel with the large riverine system of the Gascoyne River. The River Red Gums that line the river are typical of trees along the bigger rivers of the mid west and Pilbara region. Lots of raptors, such as Little Eagle, Whistling Kite, Black-breasted Buzzard, Brown Goshawk, Collared Sparrowhawk and Wedge-tailed Eagle are regularly seen along this watercourse. There are no Laughing Kookaburras here; this is the natural habitat of the Blue-winged Kookaburra and they are common in this region. Taking side tracks off the Carnarvon–Gascoyne Junction road and driving only a few kilometres south, say on the Yalbalgo North road (be careful this is reasonably remote country), you enter very good Mulga Woodland. In good seasons it is a good area for Black-eared Cuckoo and all of the common mulga species including the less common Slaty-backed Thornbill. You can decide to travel all the way around to Mullewa, travelling via Gascoyne Junction and Murchison Settlement. There is fuel at both these small townships.

The Lower South West

In the lower South West Region, the Margaret River region has some wonderful places to see and stay at and the whole region is geared to quality accommodation with wineries and restaurants galore, and stunning walks between Cape Naturaliste and Cape Leeuwin. The birdwatching is also good and the coastal heath has bird species like Rock Parrot. Red-eared Firetail. Southern Emu-wren. White-breasted Robin. Western Rosella and Crested Shrike-tit in the Karri Forest. The Margaret River area is also a good place to see Long-billed Black Cockatoo and the subspecies *naso* of the Red-tailed Black Cockatoo. Sea watching in winter for albatross can be rewarding with the common species being Yellow-nosed, Shy and Black-browed Albatross.

Travelling north to Perth there is a chain of wetlands, all the way from Busselton in the south to Mandurah just south of Perth. Most years the wetlands like Lake McLarty just south of Peel Inlet have some of our rare waders like Pectoral Sandpiper, Long-toed Stint and Ruff.

As mentioned, this publication is not a 'Where to find birds' book so the above suggested places to visit are only a very brief guide to the many areas that may be of interest.

There is a small publication titled *Birding Sites around Perth* written by Ron Van Delft et al printed by University of Western Australia Press for WA Birds Australia which gives far more information on birding localities for the Perth area.

The Western Australia branch of Birds Australia has a useful website:

http://www.birdswa.iinet.net.au/ giving detailed regional birding lists.

The keen bird watcher Frank O'Connor keeps a very detailed website:

http://members.iinet.net.au/-foconnor/ with more in-depth details than in this book, of some of the better birding localities in Western Australia.

It's a small matter but if visiting stations do remember these people have to make a living and your small contribution to stay is far outweighed by the privilege of staying there and the pleasure you will get from being there – it's a small price to pay. Also, do inform them if you wish to enter their property off a gazetted road.

BIRD PLUMAGE TOPOGRAPHY

The markings and features on a bird are known as bird 'topography'. As this publication is geared to ordinary birdwatching and not the study of true ornithology many avian biological terms have been avoided and the author does not wish to confuse or complicate the understanding of birds; however some specialised terms must be used as words like 'back' or 'head' can be too simplistic and not specific enough when describing the features of a bird so the following bird topography has been listed below to help the reader understand those features that may be described in the text.

The main features described in the body text are in bold lettering below. Little reference to the complex wing topography such as the wing coverts and scapulars have been used in the body text.

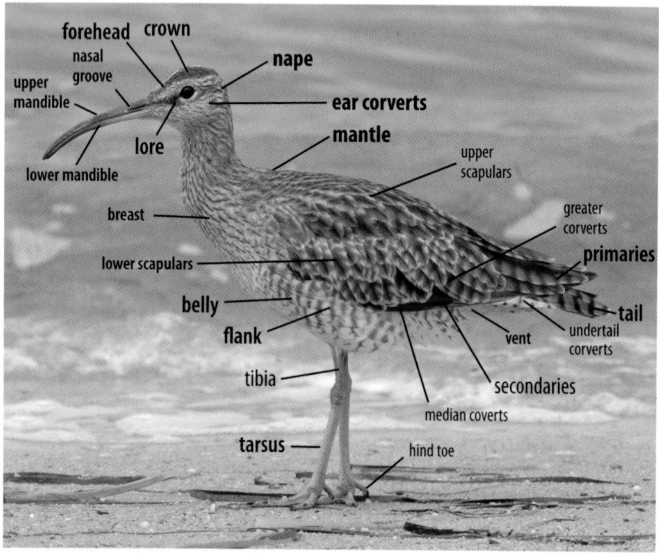

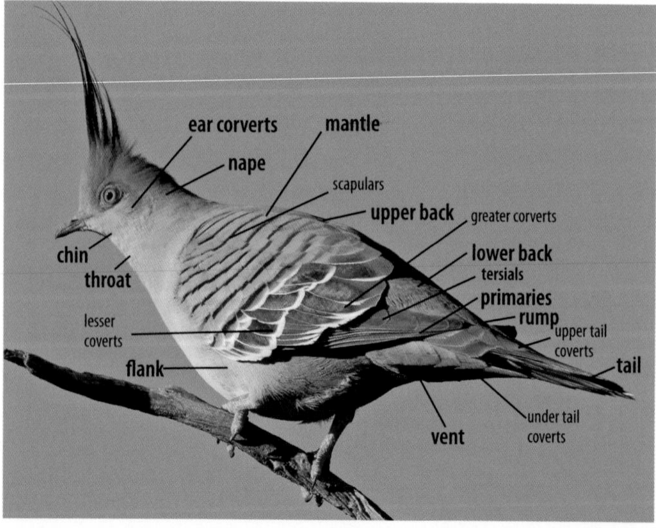

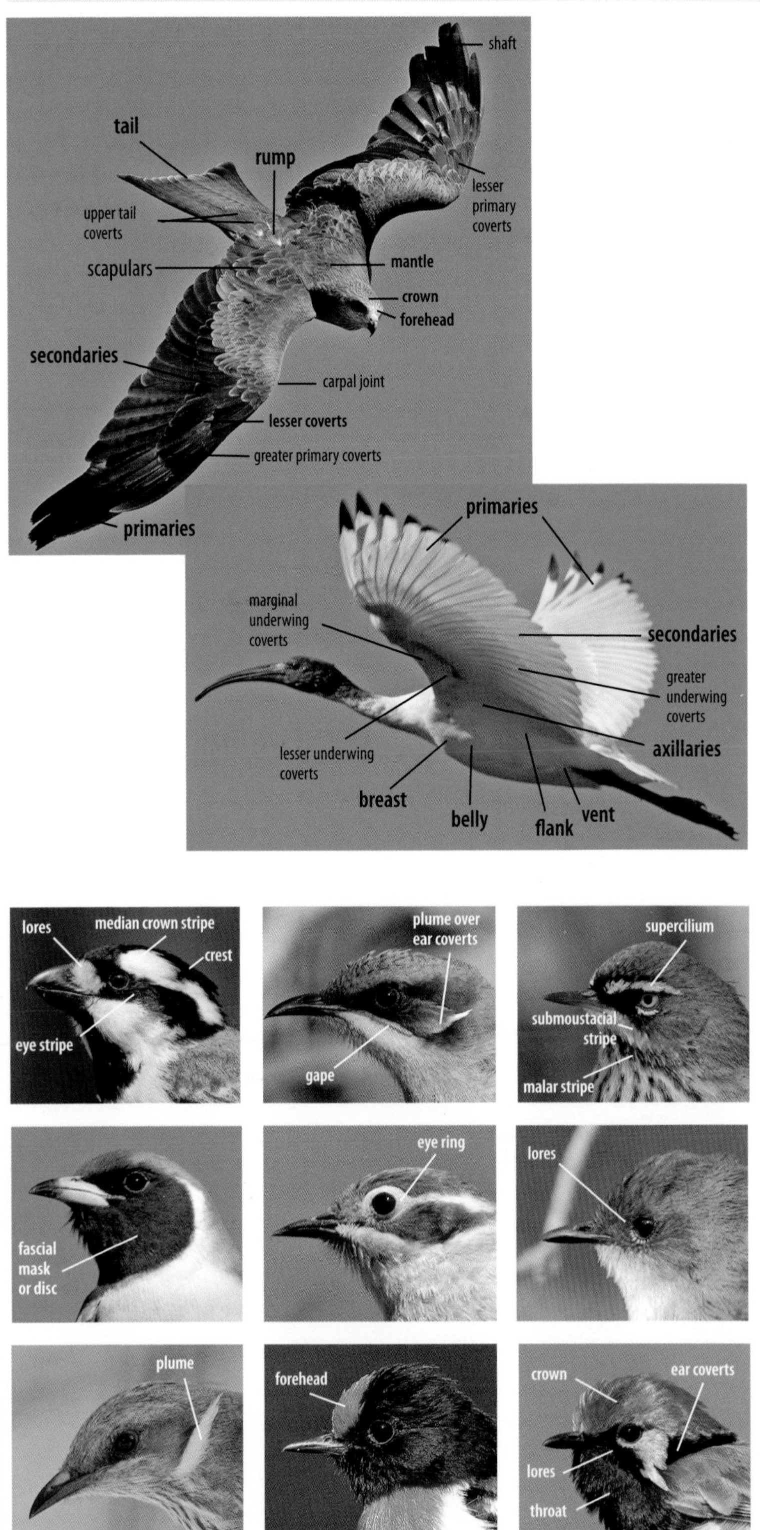
shaft
tail
rump
upper tail coverts
lesser primary coverts
scapulars
mantle
crown
forehead
secondaries
carpal joint
lesser coverts
greater primary coverts
primaries
primaries
marginal underwing coverts
secondaries
greater underwing coverts
axillaries
lesser underwing coverts
breast
belly
flank
vent
lores
median crown stripe
crest
eye stripe
plume over ear coverts
gape
supercilium
submoustacial stripe
malar stripe
fascial mask or disc
eye ring
lores
plume
forehead
crown
ear coverts
lores
throat

Birds

of the Greater South West

Introduction to the photographic guide to the birds of the Greater South West Region

This book is basic in structure and layout and is certainly not a definitive work. The emphasis is on simple descriptive text, sometimes a little more detailed than some guidebooks to generate interest in the broader knowledge of each bird. Alongside the text is the matching photograph of each species. The distribution maps should be self explanatory, highlighting the centre or core population in the darker green and the possible extent of the range shown in a lighter yellow-green.

There are over 300 species illustrated in this book. It does not include many birds of the high seas (pelagic birds) and also a few scarce or rare vagrants but it does cover the vast majority of all shore and land birds found in the Greater South West Region.

To find a bird group quickly, particularly if you are unsure of the species, use the 'fast find index' guide on the inside front cover; for the more specific species name turn to the main index at the rear of the book.

The complex procedure of grouping species to genus and genus to family and family to order is a never-ending process, no more so than in the last few years with the advent of DNA studies on several species, particularly in terms of hybridisation, that helps to define a true singular species and its origins. This will prove to be very important with subspecies that do not interbreed with the nominate race; and in some cases their populations are vulnerable, as in the South West subspecies *leucogaster* of the Crested Shrike-tit, and the studies may assist in their conservation.

The average birdwatcher does not need to get bogged down in knowing about subspecies but the author cannot avoid describing some of them. There is a good reason for this, as there is a distinct variation in plumage or size with many species and for some birdwatchers it is important to know where they occur and their differences. In years to come some of these subspecies may possibly become separate species when taxonomists have done further research.

The book has been basically structured on the taxonomic revisions made by Christidis and Boles in 2008. This applies both to the scientific names and the common names.

The photographs

The majority of the photographs have been taken by the author but a few additional photographs have been kindly supplied by other photographers. Their names are placed alongside the actual photograph and they have also been mentioned in the acknowledgments. In the case of the author, photographs at the nest have generally been avoided for obvious reasons unless there was no fear of desertion by the parent birds. Several of the raptors and a few other species have been photographed in captivity. The reason for this is that photographing, for example, raptors 20 to 30 metres up in a tree is not the author's favourite pastime and he certainly admires those like the father and son team of the Cuppers, or Michael Morcombe or the fearless Mr John Young for doing so much photography at great heights.

Some may question the ethics of having birds in captivity, even photographing them in that situation, but the author feels that it is best to show the reader a good photograph rather than a bad photograph to aid identification. Even though the author prefers birds to roam free in the wild, if well kept these captive birds bring so much joy to many who would otherwise never be able to see them in the wild and often they have been injured amd would otherwise have died in their natural environment if not cared for.

Aesthetically the author would have liked to have shown more of the background in many of his photographs, to enhance the photographs, but with little space to show each species it was felt best to enlarge and fill the frame so the bird can be seen by the reader in as much detail as possible to aid identification.

There are 301 species phtographed within the book. The author has been kindly supplied with 14 additional species. They are **Graeme Chapman** pages 54, 69, 129, 144, 186, 190, 203, 205, 207 and 209. **Michael Morcombe** 279. **Alan Collins** 132. **Adrian Boyle** 132. **Brett Barrett** 170.

Organisation of the photographic section

The order in which each species is listed and placed is loosely based on the early RAOU (Royal Australasian Ornithologists Union, now known as Birds Australia) listing but follows to some degree the more contemporary listing by Christidis and Boles in their publication *Systematics and Taxonomy of Australian* CSIRO 2008. However there have been some major changes in the sequence of bird orders in the latest Christidis and Boles taxonomic hierarchy; for example the Columbiformes (pigeons) and Caprimulgifomes (frogmouths, nightjars and owlet-nightjar) have been placed ahead of Sphenisiformes (penguins) and Procellarifomes (petrels, prions and shearwaters) etc. To the layperson this will not greatly affect the way one observes and compares one species with another, for example nightjars and frogmouths are nocturnal birds having some resemblance to owls but are totally unrelated. In this publication they are still placed together for convenience.

Taxonomic changes happen continuously throughout the natural sciences; it is part of the inevitable process of establishing a systematic classification of taxa from one species to another and under what genus, family and order they may be linked. With the advances in molecular biology in the late 1970s great changes started to take place and now, particularly in the animal kingdom with the advancement of DNA genetics, reclassification within the taxonomic hierarchy is occurring at a rapid rate. Luckily most common names will remain and the author has chosen not to complicate the layout of the book by restructuring the sequence of species in their true position in the systematic hierarchy but instead to place the birds in a more traditional manner where most waterbirds are at the front of the book and land birds like pigeons are still placed further back in the book which will simplify finding species with similar appearance but not necessarily closely related. The full list of land and shorebirds for the Greater South West species only is found on page 300.

The distribution maps

The small maps attached to the text for each species may have one or two colours. The darker green represents the main area where the species core population resides or visits on migration and will normally be the best area to see that bird. The lighter green areas show areas where either the population may occur but in low numbers or birds may occasionally expand their distribution. The maps are based mainly on the author's experience where species have been sighted in combination with the Birds Australia publication *The New Atlas of Australian Birds*, Barret et al. and Western Australian Birds Vol. 1 and 2 published by the Western Australian Museum. Ron Johnstone's work on past and current distribution is certainly the most accurate of species distribution in this state. Distribution maps are often open to debate and even the most authorative maps show major discrepancies. Also, it is not hard to find species way out of their normal range. Recently a Dollarbird was found in the middle of winter here in Perth and besides most probably feeling extremely cold for a subtropical species, its whole body clock and navigation aids would have been way out of kilter. The bird should have flown north to either Indonesia or another Asian country from the Kimberley rather than south to Perth, so do not be surprised sometimes when a bird is found way out of its normal range.

Some species have two or more subspecies located in the Greater South West and have been indicated on the distribution map. The darker green colour however still shows where the greater numbers of the species occur regardless of what subspecies it is. Where subspecies overlap, the area is known as a hybrid zone and interbreeding will normally occur within that general zone.

Species status

Various terms used to describe how abundant a species may be in the area covered by this book are as follows: Rare: simply rarely found in this region. Scarce: very low numbers in this region. Uncommon: means just that, uncommon. Common: means just that, common. Very common: the species is extremely common. Vagrant: means that a species rarely visits or is often accidental to the area. Irruptive: means that the species that will move to areas when their core centre of the habitat is experiencing severe weather conditions, normally drought, and they then move into areas where they would not normally occur. Endemic: in this case, refers to birds found only in the state of Western Australia (see below). Endemic to the region: means that the species is only found in the Greater South West (GSW).

Western Australian endemic birds

Those found in the Greater South West:

1. Baudin's Black-Cockatoo *Calyptorhynchus baudinii.* 2. Carnaby's Black-Cockatoo *Calyptorhynchus latirostris.* 3. Western Corella *Cacatua pastinator.* 4. Western Rosella *Platycercus icterotis.* 5. Red-capped Parrot *Purpureicephalus spurius.* 6. Noisy Scrub-bird *Atrichomis clamosus.* 7. Red-winged fairy-wren *Malurus elegans.* 8. Western Bristlebird *Dasyornis longirostris.* 9. Dusky Gerygone *Gerygone tenebrosa.* 10. Western Thornbill *Acanthiza inonata.* 11. Western Wattlebird *Anthochaera lunulata.* 12. Western Spinebill *Acanthorhynchus supercilosus.* 13. White-breasted Robin *Eopsaltria geogiana.* 14. Red-eared Firetail *Stagnopleura oculata.*

Those Western Australia endemics found outside the GSW.
15. Black Grasswren *Amytornis barbatus.* 16. Kimberley Honeyeater *Meliphaga fordiana.*

Although it is not conventional, written numbers throughout the text have been replaced with numerals i.e. five will be written as 5. due to space constraints.

Emu *Dromaius novaehollandiae* 1.6–2 m

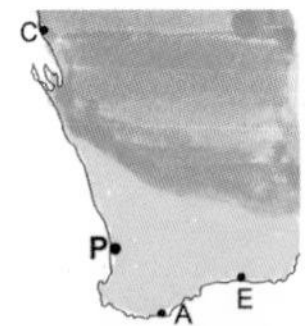

Generally a solitary bird but will mass in larger groups occasionally. Adults will pair for about 6 months, the female laying in mid winter in the Mulga and slightly later in the lower South West. The female leaves the nest area when the last egg has been laid. The male takes on the full

Immature bird

responsibility of raising the young, remaining on the nest for the full incubation period of 7 to 8 weeks without feeding or drinking through the first two weeks, and he will lose up to 8 kilos during that incubation period. After hatching the adult male remains with the young for a minimum of 6 months but in bad years will stay for a year or even longer. Emus are omnivorous, eating fruits, seeds and insects, particularly grasshoppers. Voice: deep guttural grunts by both sexes. They are a most inquisitive bird and can be easily attracted by waving an item from, say, a car window. When banging tent pegs into hard ground the author had two adult birds come from behind to see what was happening, such is their curiosity. There is a natural tendency for emus to move from the drier regions in the summer, particularly in adverse seasons, to the lower South West. Tragically in drought years many hundreds will die along the Vermin Fence trying to get to their natural south west migration route. **Nest:** No nest is made, just a scrape on the ground or eggs are laid on soft vegetation. **Similar species:** None. **Status:** Uncommon in Jarrah Forest. Uncommon in the Wheatbelt. Common in the drier pastoral country. **Where to find:** Throughout the region. Jarrah Forests. Wheatbelt. Mulga. Close to Perth areas like Julimar Forest. Wandoo. Lake McLarty near Pinjarra. More prevalent in the Mulga Region.

Malleefowl *Leipoa ocellata* 55–60 cm

A member of the Megapod family, the 'mound builders' or 'incubator birds'. Malleefowl pair for life and are long lived birds, sometimes surviving 27 to 30 years. **Nest:** The eggs of the malleefowl are entirely incubated by the heat produced from the breakdown of organic matter within a huge mound acting like a compost heap. The mound is built by both sexes but mostly by the male bird. In mid-winter the mound is opened up and leaves and organic matter are placed in the open part of the mound. With the first rains, the male bird

becomes increasingly active pushing sand or gravel over the top of the leaves. The mound may be as high as 2 metres and 5 metres wide. At the end of spring in September, the male will call to the female letting her know the temperatures are correct and she can lay when she is ready. If the temperatures are not correct, he will dissuade her from laying. The female will lay anything from between 8 and 30 eggs but normally 15–20 eggs. The male will control the temperature by opening up the mound and placing an open beak into the centre. The temperature must remain constant between 32–34 degrees C. In summer when the leaf litter is almost dry, both the male and the female play an active role in controlling the temperature by opening or closing the centre of the mound. In doing so the male and the female, but mostly the male, move literally tonnes of earth in a season backwards and forwards off the mound. During the cool night, the earth is piled high to retain heat. With the first warm rays of the morning sun, the male sometimes with assistance from the female opens up the mound to warm the vegetation, staying close to the mound. He then checks the temperature and with the warming of the hot summer day, he will pile earth back on the mound. In Dryandra Woodland Reserve there are still a few old birds surviving. In 2006 there were two active mounds; the author photographed one back in 1991 and it was active then. In another region, a small 138 acre bush block that was luckily spared from being cleared, thanks to an active conservation program and fox baiting by the farmer and the Malleefowl Preservation Group, has had as many as 5 active mounds in one season, which is a staggering quantity of nest mounds for such a small area. **Similar species:** None. **Status:** A threatened species, through predation from foxes and loss of primary habitat, the Mallee. **Where to see:** In the South West, the Wheatbelt: e.g. Dryandra Woodland NR. Buntine NR. Wongan Hills. Fitzgerald River NP. Dragon Rocks NR and Magenta NR. They still survive in parts of the station country where dense stands of mallee and mulga exist. East of Hyden, particularly around the Holland Track area, there are still reasonable populations, although their survival is always threatened by the introduced fox. Their northern range extends past Cue and across to Wiluna in the north and east right across to the northern Victoria Desert south of the Blackstone Ranges.

The mound is nearly 2 metres high.

Stubble Quail *Coturnix pectoralis* 18–20 cm

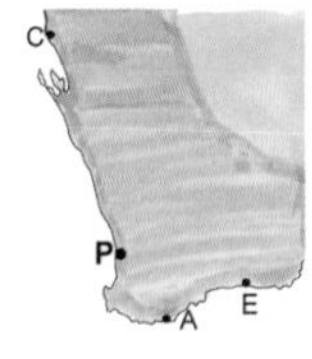

A highly nomadic quail, often travelling over 1000 km to find better feeding grounds. Heard more often than seen, mainly in the breeding season when the male makes his high pitched contact call, 'chewche-wit….chewche-wit'. Feeds mainly on seeds, both native and introduced , as well as insects. The male has an orange throat that is easily identified at close range. Seen mostly as a single bird or pair but out of the breeding season in small groups known as a 'covey' of quail. The Stubble Quail is one of the few birds that have benefited from the huge land clearing programs but this is a double-edged sword, as the breeding period can overlap with the harvest period. **Nest:** Nests are placed on a small bed of grasses in a cultivated crop or long grass, normally at the base of a thick clump. Normal clutch size 5–8. **Similar species:** Brown Quail, which is overall darker brown. Different patterning on flanks . Neither sex has an orange throat patch like the male Stubble Quail. Habitat should guide you to the correct species. Little Button-quail is much smaller with no heavy markings on the underbody. **Status:** Locally common otherwise generally uncommon. Nomadic. **Where to find:** Throughout the region. Found close to the Perth region in areas such as Harvey and Pinjarra. Easiest to see in the breeding season on the edges of paddocks that abut reserves like the northern boundary of the Fitzgerald River NP. In the drier regions in taller dry grasslands on floodplains, such as those on the Hope River floodplain some 40 km north west of Meekatharra. Also found throughout the Nullarbor Plain (not in this region).

Photo Graeme Chapman

Brown Quail *Coturnix ypsilophora* subspecies *australis* 17–22 cm

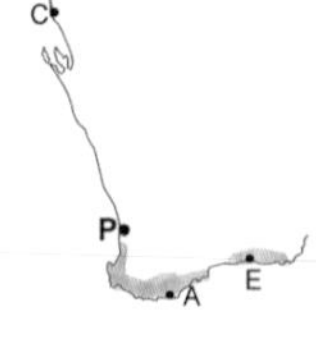

Found in wetter and denser habitat than the Stubble Quail particularly along the Southern Coastal Belt and inland where lush grasses occur. Call is different from Stubble being a more mournful and drawn out two-noted ascending call of 'too-weeee'. When flushed, flies straight upwards then drops down quickly with breaking flight. **Nest:** Nests in thick rank grasses often near water. Normal clutch size 5–8. There are nine subspecies in Australasia and some south west Pacific islands, two in Australia, *australis* on the mainland and the nominate subspecies *ypsilophora* in Tasmania. **Similar species:** Stubble Quail, refer to Stubble Quail notes. **Status:** Moderately common on the South Coastal Belt particularly adjacent to swamplands. **Where to find:** Hard to find although easiest at Cheyne Beach Caravan Park and Woody Island where they have become accustomed to people.

Magpie Goose *Anseranas semipalmata* 80–90 cm Vagrant

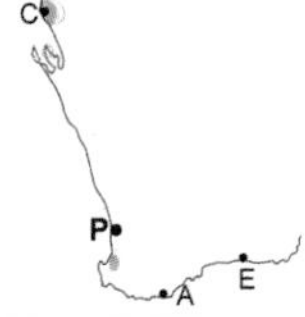

A bird primarily of northern and eastern Australia but occasionally coming all the way down to the South West wetlands. An unmistakable large bird that will roost in trees. Has unusual feathered raised knob on the crown. Continual honking noise in the larger colonies.

Nest: Nests colonially in swamplands with both male and female attending the young. Nest placed on trampled rushes often floating on top of water. Normal clutch size 4–8. **Similar species:** None. **Status:** Very common in the north although less so in the Kimberley than the Northern Territory. Rare vagrant in the South West Region as far as the Capel wetlands.

Plumed Whistling-Duck *Dendrocygna eytoni* 45–60 cm Vagrant

Rare visitor to the South West Region and then mostly in the Carnarvon region. A bird of the tropics and temperate wetlands and grasslands. Grazes on land. Congregates in large numbers on tropical wetlands in the dry season and then disperses in smaller groups during the wet. Feeds on land during the night returning to roost two hours before dawn on wetlands and river banks. Occasionally will roost in trees. Will congregate with Wandering Whistling Duck. **Nest:** Nests on ground with gathered grasses placed in long grass above flood levels. Normal clutch size 5–8. **Similar species:** WanderingWhistling-Duck, which is slightly smaller, with smaller side plumes and dark brown on the crown and rear of the neck to the mantle. **Status:** Common in the Kimberley, a vagrant to the South West Region. Has been sighted in Perth.

Wandering Whistling-Duck *Dendrocygna arcuata* subspecies *australis* 50–60 cm

Vagrant

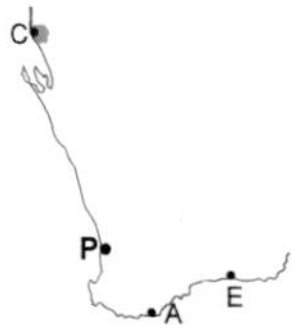

C
P
A
E

One of the two Whistling-Ducks in Australia and there are 9 species in the world. Like the Plumed Whistling Duck, the Wandering Whistling-Duck is a bird of the northern and eastern Australian wetlands but unlike the Plumed Whistling-Duck it prefers to feed on open water taking more aquatic vegetation and insects. There are three subspecies in Australasia, the Philippines and Indonesia. Subspecies *australis* is on mainland Australia and New Guinea. **Nest**: Same as Plumed Whistling-Duck. **Similar species:** Plumed Whistling-Duck (refer to Plumed Whistling Duck notes). **Status:** Locally common in some areas of the Kimberley. Rare vagrant to the Greater South West.

Black Swan *Cygnus atratus* 1–1.4 m

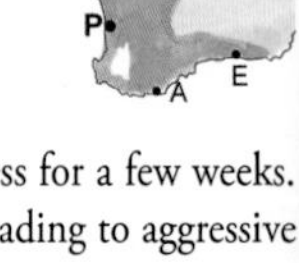

C
P
A
E

The unmistakable Western Australian icon. Found throughout the region in fresh water, brackish water and even saline waters. Feeds almost exclusively on aquatic vegetable matter, often seen tail up semi-submerged grazing on the bottom of shallow wetlands. In the breeding season gathers in smaller groups but when in post-breeding moult will gather in thousands on large permanent lakes as they will become flightless for a few weeks. Black Swans have complex territorial behaviours and social interactions leading to aggressive defence of their territory or pair bonding between breeding pairs. **Nest:** Nest is either a mass of floating grasses or reeds up to one metre high or grasses gathered on islands. Normal clutch size 4–6. **Similar species:** None. **Status:** Very common in the South West. Casual in drier areas of the GSW but will congregate in large numbers when unseasonable heavy rains fall in the pastoral region such as at Lake Anneen and Lake Austin and Wooleen Lake. **Where to find:** Throughout the South West wherever there are large bodies of water, particularly the brackish inlets along the south coast: Broke Inlet. Irwin Inlet. Wilson Inlet. Beaufort Inlet.

Mute Swan *Cygnus olor* 1.3–1.6 m

Introduced

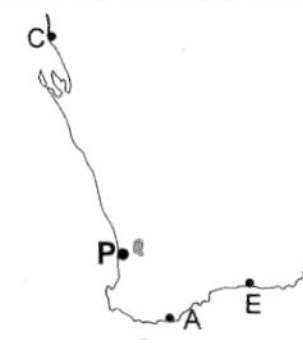

An introduced species native to Europe and central Asia, now established in Northam. In the early 1900s a pair was released on the Avon River at Northam. The population peaked in the early 1960s and now there are around 40 individuals, the number remaining stable over the last 20 years. **Status:** Locally common in the township of Northam. **Nest:** Nest similar to Black Swan.

Cape Barren Goose *Cereopsis novaehollandiae* 78–90 cm

The only member of its genus and endemic to Australia. In Western Australia the subspecies *grisea* is found on the islands of the Recherche Archipelago in the Esperance region. Seen occasionally on beaches as far west as the Fitzgerald River National Park and east to Cape Arid. It is a herbivore, feeding on native and introduced grasses on the islands and the mainland particularly around the Esperance townsite. Feral goats on some islands are having an effect on their grazing. **Nest:** Nests on several of the islands in the Recherche. Nest is a gathered pile of grasses with a hollow in the top where a quantity of down is used to cover eggs when unattended. Almost always nests on islands in Western Australia. Normal clutch size 4–5. **Similar species:** None. **Status:** Locally common on some islands and not endangered at present. **Where to find:** On the mainland in the township of Esperance, on small farmlets, particularly along Stearnes Road and on the Esperance Golf Course. To view them, there are boat trips that visit some of the islands, including Woody Island, in the late spring till autumn.

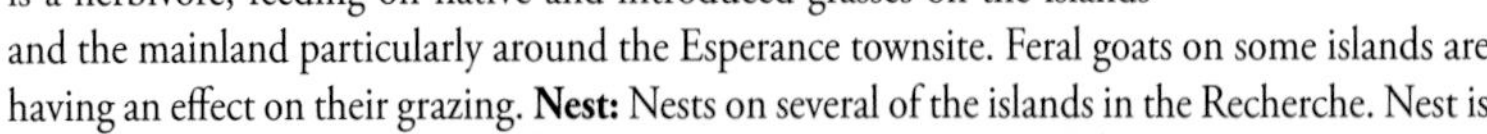

Australian Shelduck *Tadorna tadornoides* 57–73 cm

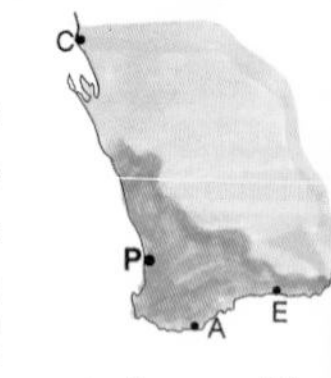

A grazing duck feeding on grasses on land or upending in shallow water to graze on aquatic plants. Formerly called Mountain Duck as in the eastern states it will graze on the high mountain grasslands. In general, it is a far more opportunistic feeder than most other ducks many of whom have very specialised feeding requirements. The most salt tolerant of all ducks. Like the Australian Wood Duck, the Australian Shelduck nests in tree hollows and has increased in numbers with the introduction of dams to the cleared Wheatbelt Region. Shelduck on Rottnest Island have adapted to nesting in the rock crevices by the sea, rather than high up in trees as on the mainland. The adult bird calls to the young from the sea whereupon they jump from the cliff, making their way to the nearest beach and then walking to the nearest salt lakes on the island. The male lacks the white eye ring of the female, no white to the base of the bill and has a brighter orange-brown chest than the duller rust-brown chest of the female. **Nest:** Most nests are located in hollow trunks with a pile of grasses or leaves laid on wood debris. Tree hollow can be as low as 2 metres or as high as 15 metres or more. Normal clutch size 6–10. **Similar species:** None. **Status:** Common in the South West particularly the Wheatbelt. Less common in the drier regions, however will congregate in large numbers on inland salt lakes after good rains. Lake Gore in Esperance has had over 7000 in one count. **Where to find:** Any wetland in

ʾerth or on or near Wheatbelt dams and wetlands along the south coast. Throughout the Mulga Region on large ephemeral lakes.

Male in foregraound

Hardhead (White-eyed Duck) *Aythya australis* 45–60 cm

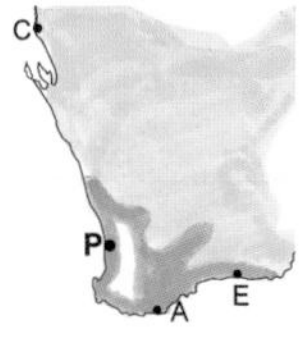

An irruptive species that will fly great distances to find new feeding grounds. Feeds on aquatic vegetation but also animals like freshwater shellfish. Prefers deep water. Can dive deeper than most ducks. Unlike some ducks, this species has declined in numbers since European settlement. The male is easier to identify with its white iris and dull white tip on the end of the bill, the female not so easy; she has a brown iris and no white on the end of the bill. **Nest:** Nest is a very large pile of reeds or other aquatic foliage with a large quantity of down used to cover eggs. Normal clutch size 6–8. **Similar species:** Female Blue-billed Duck which is smaller and has a more compact body. Bill on the Musk Duck is wedge shaped whereas the Blue-bill has a typical slim duck bill not short and wedged. **Status:** Uncommon particularly in arid regions. **Where to find:** Fairly common in most large wetlands of Perth. Found throughout the South West Region where there are large bodies of fresh water.

Musk Duck *Biziura lobata* 64–68 cm

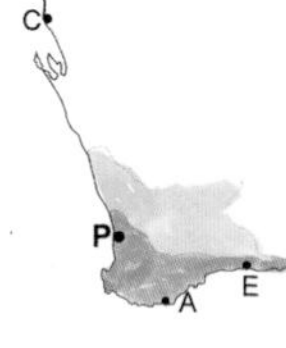

One of the stiff-tailed ducks. Male much larger than the female. Less nomadic than many other duck species, preferring the deeper permanent wetlands of the lower South West corner of WA. Normally in small numbers but occasionally out of the breeding season in summer and autumn large congregations can gather, such as on the Esperance wetlands or Peel Inlet; however it is an uncommon sight to see more than 200 birds on one wetland. The male has one of the most extraordinary courtship displays of any Australian duck. Under its bill is a leathery lobe that normally hangs as a loose appendage, but when in display the lobe becomes more rigid and its cheeks inflated, while the duck extends the head upwards and back and draws the tail forward and over its back with the wings drawn upwards, then suddenly it will let out a far carrying high pitch 'pinging' call and draw its feet to the side creating a large splash either side of its body. **Nest:** Nests mostly on a pile of aquatic vegetation, untidy with little or no soft lining. Normal clutch size 2–4. **Similar species:** Male none. Female may be confused with female Blue-billed Duck, which is smaller, has different bill shape and sits higher in the water. **Status:** Common locally but generally uncommon. **Where to find:** Common on most larger deep-water lakes in Perth. In the Esperance region Lake Gore and Lake Warden. Lake Seppings in Albany. Most other wetlands have only small numbers.

Australian Wood Duck (Maned Duck) *Chenonetta jubata* 48–58 cm

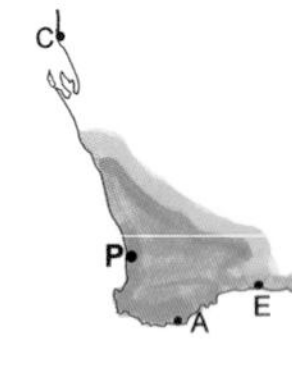

Often called Maned Duck in reference to the feathering on the lower nape. Even though this duck does not have brightly coloured feathers, when seen up close both the male and the female have exquisite detail in their plumage. The male has greyer, less mottled flanks and darker chocolate head. This duck is primarily a grazing waterfowl, preferring to eat low grasses, but in the Wheatbelt it has adapted to eating a higher proportion of grain seed. With the clearing of land and the availability of permanent water in the myriad of small dams throughout the Wheatbelt, it has found a niche habitat. Also, the need to nest in tree hollows and have water nearby for their young has made this a common bird on the edge of many Wheatbelt reserves. They nest in tree hollows as high as 15 metres from the ground. The parent bird calls constantly to the young to jump from the nest and then they freefall down to the ground extending their rudimentary wings and bounce like fluffy balls. It is an amazing sight. When all the chicks are out of the nest, the parent bird will walk them to water, often several hundred metres away. **Nest:** Nest normally 5–15 metres above ground mostly in live trees containing dead limbs with hollows, not far from water. Clutch size 6–8. **Similar species:** None. **Status:** Now common in the well watered South West but not in the thicker Jarrah Forest unless abutting farmland. Uncommon in pastoral country. **Where to find:** Throughout the region but easiest in the deeper South West Region.

Freckled Duck *Stictonetta naevosa* 50–58 cm

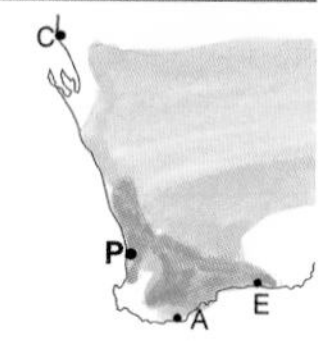

Australia's most uncommon duck other than the rare vagrants like Garganey, Northern Shoveler and Northern Pintail which visit mainly northern Australia. Seen up close, they have beautiful dark grey flecking on body. The female could be confused with a female Blue-billed Duck which is smaller and does not have the same jizz, particularly the classic feature of the 'ski slope' on the forehead of the Freckled Duck that drops down to the bill and the slight crest on its the nape. Luckily, when the male is in breeding plumage the lores are bright red allowing easy identification but out of the breeding season can be very subdued. Perth is fortunate to have a good range of permanent wetlands giving species that are highly nomadic the opportunity to have somewhere to retreat to when the desert ephemeral wetlands are dry. The bird illustrated was photographed on Herdsman Lake. One of their preferred habitats is wetlands that have dense stands of Freshwater Paperbark trees (*Melaleuca rhaphiophylia*). Not only do they feed in these wetlands but they also prefer to nest in paperbark trees in the south west, unlike their other preferred site in tall lignum in large remote ephemeral lakes like Lake Gregory. **Nest:** A large structure of twigs or flood debris placed on water in heavily treed locations often in paperbark swamps in the South West. They sometimes use an old swan's nest. Normal clutch size 4–6**. Similar species:** Female Blue-billed Duck which is smaller and its neck is shorter and its head is rounded with no steep forehead or crest on nape. **Status:** Scarce. **Where to find:** Can show up in Perth wetlands in any season. Found on wetlands such as Lake Dumbleyung (in the south east corner). Lake Tarblin.

Lake Toolibin (when both lakes have adequate water). Benger Swamp. Lake Chittering. Lake Warden. Lake Wannamal. If you are really keen to see this species in the South West, you will often require a canoe to explore many of the above wetlands, as they are mostly found in the central part of the lakes in dense stands of paperbark or sheoak thickets.

Blue-billed Duck *Oxyura australis* 36–44 cm

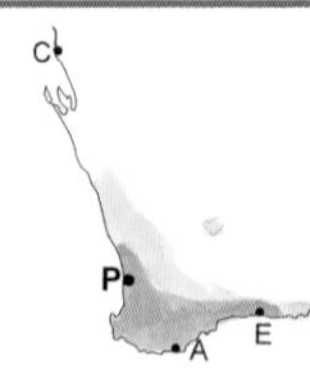

The bright blue bill of the Blue-billed Duck only lasts through the breeding period and by the autumn becomes a dull blue-grey. It is one of the two stiff-tailed ducks in Australia. It lives almost entirely in water and does not like to venture far on land. When feeding, has the ability to dive to reasonable depths preferring deeper permanent wetlands. It prefers to dive when in danger and travel up to 30–40 metres just below the surface. Like the Musk Duck, it too has a spectacular mating display which is varied and complex, including a curious movement of pressing the head to the chest then extending the head into the water while blowing bubbles and then flicking water with its bill. An uncommon duck, although locally common in the Perth region and coastal belt down to Capel, mostly in small numbers but can reach large numbers in dry years in summer on wetlands like Peel Inlet, with over 1000 birds once counted. Does not like saline waters. **Nest:** A well constructed nest on water, sometimes as thick as a metre deep with hood over nest chamber lined with soft grasses and some down. Normal clutch size 4–6. **Similar species:** Female Musk Duck or female and eclipse plumaged male Freckled Duck. Refer to notes on those species. **Status:** Locally common on the Swan Coastal Plain but tends to be uncommon throughout the southern region and very uncommon past the northern Wheatbelt. **Where to find:** All the larger lakes in Perth particularly Herdsman Lake. Peel Inlet. Wannamal Lake. Vasse Estuary. Lake Warden, Esperance.

Left: Female

Pacific Black Duck *Anas superciliosa* 50–60 cm

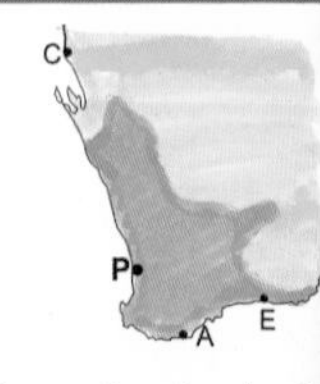

A duck that feeds in varied habitats and, unlike many other species of duck, will feed on very small bodies of water even small drainage channels. Has a preference for freshwater wetlands. It is one of the 'dabbling' ducks, taking food from the surface as well as upending to graze on aquatic plants. Normally sedentary where permanent bodies of water exist but many will migrate to inland areas after good rains. Males leave after the clutch has been laid, joining other males in large numbers on some lakes. The female is left to attend to the young until dispersal. Unlike many species of duck, the Pacific Black Duck will nest in a variety of locations including the tops of dead stumps, tree hollows and old nests and occasionally on the ground in vegetation. **Nest:** Nests vary, mostly located alongside water in grassed areas but sometimes placed in tree hollows. Normal clutch size 8–10. **Similar species:** Female Mallard. Female Garganey (rare vagrant in the Greater South West). Some likeness at a distance to Grey Teal which is smaller with no facial striping. **Status:** Very common in South West Region. Uncommon in arid regions. **Where to find:** Any wetland area.

Grey Teal *Anas gracilis* 42–46 cm

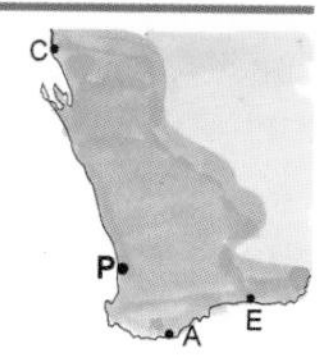

Found throughout Australia. This is one species that is extremely hard to differentiate between male and female, and colour of plumage does not separate them easily. Those who have studied the Grey Teal note that the male has a different standing posture with head held up while the female posture is lower, and that both have distinct calls. In the early

nineteenth century, it was presumed that Grey Teal were the females of Chestnut Teal. Grey Teal can be found on fresh, brackish and saline waters. Highly nomadic. Any water body in the drier region has a good chance of having Grey Teal. This propensity to feed in so many areas throughout Australia may be due to the fact that a higher proportion of the diet is made up of invertebrates, the balance being vegetable matter. They breed in any season depending on rain. **Nest:** Nests in tree hollows, bushes and on the ground but in the South West they favour nesting in tree hollows in flooded regions. Often roost in groups and will perch on logs, similar to Black Duck. Normal clutch size 5–10. **Similar species:** The female and eclipsed plumage male Chestnut Teal are both very similar in shape, size and colouration. The Grey Teal has a lighter throat but the main difference is a slight darker grey-brown colouration overall. **Status:** Common throughout the region on any wetland. **Where to find:** Any major Perth lake, more so in the summer months.

Chestnut Teal *Anas castanea* 40–48 cm

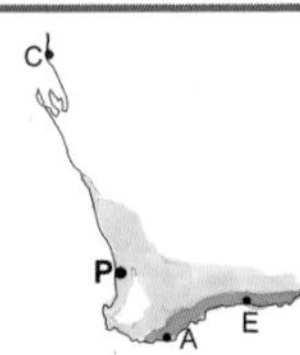

Although the Chestnut Teal is relatively common in the eastern states, particularly Tasmania, it is our second least common duck after the Freckled Duck, not including rare vagrants. It is one of the dabbling ducks, gaining most food from the surface but also upending to get at aquatic vegetation. It is well adapted to living in waters with a high salinity level such as river estuaries, mainly on the south coast, increasing in numbers as one reaches the Esperance region. **Nest:** Similar to Grey Teal. Normal clutch size 5–10. **Similar species:** Grey Teal, the main two differences being that the Grey Teal has a whiter throat and the female Chestnut Teal is generally darker overall. **Status:** Uncommon throughout the South West Region. Locally common on some of the larger Esperance lakes. **Where to find:** Occasionally in Perth but uncommon on the Swan Coastal Plain and along the coast to Geraldton. Very uncommon in the deeper South West. Best seen on the southern inland and coastal rivers and inlets including: The lake systems that lie at the northern side of the Stirling Range, including small drainage channels. The estuaries of the Bremer River. The Gairdner River. Fitzgerald River inlet including all wetlands in the Fitzgerald River NP. All lakes and inlets adjacent to the coast between Hopetoun and Israelite Bay with Lake Warden recording the greatest numbers. Uncommon to rare in the arid regions.

Australasian Shoveler *Anas rhynchotis* 47–53 cm

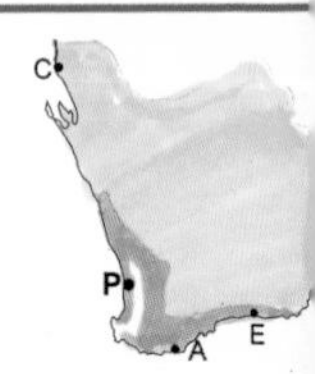

A very specialised feeder, one of the filter dabbling ducks requiring wetlands with rich aquatic vegetation as the bill is highly adapted to filter feeding. Found mostly on large deep-water lakes on the Swan Coastal Plain and the southern region. More sedentary than most ducks, remaining where food sources are reliable but have been known to wander as far north as Carnarvon and along the coast to Esperance. The male has brighter and more varied colours, with bright chestnut on belly and flanks; head is blue-grey rather than brown-grey. Male in eclipse plumage looks very similar to female but male flanks have chestnut tinge to the brown plumage, whereas the flanks of the adult female are plain brown. Also the male has a slightly darker head but these features are only noticeable when birds are close together. There are two subspecies in Australasia, the nominate subspecies *rhynchotis* in Australia, the other *variegata* in New Zealand. **Nest:** Nests close to water, nest lined with grasses and down. Normal clutch size 6–10. **Similar species:** None except the rare vagrant, the Northern Shoveler. The females are almost identical and very difficult to split. The Northern Shoveler female has a slightly lighter head and body but very difficult to note. With the male adults there is no confusion. **Status:** Uncommon to scarce throughout the region with the highest concentrations on the Swan Coastal Plain. Some authorities say the species is on the increase but the author questions this; some of the major lakes in Perth in the late 70s held far more than they do now. Between 1981 and 1985 approx. 2000 on Lake Thompson and 2000 on Forrestdale Lake (Jaensch et al. Waterbirds in Nature Reserves. RAOU 1988). **Where to find:** Any of the larger lakes in Perth and the Swan Coastal Plain such as the Peel Inlet.

Pink-eared Duck *Malacorhynchus membranaceus* 40–45 cm

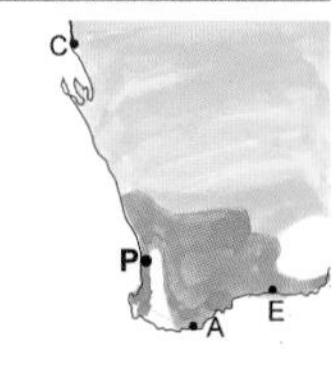

One of the most beautiful Australian ducks. A feature of the adult breeding birds not found on the juvenile is a small pink mark behind the eye, so small as to be indiscernible at distance. It has a unique bill designed for specialised filter feeding on microscopic invertebrates and algae. It is a highly nomadic duck and unlike the majority of species of duck wanders far into inland lakes and floodwaters. Has a preference for recently flooded country that is shallow with plenty of aquatic fauna and vegetation. Some ephemeral wetlands just 100 km north of Perth have had numbers as high as 2500 birds but generally Pink-eared Ducks are uncommon on the Swan Coastal Plain. They have a peculiar feeding habit whereby two birds spin very fast in a tight circle only about 60–70 cm apart, head to tail. This feeding technique stirs up invertebrates and is called 'vortexing'. At first sight it appears that it is a mating ritual but this is not the case. This form of cooperative feeding is unusual in the smaller waterbirds. **Nest:** Does not build a nest but uses other species nests or tree hollows. Large amounts of down are used and eggs can be totally covered. Clutch size 6–8. **Similar species:** None. **Status:** Generally an uncommon species but gathers in large numbers on ephemeral flooded wetlands often in remote regions. **Where to find:** In the Perth Region: Bayswater

Sanctuary. Herdsman Lake. Lake Monger. Kogolup Lake. Lake Bibra. Forrestdale Lake. In the Wheatbelt: Dumbleyung Lake. Towerrinning Lake. Capamaura Lake. Coomelberrup Lake (excellent but only good after seasonal rains, alas mostly dry). Nonalling Lake (a good wetland but often dry). In drier regions: Rowles Lagoon. Nallan Lake. Wooleen Lake.

Great Crested Grebe *Podiceps cristatus* 48–61 cm

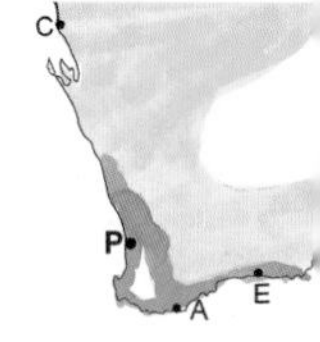

Native to Europe, much of southern Asia, parts of Africa and Australia. The Great Crested Grebe is noted for its spectacular courtship displays, in which the pair speed towards each other and meet face to face raising their necks high while leaning backwards and shaking their heads rapidly, then pull away. The most interesting display, which normally precedes mating, is known as the 'Weed Dance', where the male dives and collects weed in his bill and swims towards the female shaking his head rapidly from side to side. They then both dive and gather weed and come together both shaking heads. If you are lucky in the breeding season (August – September) on the south west corner of Lake Monger or the south west corner of Herdsman Lake opposite Lakeside Drive, you may witness this unique performance. Great Crested Grebes mostly feed on small fish and hence are very strong swimmers and can dive with ease to reasonable depths. They require unpolluted fresh water and are normally a

sign of a fairly healthy wetland although one may question this in the case of Lake Monger. There are three subspecies in the world, only one subspecies *cristatus* in Australia. **Nest:** Consists of a floating raft of reeds and aquatic grasses away from shoreline. Normal clutch size 4–5. **Similar species:** None. **Status:** Has expanded its range over the last century. It was first recorded nesting in Perth in the mid 1930s (Johnstone and Storr 1998). It now nests in several locations in Perth and the South West. **Where to find:** Lake Joondalup. Herdsman Lake. Lake Monger. Wannamal Lake. Chittering Lake. Grassmere Lake.

Hoary-headed Grebe *Poliocephalus poliocephalus* 29–30 cm

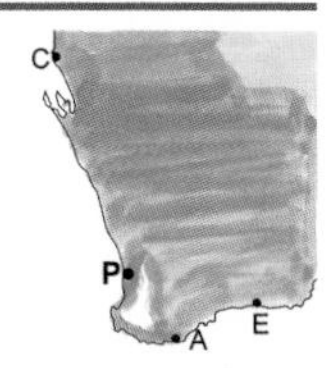

A nomadic grebe that has a high tolerance to saline waters; hence it occurs throughout the arid regions as well as the south west corner. When claypans fill after heavy rains Hoary-headed Grebes may visit in large numbers, feeding primarily on invertebrates and small fish. In the arid regions, they feed on brine shrimps. **Nest:** Nests are floating reeds or grasses often on remote lakes and sometimes in small colonies. Normal clutch size 4–6. **Similar species:** The non-breeding adult Australasian Grebe looks very similar to the non-breeding Hoary-headed Grebe and often requires the birds to be close to see the differences. The habitat tends to give you the first lead. The Hoary-headed Grebe has a longer neck. The author finds the plain grey flanks of the Hoary-headed Grebe the quickest identification detail; the Australasian Grebe always has a light chestnut-brown flank so tends to look a browner bird and the Hoary-headed a greyer bird. The dark crown meets the light cheek passing through the eye on the Australian Grebe and passes just below the eye on the Hoary-headed but these details are not easy to see unless very close. Colour shade on flanks is much easier. In breeding plumage, there is no problem differentiating both species. **Status:** Locally common on large open bodies of water with higher saline levels than Australasian Grebe can tolerate. **Where to find:** In Perth: Lake Monger. Lake Thompson. Kogulup Lake. Forrestdale Lake (Thompson and Forrestdale dry out in early summer) and Bibra Lake can be good, particularly in summer and autumn. Found throughout the Wheatbelt particularly the Esperance lakes. Found in the Mulga on inland lakes like Lake Anneen and Lake Austin when heavy rains have fallen.

Australasian Grebe (Little Grebe) *Tachybaptus novaehollandiae novaehollandiae* 23–25 cm

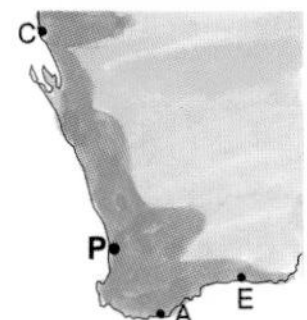

Although found together, the Australasian Grebe prefers wetlands containing fresh water whereas the Hoary-headed Grebe can tolerate saline waters, which is why on the Wheatbelt lakes you will get higher numbers of Hoary-headed Grebe. The Australasian Grebe is found more

in the deeper South West and Swan Coastal Plain but will travel to the arid regions in good seasons. Besides the bigger wetlands, they can be found on any small pool or dam. They eat small fish and aquatic invertebrates. Generally shy unless in urban areas. There are three subspecies in Australasia but only one *novaehollandiae* found in Australia and New Guinea. **Nest:** Nest is a floating pile of reeds with eggs covered over when the bird leaves the nest. Mostly close to shoreline but often concealed by reed beds. Normal clutch size 4–6. **Similar species:** Refer Hoary-headed Grebe. **Status:** Common in the southwest. Uncommon in the station country except after good rains. **Where to find:** In Perth: Lake Joondalup. Lake Gwelup. Herdsman. Bibra Lake. Throughout the south west, including: Lake Chittering. Wannamal Lake. Vasse Estuary. Lake Toolibin and all freshwater lakes east to Esperance.

Little Penguin (Fairy Penguin) *Eudyptula* minor subspecies *novaehollandiae* 40–45 cm

There are several species of penguin that may be driven onto Western Australia's shores after storms or when needing to moult, but the Little Penguin is the only resident penguin. The adult birds do not travel the great distances from their nesting colony that other penguins do; however the immature birds do not return to the colony for at least 2 years, mostly 3 years. Feed on small shoaling fish but will take crustaceans. Most colonies in Western Australia are on islands but there are a few on mainland sites. They roost during the day on land, leaving the breeding site one hour before dawn and start to return at dusk and for at least two hours after dark. Both adults will incubate the egg and rear young. There are six subspecies, only one *novaehollandiae* in Western Australia. **Nest:** Nest is located at the end of a small tunnel about one to one and

Captive bird

half metres long. The nest chamber has a small quantity of leaves or grasses. Normal clutch size is just 2. **Similar species:** None. The nearest small penguins are the Adelie and Chinstrap which are more than twice the weight. **Status**: Common throughout the South West from Carnac Island all the way around the South West coast to the far eastern colony at Twilight Cove. **Where to find:** Best and easiest location, Penguin Island. Carnac Island. Nests on hundreds of islands along the south west coast, mostly in the Recherche Archipelago.

Red-tailed Tropicbird *Phaethon rubricauda* 95–104 cm (includes tail rectrices 35 cm long)

Seen close up one appreciates what a heavy bodied bird the Red-tailed Tropicbird is, but to see a breeding pair fly and perform their courtship flight is like looking at two ballerinas in the sky, the pair flying up vertically then doing backward loops with their beautiful red central tail feathers streaming behind (the streamers can be hard to see at times). A lone species that wanders the high seas, rarely seen except when at the breeding site. Feeds on fish by diving from a good height (normally not as high as gannets) and staying under for several seconds until securing fish. **Nest:** Two types of nest location are utilised in Western Australia: either on rock ledges on cliffs or rocky outcrops using no nest material, or on sandy beaches above the high water mark normally preferring a solid overhang. The author has always found them on islands under excavated overhangs against a firm sand ridges. Normal clutch size just one egg. **Similar species:** White-tailed Tropicbird which is a slightly smaller bird with bill and central tail feathers yellow not red. White-tailed has distinct black band on the upper wing, unlike the Red-tailed which has no band. **Status:** Scarce. **Where to find:** In the Greater South West: Sugarloaf Rock and the Abrolhos Islands (both not always). The author has seen the species on Rottnest Island which is a rare occurrence and also seen it on Pelsaert Island, not rare there.

Photo Graeme Chapman

Brown Booby *Sula leucogaster* subspecies *plotus* 67–75 cm Vagrant

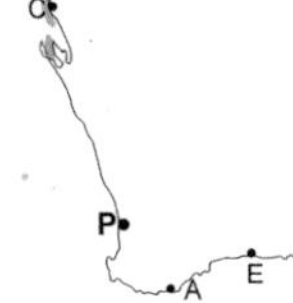

A rare vagrant to the coastal shores off Carnarvon. A bird of the north west seas. Nests on the Lacepede Islands and Ashmore Reef. **Similar species:** None in these waters.

Australasian Darter *Anhinga melanogaster* subspecies *novaehollandiae* 85–90 cm

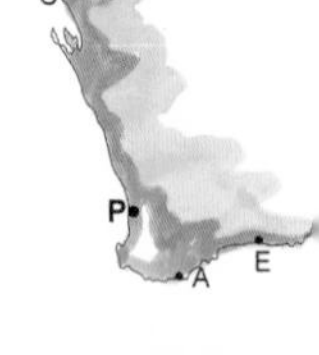

In the past, people gave the nickname Snake Bird to the Australasian Darter due to its ability to almost totally submerge its body leaving only its long neck exposed and giving it a snake-like appearance in the water. A fairly solitary feeding bird not forming feeding flocks like other wetland birds; however will congregate with other species when breeding within their colonies, particularly cormorants. Darters need to be solitary as their feeding technique requires stealth, catching their prey, mainly fish, by bending the long neck backwards and then darting out the neck, spearing the fish with their sharp pointed bill. The permanent kink in the neck is thought to be part of their powerful mechanism to spring the neck forward at great speed. In full breeding plumage, the male is a beautiful bird with a metallic black sheen to the plumage. It is distinguished from the female by having a chestnut throat, brighter when in breeding plumage, and is basically black all over, whereas the female has a cream underbody and no chestnut colour to the throat, and

Male

the upperbody and head are a lighter brown colour. It does get a little confusing with the immature male and the female as their upper and lower bodies are both a similar light brown colour but the immature male always retains a dark head with a chestnut coloured throat. The reason darters are seen sitting with wings outstretched is that their feathers do not repel water and, after constant feeding in water, they remain wet and must dry out. The absorption does however allow them to swim and feed for several hours semi-submerged. There are three subspecies in the world, only one subspecies *novaehollandiae* in Australia. Normally nests within colonies of cormorants. **Nest:** Large twig structure with hollow top lined with leaves or rushes placed on middle level branches, mostly in paperbark swamps. Clutch size 3–4. **Similar**

species: None. **Status:** Moderately common but never in large numbers. **Where to find:** Throughout the South West Region where freshwater wetlands occur. In Perth: Oldham Park on the northern side of the Narrows Bridge. Booragoon Lake. All along the Swan foreshore around the Narrows and Causeway (occasionally Fremantle North Mole).

Great Cormorant *Phalacrocorax carbo* subspecies *carboides* 80–85 cm

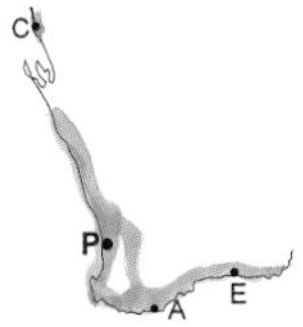

A cosmopolitan cormorant found in North America, Europe, Central and Eastern Asia, Africa and Australia. The Australian subspecies *novaehollandiae* is the largest cormorant. More of an inland species than the Pied Cormorant although can be found on coastal waters. Prefers big open bodies of water mostly in the South West Region. Dives well and can stay under water for nearly one minute. Feeds mostly on fish. A relatively solitary feeder unless food is abundant and even then it is uncommon to see more than 50 –100 birds together.

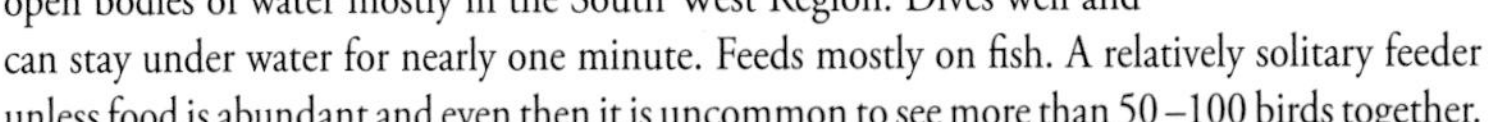

More nomadic than any of the cormorants, flying hundreds of kilometres to better feeding sites. There are six subspecies in the world but only one in Australia. Nests mostly with other cormorants in colonies. **Nest:** A large twig nest is built, often being used year after year. Clutch size 2–4. **Similar species:** Little Black Cormorant which is nearly 30 cm smaller, and lacks white on the throat and yellow facial skin. **Status:** Moderately common in the South West. Uncommon in the station country. **Where to find:** In Perth on most of the larger lakes like Joondalup and Herdsman Lake. Also Alfred Cove. Breeds at Booragoon Lake. In the South West Region: Namming Lake. Lake. Dumbleyung. Wannamal. Guraga Lake. Harvey Estuary. Peel Inlet. Not so common on southern wetlands to Esperance.

Little Black Cormorant *Phalacrocorax sulcirostris* 55–58 cm

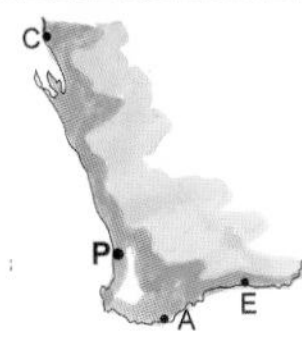

Found in greater numbers throughout the South West than the Great Cormorant. An all black cormorant with a dark green metallic sheen on the upperbody, best when seen in full sunlight. Found on a diverse range of wetlands but also in large numbers on sheltered harbours and estuaries where rafts of cormorants will work together herding fish. Seen regularly flying up or down the Swan River in 'v' formation to new feeding grounds. **Nest:** A twig nest placed in trees; nests in large colonies, as at Booragoon Lake. Nest is smaller than those of most cormorants, placed at the extremity of branches mostly over water. Clutch size 3–5. **Similar species:** Refer Great Cormorant. **Status:** Common throughout South West and mid west coastal regions. Scarce in the Wheatbelt and station country. **Where to find:** Most Perth wetlands and estuaries. Peel Inlet. Vasse. Lake Towerrinning (when flooded). Lake Toolibin (when flooded). Lake Warden.

Pied Cormorant *Phalacrocorax various* subspecies *hypoleucos* 72–80 cm

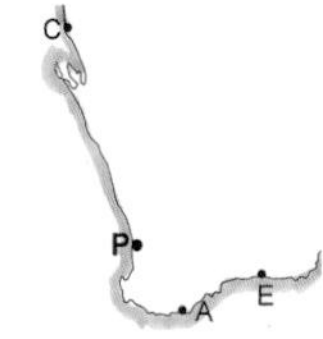

Primarily a marine species but does travel to some large inland lakes and estuaries. Mostly the adult birds stay within 30–40 km of their breeding area throughout the year. Feeds mostly on fish, some crustaceans taken. Breeds in colonies, sometimes in large numbers. Very numerous around the Denham and Geraldton regions (breeds on the Abrolhos Islands). Develops an orange patch at base of bill in the breeding season. Needs to dry wings after long periods of diving. There are two subspecies, *hypoleucos* in Australia and *various* in New Zealand. **Nest:** A large twig structure with a shallow hollow centre. Nests in trees and on the ground in colonies. Clutch size 2–3. **Similar species:** Black-faced Cormorant and to a lesser degree Little Pied Cormorant. Black-faced Cormorant has no yellow face or pink gape and no white feathers near eye. Pied Cormorant in Western Australia are uncommon in

the region around Esperance where Black-faced occur. Little Pied Cormorant is 18 cm smaller and except when juvenile does not have a black band on the flanks, and has no yellow facial patch. **Status:** Very common in Dirk Hartog Island and Denham region. Common along Geraldton coast. Uncommon mid west. Common off Perth all the way to Busselton. Not so common on the southern coast. **Where to find:** Perth coast and estuary. Alfred Cove. Rottnest Island. Vasse Estuary. Peel Inlet. The entire coastline from Shark Bay to Esperance.

Little Pied Cormorant *Microcarbo melanoleucos* 55–58 cm

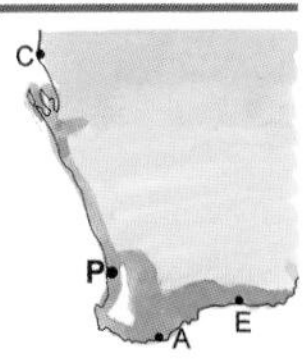

The smallest of all the cormorants. In almost a role reversal of the Pied Cormorant, it favours fresh water and inland waters but it too will feed on sheltered coastal waters though to a lesser degree. The most catholic in its choice of waters of all the cormorants. Prolific throughout most of the region, found in any small lake or dam. However, their main diet is small fish. Feeds communally when food is abundant, often with Little Black Cormorant. There are three subspecies of Little Pied Cormorant, only one in Australia namely *melanoleucos* which is also found in Indonesia, New Guinea and the Solomon Islands. **Nest:** Nests communally often with other species of cormorant and darters. Nest is small structure of twigs built in trees with small amount of leaves in central bowl. Clutch size 3–4. **Similar species:** Pied Cormorant, which is far larger and has black band on flanks and a yellow facial patch. **Status:** Very common throughout the region except inland in the drier regions. Less common in the northern part of the coastal belt gaining in numbers from Perth all the way around the south west coast to Esperance. Lake Warden can have up to 600 birds at one time. Throughout the Wheatbelt to Kalgoorlie in smaller numbers but wherever there is water there is the possibility of Little Pied Cormorants. **Where to find:** Throughout the region but only casual in the inland regions.

Black-faced Cormorant (also called Black-faced Shag) *Phalacrocorax fuscescens* 62–70 cm

Unlike most cormorants which may venture to inland waters, Black-faced Cormorants are the most sedentary birds of the cormorant group, not travelling far from their breeding and roosting sites in the southern seas. In Western Australia its range is restricted to the eastern southern coast of Western Australia. It nests on the islands off Esperance and those off Cape Arid National Park. Immature birds will fly to islands other than their original breeding site.

Nest: Nests mostly on islands either directly on rock or sometimes large seaweed structures placed on ground. Clutch size 2–4. **Similar species:** Similar to Pied Cormorant but lacks the yellow face and does not develop a pink gape during breeding. Black-faced has no blue orbital eye ring. The Little Pied is smaller again with no black band on the flanks and the eye is completely surrounded by white plumage on the face. **Status:** Locally common off the Esperance coast and further east to Daw Island. Does not come further west than the Hopetoun region. **Where to find:** The Esperance jetty often has Black-faced Cormorants at the end. A boat trip to Woody Island will pass nesting sites on lone rock islets.

Australian Pelican *Pelecanus conspicllatus* 1.6–1.8 m

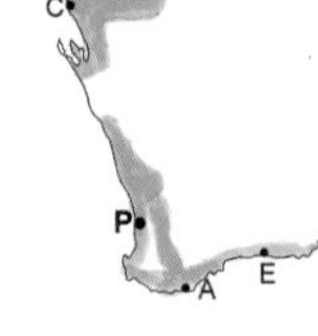

Of the seven species of pelican in the world, this is the only member of its genus in Australia. Most people know that pelicans eat fish but there is a side to their behaviour which is less well known. They will manoeuvre close to ducks or other waterbirds, particularly smaller birds such as ducklings, suddenly swing their necks and throw the body forward to try scoop up their prey; luckily for the ducklings they often fail but it shows the extent of their carnivorous and opportunistic feeding behaviour. Mostly when not feeding alone they work in groups to catch fish, plunging their heads in unison. Found along most of the

GSWcoastline and to a lesser degree on inland waters. Pelicans will fly as far as two thousand kilometres after heavy rains have fallen on inland salt lakes. They also fly regularly between the Swan Estuary and Peel Inlet by taking advantage of the thermals to carry them to great heights whence they will literally glide down to their destination. **Nest:** Nests in colonies. Two of the main nesting sites are Peel Inlet and a small rocky island opposite Emu Point in Albany. Nests mostly on islands on large bodies of water or sheltered inlets in dense colonies. Nest is scraped in sand or of small seaweed and debris on rock. Clutch size normally 2. **Similar species:** None. **Status:** Common along the South West coastline. Uncommon along the Esperance/Cape Arid coastline. **Where to find:** Most large lakes in Perth, particularly Lake Monger (not guaranteed) and the Swan Estuary. All other major inlets along the coast to Bremer Bay.

White-necked Heron (Pacific heron) *Ardea pacifica* 76–106 cm

The largest heron in the Greater South West. Unmistakable long white neck set against blue-grey body. Has a languid flight with the two white shoulder patches visible in flight, also showing its kinked neck. Normally, a very nervous heron which does not allow a close approach and soon takes flight, calling as it flies. Found on the edges of large lakes

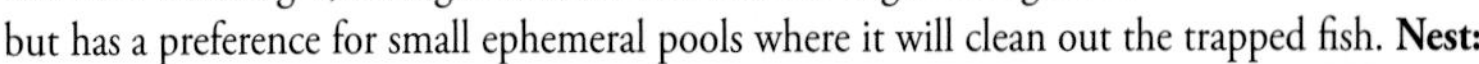

but has a preference for small ephemeral pools where it will clean out the trapped fish. **Nest:** Nests quite high in trees, sometimes a solitary nester but other times in loose small colonies. Builds a broad flat twig nest. Clutch size 3–5. **Similar species:** None in this region. In the north of the state immature Pied Heron similar but far smaller. **Status:** Moderately common throughout the Greater South West. Locally common after good seasons in the mid west, particularly from Carnarvon to Gascoyne Junction. Moves to the South West when inland wetlands dry out in summer. **Where to find:** Most of the larger freshwater lakes with shallow margins and dams particularly on the Swan Coastal Plain, also the south coast wetlands.

Captive bird

White-faced Heron *Egretta novaehollandiae* 66–68 cm

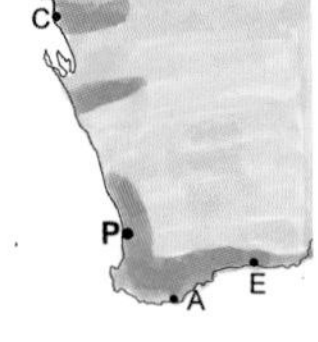

More numerous than White-necked Heron and seen on most small wetlands and small drainage channels. Feeds on fish, frogs, reptiles and invertebrates by stalking and waiting for its prey. It will gather in dry fields of stubble when grasshoppers are in high numbers, also well watered grass fields feeding off insects, and occasionally beaches. Develops additional plumes on neck and breast in the breeding season. **Nest:** Flat structure of twigs between 5 and 15 metres above ground. Mostly a solitary nester. Clutch size 3–5. **Similar species:** Dark morph of the Eastern Reef Egret, which has no white on the face, a thicker bill and shorter legs. **Status:** Common throughout the whole region. **Where to find:** All types of wetland.

White-faced Heron

Eastern Reef Egret *Egretta sacra* 60–65 cm

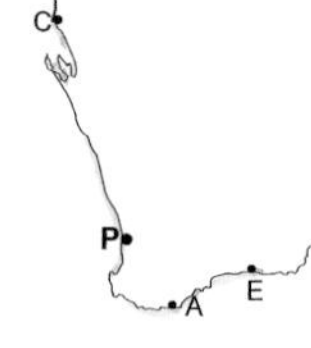

A bird found throughout Australasia and East Asia. There are two forms of Eastern Reef Egret: a white morph which occurs more in the tropics and a dark blue-grey morph which is more prevalent in the temperate regions of Australia. The two morphs do interbreed and not just in the transition zone as both occur in some areas together, although the white form is rare in the South West. They do not venture inland as other herons do but remain on the coastal belt. They mainly feed on rocky parts of the coastline rather than sandy beaches, feeding from the small tidal pools left after the retreating tides. They eat fish, crustaceans and molluscs, easily breaking shells with their robust bill. **Nest:** Nests in the south mostly on islands, nest being a small collection of twigs placed on rock ledge. Clutch size 2–3.

Similar species: The white morph is similar to Intermediate Egret but has slimmer body, finer all yellow bill, brown-black rather than pale yellow legs. Great Egret, far taller and longer necked. Little Egret, far smaller with fine black bill. It is rare for the white egrets in the South West to feed on tidal pools except the Great Egret. **Similar species to dark morph:** White-faced Heron which can feed on beaches but rarely does in the South West and does not like feeding on rocky coastlines like Reef Egret. The Reef Egret has no white on the face and has longer legs and much darker grey. **Status:** Uncommon to scarce on south coast with virtually no forms of the white morph. Moderately common on parts of the lower South West coast, increasing in the islands on the Abrolhos with a few white morphs. **Where to find:** Near Perth: on Rottnest Island, Carnac, Penguin and Garden Islands. On the south coast: Wilsons Inlet. Cheyne Beach. Can be found where extensive rocky coastlines occur.

Eastern Great Egret *Ardea alba* subspecies *modesta* 83–103 cm

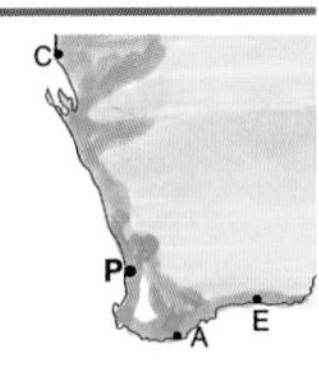

Tallest of all the egrets with very long 's' shaped neck which at full stretch is longer than the body length, a useful diagnostic feature. No other heron has the long neck to body ratio, and it is the only egret where the gape passes the eye; also has the longest legs. People talk of bill colour as a main diagnostic feature but care must be exercised as the immature bird has an all yellow bill, the non-breeding adult a yellow bill with long black tip, and then in breeding plumage the bill becomes all black. In breeding plumage the facial skin becomes lime-green. Found throughout much of the world, it was formerly a rare visitor to the South West but since the 1930s has increased in number. Will feed on inland wetlands, moist grasslands and coastal mudflats. Only one subspecies *modesta* in Australia. **Nest:** Nests mostly with other egrets and herons in small loose colonies. Flat twig nest placed in a tree mostly over water. Clutch size 3–4. **Similar species:** Intermediate Egret has neck noticeably shorter than body length. Gape stops short just below eye and does not pass it. Legs in proportion to body shorter than Great Egret. You are unlikely to see Intermediate unless a vagrant comes to the Carnarvon region. **Status:** Common in most of the lower South West, particularly on the Swan Coastal Plain. Uncommon in the western part of the Wheatbelt and Southern Coastal Regions. **Where to find:** Most large lakes in Perth. Vasse Estuary. Peel Inlet. Australind.

Little Egret *Egretta garzetta* subspecies *nigripes* 55–65 cm

Native to Africa, Asia and Australasia, the Little Egret did not establish itself in the lower South West until the early 1900s. It is still scarce in the South West being centred on the Swan Coastal Plain. The smallest of all the egrets in Australia, with a fine bill that is always black, although the juvenile has just a slight yellow colouring to the lower mandible. Long legs for its size and as they lift their feet, occasionally the yellow soles can be seen from behind. During the breeding season develops two fine plumes coming from the nape. It is a more active feeder than the larger egrets, running and darting around to get prey. Two subspecies in the world, only one *nigripes* in Australia. **Nest:** Nest and location similar to Great Egret. Clutch size 2–4. **Similar species:** None really, the Cattle Egret comes near it for size but it has shorter legs and a stocky build, a shorter thicker neck and a shorter and thicker bill that is yellow and not black. There is certainly no confusion when the Cattle Egret is in breeding plumage with its orange tinged feathers on the crown, back and chest. **Status:** Scarce in the South West and mainly on the Swan Coastal Plain. Numbers increase towards the Carnarvon region. **Where to find:** Lake Jandabup (if there is water). Lake Joondalup. Herdsman Lake. Nests in paperbark swamps near Pinjarra. One of the best places to see them is in the Peel Inlet and Australind area. Carnarvon is the next main area along the west coast.

Cattle Egret *Ardea ibis* subspecies *coromanda* 70 cm

With the clearing of land worldwide and the introduction of cattle and water buffalo, the Cattle Egret has expanded its range, coming to Australia in the late 1940s and first reported in the South West in 1952. Cattle Egrets have been recorded in several locations in the Greater South West. As the name implies it accompanies livestock, mainly cattle; the moving cattle stir up insects which the Cattle Egret retrieves. This symbiotic relationship would have been going on for centuries with Brahman cattle and water buffalo in Asia and Africa. When in breeding plumage, the bird is unmistakable with its orange head and chest, and bill that turns orange-red. When not in breeding plumage, its thickset jowls, short neck and short legs still make it an easy egret to identify. Two subspecies in the world, only one *coromanda* in Australia. **Nest:** Nest is small flat structure placed in a tree or bush mostly over water and normally not more than 5 metres above the water level. Nests in colonies with other egrets, herons and cormorants. **Similar species:** Refer to Little Egret. **Status:** Scarce in the well watered South West.

Nankeen Night Heron *Nycticorax caledonicus* subspecies *mannillensis* 55–65 cm

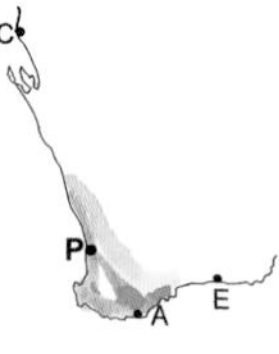

The name comes from the colour of the cotton cloth made in the city of Nankeen in China. Primarily a nocturnal feeder that roosts through the day although they will feed during daylight hours. They leave their well sheltered roosting sites at dusk to find their feeding grounds for the night. They nest and roost in colonies such as the swamp at Australind. The adults do not develop their adult plumage until the end of the first year, a rich chestnut colour on the upperbody and cream white underbody with no streaking. The crown is black with two white feathers leading from the nape of the head, called nuptial plumes. Above the eye and below the black crown is a white supercilium eye stripe. The immature birds lack the clean pure colours but have white and brown streaking on the breast and white and brown flecking on the upperbody. When very young, they have no black crown, just heavy white streaking. Six subspecies in the world, only one *mannillensis* in Australia. **Nest:** Nest normally 5–15 metres above water; mostly a solitary nester. Clutch size 2–3. **Similar species:** In the north of the GSW the Striated Heron has similarities to the immature Night Heron but the Night Heron does not feed on exposed mudflats though occasionally it can be found on saline creeks. However, the Striated Heron does not occur south of the Shark Bay region. The Little Bittern is a far smaller bird with a chestnut face, no head plumes, darker back, and no white supercilium, found mainly in long reed beds and very uncommon. **Status:** Relatively common on the Swan Coastal Plain and deep South West. Less common on the southern coast. Is found well into the Wheatbelt where there are thick paperbark wetlands. **Where to find:** In Perth: Trees in the Perth Zoo. Narrows Bridge on the north side. Fremantle Esplanade opposite the Esplanade Hotel in the pines and more so the dense cedar trees. Herdsman Lake. Bibra Lake. Lake Chandala. Lake Toolibin (if there is water) and most wetlands in the south where there are stands of paperbark.

Immature

Striated Heron (formerly Mangrove Heron) *Butorides stratus* subspecies *rogersi* 40–44 cm

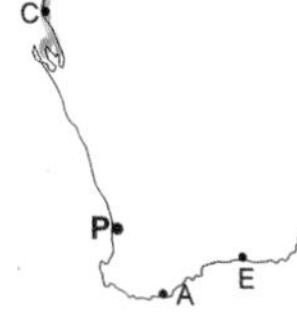

Found throughout much of Asia and Australasia. In Western Australia a bird of the northern region feeding on exposed mudflats and mud-lined tidal creeks often in mangroves along the coast. Feeds by lowering body just above the mud with neck withdrawn ready to strike, catching crabs and mud skippers. Immature birds have streaking on both the upperbody and underbody. There are 30 subspecies in the world with five in Australia, the only one in this region *rogersi*. **Nest:** Nests almost entirely in mangroves. Clutch size 2–3. **Similar species:** Immature Striated Heron has similarities to Nankeen Night Heron but does not share the same territory. **Status:** Less common in the northern parts of the GSW than the north of Western Australia.

Where to find: On some of the mangrove-lined bays on northern Peron Peninsula. In some of the mangroves between New Beach and Carnarvon. Mangroves at Mangrove Point, Carnarvon, and Miaboolia just north of Carnarvon.

Glossy Ibis *Plegadis falcinellus* 52–57 cm

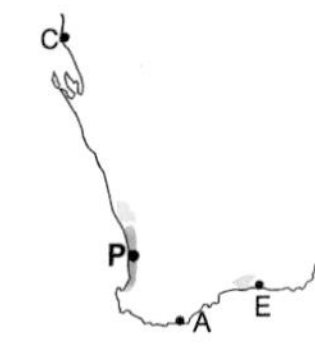

A bird found in parts of Africa, Asia and Australasia but is monotypic. The smallest Australian ibis. First recorded in Perth in 1906. Scarce to uncommon on the Swan Coastal Plain. Has nested at Chandala Lake near Chittering. Has a beautiful metallic bronze gloss when seen in full sunlight. Feeds on grassy edges of freshwater pools, has a preference for shallow waters. **Nest:** Nests either on flat rafts of reeds located in small swamps or up in paperbark trees on flat twig nests with leaves as base. Clutch size 3–4. **Similar species:** None. **Status:** Uncommon. **Where to find:** In Perth: Not common but seen at Herdsman Lake. Lake Joondalup also Thompson and Forrestdale Lakes when winter is wet. On the Swan Coastal Plain: Wallering Swamp near Gingin. Benger Swamp. Lake McClarty when winter is wet.

Australian White Ibis *Threskiornis molucca* 70 cm

C
P
A
E

First recorded in the South West Region in the 1950s. Has expanded its population to become a very common bird. Alas, has become a scavenger at waste disposal sites and has also been displacing cormorants from their breeding sites. Seen in paddocks on the Swan Coastal Plain often with Straw-necked Ibis, feeding on earthworms, insects and grasshoppers. They will also feed on freshwater mussels, fish and invertebrates. Gregarious, feeds in large groups. **Nest:** Nests both in reed beds and lignum but mostly in the South West in paperbark trees in dense colonies. Clutch size 2–3. **Similar species:** None. **Status:** Now very common on the Swan Coastal Plain expanding its range around the southern coast. Also travels to station country when seasonal rains have inundated the inland region. **Where to find:** Throughout the Swan Coastal Plain and parts of the southern region such as the Kalgan River estuary.

Straw-necked Ibis *Threskiornis spinicollis* 75 cm

Slightly smaller than the White Ibis, the Straw-necked unlike the White Ibis is endemic to Australia. Often seen spiralling up hundreds of feet to fly to new feeding grounds. Scarce in the South West until it became established in the mid 1950s in fact all ibis have expanded their range in the South West due to the massive land clearing programs, with more grasslands being created. Seen often in large numbers in paddocks taking advantage of drying ground or simply feeding on grasshoppers and other invertebrates. They are quite nomadic and banded birds have been recovered several thousand kilometres away from the South West Region. **Nest:** They nest colonially. Location and clutch size similar to the Australian White Ibis, 2–3. **Similar species:** None. **Status:** Common in the South West Region, less so in the north towards the Carnarvon area. Numbers are increasing every year and in Esperance groups of up to 500 birds have been sighted. **Where to find:** Carnarvon and inland along the lower Gascoyne catchment. South past Geraldton and all the way to Esperance. Common to very common on the Swan Coastal Plain.

Yellow-billed Spoonbill *Platalea flavipes* 85 cm

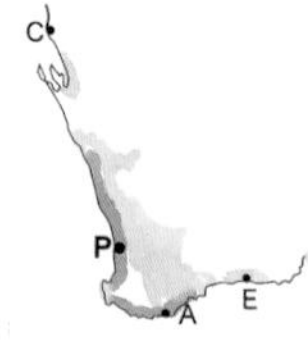

There are six species of spoonbill in the world, Australia having two of them, the Royal and the Yellow-billed. Spoonbills are related to ibis but ,through evolution, have developed a flattened bill with a spatulate end and become what is known as a 'tactile' feeder rather than developing a probing method of feeding like the ibis; by moving their open bill sideways back and forth through the water they can feel the prey, then they quickly clamp on and swallow it. The Yellow-billed Spoonbill is mostly a solitary feeder in Western Australia but will congregate with other spoonbills at times. In breeding plumage they develop nuptial plumes that grow from the lower throat and breast. They also develop a small red facial patch at the base of the bill. **Nest:** Nests in trees making a flat stick nest lined with some small leaves or twigs but also nests on flattened reed beds in swamps often in association with ibis. Clutch size 2–3. **Similar species:** Royal Spoonbill which has a black rather than yellow bill. **Status:** Like many of the ibis and egret species, the Yellow-billed Spoonbill has increased in numbers from being very rare in the 1920s to now moderately common on some wetlands on the Swan Coastal Plain. Has spread as far as the Esperance lakes. Above Moora it is scarce and not until the Carnarvon region does it occur again in any reasonable numbers. **Where to find:** In Perth: Herdsman Lake. Lake Joondalup. Bibra Lake. North Lake. Kogolup Lake. In the South West: Wannamal. Chittering. Toolibin (when water is present). Kalgan River. McCarley's Swamp (Ludlow).

Royal Spoonbill *Platalea regia* 74–81 cm

Vagrant

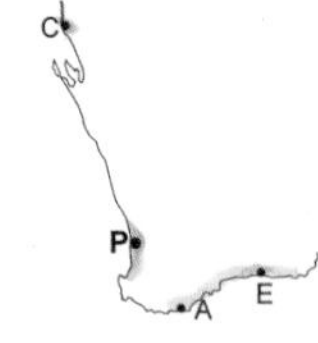

Uncommon in the South West. This species was not recorded in the South West Region until 1924 and it is still an uncommon bird . It is very common on the east coast and across northern Australia. Feeds in shallow fresh waters in the South West but, interestingly, will feed in shallow sea waters in the tropic regions of Australia. In breeding

plumage they develop beautiful long nuptial plumes from the crown and nape. **Nest:** Similar to Yellow-billed Spoonbill. **Similar species:** Yellow-billed Spoonbill which has yellow bill not black. **Status:** Scarce in the GSW. **Where to find:** Chance sightings may occur on the Swan Coastal Plain, including wetlands in Perth to Vasse and Peel Inlets areas. They have however been sighted as far east as Esperance.

Eastern Osprey *Pandion haliaetus* subspecies *leucocephalus*

50–65 cm span 160 cm

A large 'fishing eagle' found throughout the world. Feeds almost entirely on fish. Adult birds remain in their breeding territory all their life if the nesting site and feeding area are secure and food supply adequate. Can be harassed by the larger raptor the White-bellied Sea Eagle on some of the island sites. Found along all of the GSW coastline except due east of Cape Le Grand where it becomes scarce. In flight looks generally white underneath, with bands of dark brown on wings and tail and open black wing tips. When in stoop flight, tail is closed. Often seen patrolling the coastline. Female has brown flecking on breast. Male is pure white with no brown flecking. There are four subspecies in the world and just the one subspecies *leucocephalus* in Australia. **Nest:** Their nests can be huge structures particularly those on the ground such as on the Abrolhos Islands, sometimes they can be over a metre and a half high. They nest mostly on the ground on islands but also in dead trees on inland waters. Clutch size mostly 2 sometimes 3–4. **Similar species:** The immature White-bellied Sea Eagle could be confused with an Osprey but is far larger and the tail more wedge shaped. **Status:** Uncommon to common from Rottnest all the way north to Carnarvon. Common on the Abrolhos Islands. Uncommon from Augusta to Cape Arid. **Where to find:** In Perth: Alfred Cove and the Swan foreshore opposite Royal Perth Golf Club, South Perth. Also on Rottnest Island. North of Perth: Green Island. Wedge Island. Lancelin. Abrolhos Islands. Shark Bay. Carnarvon. South of Perth: Peel Inlet. Hamelin Bay. Torbay. Lower King River. Quoin Head (Fitzgerald River NP).

Black-shouldered Kite *Elanus axillaris* 36 cm span 90 cm

An elegant pale hawk often seen hovering with rapid wing beats, looking for small rodents or reptiles. White body parts seen in flight, with black carpals which lead to dark grey primaries. Adults have a completely white underbody. Juveniles have an orange-brown tinge to upper chest feathers, seen clearly in flight. An irruptive species seen more often when mice plagues occur but remains in areas where the food supply is constant. Prefers open country rather than forested areas. Rarely seen in the Darling Range. **Nest:** Placed near the top of a tree, often a solitary tree or small group of trees normally with cleared surroundings.

The nest is a small twig nest, lined with fresh leaves. Clutch size: 3–4. **Similar species:** Letter-winged Kite, which has distinct long black band running from the axillaries near the body to the primary coverts. The band follows the line of the underwing medium coverts. The black stands out clearly as a band, as the shoulders (marginal coverts) are pure white and also the rest of the underwing coverts and primaries are white. With the Black-shouldered Kite, the black is just seen on the underwing secondary coverts from the body to the centre of the leading edge wing. The Black-shouldered Kite also has a distinct black eyebrow that is not only on the lores as in the Letter-wing but also passes the eye, making it look like an extended eyebrow. **Status:** Moderately common on the Swan Coastal Plain and throughout the Wheatbelt Region and the southern coastal belt except the deep South West corner. Moderately common from Perth all the way north to Carnarvon. Many of the birds coming to the South West are non-breeding visitors and can come at any time of year. As the species is irruptive, it can be seen in station country when conditions favour rodent explosions. **Where to find:** The dry grass areas of the Swan Coastal Plain below the Darling Range. All of the inner Wheatbelt, particularly from Bindoon all the way to the Murchison. Over Kwongan heath such as that in the Fitzgerald River NP.

Black-shouldered Kite

Letter-winged Kite

Letter-winged Kite *Elanus scriptus* 33–38 cm span 90 cm Vagrant

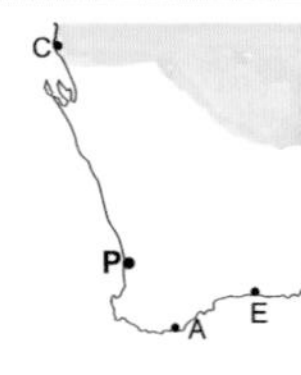

Rare in the South West. An interesting species that has evolved and adjusted to take advantage of the higher numbers of marsupials that are active at night. May not have the same nocturnal power of vision of owls, but they have developed a large retina to assist with the low light levels in which they hunt. Letter-winged Kites will often roost communally

in small numbers particularly along tree-lined watercourses. They leave to hunt just after sunset or sometimes later and return at the latest one hour before sunrise. The primary source of prey is the Long-haired Rat (*Rattus vilosissimus*). It is interesting that the distribution of Long-haired Rat stretches from northern South Australia to where the Strzelecki Desert starts, through the Simpson Desert and all the way across the southern deserts of the Northern Territory into the Tanami Desert in Western Australia, narrowing to a small band of grasslands that terminate almost at the coast near Derby and Broome; hence the plains around Roebuck Bay often get an influx of Letter-wings. The birds breed profusely where the rats are in large numbers but when the population of rats declines, the Letter-wings disperse far and wide and that is often when the GSW will receive the odd visiting bird. Letter-wings have bred in the GSW but only a few pairs have been recorded. The Birdsville and Strzelecki Deserts region is perhaps the core centre of their breeding population. **Nest:** Loose twigs and branches with fresh leaves in the centre, placed normally above 7m mostly in eucalypts along watercourses. Clutch size: 3–4. **Similar species:** Black-shouldered Kite. Refer to notes on Black-shouldered Kite. Note the photograph of a Letter-winged Kite (taken on Roebuck Plains); in flight the differences between the two species are easily visible but there are other subtle differences, as is illustrated in the two head photographs. The crown is more rounded in the Letter-winged Kite and there is no eye frown, also the eyes look larger. Note the eyebrow and the slightly conical crown of the Black-shouldered Kite. **Status:** A rare vagrant to the GSW. **Where to find:** Best chances in Western Australia are outside the range of this book, namely the lower Kimberley grasslands. Letter-winged Kites have been recorded in a few locations in the South West Region but are rare. Higher chance at Lake Gregory. The author has only seen communal roosting in South Australia and Southern Queensland. In Western Australia, he has seen one in broad daylight perched in a dead tree adjacent to Lake Gregory, also on the Roebuck Plains and at Parry's Lagoon.

Square-tailed Kite *Lophoictinia isura* 55 cm span 130 cm

A large, long and broad winged kite with open slots on the primaries. It has two favoured hunting habitats in the South West, one over trees in open or dense woodland and the other over heathland. In both habitats, it will circle often only 10–15 metres above the trees or heath looking for live prey. Most of its prey consists of small birds, although it can tackle bigger birds. When hunting, it takes a high percentage of fledglings such as the young of Yellow-plumed Honeyeaters. It will take reptiles and small mammals if the chance arises but does not like carrion. When it hunts for prey above the tree canopy, it flies in tighter concentric circles than a Little Eagle but will alternate the direction of the circle more than a Little Eagle. It will return to the same nesting site or area year after year. It migrates down from northern Australia in spring, arriving in mid to late August and nesting from September to December. Birds still are present in late January in the far south of the region such as the Torbay and Denmark region. In the drier areas like Dryandra Woodland Reserve, birds will often have left by mid December**. Nest:** Placed mostly on top of a large fork of branches either horizontal or sometimes vertical, normally 8–18 metres high, and consists of large twig saucer structure lined with fresh leaves. Has a preference for Wandoo trees or lower branches in Karri trees in the South West. Clutch size: 2–3. **Similar species:** Possible confusion with Little Eagle, which has a shorter and less broad tail. Does not twist its tail as much as Square-tailed Kite. The Little Eagle's body is stocky and thickset. Its wings are not as long and fingers on the primaries far shorter. Both have rufous colouring on parts of underwing but the Little Eagle's rufous plumage is confined to the leading edge of the wings. The Little Eagle's underbody is pale in the light morph, the most common morph in the GSW. The Square-tailed has an all rufous underbody and has light patches on the middle of the primaries looking almost like faint bullseyes, though nowhere near as prominent as a Black-breasted Buzzard's. Little Eagle has stronger contrast between underwing patterns. **Status:** Uncommon in the South West and southern coastal regions. Scarce north of Perth. The Square-tailed Kite would have been in greater numbers in the south west before European settlement as one of its favoured hunting grounds is Wandoo (*Eucalyptus wandoo*) Woodland, which extended from the edge of the Jarrah Forest almost to the Vermin Fence before it was cleared for farming. **Where to find:** In the Perth Region: On the scarp of the Darling Range. In the South West Region: Dryandra Woodland NR. Stirling Range NP. Torbay. Fitzgerald River NP. In the Transitional Woodland anywhere from Vermin Fence to Norseman.

Black-breasted Buzzard *Hamirostra melanosternon* 56–60 cm 145–155 cm

An unmistakable raptor found in the north and north east of the GSW. Their diet is more varied than some raptors, possibly including a higher percentage of reptiles than most species except the Pacific Baza. Takes many ground nesting birds. Will eat carrion (see photograph taken near Gascoyne Junction). Favoured hunting areas are open country often close to their nesting ground, which is normally in River Gums along inland river systems. Easily identified in flight by its jizz, i.e. very short tail, stocky body, distinct dihedral rocking flight more angular than Wedge-tailed Eagle's. White bullseyes in wings, in both the immature bird and adult bird but more defined in the adult bird. It is believed that some of Australia's raptors

are of an ancient lineage, not easily placed in raptor systematics. At present, it is placed in its own genus *Hamirostra*. Superficially in flight it reminds one of the African Bateleur, with its rocking motion from side to side when gliding and its short tail. In the region covered by this book, it comes down to the middle and upper reaches of the Murchison catchment and the Gascoyne River catchment (although the author has seen the bird out of its normal range near Peak Charles and also just north of the Murchison Bridge). It is predominately a carrion eater but takes birds, mostly ground dwelling, and certainly reptiles. The habit of breaking eggs open by picking up stones with its bill and then hurling them at the egg to crack it open has been known for a long time, a similar technique to some of the Old World vultures and now a common feature of various zoos showing the public how Back-breasted Buzzards do this instinctively. **Nest:** A very large twig structure with fresh leaves as a base, often replaced when a new egg is laid. Normally placed at least 12–15 metres above ground. Zebra Finches often nest in the base even when the nest is active. Most locations are along water courses with Red River Gums. Clutch size: mostly 2 but can be 3. **Similar species:** None, although possibly confused with Wedge-tailed Eagle, which is bigger, longer tailed, does not have such an angled dihedral flight, and has no white bullseyes in the wings. **Status:** Scarce in the Murchison becoming more common the further north one travels. **Where to find:** In the range of this book, on the Coastal Highway from the Murchison to Carnarvon (more so in the summer months). The birds nest on the Lyons River not far from the Kennedy Range, the northern range limit of the GSW. Some of the larger authoritative publications show extensive areas in Western Australia where Black-breasted Buzzards supposedly do not occur when in fact they do. Near the crossing on the Lyons River you may encounter Black-breasted Buzzard. If you head north on the old 'Wool Wagon Way', you may see Black-breasted Buzzards near Minnie Creek and further on they nest on Nyang Station before the North West Coastal Highway. Much of the country is open and with stony hills (classic Chestnut-breasted Quail-thrush country).

Wedge-tailed Eagle *Aquilia audax* 90–110 cm span 2.0–2.5 m

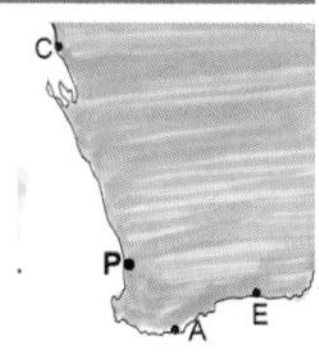

The quintessential Australian bird, found throughout all of the South West, least common in the deep South West corner. Absent from most of the islands except Dirk Hartog. It is the largest Australian raptor. Unmistakable in flight with its long wedged tail. When soaring holds wings in a semi-dihedral fashion but not as angular as a Black-breasted

Buzzard. Has a varied flight, sometimes gliding, sometimes soaring, and sometimes free falling to check prey. Often seen being mobbed or chased by birds particularly the corvids that will group together trying to gain height as fast as possible to reach a Wedge-tail before seeing it off. Feeds on carrion. There are numerous reports relating to what they feed on and the exploits they engage in to get live prey, but most birds feed on carrion particularly recent road kills, a major source of food for them. It is also a major problem for them as they get killed by vehicles, the birds being too slow to take off particularly when full. The author has pulled countless kangaroo carcasses off the Meekatharra to Newman road in a small attempt to reduce the carnage of eagles on that particular stretch of road. **Nest:** In trees mostly with commanding views over the country, sometimes on the tops of breakaways or solitary trees on open plains although they do occur in dense mulga as seen at Nallan Station. Will leave the nest long before intruders approach the site. Often maintain two to three nests in a region and will alternate which ones they use each year. Clutch size: mostly 2, uncommon to be just 1. **Similar species:** A first year immature White-bellied Sea Eagle is quite dark and has mottled plumage and can appear similar to the Wedge-tail but its tail is not as long and more a broad rather than a wedge shape. The adult Sea Eagle has strong contrasting white underwing corverts and black-brown underwing primaries making it unmistakable. The other raptor it may be confused with is the Black-breasted Buzzard but its tail looks extremely short in comparison to body size and is not wedge shaped; its flight is different and it also has no bullseyes in the wings. **Status:** Common throughout the region, more common in the station country. Moderately common in the Wheatbelt and sadly still shot. Not so common in the deep South West Region and Swan Coastal Plain. **Where to find:** Anywhere in the region and numbers increase proportionally as one travels north and east of the Vermin Fence.

White-bellied Sea Eagle *Haliaeetus leucogater* 85 cm span 200 cm

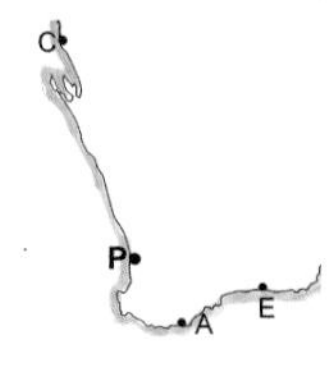

One of eight sea eagles in the world. The same genus as the American Bald Eagle and the African Fish Eagle. It is an impressive bird not common in the South West, although moderately common on the islands of the Abrolhos. Lives almost entirely on fish. It is adept at flying low and horizontally above water to take live fish, although most of its hunting is by patrolling beaches where it can take washed up carrion. It is uncommon on the south coast occurring at Broke Inlet, Wilson Inlet, Oyster Harbour and few locations along the coast to Cape Arid. It remains close to the coast except in the north where it comes in to Lake McLeod, also inland to the fresh water lakes around the Esperance area such as Lake Gore. **Nest:** Unlike the sea eagles in the north and on the east coast that normally nest in trees, the majority of sea eagles in the GSW nest on the ground and most of these are located on islands although there are some tree nesting birds on the lower south coast and also near Perth in the Peel Inlet. In the north of the region it nests on Dirk Hartog Island and the Abrolhos Islands. Clutch size: normally 2 but during the incubation period one may be ejected from the nest. **Similar species:** In adult plumage there is no like species. As immature birds, they can look similar to Wedge-tailed Eagles but the White-bellied Sea Eagle has a distinct white patch on the primaries and also the tail is rounded not diamond shaped as in the Wedge-tail. The Osprey has similar colouring but is far smaller and tail is slimmer. **Status:** Moderately common on islands to the west off the Geraldton coast and the Dirk Hartog region. Scarce on the Swan Coastal Plain. Uncommon on southern coast. **Where to find:** Abrolhos Islands. Dirk Hartog Island. Peel Inlet. Vasse Estuary. Broke Inlet. Wilson Inlet. Oyster Harbour. Fitzgerald coastline. Esperance region including the Esperance freshwater lakes.

Little Eagle *Hieraaetus morphnoides* 45–55 cm span 110–135 cm

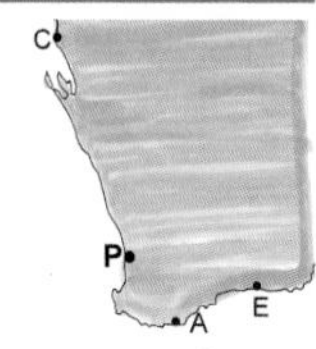

A small compact eagle with varying colour morphs throughout Australia, although in the GSW it is almost entirely the light phase. Has leg feathers on top of the feet like all true eagles. It is an attractive eagle with a small crest on the nape. Seen typically soaring over wetlands or open woodlands not far above the tree canopy at a similar height to the Square-tailed Kite. Flies in tight concentric circles more consistent and tighter than the Whistling Kite. Its habitat varies from open woodland to desert sand dunes. It has declined since the reduction of rabbit numbers in the South West and was possibly never common before European settlement. Little Eagle takes more live prey than, for example,

Captive bird

Whistling Kite, although they will eat carrion. One of 6 species in the world of the genus *Hieraaetus*. There are two subspecies in Australasia, *weiskei* in New Guinea which is smaller and the nominate race *morphnoides* in Australia. **Nest**: A large structure of branches and twigs. In desert regions can be quite low but in the South West mostly above 12 metres, rarely in solitary trees mostly in groups of trees. Clutch size: 1–2. **Similar species:** Some similarity to Whistling Kite which however has less contrasting colours on the underwing and body. Little Eagle has a richer orange-brown on the underwing coverts from the body to the carpal joint of the wing and its tail is shorter and more square cut. Again jizz is important, even in flight, as the Little Eagle looks stocky and robust whereas the Whistling Kite is slimmer and longer tailed. **Status:** Moderately common throughout the GSW except in the deep South West corner. Less common than the Whistling Kite. Prefers to be near wooded country with cleared country adjacent. **Where to find:** Throughout the whole of the GSW. Along the Gascoyne River system and upper Murchison.

Whistling Kite *Haliastur sphenurus* 50–60 cm span 120–140 cm

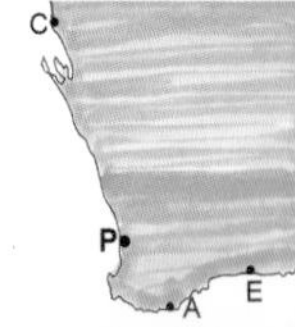

Found throughout the region. Has a preference for wooded country adjacent to wetlands in the South West. Scavenges more than Little Eagle, eating more carrion but does take live prey particularly in the breeding season, bringing fresh kills to the nest. Ducks and waterbirds

are constantly harassed by the Whistling Kite. Does not flock to the same degree as Black Kites, although will mass with Black Kites in the northern regions after fires. **Nest:** A bulky twig nest often placed in a grove of trees near water, rarely in a forested region. Clutch size: 2–3. **Similar species:** Has similarities to the light morph of the Little Eagle, the main form found in the South West. Refer to Little Eagle for details. Flies more erratically than the Little Eagle, making more turns and manoeuvres while looking for prey. **Status:** Common on the Swan Coastal Plain, less so on the south coast. Uncommon throughout the Wheatbelt. More common the further north one travels. **Where to find:** In Perth it is quite common around the major wetlands and throughout the Swan Coastal Plain. Easily seen throughout most of the GSW.

Black Kite *Milvus migrans* subspecies *affinis* 45–55 cm span 120–140 cm

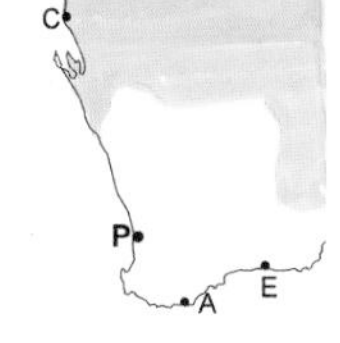

Found throughout Europe, Africa and Asia being one of the most numerous raptors in the world. It is common in the north of Australia; in the GSW Region is mainly found around Carnarvon and the Gascoyne River catchment, but nothing like the numbers further north where they can congregate in hundreds over abattoirs, rubbish dumps or stockyards, as they are basically a scavenger and opportunist feeder. Will often be found in country that is burning, its fork tail constantly twisting as it manoeuvres in flight to take insects and reptiles in front of the flames. During the breeding period, a higher percentage of live prey may be taken but at other times it relies heavily on carrion. There are 6 subspecies in the world with the Australian subspecies *affinis* being the smallest. **Nest:** A large stick structure located in groups of trees often along watercourses. Nest is lined with fur or wool or other soft materials. Clutch size: 2–3. **Similar species:** Should not really be confused with any other raptor, as the tail is so distinct.

The Whistling Kite is overall a lighter bird, noticeably so when perched; the Black Kite has an even, darker brown plumage, whereas the Whistling Kite has a light fawn head and underbody and upperbody. **Status:** In the Gascoyne catchment uncommon. **Where to find:** Anywhere in the north of this region, scarce down to Geraldton and Mullewa.

Brahminy Kite *Haliastur indus* subspecies *girrenera* 45–50 cm span 110–120 cm

A bird of coastal waters, with a preference for mangrove lined shores where it also nests. An attractive bird that feeds mostly on carrion. It does not have the powerful talons of the White-bellied Sea Eagle but can still take small live fish. Seen mostly flying low over mangroves or along beaches being an opportunistic hunter. There are four subspecies in the world and only one subspecies *girrenera* in Australia. **Nest:** A bulky structure lined with grasses, seaweed or leaves. Mostly nests in mangroves often only 4–5 metres above ground. Clutch size: 1–2. **Similar species:** None really, although the juvenile bird may be confused with Whistling Kite and Little Eagle; however, it is rare to see Little Eagles over mangroves and beaches though Whistling Kites are certainly commonly seen over beaches. At first glance the underbody of the Little Eagle has more markings and colour to the juvenile Brahminy Kite. The juvenile Little Eagle's markings are clearly defined rust on the shoulder breaks, with the greater coverts pure white and tail clearly barred and squarer. The underbody on the Whistling Kite has more even markings and colours merge. The main thing is the jizz; the Whistling Kite is slim bodied with longer slimmer tail and flies with drooped wings, the Brahminy has a stocky body and shorter tail. **Status:** Uncommon around Carnarvon. **Where to find:** Around Carnarvon between Mangrove Point and Miaboolia Beach.

Captive bird

Collared Sparrowhawk *Accipiter cirrhocehalus cirrhocehalus*

30–40 cm span 55–80 cm

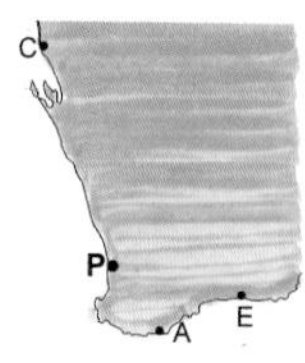

A slim, sleek small accipiter, extremely fast, having the ability to manoeuvre at high speeds between branches and vegetation in its pursuit of small birds. It can however, tackle prey nearly twice its weight. In the lower South West it has a preference for dense riverine gullies where it will perch and wait for prey to move. It may start hunting before the sun rises like so many of the falcons. It knows it needs prey to survive so it maximises the day, taking birds that are adjusting to the first morning light and may not be as alert as during the day. Similarly it will hunt at dusk when birds are moving to roosting sites and may not be as alert as in full sunlight. The female is nearly twice the weight of the male bird, the male weighing on average 140 g and the female 235 g. If you are close to the female, you can see that it is bulkier in the chest than the male Sparrowhawk; however, it is harder to split from similar sized male Brown Goshawk. Sparrowhawks in the breeding season can often be heard using their rapid high pitched contact call, which will sometimes lead you to a dependent juvenile. There are 4 subspecies in Australasia and New Guinea with 2 occurring in Western Australia. The nominate species in southern Australia *cirrhocehalus* is larger than the subspecies *quaesitandus* in northern Australia. **Nest:** A small flat twig structure lined with fresh leaves often well above 15 metres in fork near top of tree. Clutch size: 2–3. **Similar species:** Brown Goshawk. Jizz is so important here: the Sparrowhawk, including the female, is a slimmer bird than the male and female Goshawk. The much discussed frown on the Goshawk is certainly evident but one has to have it well in the binoculars to see it clearly. You can pick up more quickly the more wide-eyed look of the Sparrowhawk. The tail is square on the tip in the Sparrowhawk, more rounded in the Goshawk, but when the Goshawk is in moult it's not an easy thing to recognise. However in flight even at speed the Sparrowhawk shows what appears to be a longer tail due to the fact that it is narrow and square cut in both sexes. It is often said that the collar on the Sparrowhawk is more defined but the author finds this not a good diagnostic feature. What he does find, which is not often mentioned, is that when perched the Sparrowhawk's legs look decidedly thin and appear longer in proportion to the body than the Goshawks. The Sparrowhawk is less often seen soaring in flight than Brown Goshawk, which is one of the differences in hunting technique as the Goshawk is willing to tackle bigger prey in open country, whereas the Sparrowhawk normally relies on surprise in denser vegetation, often chasing smaller birds into thick foliage. **Status:** Moderately common in the deep South West. Uncommon in the Wheatbelt and into the station country. **Where to find:** Throughout the region, being a chance encounter in any habitat zone even mangroves.

Brown Goshawk *Accipiter fasiatus fasiatus* 40–55 cm span 70–85 cm

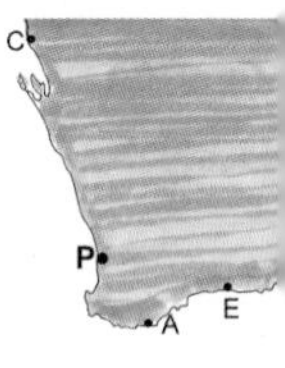

The genus accipiter is a large genera, there being 50 species throughout the world. Australia has 3, the Brown Goshawk, Collared Sparrowhawk and Grey Goshawk (not including the vagrant Variable Goshawk). The rare Red Goshawk is a different genus. The Brown Goshawk has no hesitation in tackling prey close to its own weight such as Ring-necked Parrot. In fact the parrots are a favoured prey. If one approaches waterholes particularly in the station country in the summer, there is often a resident Goshawk waiting for birds to drink: Sparrowhawks do the same but the Goshawk will soon chase off the Sparrowhawk. When taking international birding groups around Australia, the author found that even after 16–20 days, many people could still not differentiate between the two species, which is understandable. So if you have trouble with these two species, take heart, you are not alone. There are at least 12 subspecies in Australasia, parts of Indonesia, New Guinea and some of the south eastern Pacific Islands. The 3 in Australia are all found in Western Australia, the nominate subspecies *fasiatus* in the South West, *didimus* in northern Australia and *natalis* on Christmas Island (this subspecies is being reviewed and may become a separate species). **Nest:** Similar to Collared Sparrowhawk but slightly larger. Clutch size 2–4. **Similar species:** Collared Sparrowhawk. When the Brown Goshawk is soaring which it often does, the tail is often fanned out and then you can clearly see the rounded end to the tail. When fanned, the Sparrowhawk shows clearly a clean cut square tail almost like a miniature Square-tailed Kite's tail. For more details refer to the Collared Sparrowhawk text for similarities and differences between the two species. **Status:** Relatively common throughout the whole region. **Where to find:** No specific locations, can be seen in any area although has a preference for wooded and riverine habitat.

Immature

;wamp Harrier *Circus approximans* 50–60 cm span 120–145 cm

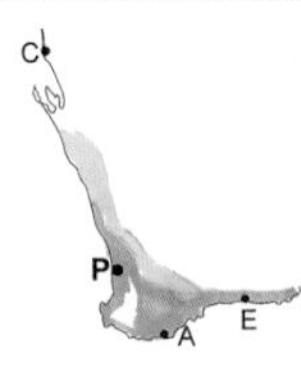

\ long and broad winged raptor having a relatively lightweight body n proportion to the wings which allows it to glide effortlessly over eed beds often only a few metres above the water. The facial disc on he Swamp Harrier is large and flattened and is thought to increase ts hearing capacity, particularly as it flies so low, so that anything that noves may be heard. Both Australian harriers have this feature. The Tasmanian Swamp Iarriers hunt over forests, grasslands, lakes and estuary margins but the south western birds re almost entirely confined to swamp habitats and lake margins although can be seen over ields but never too far from wetlands. Whether there is a migration from the south west opulation to the northern region as in Tasmania is not well known. It is known that, at Herdsman Lake for example, birds can remain all year. **Nest:** A trampled reed bed platform ocated in dense extensive reed beds. Occasionally in tall grasses close to water. Clutch size –4. **Similar species:** Spotted Harrier, however they do not share the same territory in the South West. The grey back and barred tail stand out on the Spotted Harrier and it is far nore colourful than the Swamp Harrier. The Swamp Harrier is an even brown colour on the vhole body with its diagnostic white rump seen well in adult birds. The juvenile is darker, ecomes slightly lighter with age. **Status:** Locally common on some wetlands on the Swan Coastal Plain. The southern coastal birds can be seen over heathland and fields adjacent to wamps. **Where to find**: In the Perth area: Herdsman Lake. Bibra Lake. Lake Joondalup. Lake Kogalup. Forrestdale Lake. Thomsons Lake. On the Swan Coastal Plain and South West Region: Benger Swamp. Vasse Estuary. Torbay and Elleker. Two Peoples Bay. Cheyne Beach egion. Esperance lakes. Cape Le Grand.

Captive bird

Spotted Harrier *Circus assimilis* 50–62 cm span 120–150 cm

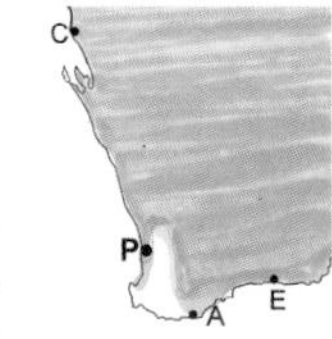

This has to be one of Australia's most beautiful raptors. Of the 13 harriers n the world, this is the only one in its genus that nests in trees. Its favoured habitat is wide open grassed plains, open bluebush plains and low spinifex plains in both rocky and sand dune country. However, since European settlement, it has adapted to feeding over cereal crops, the closest thing to native grassland habitat. It hunts just a few metres above the crops or grasses looking and listening for mice, small marsupials and small birds such as quail, songlarks or button-quail. It will take reptiles but rarely carrion. There is most probably some movement after breeding from the South West to the northern parts of Australia as is the case in the eastern

states. Sightings are certainly fewer from late summer to mid winter. **Nest:** The nest is located mostly in a group of trees rarely a solitary tree and mostly above 10 metres on a horizontal fork. A flat saucer structure lined with fresh leaves. Clutch size mostly 3 but varies between 2–4. **Similar species:** None really. Mention has been made of the juvenile Swamp Harrier but the chances of overlap with Swamp Harrier's territory would be uncommon in the South West. **Status:** Uncommon throughout the region. Very uncommon in th deeper forested region of the South West. **Where to find:** In the South West Region the bes opportunities are in the Wheatbelt Region from August through to December. Rare on th lower Swan Coastal Plain. Uncommon to moderately common from Moora to Geraldton Then uncommon throughout the rest of the region. Note: Uncommon in the drier region does not mean you will not see them; it's just they are few and far between as they require bi territories of open grasslands and spinifex covered hills to feed from.

Brown Falcon *Falco berigora berigora* 40–50 cm span 90–120 cm

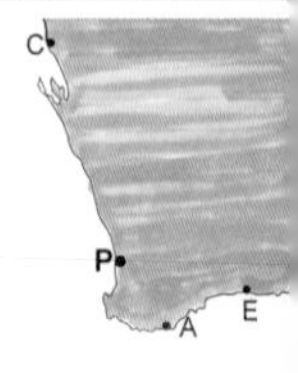

An extremely common raptor found throughout the region in a range of colour morphs from very light brown birds to blackish-brown, almost as dark as a Black Falcon; most however are just a fawn-brown. It is an unusual falcon, not related to any of the 60 world falcons except possibly the New Zealand Falcon, *Falco novaeseelandiae*. Most falcons have trouble walking on the ground as the legs and talons are designed to take prey in the air. The Brow Falcon however has long legs and short talons making it easier to walk and also grasp smaller pre such as large insects and reptiles, particularly snakes. It is one of the raptors that will sit for lon periods waiting for prey to move although most of the time it will glide and hover, pouncing o small prey. It does not develop the fast speeds in flight or the power of other Australian falcon and lacks the robust talons to take large prey, so has become more opportunistic in its hunting taking anything small that moves and even taking the opportunity of feeding on grasshoppers when they are in plague proportions. It can, however, take parrots, pigeons and other medium sized birds but this is not a common occurrence as it lacks the speed. There are 2 subspecies in Australasia, only one in Australia *berigora*. **Nest:** Normally an old raptor's or corvid's nest. Found at varying heights but rarely placed in solitary trees in wide open spaces like the Black Falcon's. Will reline the nest with leaves. Clutch size: 2–3. **Similar species:** The lighter tanned morph of the Brown Falcon can sometimes be confused with the Kestrel but the Kestrel is much smaller, has a black band on the tail in both the female and male, and when flying the Kestrel's wings are sharper at the end and not as broad as the Brown Falcon's. There are also similarities with the more powerful Black Falcon which, when perched, has an unmistakable jizz once you have become familiar with it. The first thing that you become aware of is its powerful shoulders with a relatively smaller head in proportion to the body compared with the Brown Falcon. Another feature is that when at rest, it will perch with an upright vertical posture, but in hunting mode when perched it will be the opposite of a Brown Falcon, standing more horizontally with the longer wings and tail clearly visible. In flight the jizz again shows a more powerful flyer with longer pointed wings and all black-brown body. **Status:** Very common throughout the region. **Where to find:** Throughout the region.

Black Falcon *Falco subniger* 45–55 cm span 95–115 cm Vagrant

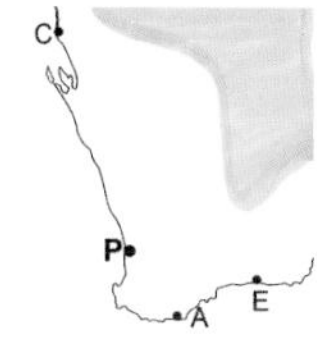

An impressive falcon and always a joy to watch in flight. One of the few raptors that can cruise in flight fairly slowly but quickly gain height by soaring and then, if it sees prey, can stoop and fly faster than most raptors. In horizontal flight when moving at high speed, its wings droop only slightly with occasional rapid wing beats. Most of the time it soars high in the sky looking for prey, being an opportunistic feeder. When fires are sighted it will move in from afar to take advantage of mammals or reptiles escaping the fire, as will the Brown Falcon. The female is the largest of all the falcons in Australia. When perched seen front on, it is almost unmistakable with its powerful square shoulders and the head looking smaller than Brown Falcon in proportion to the body. One thing to notice is that the tarsi (legs) are mostly covered by feathers whereas the Brown Falcon shows slightly longer exposed tarsi. **Nest:** Like the Brown Falcon it will not build a new nest but uses other old raptor or corvid nests. It will return to the same nest in subsequent years. Unlike the Brown Falcon, it will nest in solitary trees often on wide open stony plains or occasionally along watercourses. Clutch size normally 3 but can lay 2–4. **Similar species:** Refer to Brown Falcon. **Status:** Extremely rare in the GSW. Out of this region, but for general interest is scarce in the Pilbara, Southern Kimberley, Northern Canning Stock Route to Sturt Creek. The furthest south-west the author has seen this bird was at Lake Anneen south of Meekatharra. Other sightings by the author in Western Australia were all in the Kimberley namely: Camballin Station, Kingston Rest, Roebuck Plains, Parry's Lagoon. He has seen far more in the Queensland, South Australian deserts and in Victoria. **Where to find:** Alas, rare in Western Australia and certainly the GSW; it has been sighted by others in the Wheatbelt Region although there is a lot of misidentification with this species.

Black Falcon – captive bird

Nankeen Kestrel *Falco cenchroides cenchroides* 30–35 cm span 60–80 cm

Perhaps more common in the South West than the Brown Falcon, the Nankeen Kestrel is the smallest Australian falcon and seen in many different habitats. It has adapted well to the environmental pressures of European settlement. Seen close to the Perth city centre and throughout the entire farming region. With the clearing of land and the influx of the European mouse, it has never been short of prey. Seen hovering over beach dunes, roadside verges, fields and native grasslands. Has a diverse diet, including mice, small birds and large insects. 2 subspecies occur in Australasia, one in Indonesia and one *cenchroides* in Australia. **Nests:** Nests in a variety of locations, including trees, rock ledges as on Rottnest Island, also in hollows in trees. Will also use old corvid nests. Clutch size 3–4. **Similar species:** Refer to Brown Falcon. **Status.**: Very common throughout the South West Region, less common in the rest of the GSW. **Where to find:** Throughout the region.

Australian Hobby *Falco longipennis longipennis* 30–3 6cm span 67–90 cm

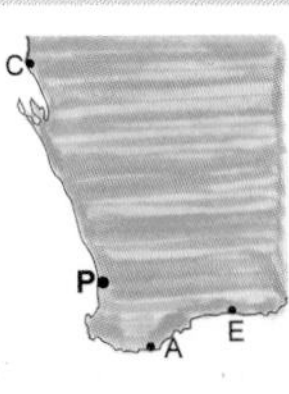

Even though the Australian Hobby is less than half the weight of a Peregrine Falcon, it still can attain extremely fast speeds when chasing prey. However, unlike the peregrine which will take on prey its own weight and more without hesitation, the hobby mostly chases much smaller birds; although it has taken birds up to a third more than its weight, the vast majority are less than half its weight. It regularly takes large insects in flight to supplement its diet. The author has always been intrigued to see which bird species will fear which type of raptor. Watching a Pied Butcherbird in the same dead tree singing its beautiful early morning song, with an Australian Hobby preening no more than 3 metres away, makes one realise that every species knows what birds to fear; it is doubtful whether the butcherbird would do the same alongside a Peregrine. Much of the Hobby's hunting is around trees, catching prey unawares and less likely to soar and dive than the Peregrine. Prefers open wooded country like Wandoo, Salmon Gum, York Gum and mulga country, and River Red Gums along inland river systems. Less likely to be in heavily forested areas of the deep South West. There are 3 subspecies in the world with two in Australia, *longipennis* in Tasmania and coastal Australia and *murchisonianus* in inland Australia. **Nest:** Does not build a nest but uses old raptor or corvid nests placed high in a tree. Clutch size mostly 3 but varies from 2–3. **Similar species:** Only the Peregrine Falcon. When perched, it is far easier to differentiate than when in high soaring flight. The Peregrine is not only bigger, nearly 3 times the weight, but it is a bulkier and more thickset bird. The peregrine has a white half collar passing from the white throat to the centre of the neck. The Hobby's collar not only goes to the centre of the neck but also curves further around to almost the height of the eye. The hobby always has a rust coloured chest whether adult or immature. The adult male peregrine does have a slight rusty tinge on the underbody but not as strong, and the female Peregrine has no rust tingeing at all. The cere is clearly yellow on the peregrine and white on the Hobby. When soaring, it's not always easy to tell as height makes size deceptive but generally the hobby has slimmer wings and a slimmer body. The Peregrine shows its white and dark brown barring much more in flight. In general, the Hobby has sharper wing tips and it beats its wings faster. The tail is squarer cut. **Status:** Uncommon throughout the whole region. **Where to find:** Anywhere on the Swan Coastal Plain particularly woodland adjacent to wetlands. Wandoo Woodland particularly near the Stirling Range. Throughout the Wheatbelt and station country particularly along river courses in arid country.

Peregrine Falcon *Falco peregrinus* subspecies *macropus* 35–50 cm span 80–105 cm

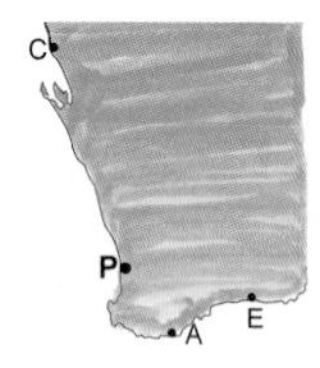

So much has been written of this master of flight. They can be found in the cold Tundra perhaps hunting for Dunlin, Curlew Sandpiper or Ruff, in North America maybe a Ring-necked Duck, maybe Torrent Ducks in the high Andes, Teal in Europe, Sandgrouse in Africa, White-bellied Pigeon in Japan. The Peregrine Falcon is truly a cosmopolitan hunter throughout the world. Here in Western Australia, it has in the past been listed as endangered, but in fact many people miss or do not see Peregrines regularly as they are such efficient hunters. They have often finished taking their prey in the first half hour of light. The author has seen a peregrine leave its roosting site on a cliff face at Glen Helen in the NT and come back with a Spinifex Pigeon before the sun has even risen. It will then slowly eat the prey at leisure and may not fly all day until hungry again. So they are often around perched on a cliff face somewhere but may not always be seen. Certainly, they are not common but there are countless locations in the South West and throughout Western Australia where Peregrines have their eyries, particularly in the Goldfields. The Peregrine's diet is almost totally restricted to birds. They will take small mammals but birds are their preferred kill. The majority of birds are taken in flight. There are many ways it will do this, either waiting on a perch and then chasing prey but more often stooping from great heights and taking birds on impact. The most spectacular kill the author witnessed was at Trephina Gorge in the Northern Territory while looking at a flock of Galahs. There suddenly appeared high in the sky something falling at high speed. It was a peregrine in a full stoop flight at an incredible speed. The wings were closed and it had gained so much momentum it passed through the centre of the flock and was able to turn and just take a Galah trying desperately to gain height and fly off. To watch the technique and timing was absolutely astonishing. There are between 16 and 22 recognised subspecies in the world, varying with different authorities. The peregrines of the South West were once recognised as a separate subspecies *submelanogenys* but they have now been grouped back with *macropus.* **Nest:** The majority of South West peregrines nest in trees, not the chosen location for most inland and northern birds. They will also nest in trees in the Wheatbelt and in other regions if food is plentiful but cliff sites are not readily available. Clutch size 2–4 but mostly 3. Established pairs will

Captive bird

remain and nest in the same territory year after year. **Similar species:** Australian Hobby. Refer to similar species under Australian Hobby. **Status:** Uncommon. **Where to find:** Fitzgerald River NP. Stirling Range NP (several pairs there). Porongurup NP. Kondinin. Peak Charles. There are many more locations north of Perth. The author prefers not to be too specific as there is still collecting of the eggs of some of our rarer raptors, particularly falcons. Only areas that are regularly visited have been included here.

Grey Falcon *Falco hypoleucos* 30–45 cm span 85–95 cm Vagrant

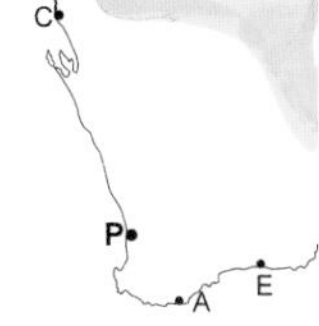

The rarest falcon in Australia and compares with the Red Goshawk as one of Australia's rarest raptors. For years the author just could not find this magnificent falcon although he had seen Red Goshawk several times before he had seen this species, which is ironical as it is not as rare. The first sighting was in its stronghold territory of the Birdsville and Strzelecki Tracks and on several repeated visits there, but it was several years before he managed to find them in WA on the Northern Canning Stock Route, in fact three of them performing aerial displays. Two days later another single bird and since that year in several other localities but never in the GSW Region, although it has been seen by others and even sound recorded on the Murchison River; it certainly is possible to see it in the Gascoyne region and catchment area of the Murchison River. The bird is smaller than a Peregrine but not much. Its flight is certainly similar. It will soar high and then glide over open country taking its prey on the wing. Even against bright sunlight, the pale body is still recognisable with slightly longer and broader wings than the Peregrine, which is surprising as it is over one third less the weight of the Peregrine. Its feet are bright yellow with long feathered socks covering the legs. Has a bright yellow cere. Mostly feeds on birds. **Nest**: Normally placed in an old raptor or corvid nest located along an inland watercourse. Clutch size: 2–4. **Similar species:** None. **Status:** Rare in Western Australia. **Where to find:** No reliable locations in the GSW. Seen mostly in the Kimberley. Pilbara and desert regions in Western Australia.

Captive bird

Buff-banded Rail *Gallirallus philippensis* subspecies *melori* 30–33 cm

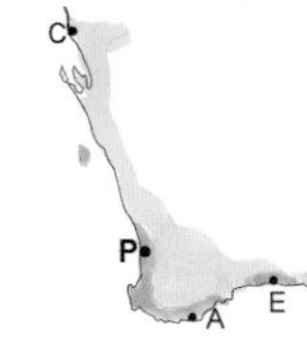

Crakes and rails can be difficult to see as they occur mostly in reed beds and thick moist undergrowth and generally are shy and elusive birds. The Buff-banded Rail can be an exception. It can tolerate a slightly drier environment and will come out into the open more than most other rails and crakes. Penguin Island is an example of where the birds venture onto open grassed areas where people gather. It is an extremely attractive rail, showing its orange breast band and barring on the underbody. It is taller and larger than all the Australian crakes and can tolerate brackish waters. It is a more opportunistic feeder than most crakes and rails, as it will eat carrion or take other birds' eggs but mainly feeds on insects, crustaceans, small reptiles and frogs. Calls mostly early morning or just after sunset. 10 subspecies have been identified throughout the world with only one *melori* on mainland Australia. There is a separate subspecies on the Cocos and Keeling Islands *andrewsi*. **Nest:** It nests in a variety of habitats, mainly reed beds and long grass. The nest is a deep saucer shape, constructed of reeds or grasses often just above water level with grasses pulled over as a hide. In dry locations such as on islands, will gather a few grasses together and lay them on bare rock. Clutch size 4–5. **Similar species:** None really, the nearest is the Lewins Rail, presumed extinct in WA. **Status:** Moderately common. **Where to find:** All larger lakes with reed beds, retreating to those that retain water through the summer. Alfred Cove in the reedy inlet. Penguin Island near the jetty. Bayswater Sanctuary. Canning River Wetlands. Herdsman Lake. Dams in the station country where permanent water runs from bores allowing reeds to grow. On islands such as Pelsaert Island in the Houtman Abrolhos Islands.

Baillon's Crake *Porzana pusilla* subspecies *palustris* 15–18 cm

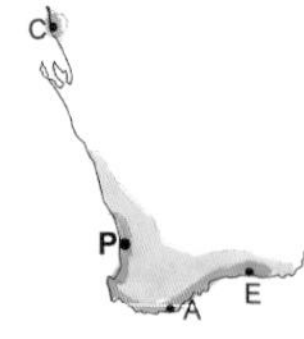

Crakes will travel far and wide to find suitable wetland habitat to feed and breed, so much so that the Asian crakes and rails occasionally, on their long sorties for better wetlands, end up in Australia. Baillon's Crake is found throughout Asia and parts of Africa, but it is presumed to be a resident bird in Australia. We still do not know where many of the crakes go to when lakes are drying, as they will sometimes be in large numbers and then suddenly disperse from a wetland. They are more common in spring and early summer in the South West. The best time of year to see crakes with some degree of success is when waters are drying and the mud becomes exposed but is still wet and full of food matter; then the crakes will venture out from the reed beds into the open, particularly early morning and late afternoon. There are several subspecies of Baillon's Crake in the world from Europe through to Asia, Africa and the Far East, as well as Australasia, but there is only one subspecies in Australia *palustris*. **Nest:** A very small deep saucer shape with reeds or grasses pulled over as a canopy either above water or amongst reeds or alongside tufts of grass close to the edge of shallow water. Clutch size 3–5. **Similar species:** Australian Spotted Crake, which has a darker blue-grey breast, small red cere at the base of the bill the bill is bright lime-green colour, the mottled back is darker and is larger. **Status:** Locally common in spring and early summer on the Swan Coastal Plain and several wetlands in the South West Region. **Where to find:** The Swan Coastal Plain, particularly Perth's wetlands: Lake Joondalup. Thomsons

Lake, Kogolup Lake. Bibra Lake, Wellard Wetlands, Namming Swamp. Found also in a few of the permanent wetlands in the South West: Benger Swamp. Grassmere Lake. Unicup Lake and Kulinilup Lake.

Australian Spotted Crake *Porzana fluminea* 22 cm

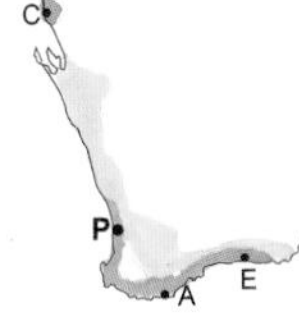

Largest of the crakes. Behaviour and habitat very similar to Baillon's Crake. Like most crakes, it moves when waters are drying in lakes. Another skulking bird, best seen in the early morning on the edge of reed beds. **Nest:** Similar to Baillon's Crake, placed at the base of or within lush grass tussocks. Clutch 3–4. **Similar species:** Baillon's Crake, which is smaller and has a brown mottled back, whereas the Australian Spotted Crake's back has white spots that can be clearly seen. Refer to Baillon's Crake for more details. **Status:** Locally common on Swan Coastal Plain and parts of south coast. **Where to find:** The following wetlands in Perth can produce good sightings of all crakes: Lake Joondalup. Thomsons Lake. Kogolup Lake. Bibra Lake. Wellard Wetlands and Namming Swamp. Found in a few of the permanent wetlands in the South West. Some wetlands in the Wheatbelt in spring and early summer when water and reeds are present. Also in the Mulga Region where permanent bore water flows into reed beds.

Spotless Crake *Przana tabuensis tabuensis* 20 cm

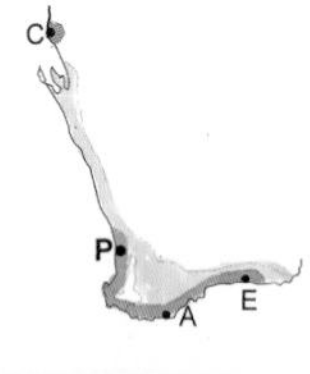

Slightly smaller than Spotted Crake. It is the easiest crake to identify being dark all over with no spotting or flecking. When seen close up, its red eye stands out against the dark purple-black head, also its red legs are a strong feature. Requires the same habitat as Baillon's Crake and Australian Spotted Crake. There are 3 subspecies in the world, 2 in Asia and the Far East and the one *tabuensis* in Australia. **Nest:** The nest is similar to other Australian crakes but is placed almost entirely over water and mostly in a higher location with a small ramp of reeds leading up to it. Clutch size 3–4. **Similar species:** None. **Status:** Locally common in well watered reed beds in any wetland in the South West. **Where to find:** The Swan Coastal Plain with Perth's wetlands being some of the best locations to see crakes. Lake Joondalup. Thomsons Lake. Kogolup Lake. Bibra Lake. Wellard Wetlands. Lake Chandala. Namming Swamp. Found in a few of the permanent wetlands in the South West. Some wetlands in the Wheatbelt in spring and early summer when water and reeds are present.

Purple Swamphen *Porphyrio porphyrio* subspecies *bellus* 47 cm

A massive rail also found in Africa, Asia and New Zealand, although not as massive as the close relative, the rare Takahe in New Zealand. The Swamphen can certainly fly and does when waters recede. In fact some birds banded in Australia have been found in New Guinea, such is the power of their flight, which is surprising considering their body weight to wing ratio. The Western Australian subspecies *bellus* is slightly larger than the eastern states subspecies and has a bluer, less purple breast colour. The bright blue-purple colour stands out on wetlands in contrast with its heavy red bill and red forehead shield. It has a tendency to be aggressive to other waterbirds. It will often corner small fledglings or other birds and kill them and is the bane of crakes and rails. Luckily most of its feeding is confined to aquatic plants, which it will hold parrot fashion in one its powerful feet, ripping off the succulent part of root. There are six subspecies in the world, with two occurring in Australia, *bellus* in the South West and *melanotus* in the east and northern Australia. **Nest:** Builds a broad rush platform amongst reeds. Clutch size 2–4. **Similar species:** None, except the Purple Gallinule not found as yet in Australia. **Status:** Common in the South West only. **Where to find:** Most larger wetlands in Perth and the South West from Wannamal south east to the Albany region with an outlying population in Esperance.

Dusky Moorhen *Gallinula tenebrosa* 35–40 cm

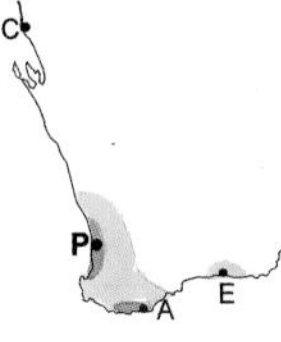

A medium sized waterhen. Has adapted well to urban developments where there are grassed areas adjacent to wetlands, and it is common and far more confiding in city environments than birds found on remoter wetlands where they tend to be shy and at times elusive. Feeds on the edges of wetlands, mostly near reeds where it can seek refuge if threatened. Like many rails and waterhens, they have white feathers on the vent that one normally does not see, but when threatened will raise their tail, flicking it constantly, exposing the white as warning to other birds while at the same time giving its warning call. This cooperative early warning system is used by most rails and crakes and is a self protective instinct aiding all waterbirds, mainly against raptors particularly Swamp Harriers and Whistling Kites. Feeds on aquatic vegetable matter, insects and seeds. Its red forehead shield and yellow tip to its bill stand out from its dark body. Tends to swim more than most waterhens and will feed on the water surface for insects, it will also eat shoots. There are 3 subspecies in the world with the nominate race *tenebrosa* occurring in Australia. **Nest:** Similar to Purple Swamphen, but smaller and can be located up in a fork in a paperbark tree. Clutch size 5–7. **Similar species:** None. **Status:** Common. **Where to find:** Any water body in the South West. Most lakes in Perth.

Black-tailed Native-hen *Gallinula ventralis* 32–38 cm

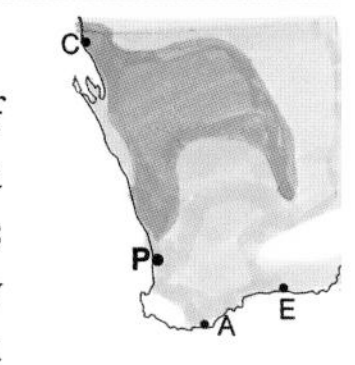

This is one of the few waterhens that have a preference for bodies of water located in semi-arid and arid regions of inland Australia. It is a highly irruptive species that is often seen in large numbers, sometimes as many as 200–300 birds on large inland ephemeral wetlands, particularly where there are lignum swamps. In fact, out of the range of the GSW on some of the larger wetlands like Lake Gregory, they can occur in their thousands after good rains. When wetlands recede, they fall back on the station dams that may have permanent water from bores. Sometimes they will come to the northern edge of the metropolitan region of Perth. They feed on plants, insects and small reptiles. **Nest:** A small reed platform, with a hollow centre placed in reeds or lignum, often located on ephemeral lakes on claypans. Clutch size 5–6. **Similar species:** Tasmanian Native-hen, not in this region. Swamphen far bigger with blue underbody. Black-tailed Native-hen is an overall dull brown bird. **Status:** Locally can be very common in the arid zone, overall uncommon. May have suffered from loss of habitat in station country. **Where to find:** Permanent bores supplying large dams with reeds. Any large inland lake after receiving heavy rains, also in the Wheatbelt.

Black-tailed Native-hen

Eurasian Coot *Fulica atra* 35–39 cm

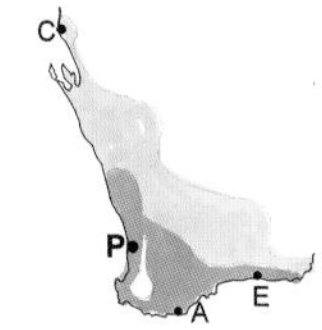

Found throughout Europe and Asia but not Africa or the Americas. An extremely common waterhen, seen on most wetlands through much of the South West. A pugnacious bird, if not chasing other coots in the breeding season they are chasing other birds from their feeding territory. Being an all black bird with a white bill and white forehead shield makes it easy to identify. It is mainly herbivorous but also eats insects. **Nest:** A small neat platform with hollow dish centre, constructed of water weeds and placed over water, often within reed beds or at the base of a paperbark tree. Clutch size 4–6. **Similar species:** Dusky Moorhen is the same size but different in body colour and has a red bill and forehead shield making it easy to differentiate. **Status:** Extremely common. Wetlands throughout the South West. Scarce in the arid zone. Seen at most large or small wetlands in Perth.

Australian Bustard *Ardeotis australis* Male 110–120 cm Female 80–90 cm

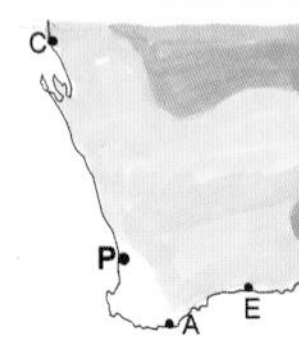

The Australian Bustard is one of the many bustard species found throughout the Old World, most of them occurring in Africa. Australia has just the one species but it is one of the largest, in fact is our third largest bird and our heaviest flying bird. When it is taking flight, it requires a reasonable distance from which to run before it can actually take off. It has always been one of the favoured foods of the desert Aborigine. Bustards are no longer common in the lower South West, but when the inland arid regions are experiencing severe droughts bustards will fly long distances to get to better feeding grounds and the South West in some years will receive several visiting birds. Farming friends have had them on their Tenterden farm several times over the last 20 years. When caught unawares, will stand with neck outstretched, bill to the sky, hoping the intruder will not see them; however, will soon take flight if they feel there is imminent danger. The male is much larger and his breeding display is very interesting. He will inflate his throat and loose neck skin into a huge bag that almost touches the ground. He then flicks the tail vertically with its white undertail coverts showing well and proceeds to utter deep booming grunts, while walking in circles. The female is attracted to this performance and they may mate. Other younger subordinate males may be present, witnessing and learning the complex procedure. Sadly, the bustard is still shot in many areas and it only remains common away from human disturbance. Its diet consists of small mammals and reptiles but when grasshopper plagues occur, it will gorge itself for several days. It also will come into areas that have been and are being burnt, to take advantage of the fleeing small animals. **Nest:** No nest is made but just a simple scrape on the ground, often located below a bush or mulga tree. Clutch size, mostly just one egg. **Similar species:** None in Australia. **Status:** Scarce in the South West. Uncommon in the drier regions of the GSW. Locally common in the desert regions and the Pilbara outside the GSW. **Where to find:** Heavily grassed areas in the Mulga Region.

Bush Stone-curlew *Burhinus grallarius* 54–59 cm

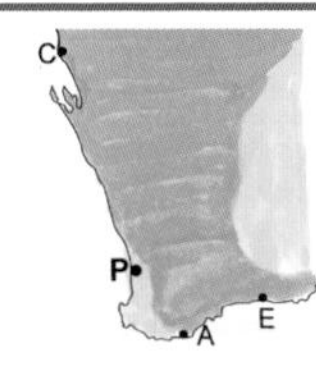

There are 5 thick-knees (Stone-curlews) in the world; Australia has two, the Bush Stone-curlew and the Beach Stone-curlew. Sadly, both have been driven out of much of their former territory The Bush Stone-curlew has certainly gone from much of the Wheatbelt. This is not only due to land clearing but also to persecution from the feral fox. Being a sedentary bird, once removed from an area they rarely return. The sound of the Bush Stone-curlew wailing at night to many is an eerie sound and those who have never heard their call often wonder who and what are making these screeching calls. They prefer dry open woodland areas and also mulga woodland. When approached will freeze on the ground with head and neck stretched horizontally. If the nest is approached they do their classic wing spreading defence posture. The chicks are well camouflaged and the streaked bodies make them difficult to see in the leaf litter or stones, where they have their nest. Bush Stone-curlews feed mostly on insects, some reptiles and seeds. They are very active at dusk and dawn before they go to their daytime roost. Feeding is mostly done at night, hence their large eyes aiding nocturnal vision. **Nest:** No nest is made, only a few twigs are drawn close to the nest but actually serve no purpose, almost a relic of an ancient instinct to create a nest. Will normally select a nest site which has a clear surrounding view. Clutch size normally 2. **Similar species:** Only the Beach Stone-curlew and that is not found in the GSW. **Status:** Scarce in the Wheatbelt. Uncommon on the edge of the Wheatbelt and into the mulga and York Gum and Salmon Gum Woodland. **Where to find:** Luckily at present, the small reserve known as Dryandra Woodland Reserve near Narrogin has a few families still surviving, one of the few populations in the western Wheatbelt. They are occasionally found in the eastern and northern Wheatbelt but more so in the Mulga Region and Transitional Woodland.

Australian Pied Oystercatcher *Haematopus longirostris* 45–50 cm

Oystercatchers are stocky birds with sturdy short legs and a strong thick bill, which they certainly need particularly when hammering on molluscs attached to rocks because the impact on the neck is immense. In the breeding season a pair can be very territorial, protecting their feeding and nesting area. It is interesting how oystercatchers manage to feed on hard shelled mussels and oysters. Shellfish have a strong adductor muscle that controls the opening and closing of the shell. The Pied Oystercatcher will stab at the shell and open it, quickly trying to strike the muscle and thus sever it, then eat the body parts. If it is not successful in opening the shell, it will peck hard into the side of the shell again, trying to cut the muscle. Both Pied and Sooty Oystercatcher use this technique. Pied Oystercatchers are more diverse in their choice of food than Sooty Oystercatchers. Pied Oystercatchers mostly

work the sandy beaches where they run backwards and forwards with the tides eating exposed molluscs, worms and small fish, whereas Sooty Oystercatchers feed mostly on rocks. **Nest:** Above high water mark with no nest made except a scrape in the ground. Birds prefer to have locations where they can see approaching predators. Clutch size 2–3. **Similar species:** Sooty Oystercatcher, which instead of a pied plumaged body is all black. **Status:** Moderately common along the GSW coastline. **Where to find:** Near Perth common on Rottnest Island. Common on the Abrolhos Islands. Common in the Albany region all the way to Esperance.

Sooty Oystercatcher *Haematopus fuliginosus* subspecies *fuliginosus* 40–52 cm

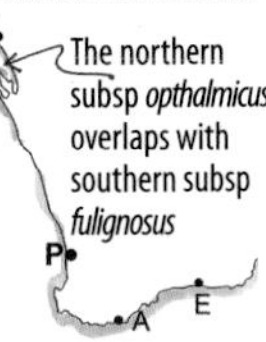

Slightly thicker set than the Pied Oystercatcher. Has a preference for rocky coastlines, where it feeds off the molluscs on the rocks, either piercing the shell or hammering it on a rock or simply using a scissor action to prise open the shell. More solitary than Pied Oystercatchers and seen more often on remoter rocky coastlines. They are found from Quobba north of Carnarvon, all the way around the coast to the Cape Arid region wherever there are rocky shorelines. There are two subspecies in Australia, *fuliginosus* on the southern coastline and *opthalmicus* on the northern coastline, the latter having a thicker bill and larger yellow-orange orbital eye ring. They overlap between Shark Bay and Ningaloo. **Nest:** No nest is made, just a scrap in the ground but will draw debris close to nest site if available. Nest commonly placed between rocks and often on islands. Clutch size normally 2. **Similar species:** Pied Oystercatcher, which has pied plumage. **Status:** Uncommon throughout the region, locally common between Walpole and Bremer Bay, then to a lesser degree along the eastern coast to Cape Arid. **Where to find**: Mostly on the south coast and particularly on offshore islands in the Archipelago of the Recherche.

Black-winged Stilt *Himantopus himantopus* subspecies *leucocephalus* 33–37 cm

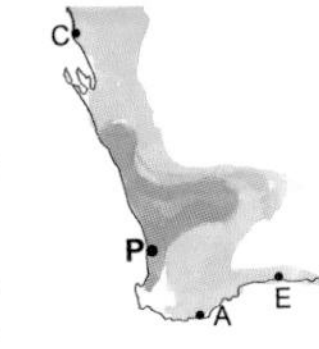

There are only four stilts in the world and Australia has two of them, the Black-winged and the Banded. Stilts are the longest legged waders of all, with extremely long fine bills. The Black-winged Stilt delicately prods on the surface of the water for aquatic invertebrates that swim on the surface. If they don't surface feed, they will select muddy areas where they can pick off small invertebrates and worms. Unlike the Banded Stilt, Black-winged Stilt will nest as a solitary pair on a small wetland, or more often just a small colony of 5–10 birds, occasionally as many as 100 but that is very uncommon in the west and nothing like the incredible numbers that the Banded Stilt colonies reach. Also unlike Banded Stilt, Black-winged Stilt prefer freshwater lakes and will feed on lake edges, swamps and samphire flats that have fresh water. There are five subspecies in the world with one in Australia *leucocephalus* . **Nest:** Sites vary, sometimes a scrape in the ground if on sandy islets, or if near or on water a pile of grasses are pulled together above the high water mark. Will nest in small colonies. Clutch size 3–4. **Similar species:** Banded Stilt. Easy to differentiate when they are adult birds as the Banded has a chestnut band passing from the shoulder right around the belly to the other shoulder. Also has an all white head, whereas the Black-winged Stilt adult has black on the back of the neck, stretching from the nape to the base of the neck. Juvenile Banded Stilt and Black-winged Stilt can be a little tricky, although it's rare for them to be feeding on their own without some adults nearby. The juvenile Black-winged Stilt has a white head like the Banded, with a faint black patch around the eye and on the crown. The main feature to note is that even if the Banded Stilt does not have a chestnut band it will still have a white back between the wings, whereas the Black-winged Stilt has a completely black back whether juvenile or adult. **Status:** Common on the Swan Coastal Plain. Can be in large numbers after breeding. Over 1000 birds have been recorded at the Vasse Estuary and Peel Inlet. Locally common on some Wheatbelt lakes. Uncommon on the southern coast. **Where to find:** Many large lakes in Perth with shallow margins. Small Wheatbelt wetlands often with samphire edges may have only one or two birds at times.

Banded Stilt *Cladorhynchus leucocephalus* 35–43 cm

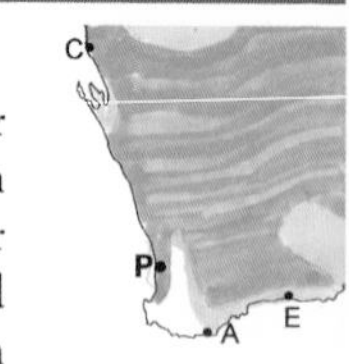

A bird that feeds on some of the most saline waters in Australia, wherever small crustaceans occur particularly brine shrimps. They will wade in water picking off small invertebrates and crustaceans or swim in deeper water using the same pecking technique as Black-winged Stilt. Banded Stilt gather in some of the largest concentrations of any species, with numbers over 150,000. For years ornithologists did not know where Banded Stilt bred. It was not until 1930, when a large colony was found at Lake Grace, that observers realised how and where they breed. The colony found at Lake Ballard in Western Australia had an estimated 179,000 nests. Because Banded Stilt are opportunistic breeders, they will fly long distances to remote salt lakes if sufficient water is present. For nesting they will normally select large islands located in remote inland ephemeral lakes. Sometimes the water evaporates so fast that by the time many of the chicks have hatched the lake may have dried up and thousands of birds will perish. There is still so much that is not known about movements of this fascinating bird. We know that small groups can occur, say 50–200 birds feeding on the odd salt lake or brackish waters, like Lake McClarty near Pinjarra. We also know that very large numbers can visit the salt lakes on Rottnest Island. Recently over 11,000 birds were gathered on one of the lakes on Rottnest for a brief period. It would be fascinating to know whether that massive group stayed together and also where they dispersed to. **Nest:** No nest is made, just a scrape in the sand. They invariably nest where brine shrimps are available close by. Nest colonially in their thousands. Clutch size 2–4 eggs. **Similar species.** Refer Black-winged Stilt. **Status:** Locally very common on selected salt lakes. Uncommon throughout most of the region. Always present on Rottnest, hence the ridiculous nickname of Rottnest Snipe was given to this specie in bygone days. **Where to find:** Often on the Esperance lakes after breeding may have occurred in the remote Goldfields salt lakes. Rottnest Island is normally reliable for a few birds. Sometimes Peel Inlet. They can occur when not breeding on lakes in the Wheatbelt, like Lake Marmion near Dowerin or Lake Hinds near Wongan Hills. Lake Grace. Lake Cowcowing and Lake Campion.

Red-necked Avocet *Recurvirostra novaehollandiae* 40–48 cm

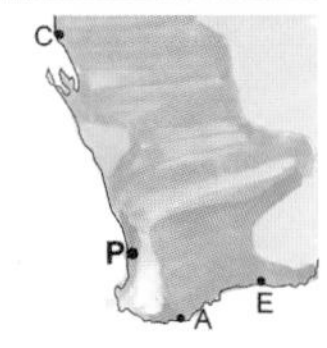

A beautiful avocet, one of four in the world. It is endemic to Australia. Has the typical avocet bill that it uses in a scything action backwards and forwards with bill slightly open so it can feel prey, just like the spoonbills do, being another tactile feeder. Like the Banded Stilt, it can swim whilst feeding but mostly wades in water. Prefers to feed in saline or brackish

waters particularly ephemeral lakes. **Nest:** It nests in a variety of locations including islands in small salt lakes, freshwater swamps. Often nests on remote inland lakes like the Banded Stilt but never in such large concentrations, normally in colonies of 6 to 20 birds but sometimes reaching larger numbers. Will nest with other birds like Black-winged Stilt. No nest is made, just a scrape on the ground in sand or earth but some soft material like grasses or samphire is often used as a base. Clutch size normally 4. **Similar species:** None. **Status:** Locally common, normally only individuals or small groups of 6 to 10 birds. Occasionally bigger groups 30–100 birds at most. **Where to find:** Rottnest Island. Joondalup. Lake Thompson. In the Wheatbelt any salt lake after good rains. Station country like Lake Anneen and Lake Austin.

Painted Button-quail *Turnix varia* 17–19 cm

Much of the Painted Button-quail's original territory has been cleared. It prefers open dry woodland, particularly Wandoo and Salmon Gum Woodland. It requires a reasonable cover of leaf litter on top of the base soils from which it gets most of its food. It feeds mostly in small family groups or in pairs, constantly turning in circles, using one foot and then another to kick away the leaf litter to expose the insects and seeds. You can see where button-quail have been feeding as small plate sized areas are left cleared on the ground, the depressions left are known as 'platelets'. The Painted Button-quail is one of the larger button-quails, not much smaller than the Brown Quail (unrelated). Sometimes you can catch them unawares. In open country they will try and walk away extremely slowly, rocking the body backwards and forwards. Most of the time they surprise the walker as suddenly, like all quail, they fly just in front of you with a loud 'brrrrrrrrr' sound coming from the rapid wing beats as they fly off, normally landing about 30–40 metres away. They also give themselves away with their low soft booming call repeated every two or three seconds 'ooow… oooow…oooow'. There are three subspecies in Australasia, with two in Australia. subspecies *varia* is found in the South West and in the eastern states. There is a small population of the subspecies *scintillans* on the Houtman Abrolhos Islands. **Nest:** No nest is made, just a scrape in the ground, although some dry grasses may be used as a base. Built normally below a bush or alongside a tuft of grass. Clutch size 3 to 4. **Similar species:** Nothing in their distribution range, the closest in terms of colour is the Little Button-quail which is smaller and a plainer lighter colour overall. The Painted Button-quail is more attractive with chestnut–brown flank and a dark mottled crown whereas the Little Button-quail has no chestnut coloured patch on the flank. **Status:** Locally common in uncleared Wandoo, Salmon Gum and some mallee regions in the south west. Distribution stops past the Mulga/Eucalypt Line. **Where to find:** Most Wheatbelt reserves with reasonable acreages. Dryandra Woodland NR. Boyagin Rock NR. Dongalocking NR. Lake Magenta NR. Dunn Rock NR. Durokoppin NR. Billyacatting

NR. Stirling Range NP. Throughout the Transitional Woodland from Lake Cronin all the way east to past Dundas NR. North and east of Billyacatting, although one must be careful as it is possible to get Little Button-quail there. Little Button-quail have been recorded in much of the Wheatbelt as they have moved into the South West and have adapted to crops and stubble.

Little Button-quail *Turnix velox* 12–14 cm

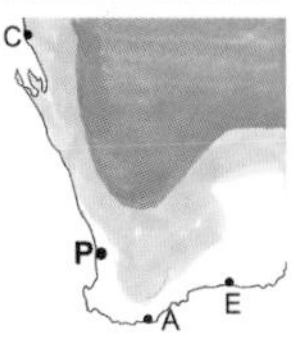

One of the smallest Button-quails along with the Red-backed Button-quail. You realise how small they are when you find dependent young chicks sitting motionless on the ground with heads outstretched, just slightly bigger than a 50c coin. Even the best birdwatchers have trouble with quail; the author has seen this first hand as you don't get long to identify them sometimes as they fly off at speed. The Little Button-quail look paler when flying off, having an even coloured fawn back contrasting with its darker wings. Painted Button-quail have greyer brown but colours on their back are more mottled and darker. Definitely a quail of the semi-arid and arid regions, in fact one of the most common birds to be found in the desert regions. Feeds mostly on grass seeds and insects. Can often be missed when walking through tufts of grass, as it will scurry off at an incredible pace if it has not already flown. **Nest**: Similar to Painted Button-quail. Clutch size 3–4. **Similar species:** Refer to Painted Button-quail for details. **Status:** Locally common where large tracks of grass plains occur or stubble between mulga. Throughout the drier areas. Does not like rank grass, wet conditions like Brown Quail. **Where to find:** Anywhere past the Vermin Fence where there is a good cover of native grasses. The further away from the South West Region the better your chances, particularly in deserts and the Nullarbor.

Captive bird

Pacific Golden Plover *Pluvialis fulva* 23–26 cm

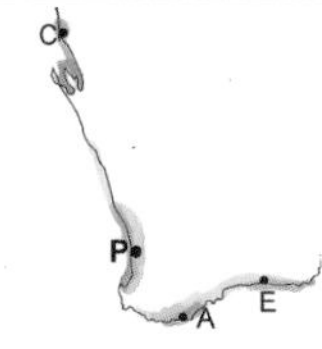

There are three Golden Plovers in the world: the American, Eurasian and Pacific Golden Plover. The species that primarily comes to the western shores is the Pacific Golden Plover. The Pacific Golden Plover is a slim upright wader of coastal beaches, estuaries and salt marshes. Breeds in the central and eastern Tundra and western part of Alaska. **Similar species:** None in breeding plumage but in non-breeding plumage the Grey Plover has similar features. If you manage to see the Grey Plover in flight (see illustration) it has a black 'armpit', the Golden has no black 'arm pit'. When resting, the Golden has a rounded head less flattened on the crown (subtle difference but noticeable), and a slightly more upright stance. Grey Plover looks bulkier and is bigger, weighs a third more. Bill is larger and longer in the Grey. Pacific Golden Plover also has a golden tinge to plumage, not as strong as when in breeding plumage but quite noticeable. Small brown facial patch to the rear of the ear corverts. **Status:** Moderately common in a few areas. Mostly uncommon in the South West. Visitor from October to March. **Where to find:** Mangrove Bay, Carnarvon beaches with mud south to Gladstone. All the way down to Vasse Inlet. In Albany in Oyster Harbour near the fishing boat harbour. Kalgan River. Occasionally seen in inland lakes not far from coast.

Grey Plover *Pluvialis squatarola* 27–31 cm

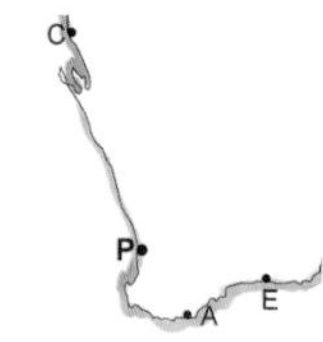

Nests throughout the Siberian and the North American Tundra. More coastal than the Pacific Golden Plover and certainly in greater numbers on the Western Australian coast. Has a typical plover technique of feeding, that is look for prey while motionless, then run and pick and continue the process. Found on coastal beaches, particularly estuaries, coastal marshes. **Similar species:** None in breeding plumage. In non-breeding plumage Pacific Golden Plover. The Grey Plover stands more horizontally, has a thickset body, flattened crown, larger bill, black armpit, grey body rather than golden tinge. In flight bold white wing bar. **Status:** Uncommon to moderately common locally. Generally uncommon. Visitor from September to April but some over-winter. Normally solitary or in small numbers. **Where to find:** All suitable beaches and mudflats from Carnarvon to Bunbury including the Abrolhos and Dirk Hartog Islands. Uncommon along the southern coastline. Oyster Harbour. Kalgan and King Rivers.

Showing black arm pits

Red-capped Plover *Charadrius ruficapillus* 14–16 cm

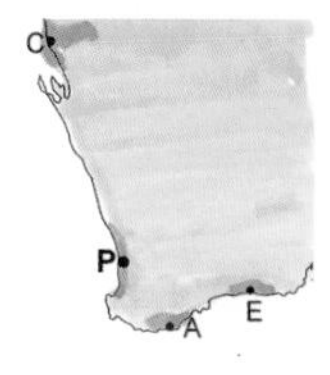

An endemic plover, very common and found in many habitats including sandy beaches, salt marshes, margins of freshwater lakes, inland salt lakes. A very small plover feeding with typical plover run and pick and stop technique. In breeding the male cap is bright chestnut, the female a duller chestnut colour. The male cap becomes duller out of breeding plumage. The male has a black lateral band coming from the neck and stopping before the chest. Female has no black only a shorter chestnut band. **Nest:** No nest is made, just a scrape in the sand or soil out in the open but often with tuft of grass or beach washed piece of timber adjacent to nest. Clutch size 2–4. **Similar species:** Only one and extremely rare, the Kentish Plover seen by John Darnell at Leslie Saltworks. Very difficult to split but has broader black forehead band, is slightly larger but main feature is complete white collar, whereas Red-capped Plover has no white collar. **Status:** Very common throughout the coastal region of the GSW. Most small lakes near the coast. Largest numbers on inland lakes. In 2007 the author had at least 1100 on Lake Thompson as it was drying out. On Jandabup 3000 have been recorded by others. **Where to find:** Rottnest. Lake Mclarty particularly when water is receding in early summer. Lake Forrestdale. Most inland salt lakes in the Wheatbelt. Esperance lakes.

Lesser Sand Plover *Charadrius mongolus* 18–21 cm

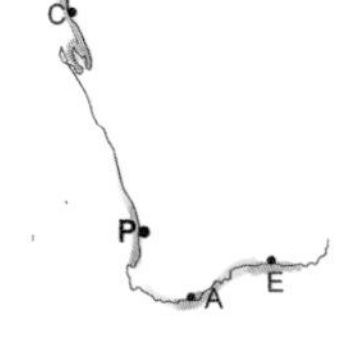

Breeds in Mongolia and parts of eastern Siberia, often as high as 5000 metres in the Himalayas on the western edge of Mongolia. Arrives in Australia mid September moving slowly down the coast then returning slowly north by December and leaving March to April. Common in the north west of Western Australia. Scarce in the South West. **Similar species:** Greater Sand Plover. Lesser Sand Plover is only slightly smaller but looks in proportion to other small plovers. The Greater Sand Plover head looks large compared to the body and the bill is larger and heavier than the Lesser. The legs are longer on the Greater. The head is flatter on the top, dropping steeply down to the bill on the Greater, whereas the Lesser has a more rounded head. If the birds are side by side you will see the differences. Sometimes you may get them in eclipse or even full breeding plumage, then the task of splitting them is made much easier. The Greater has a smaller orange–brown collar band than Lesser but the important thing is that the Lesser has a black edge band to the top of the breast band (in the male only). Having said all this, unfortunately it is very uncommon in this region. There are 5 subspecies in the world with 3 that come to Australia's shores, mostly the subspecies *mongolus*

but *stegmanni* and particularly *schaeferi* may come to Western Australian shores mostly to the north west. **Status:** Scarce to uncommon in the South West but uncommon in the Carnarvon region. From Mangrove Bay down to New Beach. **Where to find:** In this region mainly in the Carnarvon and Denham region.

Greater Sand Plover *Charadrius leschenaultii* 22–25 cm

Breeds in central Asia in highland open plains, mainly the Gobi Desert in Mongolia. Arrives in Australia late August to mid September moving slowly down the coast or may remain in north west all summer. Some come down the coast as far as Busselton but numbers decrease from north to south. A few birds pass on down to the southern coast. Feeds almost entirely on the coast on estuaries and beaches. There are 3 subspecies in the world but only *leschenaultii* comes to these shores. **Similar species:** Lesser Sand Plover and Oriental Plover, refer to notes on Lesser Sand Plover. Oriental Plover is much easier to differentiate. Its neck is longer, it has a finer bill, no dark eye band, legs longer and paler yellow, breast less marked. In breeding there is no confusion, breast colour configuration is different with black base to orange chest and white neck and face and no black eye stripe. **Status:** Moderately common in the northern part of this region. Uncommon from Geraldton down to Busselton and on the south coast. Locally common Peel Inlet. Oyster Harbour. **Where to find:** Carnarvon region. Mangrove Bay. New Beach. Denham. Alfred Cove. Peel Inlet. Oyster Harbour.

Inland Dotterel *Charadrius australis* 19–23 cm

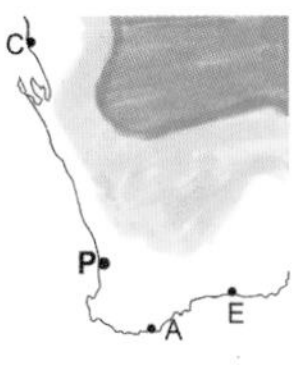

One of the most cryptic birds in Australia with its transverse band running from the crown through the eye as well as a distinct 'v' shaped breast band. It can be very hard to see in the stony country where it occurs. A bird of the drier regions of the GSW, found on open stony plains to samphire flats and claypans. It is one of the few birds that have encroached into the northern Wheatbelt after the land clearing program, finding suitable habitat in ploughed fields or fallow pastures. It is both a nocturnal and diurnal feeder having large eyes to aid in low light. In winter it can be seen far more in the day time but in the hot summer months it does much of its feeding during the night. Feeds on insects and seeds. Often overlooked and best seen in the cold winter months when it can be more active during the day. Occasionally seen at night with headlights on the edge of remote outback roads. **Nest:** No nest is made only a shallow depression, sometimes uses the base of a ploughed trough in field. Nest site can be located in fields, open samphire plain and more often open stony country. Clutch size usually 3. **Similar species:** None. **Where to find:** In the northern Wheatbelt. Mullewa. Koorda. Bonnie Rock. Better chance in the Cue region on Austin Downs west of Cue. Stony country south of Gascoyne Junction. Has come into the Swan Coastal Plain to Lake Clifton and Lake Wannamal. Also into the Southern Wheatbelt. For those that really wish to see it, best chances are out of this region on the Nullarbor Plain particularly south and just north of Rawlinna.

Black-fronted Dotterel *Elseyornis melanops* 16–18 cm

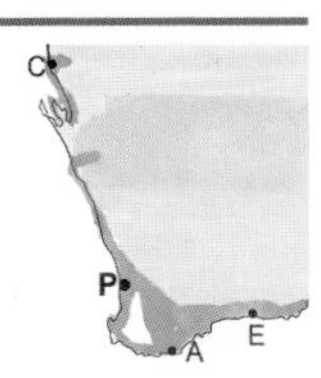

A common bird throughout the GSW. Found on the margins of freshwater and brackish pools. Feeds on crustaceans and insects. Slightly larger than the Red-capped Dotterel but shares the same habitat. Tends to be found near freshwater pools rather than saline. The Red-capped Dotterel can tolerate more saline waters. **Nest:** No nest is made, nests in a variety of locations, in depressions in sand alongside water, on stony plains alongside creeks, even in gravel on roadside verges where streams are close by. Clutch size normally 3 sometimes 2. **Similar species:** Only the immature Red-capped Dotterel, which is smaller, stands more upright and has black eye line. **Status:** Locally common, overall uncommon. **Where to find:** Most large lakes in Perth with grassed and muddy margins. Lake Kogolup. Lake Thompson. Herdsman Lake.

North Lake and Bibra Lake. Lake Joondalup. Throughout the southern wetlands and the Swan Coastal Plain. Found alongside pools and rivers on south coast. Gairdner River. Kalgan River. In the northern region, common on pools remaining on larger rivers like the Gascoyne and Murchison. Found on station dams particularly large permanent dams.

Hooded Plover *Thinornis rubricollis* 19–23 cm

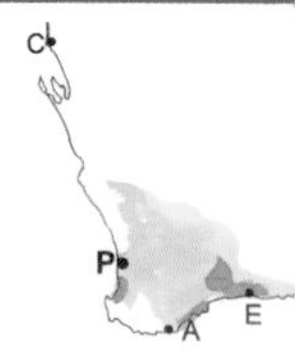

A species that has suffered since European settlement having lost much of their original habitat and now confined to the more remote beaches where there is less interference. The Hooded Plover population in Western Australia is the only one in Australia that can be found on inland salt lakes as well as coastal beaches. They nest on remoter beaches avoiding continual disturbance of their territory by human activities. After breeding many will migrate to larger salt lakes like Lake Clifton south of Mandurah, or Lake Gore and Lake Warden in the Esperance region, sometimes gathering in reasonable numbers normally 40–50 but as many as 350 have been recorded, which are large numbers for such an uncommon species. They feed by running along the beach stopping and starting, picking small molluscs and crustaceans, they will also walk along the base of sand dunes feeding on seed. Have a preference for wide sandy beaches. Their distribution extends from Horrocks near Northampton to Eyre on the Nullarbor. **Nest:** No nest is made, just a scrape in sand or gravel, mostly very close to a waterline but commonly near fallen log or branch. Clutch size 2–3. **Similar species:** None. Unmistakable with an all black hood. Juvenile could be confused with juvenile Black-fronted Dotterel but it has a black eye stripe not black hood. **Status:** Locally common but generally uncommon. **Where to find:** Lake Clifton. Lake Preston. Beaches from Nornalup to Wilson Inlet. Bremer Bay (threatened there by beach vehicles). Beaches in the Fitzgerald River National Park. Largest numbers on the Esperance lakes. Inland on some of the smaller ephemeral salt lakes, particularly in the Salmon Gum Woodlands north of Esperance and those north east and south east of Hyden.

Red-kneed Dotterel *Erythrogonys cinctus* 17.5–19.5 cm

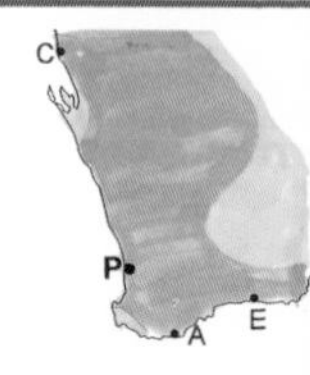

Often shares the same habitat as Black-fronted Dotterel but Red-kneed Dotterel does not like coastal saline waters or gravel beaches which the former can occupy. Likes freshwater lake margins and swamps or inland large dams. An attractive Dotterel, having strong black and white markings and a chestnut flank with red on the leg from the thigh to the knee, hence the name Red-kneed. Feeds on insects, molluscs and seeds. Is nomadic and will travel long distances to get good feeding sites. Found on many outback station dams.

Nest: No nest is made, just a deep scrape but may put loose grasses or other debris in base of depression. Nests mostly close to waterline of inland lakes and swamps particularly small islands. Clutch size 3–4. **Similar species:** None. **Status:** Moderately common throughout most of its range, increases near the coast in summer as inland freshwater pools dry up. **Where to find:** In Perth on many of the large lakes. Herdsman Lake. Bibra Lake. Kogolup Lake. Lake Joondalup. Lake Claremont. Odd inland Wheatbelt lakes like Lake Coomelberrup. Nonalling Lake near Corrigin. Towerrinning but only after good winter/spring rains. Large numbers gather in the Cue region on various ephemeral wetlands and then disperse to station dams.

Banded Lapwing *Vanellus tricolour* 25–29 cm

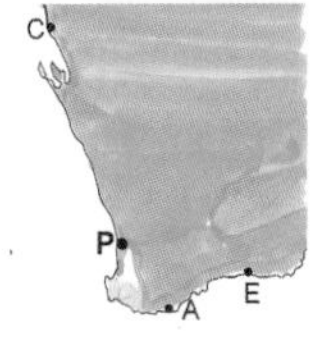

This attractive lapwing has a preference for open plains with short grasses unlike the Masked Plover which is happy to feed in longer lush grasslands. There are a few species like the Inland Dotterel and the Banded Lapwing that most probably have gained from the clearing of land in the northern Wheatbelt. We know that early historical records make little mention of Banded Lapwing in the South West. What has been recorded is the expansion into many areas by the 1930s, breeding as far south as Bridgetown. Banded

Lapwing can be found throughout most of the GSW except the deep South West forests and the Salmon Gum/York Gum Woodland. They feed on seeds and mostly insects and worms with the typical plover action of see, run and pick. Its preferred habitat and where it can easily be seen are the various small open stony or flat clay plans that occur throughout the Mulga Woodland. Like so many plovers, they will perform their broken wing act to distract you if you get too close to the nesting site. **Nest:** No nest is made just a hollow depression is scraped with some dry materials used as a base for the nest. Mostly located on open plains with a good surrounding view. Clutch size 3–4. **Similar species:** Masked Plover that is scarce in the GSW. One should not have problems with these two species, the Banded Lapwing has a black band starting from the lores all the way around the belly, and a red cere. Masked Plover has no band on belly and a prominent yellow wattle. **Status:** Found throughout the region. Uncommon on the southern coastal regions and Swan Coastal Plain. Moderately common in certain areas of the Wheatbelt particularly the northern and north eastern areas. Common in the MulgaWoodland. Locally common on Rottnest Island.

Bar-tailed Godwit *Limosa lapponica* 37–39 cm

Of the world's 4 godwits, 2 migrate to Australia, the Black-tailed Godwit and the Bar-tailed Godwit. They breed in different regions, the Black-tailed in Europe, Iceland, Central Asia and western China, the Bar-tailed in Scandinavia, Russia and Western Alaska. Just over twice the number of Bar-tailed Godwits migrate to Australia than the Black-tailed Godwit and the population of Black-tailed Godwits is even less in the GSW than Bar-tailed. There are three subspecies in the world and most probably the main migrant to Western Australia's shores would be the subspecies *menzbieri* as the majority of retrieved banded birds have been that subspecies.

Bar-tailed showing barring on rump

ll godwits have long necks, long legs, small heads and long slim bills. They feed by probing nto the mud with rapid probes searching for aquatic invertebrates, finding food by touch. hey also feed in wet grassed areas probing for worms. **Similar species:** Black-tailed Godwit. n non-breeding plumage the Bar-tailed has mottling on the wing corverts (mostly on the pperbody), looking overall a fawn-brown colour. The Black-tailed has a decidedly dull grey-rown look to the wing corverts (mostly on the upperbody). So in essence, one looks dull rey-brown, one lighter fawn-brown. The Bar-tailed has a slightly upturned bill and shorter egs than the Black-tailed and breast and flanks have slight flecking. Black-tailed has a fine traight bill, breast and flanks are plain light grey-brown. It is easily identified in flight. The ar-tailed has three thin dark black-brown bands on the tail, no white bar in the wing. The lack-tailed has a complete wide black band from the middle of the tail to the base of the tail ith a clear white rump above the black band, darker wing feathers with a distinct lateral bar unning the full length of the wing. **Status:** Moderately common in north of GSW, getting ess common towards southern coast. Arrives in October in the South West, departing end of Iarch, early April. **Where to find:** Carnarvon estuary and Mangrove Bay south to Gladstone. he Abrolhos. Geraldton to Bunbury. Alfred Cove. Then a few estuaries on the south coast ncluding Kalgan River mouth and Oyster Harbour.

lack-tailed Godwit *Limosa Limosa* subspecies *melanuroides* 40–44 cm

C
P
A
E

ess common than Bar-tailed in the South West Region, although in the orth west of the state you can see hundreds and even more in the Gulf f Carpentaria. Tends to feed in small groups. Migrates to Australian hores from late August onwards and leaves April–May. There are three ubspecies in the world but the predominant one that comes to Australia *melanuroides* which breeds in Mongolia and iberia. **Similar species:** Bar-tailed Godwit, efer to notes. **Status:** Moderately common in he north of the GSW. Uncommon down to unbury. Scarce in the South Coastal Region. **Where to find:** Carnarvon. New Beach. Denham. Alfred Cove. Black-tailed have a endency to enter freshwater regions a little more han Bar-tailed and can be found occasionally n lakes like Thompson. Forrestdale. Lake McClarty and Benger Swamp.

Black-tailed showing white rump

ack tailed right of Bar-tailed

Little Curlew *Numenius minutus* 28–31 cm Vagrant

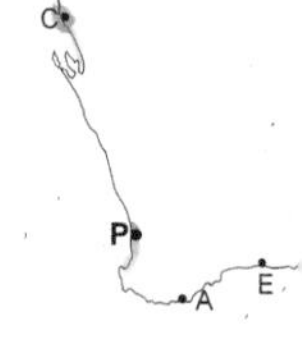

A bird that migrates from the Russian Tundra. Very rare in the South West, although the author has seen the species at Woodmans Point with a group of birdwatchers. There are chances of Little Curlew in the Carnarvon region but they rarely come past Port Hedland. The smallest curlew with a very short bill most unlike all other curlews, more like a Whimbrel but much smaller and the bill is shorter and straighter. Has an upright stance. Likes feeding on well watered grassland, often seen on playing fields and parks in northern towns such as Port Hedland, Karratha, Broome and Derby. Also freshwater wetlands. Found in the north west of the state in their hundreds, even more so in the north of the Northern Territory and especially the Barkly Tablelands. **Similar species:** Only the Whimbrel could possibly be confused but is a larger bird with a bill almost twice as long and longer legs. **Status:** Rare in the GSW and scarce in the Carnarvon region.

Whimbrel *Numenius phaceopus* subspecies *variegates* 40–45 cm

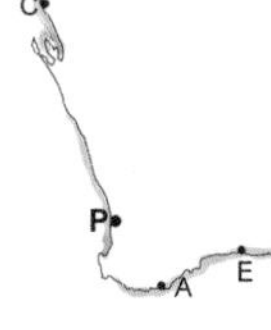

Breeds in eastern Siberia. A medium sized curlew with a long down curved bill, dark crown with a slight eye stripe, short legs. Important feature is the white rump, in flight it looks wedge shaped. Mainly a solitary wader or in small groups, feeding on beaches, mangrove mudflats and estuaries, although tends to prefer mangrove habitats where it will also roost. When it does roost it will come together with other waders. Eats small crab worms and shrimps. There are four subspecies in the world but most probably the only tw

ıat come to Australian shores would be *variegates* that breeds in Siberia and *hudsonicus* that :eeds in Alaska and northern Canada; most Western Australian birds are *variegates*. **Similar** **ɒecies:** Eastern Curlew. Far larger with very long bill more down curved. No eye stripe. Main ature, has no white on the rump. Little Curlew is far smaller in size and the bill is one third ıorter and only slightly curved. **Status:** Common in the north out of this region. Moderately ɔmmon Carnarvon south to Gladstone and in Denham and Shark Bay region. Scarce in the ɔuth West Region. **Where to find:** Best in the north of this region.

astern Curlew *Numenius madagascariensis* 60–66 cm

he largest wader to come to Australia, with a long neck, long legs, thickset ɔdy and very long bill, particularly the female which is larger than the ıale. Breeds in eastern Siberia in wet marshes. The call is familiar to those ho wader watch regularly, sounding 'cur-loo' like, although less so than ıe European Curlew. Feeds in a variety of habitats in marshes, beaches, ltworks, muddy creeks but prefers large muddy estuarine habitat. Feeds on crustaceans. **Similar** **ɒecies:** European Curlew *Numenius arquata* subspecies *orientalis* which has a white rump and

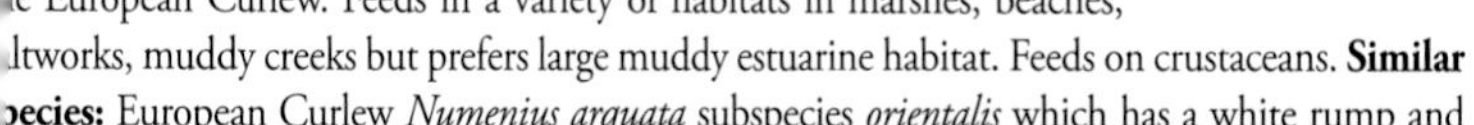

ɔwer back, also white on the nderwing at the axillaries and nderwing coverts and the bill not as long as the Eastern :urlew. The Whimbrel is ıuch smaller and has a much ıorter bill. **Status:** Moderately ɔmmon around Carnarvon om Miaboola Beach down to ong Point and Denham region. Incommon further south. **Vhere to find:** Carnarvon stuary down to Long Point and)enham region. Alfred Cove. eel Inlet. Albany region.

larsh Sandpiper *Tringa stagnatilis* 22–26 cm

. medium sized wader, looking like a delicate miniature Greenshank. Iigrating to Australian shores between September and March. The Iarsh Sandpiper has a needle-like bill, small head and very long legs. reeds in eastern Europe and central and far eastern Asia. This is one ader that has a preference for freshwater lakes and dams. It will feed on ıudflats and beaches but not as ıuch in the GSW. It does mass in ıe north west of WA to migrate orth for the breeding season. eeds on aquatic invertebrates nd crustaceans, mostly on the ıargins of small freshwater ıkes but will venture deeper ıto lakes past the tarsus, even ı water to the base of the belly, icking at swimming insects. **imilar species:** Greenshank, ıat is larger and much thicker et, weighing more than twice the Iarsh Sandpiper. Bill thicker and

slightly upturned. Marsh Sandpiper has a fine and straight bill and loger legs in proportio to body. **Status:** Uncommon throughout most of the GSW, locally common on a fev freshwater lakes. **Where to find:** Chinaman's Pool in Carnarvon. Inland bores with overflo drains between Carnarvon and Overlander Roadhouse. Pools on the Murchison River. Man freshwater pools inland after heavy rains have fallen. In Perth: Kogolup Lake. Bibra and Nort Lake. Thomsons Lake. Herdsman Lake. Lake McClarty. Kalgan and Lower King River i Albany. Lake Gore in Esperance.

Common Greenshank *Tringa nebularia* 22–26 cm

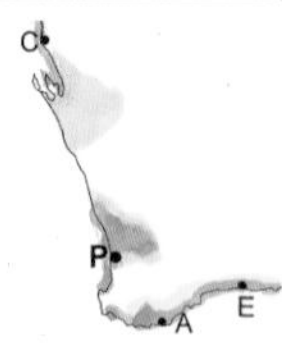

A large long legged wader, with a long slightly upturned bill. Its breeding range is vast, stretching from Britain right across Europe, northern Asia and as far as eastern Siberia. A visitor to Australia from August to April/ May. Far more diverse in its range of feeding habitats than the Marsh Sandpiper, including mudflats, sandy beaches with some soft sand, salt marsh and mangroves and inland ephemeral lakes and permanent dams. Feeds on crustacean molluscs and small fish. Is the equivalent of the Sulphur Crested Cockatoo in the rainfores in that it is the first bird to warn waders of imminent danger, giving its three note rapid 'teu teuu teuu' call while normally flying off as it does, not always appreciated by birdwatcher **Similar species:** Marsh Sandpiper. The Greenshank is a larger bird, thicker set with heavie upturned bill, larger head and thicker neck. Unfortunately both have similar plumage feature in flight with fine bars on the tail and white rumps looking wedge shaped. **Status:** Moderatel common throughout suitable habitat in the GSW. **Where to find:** Lake MacCleod. Th Carnarvon mudflats but also the Gascoyne River pools. All mangrove-lined beaches fron Carnarvon to Long Pont. Denham beaches. Wannamal Lake. Many of the Perth lakes. Alfre Cove. Peel Inlet. Vasse Estuary. Harvey Estuary. Albany region. Esperance lakes.

Wood Sandpiper *Tringa glareola* 19–23 cm

An attractive wader, breeding in Europe through to eastern Siberia. Medium sized wader with a distinct darker back than most waders, although not as dark as a Common Sandpiper; the same size as a Sharp-tailed Sandpiper. Strong white markings to the edges of the scapulars and wing coverts, giving the appearance of a spotted upperbody. Long sharp straight bill, distinct supercilium eye stripe, yellowish green-legs. A feature of the Woo Sandpiper is that it bobs its tail constantly when on the move. Has a preference for fresh wate more so than most waders. Found on the margins of shallow freshwater lagoons and swamp ften with emergent vegetation. Will feed in flooded grass plains. **Similar species:** Sharp-tailed andpiper which does not have the same coloured upperbody, being lighter plain brown; has igger wing coverts and the supercilium eye stripe is not as prominent as the Wood Sandpiper's. narp-tailed has a rufous crown and shorter legs. Common Sandpiper can share the same habitat ut unlike the Wood Sandpiper feeds mostly on estuaries and mangrove areas. Is a similar ze but has shorter legs, distinct collar and a rong green tinge to ne back, which should ot be confused with Vood Sandpiper. **Status:** Uncommon throughout ange. **Where to find:** Carnarvon region down to ong Point. Base of Shark ay around Hamelin Bay. ound on inland bores etween Carnarvon and Overlander. Pools on the ower Murchison. Many of erth's wetlands including rainage channels. Inland Vheatbelt ephemeral kes but not if too saline. Uncommon on the south oast.

erek Sandpiper *Xenus cinereus* 22–24 cm

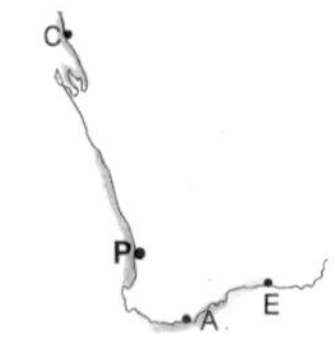

n unmistakable wader with bright orange legs and an upturned yellow-range bill and a stocky body. The only species of its genus. Breeds in the igher regions of Asia and Siberia but not the Tundra and migrates down o Africa, the Indian subcontinent, east Asia and Australasia. A coastal ird of mud banks, estuaries and mangroves. Whenever it lands it bobs s tail and rocks its head. A fast feeder running erratically to various mud pools, digging its ill into mud or running with head down chasing small crabs. **Similar species:** None. **Status:** carce in the whole of the GSW. **Where to find:** Occasionally Lake McLeod. Mangrove Bay.

New Beach. Alfred Cove. Peel Inlet and Mandurah Harbour. Can turn up at any mudd estuary in the South West. Found along the line of mangroves south of Carnarvon as it love small crabs.

Common Sandpiper *Actitis hypoleucos* 19–21 cm

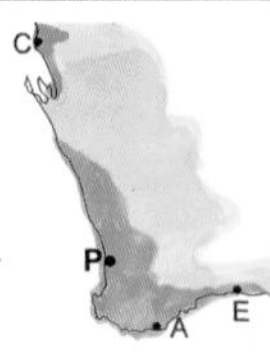

A long bodied small wader. Breeds over a broad band from Britain right across central Russia to the Far East. Found in a variety of habitats including estuaries, mangroves, beaches, rocky coastlines, lagoons, marshes, small inland ephemeral lakes as well as larger lakes and particularly lower pools on the large rivers like the Murchison and the Gascoyne Rivers. Like the Wood Sandpiper, can be found a long way inland. Is one of the most active feeders constantl running here and there chasing insects and aquatic crustaceans. Bobs its tail constantly, eve when standing on rocks. Is often seen running over small boulders to snatch food in sma tidal pools. Main diagnostic feature is the neck collar that passes around the chest but ther is a distinct white break from the wing shoulder and the dark green-brown collar. Has a lon tail passing well past the wing tips. Has a prominent white eye ring. Green-brown tinge to a the upperbody. In flight has a very noticeable thin white wing bar standing out from the dar wing. When approached, tends to fly low over water with stop-start wing beats with its wing drooping. **Similar species:** None that can be confused in the GSW. **Status:** Moderately commo in the northern region. Uncommon in the South West. **Where to find:** All mudbanks in th Carnarvon area south to Long Point. Throughout Shark Bay region. Inland along the Gascoyn and Murchison Rivers. Also some inland pools and dams. On many of the islands including th Abrolhos group. Locally common on Rottnest Island. Penguin Island. Found along the sout coast all the way to the Esperance region, including the inland lakes like Lake Warden.

Grey-tailed Tattler *Tringa brevipes* 25 cm

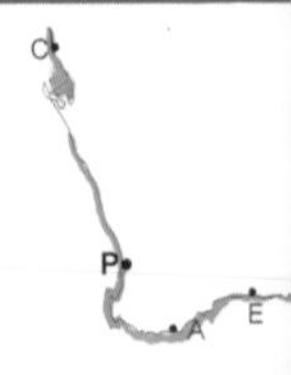

There are only 2 tattlers in the world, Grey-tailed Tattler and Wandering Tattler; both come to Australia, although the Wandering Tattler is far less common than the Grey-tailed and is almost entirely restricted to the eastern shores of Australia where it over-winters. We all marvel at the long flights that waders make to get to Australia but some of the locations they breed in are very interesting. The Grey-tailed nests in rocky stream beds but also occasionally nests way up in trees in old birds nests high in the mountains of remote eastern Siberia Apparently quite adept at perching on tree branches, something we don't see in Australia. It is medium sized wader with short yellow legs, wings almost touching the tail when at rest. Whit supercilium eye stripe that passes just over the eye. Plain grey upperbody and crown with greyis front to the breast, bleeding out to a white throat. Bill straight and slightly yellow. **Simila**

ecies: Wandering Tattler. You will be lucky to see the Wandering Tattler in the west but if you o it is, perhaps of all the regular waders visiting these shores, one of the hardest to split from e similar Grey-tailed Tattler. All the described features are very subjective. It often gets down jizz as the Wandering is thicker in the body but not much more. One of the main differences the Wandering Tattler is definitely a darker grey but it's really best to have these birds side y side then you can get used to the shape and colour. Features like nasal grooves, supercilium e stripe size, and primaries to the tail are variable and can be unreliable. Wandering has a reference for feeding on rocky coastlines and that certainly aids identification as they rarely feed n mud banks. In breeding plumage, it is much easier as the barring on the underbody on the Vandering is heavier and passes right under the body whereas the Grey-tailed has lighter barring at diminishes on the flanks to a white belly. **Status:** Moderately common in the northern gion. Uncommon in the South West Region. **Where to find:** Carnarvon region down to Long oint also in the Shark Bay inlet and Peron Peninsula. Kalbarri down to the Vasse Estuary. On me of the western islands including Rottnest Island. Uncommon on the south coast.

uddy Turnstone *Arenaria interpres* 22–24 cm

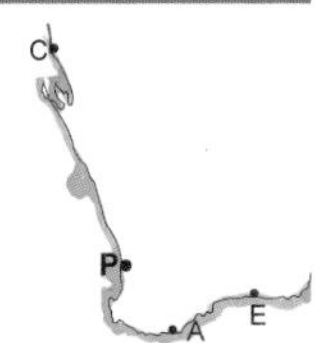

. small very stocky wader but its size certainly belies its capacity to avel. The Ruddy Turnstone nests as close to the Arctic Circle as you can ossibly get. The breeding grounds in the Tundra stretch the full circle f the globe; there are five identified separate populations but they come

together when flying south to their over-wintering grounds, which include Australia. The make this phenomenal journey leaving the Tundra in July and slowly make their way throug Asia arriving in the north of Australia in August. So when you see these small waders, say o Rottnest Island salt lakes, spare a thought for the journey they have made to get here, losin up to one third of their body weight in the process. Turnstones cannot be confused with an other wader. They are small, very dumpy waders with a black chest, partly broken by a whit collar that is not clear cut until in breeding plumage. Dark brown coverts, turning to brighte rust-orange coverts in breeding plumage. Has short bright orange legs. A very short stout bil Feeds in a variety of habitats but prefers scrambling over rocks feeding in small tidal pools Also feeds on sandy and gravel beaches and estuaries. There are two subspecies in the worl and both come to Australia but the main subspecies to Western Australia's shores is *interpre* that breeds in northern Europe and northern Siberia and part of Alaska. **Similar species** None. **Where to find:** Moderately common in the Carnarvon region down to New Beach Also in the Shark Bay region. Common on all the larger islands south to Penguin Island. Mos common on Rottnest Island. Uncommon from Augusta to Cape Arid.

Asian Dowitcher *Limnodromus semipalmatus* 33–36 cm Vagrant

P
A
E

A similar wader to the Godwits but the bill is more reminiscent of a snipe bill. Uncommon in Australia. Some authorities put the estimated population to Australia at less than 500 birds, however Broome and Eighty Mile Beach receive reasonably large numbers in a season but it is still an uncommon wader. Once you have seen a few Asian Dowitchers, you soon get to pick them. They are smaller than the godwits, with similar plumage but th bill is distinctive being snipe-like and long and heavy. If the author had to give it a name, h would call it the 'sowing machine' bird as it prods in snipe fashion faster than most wader into soft mud but will also stretch forward as it is walking looking for food. It requires soft sandy beaches and more so mudflats and estuaries. **Similar species:** Bar-shouldered Godwit, which is taller with a larger body and thinner upturned bill. **Status:** Rare in South West. Uncommon north of this region. **Where to find:** Seen in Albany region. Lake McClarty and Lake McLeod. Possible on any mudflat or salt marsh in the GSW but more likely out of the region in the Broome and Eighty Mile Beach area.

Great Knot *Caliddris tenuirostris* 26–28 cm

P
A
E

Great Knot breed in remote subarctic mountains in far eastern Siberia. For a bird that comes to these shores in greater numbers (approximately 350,000 +) than most waders, little is known of its breeding habits. There are two knots in the world and both migrate to Australia, the Great Knot and Red Knot. The Great Knot is a medium sized wader with a thickset body, stout bill and relatively short legs in proportion to the size of its body **Similar species:** Red Knot is smaller, bill is less than the depth of its head, whereas the Grea

Knot's bill is larger than the depth of its head. The chest is more pronounced on the Great Knot, giving it a sturdier look. If in breeding plumage there is no problem identifying the two species. The scapulars on the back of the Great Knot are larger and appear more contrasting, **Status:** Uncommon to moderately common in the Carnarvon region and Peron Peninsula. Scarce to uncommon in the South West. **Where to find:** Gascoyne estuary and Mangrove Bay. Less so down to New Beach. Beaches in the Denham region. Murchison and then further down the coast to Bunbury. In the Perth region. Alfred Cove. Woodmans Point. Peel Inlet. Scarce on the south coast.

Red Knot *Calidris canutus* 23–25 cm

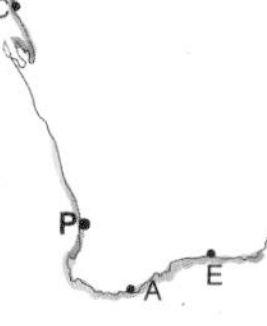

Breeds in several separate areas in the Arctic from Canada through to parts of Russia and the far eastern tip of Siberia. Unlike on the east coast, the number of Red Knot in Western Australia could exceed Great Knot. They feed together which makes identification easier. A medium sized thickset wader with short legs. Thick bill, in length less than head depth. Scalloping on flanks bolder than on Great Knot. There are 5 subspecies in the world and it

Graeme Chapman

is still not totally clear which are the main subspecies that migrate to these shores but *rogersi* and *canutus* are considered the primary migrants. **Similar species:** Refer to notes on Great Knot. **Status:** Uncommon to moderately common. **Where to find:** In the Gascoyne Estuary, Mangrove Bay and parts of the Shark Bay region including Dirk Hartog Island. Mudflats and estuaries from Murchison to Bunbury and then uncommon from Wilson Inlet to Esperance. In Perth region mainly Alfred Cove and Peel Inlet.

Sanderling *Calidris alba* 20–21 cm

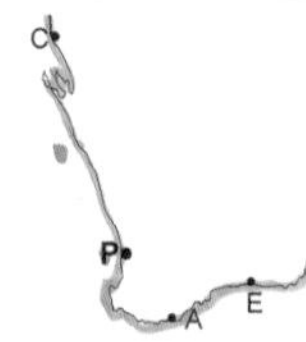

Breeds in various locations as close to the Arctic Circle as possible, just 800 km from the North Pole, having the briefest period in which to nest and raise young before it makes its massive journey to the Southern Hemisphere. It migrates south to coastal beaches in more countries than almost any other wader, including North America, Central America, South America, Africa, the Middle East, the Indian subcontinent and parts of South East Asia and Australasia. The numbers visiting Australia are not enormous, estimated to be around 10,000 birds. A bird similar and slightly smaller, the Red-necked Stint, arrives on the these shores in numbers around the 250,000 mark. Sanderling are dumpy little birds, smaller than a Curlew Sandpiper and slightly bigger than a Red-necked Stint. Birdwatchers can overlook them in non-breeding plumage, thinking they are Red-necked Stint. Sanderling prefer sandy beaches but will visit salt lakes such as on Rottnest Island. **Similar species:** Red-necked Stint. Sanderling are not only larger but much thicker set in body. Upperbody has pale grey plumage not grey-brown. The Sanderling has a distinct black shoulder patch, head looks paler. It is one of the most active waders, typically running backwards and forwards as the tide ebbs, exposing crustaceans and other food. Broad-billed Sandpiper is slightly smaller, with a distinct, longer bill with a down turned end and distinct supercilium eye stripe. **Status:** Moderately common. **Where to find:** All sandy beaches throughout the whole region. Patchily distributed on select beaches. Every year can be found on Rottnest beaches and salt lakes.

Red-necked Stint *Calidris ruficollis* 13–16 cm

One of the most common waders to arrive on the shores of Australia, breeding directly north of Australia in the far north of Siberia; also a much smaller population in Alaska that flies down to the west coast of North America. Besides the very rare Little Stint and the scarce Long-toed Stint, the Red-necked Stint is our smallest wader to migrate to these shores and smaller than any of our endemic shorebirds. In non-breeding plumage, the Red-necked Stint has grey-brown back, with mottled markings on the neck collar. Slight flecking on the crown, which will turn red-brown with darker brown streaks in full breeding plumage. It has short legs and small straight bill. Does not develop the rich rust red on the face and upper breast until in breeding plumage. Has a white supercilium. In flight on the upperbody it has a white wing bar, not pronounced. What is clearer on the upperbody, which all stints fortunately have, is a white tail with central black tail coverts showing as a long black centre stripe. Can be found in fresh water as well as saline waters but primarily is a bird of the coastal regions, estuaries, islands and saltworks ponds. Almost always in groups, from a few birds to several hundreds in the south west and in the north west into their thousands. **Similar species:** Long-toed Stint, which is slightly bigger and could be described as a miniature Sharp-tailed Sandpiper with its black streaking on a chestnut crown and browner back. Longer legs that are yellowish-green. Has a slightly longer neck and will stretch neck to feed or when alarmed which Red-necked Stints do not do as much. **Status:** Red-neck Stints are one of our commonest waders in the GSW. **Where to find:** From Lake McLeod all the way down to Hamelin Bay including Dirk Hartog and Useless Loop. Murchison down to Busselton and Augusta to Cape Arid. Common on islands particularly Rottnest.

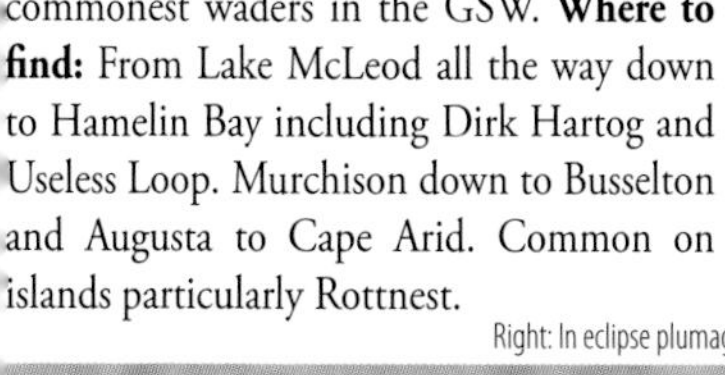

Right: In eclipse plumage

Long-toed Stint *Calidris subminuta* 13–16 cm

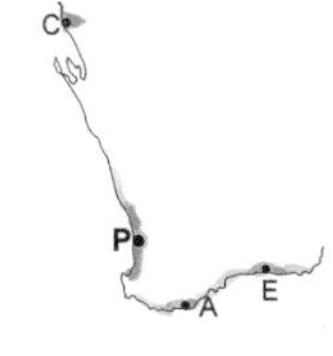

Breeds in central eastern Siberia and parts of Mongolia. One of the few rare waders that have a higher population in Western Australian than in eastern Australia. It is estimated that Australia receives about 1000 birds each year. Prefers shallow freshwater and brackish wetlands, particularly with emergent grasses. A more solitary wader found normally in no more than groups of 5–10 birds although larger numbers have been seen. **Similar species:** Has a distinct shape, being slightly bigger than Red-necked Stint, with small head and longer neck which it will stretch to feed or when alarmed standing upright. Dark streaking over chestnut crown. Darker back and shorter rear body. Legs are longer with distinct yellow-green tinge that shows well in good light. Flies at a steep incline when alarmed, with a distinct call. The author often thinks of it as looking like a miniature Sharp-tailed Sandpiper with its slightly rufous crown with faint streaking and heavier markings on the scapulars. **Status:** Scarce to uncommon locally in the GSW. Very scarce in the Carnarvon region although seen on Lake McLeod. **Where to find:** Most birds are seen on the Swan Coastal Plain with Jandabup, Lake Thompson and Lake Kogalup being the favoured wetlands when they have sufficient water.

Lake Mclarty is a particularly good site. During the last 30 plus years, the author has seen several small grassy wetlands that were favoured by Long-toed Stints, filled in for new housing developments particularly in the Jandakot and Banjup suburbs.

Photo: Adrian Boyle

Pectoral Sandpiper *Calidris melanotus* 19–24 cm

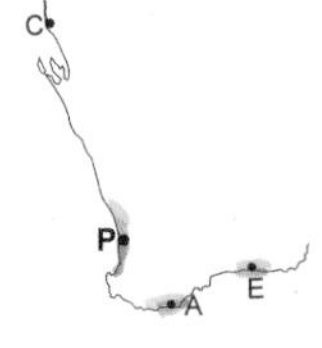

Breeds in the far north of central and eastern Siberia and northern Alaska and Canada. Most birds fly down to South America but a few migrate to the Australian shores each year, however it is generally scarce in Australia with a few coming to the South West. A medium to small wader with small head on longish neck. Body tapers at rear. Well streaked brown crown, nape and upperbody. Bill often slightly down curved with yellowish tinge to the wide part of the bill. Has a distinct break from the streaked throat and breast to a pure white belly. Shortish yellowish legs. Found on freshwater wetlands but will feed on the remaining exposed mud on large lakes. **Similar species:** Sharp-tailed Sandpiper. Let's compare them; the Pectoral Sandpiper is best seen with Sharp Tailed Sandpipers as you can compare the differences quicker. One of the main diagnostic features of the Pectoral Sandpiper and from which it derives its common name is the clear cut division of the heavy brown streaking and beige background on the neck and upper breast from the pure white on the lower breast and underparts. This remains a constant whether it's male or female, breeding plumage or non-breeding plumage. If you are lucky to get a male in eclipse or even better breeding plumage, the contrast between the upper breast markings and the white lower breast is one of the strongest in any wader.

Right: Showing clearly the pectoral band Photo: Alan Collins

The Pectoral Sandpiper has a slightly longer neck which, when you get used to them, stands out from the Sharp-tail's neck length. Mention is always made of the longer and slightly down curved bill of the Pectoral Sandpiper but I find this not a great feature as the beaks are very close in length and anyway the Sharp-tailed also has a slight down curve though not as pronounced. The Pectoral Sandpiper shares the same feeding habitat, that of emergent grasses in freshwater. Has a more upright stance than the Sharp-tailed Sandpiper.. Similar markings in flight make it difficult to split. **Status:** Very uncommon in the GSW Region. **Where to find:** Mostly on the Swan Coastal Plain but rare to scarce on Lake Thompson. Can be seen on any freshwater wetland in the South West Region which has shallow well grassed margins. Seen at Lake Warden, Esperance, and best at Lake McClarty.

Sharp-tailed Sandpiper *Calidris acuminata* 17–22 cm

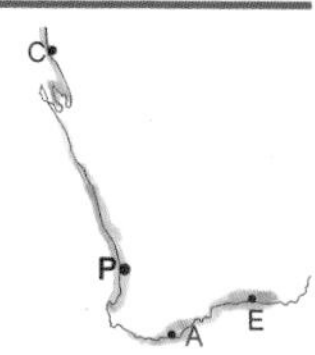

It is an interesting fact that the Sharp-tailed Sandpiper breeds in the same remote Siberian region as the Pectoral Sandpiper, both in large numbers, but one flies almost entirely down through the Americas to South America and the other chooses to come to Australia. Both look similar and both require similar feeding habitats. The Sharp-tailed Sandpiper is another common visiting wader with an estimated population of 140,000 birds. A reasonable number come down the west cost to the GSW region. Sharp-tailed Sandpipers are a small-medium sized wader with rufous streaked crown, white supercilium eye stripe, a longish slightly down curved bill, short yellow-green legs, long pointed rear body. The main feature is not so much size but the overall colour that is a richer brown compared with many of the waders that are greyish looking. The Sharp-tailed Sandpiper has warmer colours particularly the rufous streaked crown. Has a habitat preference for feeding on muddy edges of freshwater and brackish wetlands. Feeds in water that has emergent grasses and sedges but will feed on open mud when the need arises. **Similar species:** Refer to Pectoral Sandpiper. **Status:** Common on selected wetlands throughout the range. **Where to find:** Found from Carnarvon down to Hamelin Bay occasionally on the coast but mostly in flooded samphire or the many bores with overflow pools that create wet grassy areas. Found throughout many wetlands on the Swan Coastal Plain. In Perth can be found on a few lakes with wet grassed margins and receding waters like Thompson, Forrestdale, Jandabup and Joondalup Lakes. Masses can gather on the edge of Peel Inlet in the samphire marshes also Lake Mclarty near by. Also Vasse Estuary. Harvey Estuary and Busselton Wetlands mainly Broadwater. Less common on south coast until the Esperance region where there can be larger numbers.

Curlew Sandpiper *Calidris ferruginea* 18–23 cm

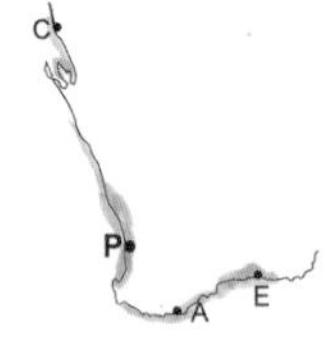

Breeds in the far north of central Russia migrating to Africa, the Middle East, Indian subcontinent and East Asia and Australasia. One of Australia's most common waders. One of the easiest of the small waders to identify with its long down curved bill from which it gets its name. It has longish legs for its size, slender neck and small head. An important diagnostic feature is that most sandpipers and stints have black tail coverts and central tail feathers running down the length of the tail. It contrasts well with the white outer tail feathers. The Curlew Sandpiper has an all white rump and upper tail coverts. Has distinct white wing bar. Found in sheltered bays and estuaries, preferring softer mud conditions. Will feed in freshwater lakes and will go inland although not as much as those that visit Africa.

Similar species: Only the White-rumped Sandpiper which is extremely rare, has a shorter and blunter bill and is a smaller and slimmer wader. **Status:** Common along much of the coastline along the GSW Region. **Where to find:** From Lake McLeod, Mangrove Bay all the way down to Hamelin Bay and then much of the Shark Bay region. Also will visit bore overflows and ephemeral wetlands near coast. Common on the Swan Coastal Plain particularly large drying lakes like Thompson and Forrestdale. Peel Inlet can get several thousand birds in a good season. Is less common along the southern coast to Esperance.

Eclipse plumage

Broad-billed Sandpiper *Limicola falcinellus* subspecies *sibirica* 16–18 cm

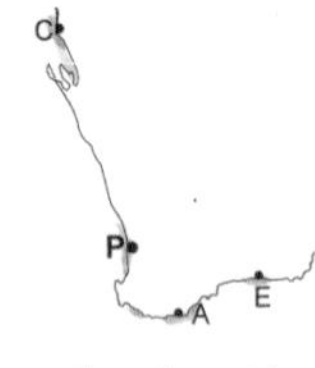

One of the uncommon waders in the world, found breeding in a few fragmented areas from northern Europe and Russia. Most birds remain in the north west of WA. Massive numbers for such an uncommon bird have been recorded just north of the GSW in the Leslie Saltworks, Port Hedland, with over 3000 birds sighted. A few come down the coast to the Swan Coastal Plain and rarely to the southern coastal belt. It is a small wader with a distinct bill, some people presume it is called Broad-billed because its bill is relatively broad at the base, which it is, but when looking from above the bill, the tip slightly broadens, which is an unusual feature in waders. The Broad-billed Sandpiper is a small wader not much bigger than a Red-necked Stint and smaller than a Curlew Sandpiper. The head is distinctly striped, seen well even in non-breeding plumage. The bill is not only broad at the base but also relatively long, nearly as long as a Curlew Sandpiper in relation to head size, also bent downwards near the tip. Legs short. In the GSW not seen in large groups but mostly solitary with Curlew Sandpipers and Red-necked Stints. There are two subspecies and only one *siberica* which breeds in Siberia, comes to Australia. **Similar species:** No other wader visiting Australian shores. **Status:** Very uncommon in the GSW. **Where to find:** Lake McLeod. Gascoyne Estuary and Mangrove Bay. Found south to Hamelin in the more muddy beaches and estuaries. More likely to fly down to Swan Coastal Plain and Peel Inlet. Best place in Perth is Alfred Cove. Scarce on south coast.

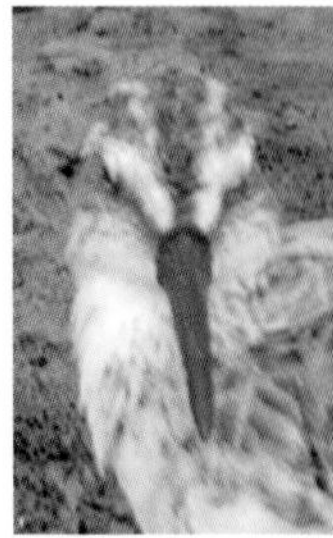

Above: Showing lateral stripes on crown.

Oriental Pratincole *Glareola malddivarum* 23–24 cm Vagrant

Oriental Pratincole breed in southern Asia and migrate down to Australia in the wet season in massive flocks, often following storms where insects are swept up in the turbulence. Found on open plains where they will run and pick insects or more often fly with incredibly fast manoeuvres hawking for insects. When in full feeding frenzy, it is like watching jet fighters flying in all directions as they fly over the treetops taking advantage of swarms of insects in the wet season. Their movements are unpredictable but they can gather in their thousands, such as on Eighty Mile Beach. **Similar species:** Australian Pratincole, similar in shape only. Australian Pratincole has a brown-fawn coloured body, the Oriental Pratincole has a grey-brown duller body with a distinct throat pattern seen best in full breeding plumage. Australian Pratincole has a distinct dark chestnut band on the flanks and belly and longer legs. **Status:** Rare in the GSW where you are unlikely to see this bird; it has been seen in Perth on Jandabup Lake but is extremely rare this far south. **Where to find:** Mainly north of Karratha and common in the Kimberley in summer.

Australian Pratincole *Stiltia Isabella* 19–24 cm Vagrant

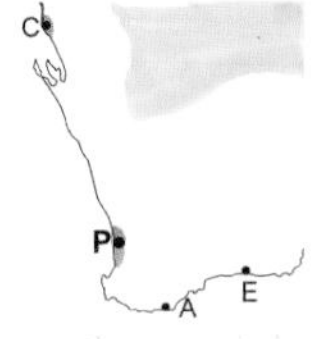

There are 8 pratincole in the world and Australia has two of them, the Oriental Pratincole which migrates here in the summer months and the Australian Pratincole, which is a resident endemic bird and the sole member of its genus. A long slim bird with longer legs than other pratincoles. Has a rust coloured band on the flanks and belly which in flight contrasts well with the white vent, has black along the underwing coverts. Bill is slightly down curved on the tip, and in breeding plumage it is bright red from the base to half way along. Has very pointed wings shown clearly in flight and is a graceful flyer. A bird of open stony plains and grasslands of the inland arid regions. Does not hawk for insects as much as Oriental Pratincole but rather runs and picks at insects mainly on exposed stony or very short grassed plains. Even though found on remote open plains, they still need to be near bodies of drinking water. **Nest:** No nest, only a scrape made on bare ground and located where the bird has good all round vision, often on a rise. Clutch size 2. **Similar species:** Oriental Pratincole which has grey-brown upperbody and not pale chestnut. Legs almost half the length of the Australian Pratincole. In flight easy to split as Oriental lacks chestnut band on the belly but does have pale chestnut axillaries and median coverts. **Status:** Scarce in the GSW. **Where to find:** Occasionally on open plains in the north west of this region. Rare vagrants have been reported in the Perth region.

Pacific Gull *Larus pacificus* subspecies *georgii* 50–67 cm

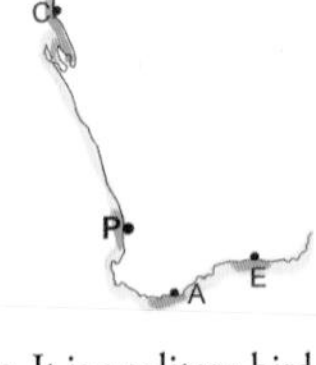

Endemic to the shores of southern Australia reaching the highest latitude in Australia on the west coast as far as Carnarvon. Scarce north of Carnarvon. The largest gull in Australia with a heavy bill, dark back, wings at rest extending past the tail. Feeds mainly on fish and molluscs but is also a predator taking the young of other seabirds during the nesting period. Will hunt at night as well as day over some seabird colonies. It is a solitary bird and rarely feeds in groups. Pacific Gulls do not reach full adult plumage until the fourth year and that makes identification of the first, second and third year birds more difficult to split with Kelp Gull. There are two subspecies in Australia with one *georgi* in the South West. **Nest:** No nest is built but a relatively deep scrape is made and lined with seaweed if near a beach but on islands the nest hollow is lined with any soft material adjacent to nest site. Clutch size 2–3. **Similar species:** The Kelp Gull is a smaller less stocky bird. Bill is not as massive. The nostrils are an interesting feature of the Pacific Gull, in so much as they are round, except in the subspecies *georgii* in the Shark Bay region which has slightly narrower nostrils. The Kelp Gull's nostrils are the narrow long slit typical of most gulls. Two important differences involve colour in the adult birds. The bill on the Pacific Gull has a red-orange tip on both the upper and lower mandible; on the Kelp's bill, it is only on the lower mandible. The tail of the Pacific Gull has a distinct broad black band whereas the Kelp Gull has no band but an all white tail. Juveniles of the Pacific Gull still have the massive bill and bigger more rounded head but are a darker more even brown all over, getting less brown into adult plumage by third year, but do not have any yellow on bill until becoming an adult bird in the fourth year. **Status:** Moderately common in the Shark Bay region. Uncommon on the Swan Coastal Plain. Common on the south coast. **Where to find:** Carnarvon, Denham and most of the Shark Bay region. Kalbarri. The Abrolhos Islands. Most islands off the Swan Coastal Plain. Numerous beaches on the South Coast particularly on rocky coastlines. Common in the Albany region and Esperance region.

Immature

Silver Gull *Chroicephalus novaeholladiae novaehollandiae* 36–44 cm

The ubiquitous scavenger we know in our coastal cities throughout much of Australia. It is however an attractive gull, particularly the adult bird in breeding plumage with its bright red legs and bill. Found only in Australasia, it has adapted well to European settlement and most probably increased in numbers. Found along the entire Australian coastline including all the northern coastline, and throughout New Zealand (subspecies *scopulinus*). An opportunistic scavenger that now relies heavily on human organic waste found at fishing harbours, waste dumps, and ornamental parks and gardens. Can be found in the hinterland where ephemeral lakes occur. On the coast fish is still an important part of its diet. There are three subspecies in the world with only one *novaeholladiae* in Australia. Breeds mostly

on islands that dot the whole GSW coast. The Perth region has the largest populations of Silver Gull, nesting on Rottnest, Carnac, Flat Rocks, Gull Rock and Penguin Island. Silver Gulls are basically sedentary in the Perth region and tend not to travel further than 50 kilometres from their breeding grounds. **Nest**: A scrape on the ground lined with any soft material available. Nests mostly on offshore islands but also on islands on inland lakes. Clutch size 2–3. **Similar species:** None in WA. In New Zealand there can be slight confusion between immature Silver Gulls and the endemic Black-billed Gull. **Status:** Very common. **Where to find:** From Carnarvon all the way around the South West coast to Cape Arid.

Gull-billed Tern *Gelochelidon nilotica* subspecies *macrotarsa* 35–38 cm

Gull-billed Terns are patchily distributed throughout all the continents of the world. The Australian subspecies *macrotarsa* occurs both on the coast and inland WA. The subspecies *affinis* that breeds in China comes down to northern Australia and would be extremely rare in the GSW. Gull-billed Terns are a medium sized tern with a black crown, short gull-type bill which is completely black both in and out of breeding plumage. In non-breeding plumage there is no black crown, only a black patch remaining around the eye and on the ear coverts. They are gregarious birds and will normally

Above: In non-breeding plumage

be accompanied by other Gull-billed Terns. Has a slow languid flight. Even though it can be found on beaches and mudflats in the GSW, has a preference for ephemeral freshwater or brackish lakes. Highly nomadic and will disperse to inland lakes like Yarra Yarra Lake, Lake Austin or Lake Anneen. There are 6 subspecies in the world and one in Australia. **Nest:** No nest is made, only a scrape in sand or earth. Located mostly on islands off shore. It does however, nest on islands on inland lakes more than any other tern. Clutch size 2–3. **Similar species:** None. **Status:** Generally uncommon but locally common in the north and north east of the GSW. Uncommon on the Swan Coastal Plain. Scarce in the southern region. **Where to find:** In the Carnarvon region particularly after good rains. Seen at Mc Neill Claypan. Hutt Lagoon north of Geraldton. Yenyening Lakes. Camel Lake north of the Stirling Range. Any inland lake after heavy rains, particularly Anneen, Austin, Wooleen. Yarra Yarra and Hinds.

Caspian Tern *Sterna caspia* 47–54 cm

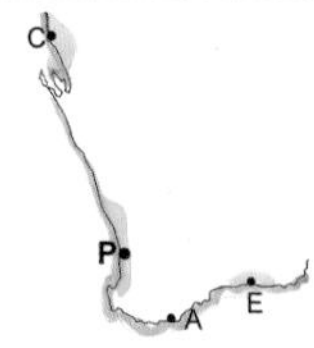

A very large tern found in many parts of the world. Largest of all the Australian terns. Has large orange-red bill, slightly down curved with a black tip, black crown passing under the eye to the base of the nape, short black legs. In non-breeding plumage the crown is mottled with some white flecking in the black. Juveniles have black edging to the scapulars on the back. Has short tail with slight wedge, in flight shows black tips to the wings. Often calls with typical rasping harsh note similar to a White-necked Heron's call. Feeds entirely on fish. Found on sheltered inlets and bays, coastal lakes mainly brackish, harbours and reservoirs. **Nest:** No nest is made but places soft material in a scrape. Nests mostly on islands either on sand above the high water mark or in the centre of islands. Can be a solitary nester or form small colonies. **Similar species:** None. **Status:** Moderately common in the Great South West. **Where to find:** Carnarvon region including Lake McLeod. Mangrove Bay down to Hamelin Pool. Throughout the Denham, Useless Loop region in small numbers. From Murchison all the way to Bunbury. In Perth often at Alfred Cove and also on Rottnest Island where it nests. The Rockingham area and Penguin Island. Peel Inlet. On the south coast from Augusta to Esperance, particularly in the large inlets like Nornalup Inlet and in Oyster Harbour easily seen at Emu Point.

Crested Tern *Sterna bergii* subspecies *cristata* 40–50 cm

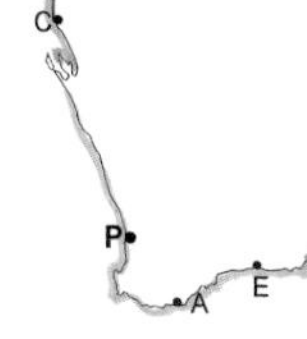

Found in countries abutting the Indian Ocean, west Pacific Ocean and Australasia. A large tern with a black crown and crest, narrow white gap between bill and crest on the forehead in breeding plumage, pale long yellow bill, long forked tail, black legs. Feeds almost entirely on fish, hovering in true tern-like fashion just a few metres above the water to look for fish and then dive and catch. Is a colonial breeder and will also roost colonially but tends to feed individually. Found throughout the coastal region of the GSW on open beaches, estuaries, and brackish waters, islands and mangrove-lined shores. Breeds on many islands throughout range sometimes in large numbers. On Pelsaert Island in the Abrolhos there can be over 1000 birds in one colony. When breeding, nests very close to other birds mostly just out of pecking range. The crest remains extended in bristle fashion when breeding or threatened, other times crest is dropped. There are four subspecies in the world with only one in Australia *cristata* being one of the smallest subspecies. **Nest:** No nest made, just a hollow scrape in sand. Nests in colonies, often with other species of tern almost always on islands. Clutch size normally one egg only but occasionally 2. **Similar species:** Lesser Crested Tern, although scarce in this region, is a smaller, slimmer bird. Has a finer orange to orange-yellow bill not pale lemon-yellow. Important feature with adult birds is that the black cap touches the base of the bill on the Lesser Crested Tern. The Crested has a small gap of white between the bill and the black crown. In immature birds it's not a distinctive feature, best to look at size, shape and bill colour. **Status:** Common on the coast and islands throughout the region, often very common locally. **Where to find:** Carnarvon down to Hamelin. Throughout the Shark Bay region. Nests throughout the Abrolhos region on selected islands and from the Murchison all the way down to Busselton. Augusta to Cape Arid. In the Perth region nests on Rottnest. Lancelin. Carnac and Seal Islands. Can be seen in most areas. Carnarvon estuary. Swan River. Rottnest. Mandurah. Oyster Harbour.

Roseate Tern *Sterna dougallii* subspecies *gracilis* 31–38 cm

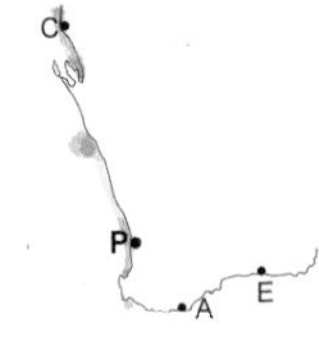

Found throughout many coastal regions in the world including parts of America (on the east coast), Europe, Africa, Asia and Australasia. A beautiful elegant tern with a slick black crown that touches the bill and passes down the back of the nape in the breeding season. Out of the breeding season the forehead and lores become white and streaking into the top of the crown. Has red legs except when a juvenile. Long down curved bill which is black in the immature and non-breeding adults, but during the pre-nuptial and incubation period is bright red then darkens when chicks hatch. Has a long tail. Has a beautiful pinkish flush on the underbody in the breeding season. Feeds on fish and occasionally molluscs. Prefers to feed in what is known as 'blue waters', that is waters that are clear for feeding. Not found on the south coast. There are at least four subspecies in the world with one subspecies *gracilis* in Australia. **Nest:** No nest is made, just a scrape in sand. Nests in colonies on islands. Clutch size normally 2. **Similar species:** Common Tern subspecies *longepennis* is very similar but is a bigger and thicker set bird, the upperbody is darker grey, the bill is shorter and thicker, the tail not as long or as forked, neck shorter, legs are black and slightly shorter and it has a grey flush to flanks. The rare nominate race *hirundo* has a red bill with black tip and red legs closer in colour to a Roseate Tern. **Status:** Moderately common in the north of the region. Common on the Abrolhos. Uncommon south of Murchison. Vagrant on the south coast. **Where to find:** Off Dirk Hartog Island and in Denham region. Has nested on Meade Island near Dirk

Hartog Island. Bird Island. Peron Peninsula. Common on some of the Abrolhos Islands. Has nested in the Peel-Mandurah region in past years. Bathurst Point, Rottnest Island.

Fairy Tern *Sterna neresis neresis* 22–27 cm

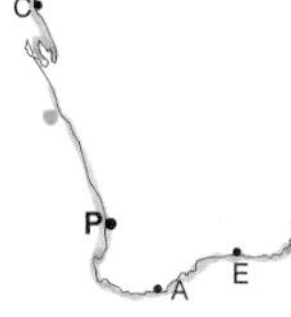

Unlike the Little Tern, which is found throughout much of the coastal waters of the world, the Fairy Tern is restricted to Australasia. Sadly the population of Fairy Terns has been diminishing over the years since European settlement. The Western Australian population is estimated to be around 1400 pairs (Hill et al. 1988). Much of the disturbance and loss of nesting colonies results from the consistent expansion of towns such as Mandurah, and disturbance by recreational vehicles near breeding colonies. The Fairy Tern is a delicate small tern, found mostly in the southern part of Australia including most of the coastline in the GSW. Feeds almost entirely on small fish and, like many terns, the male will present to prospective mates an offering of a small fish to try and instigate the breeding process. In breeding plumage has black crown, which drops down to the front of the eye and stops before the bill, showing white between the bill and the black eye stripe. The primaries are an even grey colour. The bill colour is bright yellow-orange. In non-breeding, the bill is still yellow-orange but has some black at the base and a small black band just before the tip. Feet yellow. There are 3 subspecies in the Australasian region with one subspecies *neresis* in Australia. **Nest:** No nest is made, just a small scrape on sand. Nests both on islands and narrow sandy spits or headlands. Clutch size normally 2. **Similar species:** The Little Tern is slightly smaller and slightly slimmer. The bill is yellow colour rather than yellow-orange, with a black tip. The black crest comes closer to

the forehead and forms a white eyebrow rather than just coming across the head and straight down to the eye as in the Fairy, and the back is greyer. **Status:** Uncommon throughout the west coast and its islands and the southern coast, except the Abrolhos Islands where it is common. Moderately common locally. Population may be on the decline. The Little Tern does come down to Carnarvon, occasionally overlooked. **Where to find:** Good chances in the Denham region as it has nested on Peron Peninsula and also on Dirk Hartog Island. Rottnest Island. Garden Island. Alfred Cove. Woodman Point. Halls Head. Penguin Island. Mandurah Harbour. Esperance lakes particularly Lake Warden.

Bridled Tern *Onychoprion anaethetus anaethetus* 30–32 cm

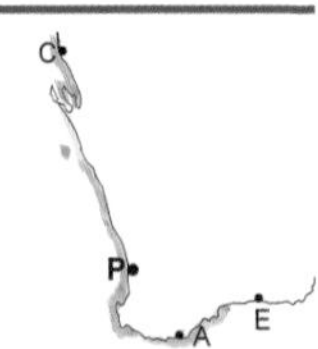

The nominate race is found throughout much of South East Asia and most of Australasia. A medium sized tropical tern very similar to the Sooty Tern with whom it shares much of the same distribution, although the Bridled Tern nests in smaller numbers than the Sooty Tern. Bridled Terns nest on many of the GSW islands, including islands just off the east side of Dirk Hartog and in Freycinet Harbour including White and Mary Anne Islands. Nests on many of the Abrolhos Islands in small colonies, often amongst the more populous Common Noddy. The estimated population in excess of 7000 birds, breeding on over 60 islands. Further north out of this region there are larger nesting colonies particular on Barrow Island and in the Montebello Islands. Other islands closer to Perth include Cervantes, Lancelin, Rottnest, Carnac. Little (near Whitfords Beach), Garden and Penguin Islands. Bridled Terns have expanded their breeding range over the last fifty years moving further south. There are 4 subspecies in the world with one *anaethetus* in Australia. The Western Australian birds are slightly smaller than the east coast birds. **Nest:** No nest is made, just a scrape in the sand. Nests in colonies on offshore islands. Clutch size one egg. **Similar species:** Sooty Tern. The Bridled Tern is slightly smaller and slimmer than the Sooty. Has a dark black-brown upperbody getting grey-brown below the nape. Shortish neck. The important feature is the white supercilium eye stripe running from the forehead past the eye as a thin eyebrow. Long tail that passes the wing tips at rest. The Sooty Tern is slightly larger and thicker bodied. The main differences from Bridled Tern is that the Sooty Tern's upperbody is black not dark brown. The forehead is white stopping just above the eye as a broad patch not a narrow long eye stripe passing the eye to a point as in the Bridled Tern. The black crown runs down the nape and continues as a solid black back. There is not a break at the base of the nape that changes to grey as in the Bridled**. Status:** Very common on most islands in the mid west and off the Perth coast. Scarce on the southern coast. **Where to find:** All the islands listed above. Easiest to access near Perth on Penguin Island and Rottnest Island.

Sooty Tern *Onychoprion fuscata* subspecies *serrata* 33–36 cm

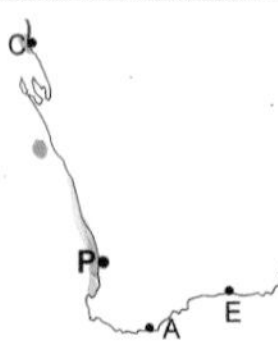

A bird that is found throughout the southern hemisphere oceans. Some of the colonies in the Pacific have as many as 300,000 birds. Colonies in Australia are far smaller but, in terms of many other seabirds, they are still in large numbers and the largest colony is here in Western Australia on the Abrolhos Islands where the numbers are in excess of 25,000 birds. As described under Bridled Tern, the Sooty Terns have a jet-black crown that passes down the nape to the upperbody. The forehead is white, stopping just above the eye as a broad patch not a narrow long eye stripe passing the eye to a point as in the Bridled Tern. There is no break at the base of the nape that changes to grey as in the Bridled. They arrive in the breeding season in October and November and depart February and March. Possibly 7 subspecies in the world with 3 in Australia, *serrata* on the Abrolhos Islands, *oahuensis* on Christmas Island and *nubilosa* on the Cocos and Keeling Islands. **Nest:** No nest is made, just a scrape in the sand. Nests in large colonies on offshore islands. Clutch size one egg. **Similar species:** Refer to Bridled Tern. **Status:** Very common on the Abrolhos. South of the Abrolhos it is accidental and only seen or found dead on beaches after severe storms. **Where to find:** The Abrolhos Islands and north of the GSW to Ashmore Reef.

Whiskered Tern *Chlidonias hybrida* subspecies *javanicus* 23–25 cm

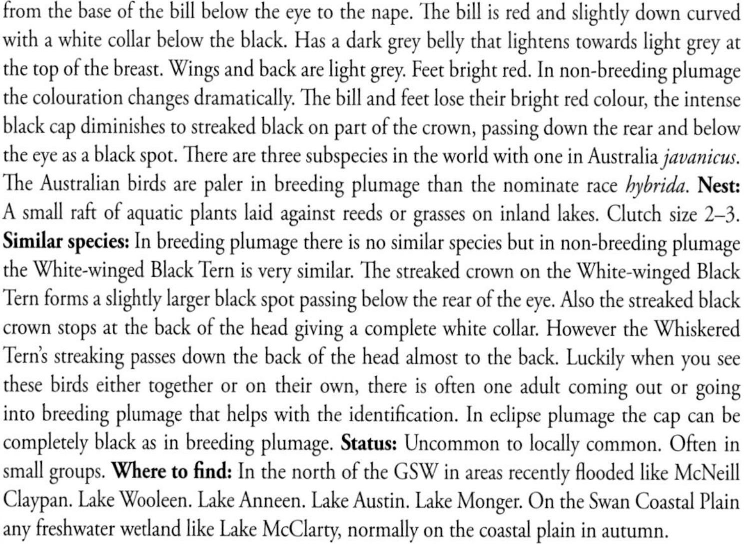

One of the 'marsh terns' found in Africa, Europe, Indian subcontinent, South East Asia, China and Australasia. A bird of freshwater lakes, swamps, reservoirs and flooded samphire. Will nest on inland or coastal wetlands, often with preference for recently flooded lowlands with emergent grasses. The adult breeding birds have a black cap running from the base of the bill below the eye to the nape. The bill is red and slightly down curved with a white collar below the black. Has a dark grey belly that lightens towards light grey at the top of the breast. Wings and back are light grey. Feet bright red. In non-breeding plumage the colouration changes dramatically. The bill and feet lose their bright red colour, the intense black cap diminishes to streaked black on part of the crown, passing down the rear and below the eye as a black spot. There are three subspecies in the world with one in Australia *javanicus*. The Australian birds are paler in breeding plumage than the nominate race *hybrida*. **Nest:** A small raft of aquatic plants laid against reeds or grasses on inland lakes. Clutch size 2–3. **Similar species:** In breeding plumage there is no similar species but in non-breeding plumage the White-winged Black Tern is very similar. The streaked crown on the White-winged Black Tern forms a slightly larger black spot passing below the rear of the eye. Also the streaked black crown stops at the back of the head giving a complete white collar. However the Whiskered Tern's streaking passes down the back of the head almost to the back. Luckily when you see these birds either together or on their own, there is often one adult coming out or going into breeding plumage that helps with the identification. In eclipse plumage the cap can be completely black as in breeding plumage. **Status:** Uncommon to locally common. Often in small groups. **Where to find:** In the north of the GSW in areas recently flooded like McNeill Claypan. Lake Wooleen. Lake Anneen. Lake Austin. Lake Monger. On the Swan Coastal Plain any freshwater wetland like Lake McClarty, normally on the coastal plain in autumn.

White-winged Black Tern *Chlidonias leucopteris* 20–23 cm

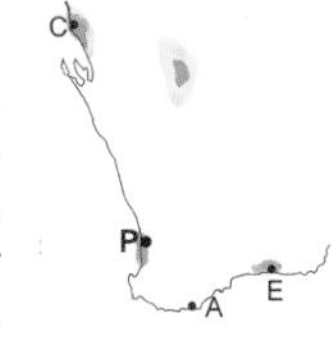

Two fresh water frequenting terns come to these shores, the Whiskered and the White-winged Black Tern. Both can be found throughout many regions of the world, often feeding together on the same wetlands. The White-winged feeds in coastal waters and can be seen in the company of Fairy Terns and Little Terns. The Whiskered Tern nests in Australia but the White-winged does not, breeding in the northern hemisphere. In breeding plumage, the White-winged Tern is a stunning bird but alas we do not get to see it that often in Australia except just before they set off from these shores at the end of March to May. In full breeding plumage, the White-winged Black Tern has a complete black head, underbody and upperbody breaking at the rump to grey. The vent is white and the wings contrast with the black head and body being pale grey. The tips of the primaries are dark grey. The legs are bright red. Adult non-breeding plumage totally different. Refer notes on Whiskered Tern. **Similar species:** Refer to Whiskered Tern. **Status:** Scarce in the GSW but is an irruptive species that will come down when cyclones are present. Flies with Whiskered, which is far more common in the South West. **Where to find:** Chance sightings on any major lake especially Lake McClarty and Peel Inlet.

White-winged Black Tern in breeding plumage Photo: Graeme Chapman

Common Noddy *Anous stolidus* subspecies *pileatus* (may change) 40–45 cm

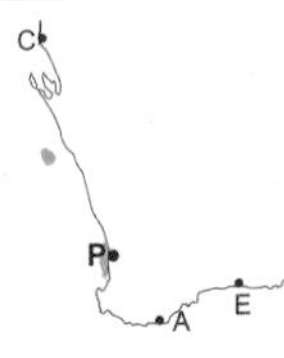

Found throughout all the southern oceans of the world and as far north as the Caribbean. The largest of all the Noddies. A dark brown tern that in West Australian waters leaves their breeding sites in April to May returning in late August through to October. Plumage is dark chocolate-brown on all

of the body with prominent white cap. The important feature is that the white cap stops abruptly above the eye and above the lores and touches the bill. The white fades down the nape into the dark brown back, level with the eye. There are 4 subspecies in the world with one *pileatus* in Australia. The populations in Western Australia are slightly smaller and paler than those found on the east coast. **Nest:** Consists of a large pile of seaweed and other plants on top of or below prostrate plants on offshore islands. Clutch size one. **Similar species:** Lesser Noddy is slightly smaller and certainly a slimmer bird. Plumage is darker chocolate-brown almost black, although not as dark as Black Noddy, which has not been seen in these waters as yet. White cap passes below eye and at base of bill. Importantly, the white cap grades into the dark brown more gradually not reaching its darkest brown until the upper back and belly. So in simple terms, the head of the Lesser Noddy is overall lighter in colour than the Common. In flight when seen together, which is common in the Abrolhos, the Lesser Noddy has faster wing beats. The generic name 'Anous' means silly or foolish in Greek and the early mariners found them easy birds to take as they were so accepting of humans. To walk alongside (not through) colonies of Common and Lesser Noddy is an experience never to forget as they allow such a close approach without fear, a rare privilege in these times. **Status:** Very common in the Abrolhos during the breeding season. Accidental in the South West , often found dead after cyclonic storms. They did breed on Lancelin Island in 1989 and 1992. **Where to find:** The Abrolhos Islands. Pelsaert Island can have in some years in excess of 130,000 nests.

Lesser Noddy *Anous tenuirostris* subspecies *melanops* 29–34 cm

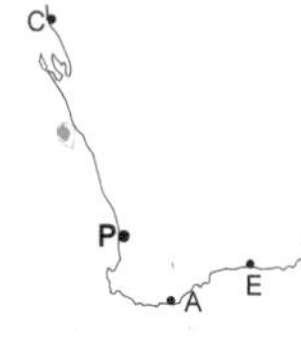

There are 2 main breeding regions in the world for Lesser Noddy both restricted to remote islands. The nominate *tenuirostris* occurs on a scattered group of islands centred on the Seychelles and Maldives Islands in the Indian Ocean. The subspecies *melanops* occurs in the GSW on the Abrolhos Islands. On the Abrolhos they are found on only a few islands, the reason being is that they require mangrove trees as a nesting habitat. On Pelsaert Island, they share the island with a larger colony of Common Noddy but both require different nesting locations. To see a Lesser Noddy nest in mangrove trees is like looking at a Jewish candelabra with various nests branching off the main trunk all incredibly close together. The noise from the whole colony is continuous as parents locate their young. **Nest:** The nest is a small platform consisting of branches and mangrove leaves cemented together with the bird's excreta and placed on the fork of a mangrove branch. Clutch size one. **Similar species:** Refer to Common Noddy for plumage details. **Status:** Locally very common on a few islands in the Abrolhos. As for Common Noddy, accidental in the South West, often found dead after cyclonic storms.

Rock Dove (Feral Pigeon) *Columba livia* 31–34 cm Introduced

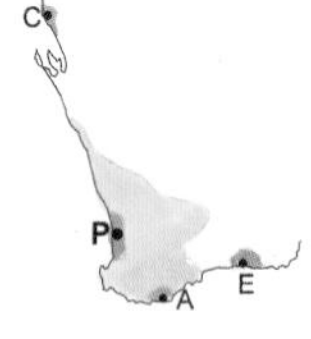

The pigeon that is so common in many cities of the world is now widespread in most large southern cities of Australia being introduced in the mid 1800s. Its origins are difficult to define, as there is so much interbreeding between domestic pigeons and wild pigeons throughout the many countries in which it occurs. They most probably originated in northern Africa and the Middle East where wild populations still occur, in fact there are still wild populations in the north of Britain. Even though introduced to Australia, they still instinctively go back to their roots, nesting in rock ledges as can be seen on Penguin Island where they nest in the small limestone caves and crevasses on the island. The wild populations are often augmented by stray racing pigeons. There are approximately 14 subspecies spread throughout the world. **Similar species:** None. **Status:** Common to uncommon in large towns. **Where to find:** Found in most of the larger South West cities in Western Australia from Esperance all the way to Geraldton.

Laughing Dove *Streptopelia senegalensis senegalensis* 25–27 cm Introduced

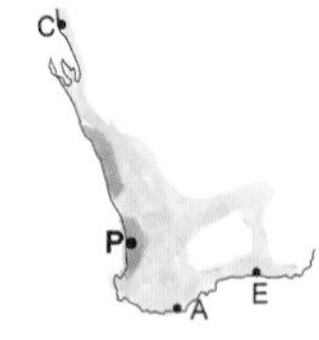

Laughing Dove is a small pigeon with general pinkish tinge to the upperbody and breast. Grey on the wings with distinct black and pink mottling on the throat, its main diagnostic feature. Introduced to Perth in 1898 its origins are not clear, however there are 7 subspecies in the

world, found on the African continent, part of the Middle East and the Indian subcontinent. One of its common names is Senegal Dove from where the nominate race occurs. Laughing Dove in Australia only occurs in the GSW. The dove has spread to most of the major towns in the GSW. In one of his maps, Sedgwick showed that the Laughing Dove had reached Geraldton, Kalgoorlie, Esperance, Albany and Bunbury by 1958. It is uncommon north of Geraldton. Like all pigeons, its staple diet is grain and consequently it has followed the railway lines that fan out from Perth. Luckily, Laughing Doves do not inhabit native woodlands but have a preference for city parks, roadside verges in cities and railway lines wherever seed are abundant. There are 7 subspecies in the world and it is presumed the nominate *senegalensis* is the one that was introduced into Perth. **Nest:** The nest is a flimsy structure of twigs placed in a variety of trees or bushes mostly exotic. Clutch size 2–3. **Similar species:** Spotted Dove, which is a larger pigeon with a distinct black collar with white spots forming a half collar, that passes from the centre of the neck around the back. Has a grey head, its tail is longer and dark grey-brown not pink. Laughing Dove's tail is blue-grey. Spotted Dove's eye is yellow and Laughing Dove's eye is black. **Status:** Locally common. **Where to find:** Throughout the major towns in the South West.

Spotted Dove *Streptopelia chinensis* 30–33 cm Introduced

An introduced bird from the Indian subcontinent and South East Asia. The first birds released into the wild were those from Perth Zoo between 1898 and 1899. Other birds were released over the years in all the eastern states unlike the introduced Laughing Dove which was only introduced to Perth. There are 8 subspecies in the world, 2 subspecies *tigrina* and *chinensis* have been introduced to Australia and interbreeding has certainly occurred between them. The Spotted Dove has spread not quite as far as the Laughing Dove in the GSW. Has expanded down to Augusta but has not passed Dongara in the north. Was also released in Kalgoorlie but is not found in the outer Wheatbelt or most of the Southern Coastal Region. **Status:** Locally very common around Perth. Uncommon to scarce south and north of Perth. **Nest**: Clutch size and nest structure similar to Spotted Dove. **Similar species**: Laughing Dove which lacks the black neck band with white spots to the rear of the neck. **Where to find:** Most coastal major towns including Perth, Rockingham, Mandurah, Bunbury, Also many of the Darling Range suburbs on the outskirts of Perth.

Common Bronzewing *Phaps chalcopters* 28–36 cm

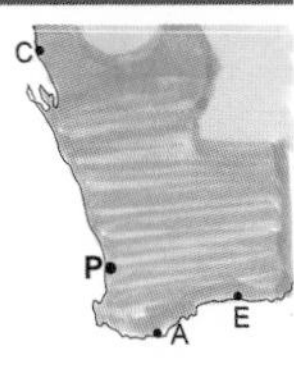

Found throughout the GSW Region. A bird of open woodlands, open fields with adjacent cover, roadside verges, Mulga Woodland, Mallee Woodland and rocky terrain. It is a generally a solitary feeder but when grains are spilt and food abundant small groups can congregate to feed. Feeds on seeds and some insects, however cannot bite so must swallow whole. Also must come to water to drink. Often found by hearing its low booming call of 'ooom…ooom…ooom' repeated slowly. A nervous bird that will often leave its nest when one is not even close to the nest. There are small differences between the male and the female. The male has a pale yellow-cream patch on the forehead, female white. Male has red-brown crown, female plain brown. Male has pink flush to all the underbody, female grey-brown. Bronzing on wing coverts more iridescent in the male. **Nest:** A loose collection of twigs in a saucer shape placed from 3–15 metres on a fork or horizontal limb. Clutch size normally 2. **Similar species:** Brush Bronzewing which is smaller in size with shorter tail, bronzing on wing restricted to two central bars on the median and greater coverts. Forehead on male has more buff-cream and goes to just above front of eye. Dark chocolate-brown above white eye stripe. Blue-grey underbody and throat. Most important feature is a distinct deep red-brown throat patch on the male. Nape and shoulder on male rich chestnut-brown passing to a point on the upper breast. Female lighter copper-brown nape and neck contrasting with the blue-grey neck and underbody. **Status:** Common to uncommon throughout the range. **Where to find:** Darling Range near Perth. All of the Wheatbelt particularly where there is remnant woodland and dams close by. Common in all the inner Wheatbelt reserves. Found throughout the Mulga Woodland.

Male

Female

Brush Bronzewing *Phaps elegans* subspecies *occidentalis* 25–33 cm

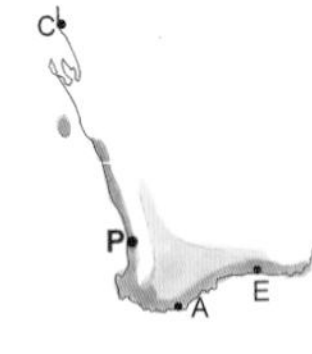

There are two subspecies in Australia, *elegans* in eastern Australia and *occidentalis* in Western Australia. There are subtle differences in the Western Australian subspecies. It has a buff-cream forehead not orange-brown, back and nape darker chestnut-brown and lighter grey underbody than nominate race *elegans* in the eastern states. A shy bird found close to the coast in coastal thick scrub, heath and wet gullies from just south of Dongara all the way to north of Perth. Most of its former habitat on the Swan Coastal Plain is now cleared so does not become locally common till the Busselton region and then found all along the coastal belt and just inland from Cape Naturaliste to Cape Leeuwin. Becomes more common from Augusta to Cape Arid where its favoured habitat of lusher heaths and well watered gullies occurs. The Jarrah Forest is not one of its preferred habitats, although it certainly is for the Common Bronzewing. However when the Wandoo Woodland commences after the Jarrah Forest in the inner Wheatbelt, the Brush Bronzewing can be found, particularly if there is an understorey of heath and plants of the poison pea group (*Gastrolobium*). Does not congregate in a group as does the Common Bronzewing. The Brush Bronzewing has the bronzing on its wing restricted to two central bars on the median and greater wing coverts. Forehead on male more buff-cream, which goes to just above front of the eye. Dark chocolate-brown above white eye stripe. Blue-grey underbody and throat. Important feature is a distinct deep red-brown throat patch in both sexes. Nape and shoulder on male is a rich dark chestnut that passes to a point on the upper breast. Female lighter copper-brown nape and neck contrasting with the blue-grey neck and underbody. **Nest:** Similar to Common Bronze but much lower and often placed in thicker foliage. Clutch size 2. **Similar species:** Refer to Common Bronzewing. **Status:** Uncommon in selected habitat. **Where to find:** Coastal heaths between Dongara and Yanchep. Between the two capes in the deep South West. All along the south coast particularly in heath, including the following parks: Stirling Range NP. Two Peoples Bay NP. Waychinicup NP. Fitzgerald River NP. Stokes Inlet NP. Cape Le Grand NP. Cape Arid NP. Also many of the Wheatbelt reserves including Boyagin Rock NR. Tutanning NR. Dryandra Woodland NR. Dongalocking NR. Tarin Rock NR. Unlike the Common Bronzewing, you will not find this bird in the dry Mulga Woodland. Unusual remnant population on the Abrolhos Islands.

Flock Bronzewing *Phaps histrionica* 28–31 cm Vagrant

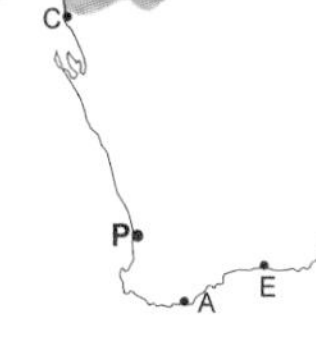

A gregarious species that is centred in the Barkly Tableland in the Northern Territory and the southern channel country in Queensland and the northern South Australian deserts. A rare visitor to the north of this region in the upper reaches of the Gascoyne catchment. Found in open grassy plains mainly in northern grass plains of the Pilbara, but mostly in the Kimberley and Great Sandy Desert particularly near Lake Gregory; all of these areas are out of this book's region. Main feature to look for is a white mask to front of head contrasting with a black band that covers the head and throat, broken with a white circle surrounding the lores and with patch on upper breast. Both features occur in the male and female but crown and lores are brown instead of black on the female. Fawn upperbody in both sexes, blue-grey chest and underbody in male contrasting with white throat. Female grey-blue only on the underbody. If you see a large flock of pigeons flying faster than any other species of pigeon you have ever seen before, then the chances are you have just seen Flock Bronzewing as no pigeon flocks in the numbers that Flock Bronzewing does. If you see them land normally away from water, try to get close and well hidden from the dam or pool you think they are coming to. They will eventually walk one by one through the grass checking all is clear then group and come down to the water and drink fast, and then all will fly off together at the same time, circling first and then flying off. In flight the white facial patch on the male stands out from a chestnut-orange back and wings as well as distinct white patch on the leading edge of the shoulders (inner primaries and outer secondaries) which is clearly visible in flight but not shown in many books. **Nest:** No nest is made, only a slight hollow if soil is soft enough to scrape. Mostly placed between high grasses on black soil plains. Clutch size 2.

Similar species: None. **Status:** Rare in this region. **Where to find:** Remote chance in grassed areas on the Gascoyne floodplain. To get reasonable chances, out of this area in WA. Sometimes near Lake Eda. Black soil plains on Meda and Kimberley Downs Station, Camballin, Parry's Lagoon, Lake Gregory. Less chance in the Pilbara although chances on the grass plains between the Jones, Sherlock and Yule Rivers in the north west or on the Fortescue floodplain.

Crested Pigeon *Ocyphaps lophotes* 31–36 cm

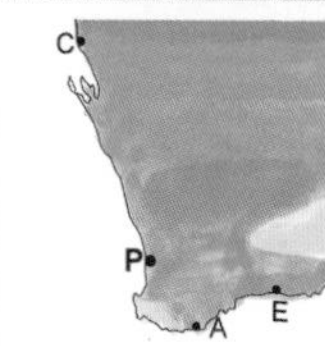

A bird that is found throughout most of the GSW Region except the lower South West forests and the Salmon Gum Woodland east of Hyden. It was a bird of drier regions being the dominant Bronzewing in the arid areas and still is, but since land clearing in the early nineteen hundreds the Crested Pigeon has slowly encroached into the South West Region eventually coming to Perth. You can imagine the Swan Coastal Plain where Perth stands today was either thick with coastal heath or thick Jarrah Forests or swamps with heathland, not the habitat preferred by Crested Pigeons but that of Brush Bronzewing. Now with crop fields, it is understandable that this bird that requires dry grains finds food in abundance in the South West with permanent water readily available on dams, which it must have. Even though the Crested Pigeon has moved into the South West it is basically a sedentary bird and will remain in the territory that it feeds in. It is a gregarious pigeon and will often be seen with other birds, particularly coming to drink. It is an unmistakable pigeon with its high crest. There is no marked difference between the male and the female, the main feature is that the female has a duller lustre to the bronzing on the wing and the body is a little duller grey. In the GSW there are 2 subspecies, the nominate *lophotes* found in the southern part of Western Australia and *whitlocki* found in central and northern Western Australia, which has a narrower white tail band. The central and northern birds are slightly smaller. **Nest:** Is the same as Common

Bronzewing. Clutch size 2. **Similar species:** None. **Status:** Common throughout most of the GSW, even in the areas it has expanded to but still not in the forested lower south west. **Where to find:** On the outskirts of Perth and throughout the Wheatbelt and in the mulga coming to dams. The subspecies *whitlocki* is centred in the Pilbara but can come as low as the Gascoyne area.

Spinifex Pigeon *Geophaps plumifera* subspecies *ferruginea* 20–24 cm

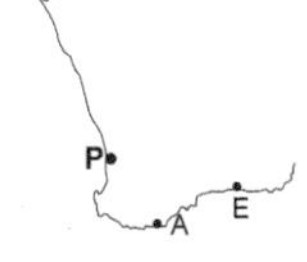

The Spinifex Pigeon can come down to the Gascoyne region although the main populations are in the north west, centred in the Pilbara region. This is a separate subspecies from the nominate race *plumifera* found in the Kimberley and Northern Territory, having an entirely rust red underbody rather than a white underbody. It also is slightly smaller. It's a bird of rocky terrain with spinifex being the principal plant from whose seed it feeds. The Spinifex Pigeon can remind one of a clockwork toy as it scurries fast with its short feet and body hardly moving as it runs over stony ground and rocks. Mostly seen coming down to water points in small groups as a safety measure. Its crest is a very distinct feature and it has an all orange-red body. If you see one bird there are likely to be others hidden very close. **Nest:** They nest on the ground next to spinifex clumps, often between small boulders. Nest consists of a few leaves or grasses either placed alongside spinifex plant or on a rock ledge. Clutch size 2. **Similar species:** None. **Status:** More common north of the GSW Region. **Where to find:** The most southerly the author has seen this species is just south of Dairy Creek on the Gascoyne-Murchison Road but mainly north towards the Ashburton and the Pilbara region.

Diamond Dove *Geopelia cuneata* 19–24 cm

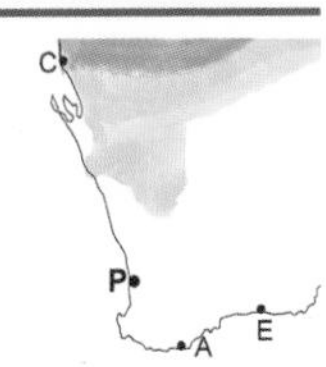

The smallest Australian dove with an overall grey body, darker grey wings covered in white spots on the scapulars and coverts. Has a prominent red orbital eye ring that stands out from its blue-grey head and has pink legs. Found in the semi-arid regions of the GSW. More common above the Murchison River but does come down to the northern Wheatbelt. Not found on the Swan Coastal Plain or most of the central Wheatbelt, southern coast or deep South West. Often found feeding in small group up to 10 birds. Prefers even drier country than the Peaceful Dove found throughout the mulga, although it overlaps with the Peaceful Dove. **Nest:** A small saucer shape of twigs placed in any position in a tree or bush, normally between 3–10 metres at the most. Clutch size 2. **Similar species:** Peaceful Dove, which is slightly larger. Has a light blue orbital eye ring rather than a bright red eye ring. Has black barring on the nape running down to the neck and chest, forming a band. Dark edges to the wing coverts and scapulars. Barring on back, rump and tail. **Status:** Locally commo[n] but overall uncommon in the northern part of the GSW. **Where to find:** Yalgoo region Murchison Settlement. Wooleen Station. Austin Downs.

Peaceful Dove *Geopelia striata* subspecies *clelandi* 20–24 cm

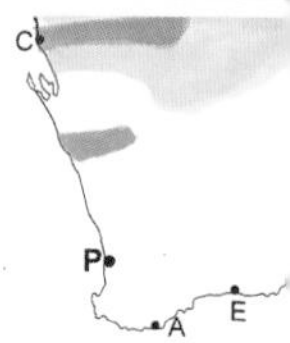

Most common in the north of Western Australia preferring less arid parts of Australia. In Western Australia the subspecies *placida.* is found throughout the Kimberley. Then the Great Sandy Desert breaks the distribution until the Pilbara and Gascoyne River region where the subspecies *clelandi* occurs, which is overall paler and has a fawn tinge to the grey upperbody and tail compared to the Kimberley birds. Like the Diamond Dove they have attractive markings. The Peaceful Dove has a light blue orbital eye ring. Has black barring on the nape running down to the neck and chest, forming a band. Dark edges to the wing coverts and scapulars. Barring on back, rump and tail. Their pleasant 'cooing' call is always a reminder that you are in the north where the warmer climates occur. **Nest**: Clutch size is the same as for the Diamond Dove. There are 6 subspecies in the world with 2 in Australia. **Similar species:** Refer to Diamond Dove. **Status:** Common in the Gascoyne catchment and Murchison Settlement area. **Where to find:** Carnarvon and along the lower Murchison where pools occur and River Red Gums (*E. camaldulensis*). On the Butchers Track on the Murchison River where the Wooleen road crosses. Along the Gascoyne River to the start of the Lyons River.

Red-tailed Black-Cockatoo *Calyptorhynchus banksii* subspecies *samueli* 55–60 cm

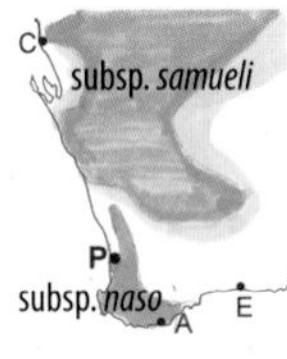

One of the largest cockatoos in Australia. In Western Australia there are 3 subspecies: *macrorhynchus* found in the Kimberley and the rest of northern and eastern Australia, subspecies *samueli* in the Pilbara down to the northern Wheatbelt and also central Australia and subspecies *naso* found solely in the South West. Of the two subspecies in the GSW Region, *samueli* and *naso*, there is clear evidence from historical records that the mid west birds (*samueli*) are slowly moving south into the South West Region. They have in fact increased in numbers in the northern Wheatbelt where they rarely occurred before. With the advent of land clearing and permanent water on dams the Red-tailed Black-Cockatoos have found abundant new sources of food, with seeds from weeds and grains. Some of the largest flocks in the state, often over 200 birds can be found in the northern and north eastern Wheatbelt adjacent to the Transitional Eucalypt Woodland. Red-tailed Black Cockatoos will begin nesting in the northern Wheatbelt in the months of April and May. The South West bird, the subspecies *naso*, may be on the decline due to loss of habitat. They have adapted to feeding almost entirely on the South West eucalypts, mainly Jarrah, Marri and Blackbutt. The male's plumage is entirely glossy black except for the broad bright red panels half way along the tail feathers, seen best in flight or when alighting. The female's entire body is a duller black without the lustre of the male but is covered with pale cream-yellow spotting, which occurs on the head and wings as flecking. The underbody is slightly greyer black with cream-yellow barring. The tail, seen best in flight, has orange-yellow barring that goes closer to the end of the tail shafts but also bleeds into a brighter orange colour near the outer tail feathers. The Red-tailed Black-Cockatoo's call has similarities to the White-tailed Black-Cockatoo but is much softer, more mournful and less harsh. **Similar species:** The Short-billed and Long-billed Black Cockatoos are similar large black cockatoos but both species have white in the tail, and have different calls from the Red-tailed. Crest on the Red-tailed is longer and extends higher when alarmed or making contact calls than the crest on the White-tailed Black Cockatoo. **Status:** Subspecies *samueli* is

Female

Male

locally common in the Transitional Woodland, uncommon in the Mulga Region and Gascoyn region. Subspecies *naso* is uncommon in the Jarrah Forest found in small groups of 8–1 birds. **Where to find:** subspecies *naso,* in the Hills suburbs like Roleystone and Kalamunda Bungendore. Throughout the Jarrah Forest. Seen on the Brookton and Albany Highway particularly around North Bannister. Margaret River area. Subspecies *samueli*: seen best in th northern and north eastern Wheatbelt Region and the Transitional Woodland, particularl in the area around Eurady Station in the York Gum woodland. Wandana NR. Along th Warriedar Road east of Perenjori. The Ninghan area. On the road from Beacon to Bimbijy. I the Salmon Gum Woodland in reserves like Korrelocking NR near Wyalkatchem.

Carnaby's Black-Cockatoo (Short-billed Black-Cockatoo)

Calyptorhynchus latirostris 54–56 cm Endemic to Western Australia

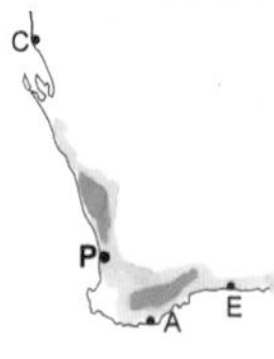

There are two very similar white-tailed black cockatoos in the GSW both endemic to WA, the Short-billed and the Long-billed Black-Cockatoo. The Short-billed Black-Cockatoo (also known as Carnaby's Black-Cockatoo) favours a different habitat to Long-billed Cockatoos (also known as Baudin's Black-Cockatoo). However, they do share similar habitats at time particularly in the Perth region and nesting Short-bills have been found in the Jarrah Fores close to the nesting sites of Long-bills. The main fact is that the majority of the Short-bille Black-Cockatoos, particularly the southern and northern populations, prefer heathlan habitats. Sadly much of their preferred habitat has been cleared and there has been a movemen of the northern populations into the deeper South West. The northern populations can b found in their breeding and feeding areas of Lesueur National Park, Eneabba, Watheroo Coorow, New Norcia and Rica Erickson Reserve. Also the armed forces' prohibited site nort of Julimar State Forest and the north west section of Julimar Forest. They require habitat tha combines their nest sites, primarily *Eucalyptus wandoo*, with rich flora habitat to feed fron which includes plants mainly of the Proteaceae family, namely dryandras (soon to be groupe as banksias), hakeas and banksias found on the heaths of the northern sand plain. With th loss of much of their territory, many now move after the breeding period finishes from Januar through to April into areas where there are pine plantations, often massing in numbers of ove one hundred birds. Mostly though they break up into flocks 10–40 birds. One can see ther in the summer feeding in suburban gardens. They can strip fruiting trees of all their seed an are catholic in their choice of food, from native plants as diverse as bottlebrush (*Calothamnus* to the eucalypt Illyarrie (*E. erythrocorys*). The southern populations have the same problem a they too have lost much of their favoured tree, the Wandoo, to nest in, as well as countles hundreds of square kilometres of Kwongan heath that they would have previously fed from They are found throughout much of the southern Wheatbelt Region, including the Stirling Range NP, Fitzgerald River NP and woodlands in the eastern Wheatbelt east of Hyden wher there are extensive heaths. On the author's previous property adjacent to the Stirling Range there was a breeding group of 14 birds with 4 nesting pairs, the remainder being dependen young. They selected nest sites in the third week of September, two pairs returning to thei previous nest hollow from the season before. Sometimes, the female would improve the entr to the nest hollow, while the male would give encouragement to the female, calling constantl with a repetitive rasping soft call, totally different from his harsh contact call. The small grou would call just after dawn, making contact with each pair from the group. They would gathe at a central meeting point, normally a large dead Wandoo tree and then leave together for thei feeding grounds on the heaths on the eastern side of the Stirling Range. The female become quite aggressive to the mature dependent young, while she and the male are feeding the newbor chicks and possibly this constant harassment, combined with the harshest screeching calls tha they ever make are possibly the trigger for the dependent young to finally leave the breeding area. This practice is common among so many species whose dependent young remain with th parents for extended periods. Clutch size is 2. **Similar species:** The Long-billed Black-Cockato is almost identical and certainly gives even the most knowledgeable eastern states birdwatcher

some initial difficulty. When you can get close views with binoculars, you can soon see, as in the photograph next page, that the Long-billed has a long fine bill and if you manage to view it front on, you will notice it is a slim bill. The Short-billed has a broader bill and shorter top mandible particularly near the tip of the bill. The call is slightly harsher than the Long-billed and has slightly longer intervals between their repeat calls but you need to be accustomed to listening to the two species regularly to hear this difference. **Status:** Overall uncommon but can be locally common. There is concern for the Short-billed Cockatoo's status as the population has indeed decreased since European settlement but in general it has stabilised. But there are a few far more vulnerable species like the Crested Shrike-tit subspecies *leucogaster*, also the Australian Bittern and, most crucial of all, the western subspecies of the Ground Parrot. **Where to find:** Mt Lesueur area. Near Manmanning NR. Rica Erickson NR. North Julimar Forest. Durokoppin Reserve. Between Carnamah and Perenjori. Dryandra Woodland NR (but does not breed there). Stirling Range NP both east and northern boundaries. 70 km east of Hyden. Esperance region to 50 km north. Throughout north and central Swan Coastal Plain including Yanchep and Gnangara Pine Plantation between January and May. Moves south through Fremantle to the southern suburbs February to April.

Baudin's Black-Cockatoo (Long-billed Black-Cockatoo)

Calyptorhynchus baudinii 52–57 cm Endemic to Western Australia

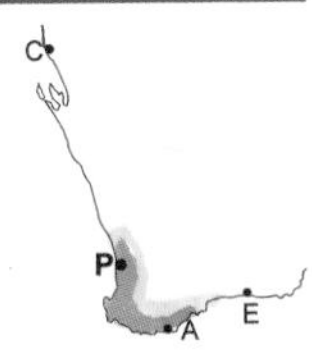

Found in the South West Region, principally in the Jarrah Forest although Jarrah (*Eucalyptus marginata*) is not the primary eucalypt from which it feeds, that being Marri (*Corymbia calophylla*). Found as far north as Muchea and east between Wandering and Pumphreys Bridge and south to the Porongurups and Albany, all the way across to Augusta. The Long-billed Black Cockatoo as the name implies, has a longer bill than the Short-billed and sometimes, looked at from the side, the upper mandible tip appears so fine that it would simply break with the hard marri nuts it feeds on, however the long bill is used to dislodge the seed from the internal base of the nut in just the same manner as the Red-capped Parrot while the heavier cracking of nuts is done at the back of the two mandibles. Long-bills also have the unusual habit of ripping bark from the trunks of Jarrah and Marri trees, looking for larvae. The male has the distinct red orbital eyering, a common diagnostic feature in many male parrots whereas the female has a dull grey eyering. **Nests:** Selected hollows in Jarrah and Marri trees. Clutch size is 2. **Similar species:** Refer to Short-billed Black-Cockatoo. **Status:** Some reduction in population since European settlement but relatively stable population now restricted to the Jarrah Forest. Is still shot by orchardists, as the cockatoos will eat cultivated fruit and take the seeds. **Where to find:** Throughout the Jarrah Forest: including Bungendore Reserve. Jarrahdale. Dwellingup. West of Quindanning. Darkan. Albany. Porongurups. Denmark. Walpole and all the deepe South West Region which has the highest concentrations of this species.

Baudin's

Carnaby's

Galah *Eolophus roseicapillus roseicapilla* 35–37 cm

Since European settlement this species has expanded its range, with the onset of land clearing and availability of abundant crops producing seed and permanent water from farm dams. It has also moved into the Swan Coastal Plain, a region it never was found in before. It has adapted to urban environments and is seen in most areas of Perth. It typically masses in large flocks throughout its range not only in the farming country but also in the Mulga Region. The habitat it least prefers is the dense forested areas of the lower South West Region. There are three subspecies in Australia, two of them in WA: *kuhli* in the Kimberley and the rest of Northern Australia and *roseicapilla* found in the Pilbara, the GSW and central Australia. In the context of this book the differences are marginal but suffice to say that the subspecies found in this region *roseicapilla* has a larger and more extensive crest extending partly down the nape. The 'play' behaviour of Galahs are not entirely understood but they certainly play, turning somersaults on wires, hanging on windmills, sliding down corrugated roofs, similar behaviour to the Keas in New Zealand, often accompanied by screeching. **Nest:** In a variety of eucalypts

hroughout its range. Clutch size 3–5. **Similar species:** None. **Status:** Common throughout he region, very common locally sometimes in flocks in excess of 200 birds. Uncommon on nuch of the south coast. **Where to find:** Throughout the region.

ong-billed Corella *Cactua tenuirostris* 40 cm Introduced

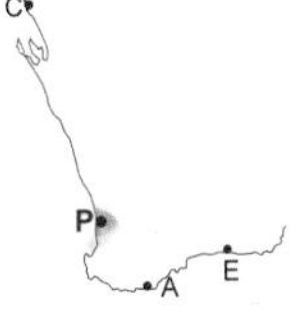

n introduced bird from Victoria, its natural population occurring in n area centred in the region of the Grampian Range. Found in Western ustralia in Perth, where captive birds were released. Often seen with ittle Corellas and occasionally with Western Corellas. Has the longest op mandible of all corellas and has extensive bright scarlet-pink around ores and lower forehead above the base of the bill; scarlet passes over the eye and finishes at he rear of the eye. The only corella with the upper chest feathers coloured scarlet. Has distinct carlet colouring to the base feathers on the top of the chest. When the neck moves, more carlet can be seen on the base of the feathers on the neck. **Similar species:** The most similar pecies is the Western Corella which also has a long top mandible and scarlet to the lores ut the colour is not as intense r as extensive, being restricted o between the eyes and the base f the bill and does not pass over r behind the eye as in the Long-illed. Does not have the red on he upper chest feathers. The rest of the Western Corella is aller and more erect than Long-illed when extended. Also the Western Corella is larger than the ong-billed. The Little Corella s the least similar with a much horter bill and only a faint pink atch between the eye and the ase of the bill, and it is slightly maller than the other corellas. **tatus:** Only a small population n Perth. **Where to find:** Lake oondalup. Lake Monger. Bold Park. Manning Lake.

Western Corella *Cacatua pastinator* subspecies *derbyi* 40–45 cm

Endemic to Western Australia

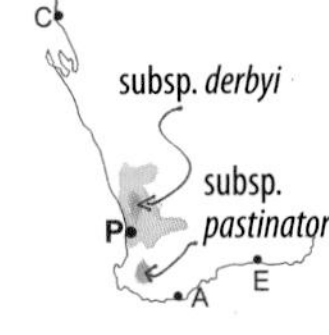

There are two subspecies in Western Australia, *derbyi* occurs between Dongara and Three Springs in the north, mainly in the following areas: Hill River in the west, Reagans Ford, New Norcia, Goomalling in the south and Wubin, Latham, Kalanie in the east. The other subspecies *pastinator* is centred in the Lake Muir, Rocky Gully and Frankland areas. The Western Corella has a high crest and when displaying or agitated raises the crest forward. Has a very long pointed bill and slightly more yellow on the underwing than the Little Corella. The Western Corella can be found digging up roots in crop stubble in the process of which the underbody gets covered in dust so the birds tend to have a red ochre coloured underbody. Normally in large flocks from 30–60 birds. For such a restricted species it is very common in the central areas of its range like Wongan Hills, Moora and Wubin. The other main area for the northern subspecies *derbyi* is around the Mt Lesueur and Hill River area. **Similar species:** Refer to Long-billed Corella. The only species that overlaps the northern population of Western Corella is the Little Corella. The Long-billed and Western Corella only overlap in the Perth region where they both occur. The differences between Little and Western Corella are far easier to defin The long bill on the Western is the obvious feature and can be noticed even in flight such the bill's shape and size. It is also a longer and larger looking bird. The pink between the bas of the bill and eye is always weak on the Little Corella but even so not a good feature whic to identify the two species. **Nests:** Located in tree hollows of Salmon Gum, Wandoo an sometimes York Gum. Clutch size 2–3. **Status:** Locally common. **Where to find:** subspecie *derbyi* can be found around Moora, where they also nest in the few remaining Salmon Gum north of the town on the road from Moora to Three Springs. Perhaps the closest site t Perth is just south of New Norcia, where there is a resident flock. Another general region i between Wongan Hills and Wubin and east to the first Vermin Fence; however, Wubin can ge Little Corella so be careful. In the Hill River and Mt Lesueur area is another population. Th subspecies *pastinator* has a more restricted range centred around Boyup Brook in the nort and south around the Lake Muir area.

Western Corella

Long-billed Corella

Little Corella

Little Corella *Cacatua sanguinea* subspecies *westralensis* 35–40 cm

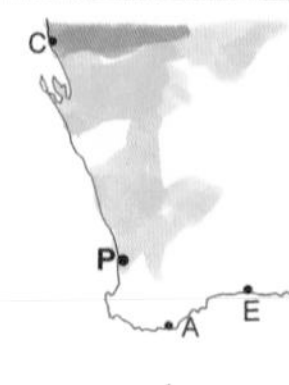

Little Corellas are found in much of the arid and semi-arid regions of Australia including Tasmania. The only areas where they are not found are in some of the central deserts, the Nullarbor and obviously rainforest. In the Pilbara and part of the GSW Region only the subspecies *westralensis* occurs. It is slightly larger, has more red on the lores and longer wings than the eastern states subspecies *gymnopis*. More than 1000 kilometres separate these tw subspecies. In the northern Wheatbelt Little Corellas are often found near wheat bins or ou in paddocks digging for seed and can be found in very large numbers in excess of 200 birds They overlap with Western Corella particularly near Three Springs. There are four subspecie in Australia but only one in this region. **Nest**: Nests in a variety of eucalypts. Clutch siz mostly 3. **Similar species:** Refer to Western Corella. **Status:** Very common locally an uncommon throughout the north of the region. **Where to find:** Northampton to Mullew and south to Three Springs. Occasionally found further south as far as Dumbleyung. Fron

;arnarvon to the upper reaches of the Gascoyne catchment. A population now established in 'erth, presumably from escapees.

'ink Cockatoo (Major Mitchell's Cockatoo) *Cacatua leadbeateri*

ubspecies *mollis* 39 cm

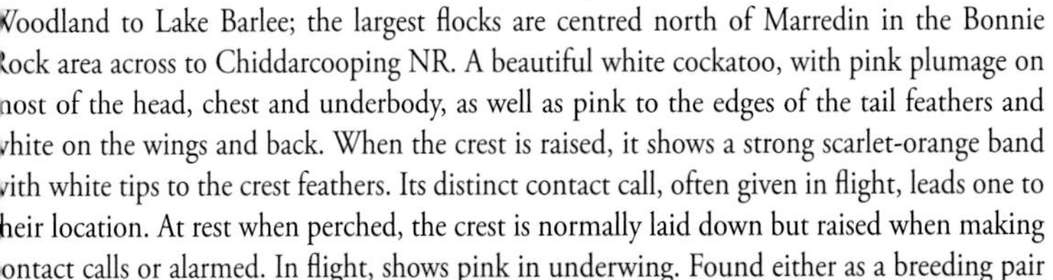

[he distribution of the Pink Cockatoo in Australia is intriguing, as there re distinct populations in specific areas. Here in the GSW, they are ound in two areas: along the Murchison River where it is not common, nd in the northern and eastern Wheatbelt, through the Transitional Voodland to Lake Barlee; the largest flocks are centred north of Marredin in the Bonnie Rock area across to Chiddarcooping NR. A beautiful white cockatoo, with pink plumage on nost of the head, chest and underbody, as well as pink to the edges of the tail feathers and vhite on the wings and back. When the crest is raised, it shows a strong scarlet-orange band vith white tips to the crest feathers. Its distinct contact call, often given in flight, leads one to heir location. At rest when perched, the crest is normally laid down but raised when making ontact calls or alarmed. In flight, shows pink in underwing. Found either as a breeding pair r in small feeding groups. n the northern Wheatbelt n locations like Bonnie Rock or north of Beacon, hey have adapted to eeding on grain in pen paddocks. Tends o hug the Transitional Voodland line where 'ork Gum (*E. loxophleba* ubsp. *loxophleba*) grows nd sometimes shares the ame habitat with Red-ailed Black-Cockatoos. There are 2 subspecies in Australia, the nominate *eadbeateri* in central astern Australia and *nollis* in west and central

Australia. Western birds have no yellow banding in the crest. **Nest:** Nests in a variety c eucalypts mainly Salmon Gum, Red River Gum, York Gum, Ghost Gum and occasionall large Callitris pines. Clutch size 2–4. **Similar species:** None really. The Galah has a grey bac and tail, stronger red-pink underbody and a small white crest with no red. **Status:** Overa uncommon but locally can be in large numbers. **Where to find:** Between Mereberie an Milly Milly but scarce. Around Karara area, north east of Perenjori. Southern end of Lak Monger off the Great Northern Highway down to Kalannie. 40 km south of Bimbijy on th Beacon Road. North east of Mukinbudin and Bonnie Rock (some of the largest flocks in th state here).

Cockatiel *Nymphicus hollandicus* 29–32 cm

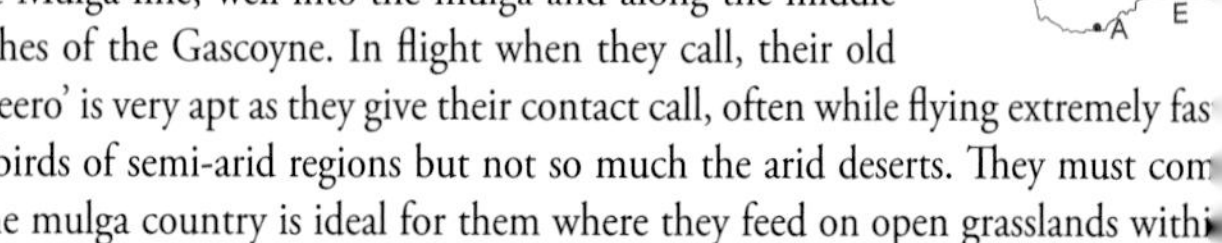

Even though distribution maps show cockatiels located in the South West Region, they are casual visitors to much of the South West Region and in the GSW are found principally north and north east of the Eucalypt-Mulga line, well into the mulga and along the middle and upper reaches of the Gascoyne. In flight when they call, their old nickname of 'weero' is very apt as they give their contact call, often while flying extremely fas Cockatiels are birds of semi-arid regions but not so much the arid deserts. They must com to water and the mulga country is ideal for them where they feed on open grasslands withi the mulga habitat and along watercourses. Most large inland river systems have their sha of cockatiels where they also nest. A gregarious parrot normally in small groups of 10 to 16 birds but bigger groups can occur in the summer months. They are nomadic and will move to areas with the best feeding conditions. The female has a greyer head, less white on the face and the orange spot on the lores is duller. **Nest:** Nests in a variety of eucalypts, mostly in dead hollows of Red River Gums. Clutch size 4–5. **Similar species:** None. **Status:** Uncommon in the northern part of the GSW mainly in the middle and upper Gascoyne catchment. Increasing in numbers out of the region to Minilya, Ashburton and Fortescue Rivers. **Where to find:** Mainly in the Mulga Region. Found along the Murchison to Sandstone and east.

Rainbow Lorikeet *Trichoglossus haematodus* subspecies *malaccans* 30 cm Introduced

Found in Australia, New Guinea, islands in eastern Indonesia and the south west Pacific. In the GSW Region we have a population in the Perth area that was introduced from the east coast namely the subspecies *malaccans*. There are Rainbow Lorikeets naturally occurring in the Kimberley, being the subspecies *rubritorquis*. The eastern Australian birds introduced to Pert subspecies *malaccans* has a yellow collar on the rear of the neck below the nape, wherea *rubritorquis* has an orange collar. Also *malaccans* has a completely green back and yellow o the side of the breast whereas *rubritorquis* had blue-purple patch below the orange collar a well as a complete orange breast. Rainbow Lorikeets are pugnacious parrots and, even thoug considerably smaller than the endemic Ring-neck Parrot, will challenge and displace them from nesting in selected tree hollows that the Rainbow Lorikeet wishes to use. **Nest:** Nests in a variety of eucalypts particularly introduced eucalypts. Clutch size 2. **Similar species:** None. **Status:** Sadly, increasing in numbers and should have been eradicated years ago when the population was small. Locally common in central Perth and moving to the outer suburbs including the Hills suburbs. **Where to find:** Kings Park. Perth Domestic Airport. Cottesloe, adjacent to the beach in the Norfolk Pines. Perry Lakes.

Purple-crowned Lorikeet *Glossopsitta porphyrocephala* 17–18.5 cm

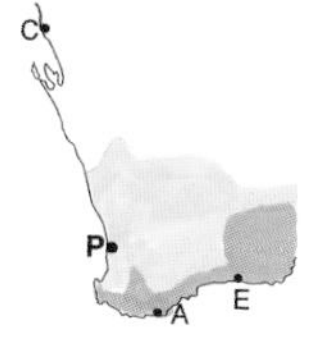

Western Australia's smallest parrot, feeding almost entirely from the pollen and nectar of flowering eucalypts. It is highly nomadic in its search for flowering trees and will move into areas when certain eucalypts are in full bloom. Often seen flying at very fast speeds over the treetops, while they call continuously with their high pitched 'zit zit' to keep the group together. They can be difficult to locate when feeding high up in the tall flowering eucalypts but when a good view is had, the multi-coloured head makes it well worth finding. Its range in the South West is linked to the occurrence of stands of flowering eucalypts. In the deep South West it feeds off the Karri (*E. diversicolor*), Marri (*Corymbia calophylla*) and Jarrah (*E. marginata*); in the Wheatbelt Wandoo (E. wandoo). Powder-bark Wandoo *(E. accedens)*, Wheatbelt Wandoo *(E. capillosa)* and Salmon Gum (*E. salmonophloia*). In the mallee region they feed on many mallees particularly Sand Mallee *(E. eremophila)* and Capped Mallee (*E.*

pileata). A major region with high populations of Purple-crowned Lorikeets is the Transitional Woodlands of the south western Goldfields from the Vermin Fence 50 km east of Hyden to Norseman and beyond. There are well over 100 species of eucalypt in this region and there are always one or two eucalypt species in bloom at any given time of the year. **Nest:** Nests in a variety of eucalypts including Karri, Wandoo, Swamp Yate, Goldfields Blackbutt, Black Morrell and Salmon Gum. Clutch size 2–3. **Similar species:** None. **Status:** Locally very common. **Where to find:** The deep South West where Karri grows, from Pemberton all the way along the southern coast to well past Esperance, including: the Walpole National Park, Porongurups, Stirling Range and Fitzgerald River National Park. On the Hyden to Norseman and the Lake King to Norseman roads. Occasionally in Dryandra Woodland NR depending on how the Karri Forest is blooming in the deep South West Region.

Regent Parrot *Polytelis anthopeplus* subspecies *anthopeplus* 40–42 cm

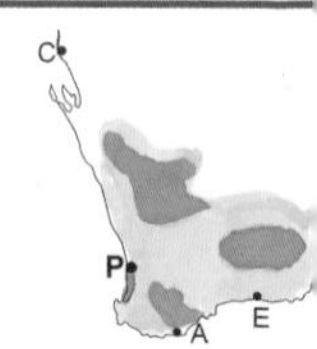

There are 2 subspecies of Regent Parrot in Australia; in the South West is the subspecies *anthopeplus*. There are very slight differences in the two subspecies. The eastern Australian birds are a duller yellow, the Western Australian birds have slightly darker lime-green body and other minor differences. All the *Polytelis* group are extremely fast flying parrots, normally identified in flight with their contact calls, a plaintive soft screech. The call is similar when perched but softer to the ear. Has an extremely long tail although not quite as long as Princess Parrots. The male is a brighter lime green with brighter red on the wings, bill brighter red, contrasting vividly with the lime-green head. Has a long dark blue tail. Female has similar colouring but body is duller and darker lime-green. Bill is a less intense scarlet. Main difference is the tail, which is dull green not dark blue. They favour certain eucalypts from which to feed and also nest in. On the Swan Coastal Plain it is the Tuart (*E. gomphocephala*). They do not favour Marri or Jarrah hence they are rarely found in the deep South West. In the Wheatbelt they favour Wandoo Woodland where they also nest. In the Salmon Gum Woodland east of the Vermin Fence between Hyden and Norseman they nest and feed in a variety of large eucalypts. In the north eastern Transitional Woodland inland from Wubin, they feed and nest in York Gum (*E. loxophleba* subspecies *loxophleba*), *E. oldfieldii* and Salmon Gum (*E. salmonophloia*). **Nest:** Normally above 15 metres. Clutch size 3–4. **Similar species:** None in this region. **Status:** Overall uncommon, moderately common locally. The Regent Parrot population in the South West expanded with land clearing and the growing of grain crops and by the mid 1940s it was one of the most common parrots of the Wheatbelt and in fact was declared vermin; but then numbers drastically declined. They have slowly reduced since the 1950s particularly in the northern Wheatbelt. Only in the last 20 years has their population stabilised but they do not occur in the numbers as in previous years.

Where to find: There are distinct areas where Regents may be seen and this is related to where they have nesting sites, although they will move in summer returning back to favoured nesting locations. The Wandoo Woodlands in the South West on the western and northern sides of the Stirling Range. The Woodanilling–Kojonup area. Narrogin to Dryandra Woodland NR. On the Swan Coastal Plain on the Mandurah to Bunbury road and in the Pinjarra area. On the Hyden to Norseman road and the Lake King to Norseman road. 60 km north of Beacon on the Bimbijy road and between 40 and 60 km north east of Wubin.

Western Rosella *Platycercus icterotis* subspecies *icterotis* 25–30 cm

Endemic to Western Australia

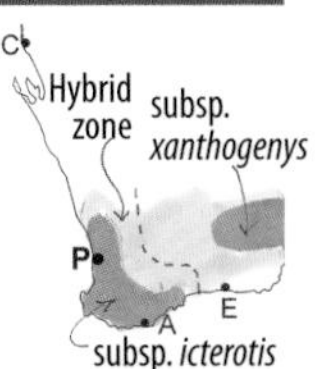

The Western Rosella is the smallest of all the rosellas in Australia. There are two subspecies in the GSW: *icterotis,* which occurs in the wetter forests of the deeper South West and *xanthogenys* in the Wheatbelt and eastern and north eastern Transitional Woodland. There is a hybrid zone, roughly running from north of Perth down past the Stirling Range to Bremer Bay. The Wheatbelt *xanthogenys* male birds' main contrasting feature, particularly in areas like Hyden and Bruce Rock, is red to the back (mantle) rather than green. They also have more blue in the wing coverts and a dark blue tail rather than a dark blue-green tail. There are other minor differences in rump and cheek colour. Also the outer Wheatbelt birds are slightly smaller and slimmer than the deep South West Region birds. The female of the subspecies *icterotis* has duller colouring, lacking a bright red head and underbody, and a red patch on the forehead and mottled green crown and upperbody. Cheek patch is duller cream-yellow compared to bright yellow in the male. The female subspecies *xanthogenys* is far redder on the underbody and redder on the head like the male. The South West birds are particularly prevalent in the lower strata of the Karri Forest, feeding off acacia and other understorey plants. Both in the wetter zone and the drier zone they prefer to feed off casuarinas and allocasuarinas. Often when walking through groves of Rock Sheoak (*Allocasuarina huegeliana*) in the outer eastern Wheatbelt, suddenly you can come across these beautiful small parrots that seem so out of place in drier environments compared with the other subspecies that occur in the damp Karri Forests in the deep South West. All rosellas throughout Australia have as part of their calls a bell-like note and this will often lead you to where the birds are located. **Nests:** The South West birds nest in Karri, Marri, Jarrah and Wandoo; the eastern Wheatbelt birds nest in Wheatbelt Wandoo and Black Morrell as well as other Transitional Woodland eucalypts. Clutch size 3–5. **Similar species:** None. **Status:** The subspecies *icterotis* is common in the wetter forest of the deep south west. Uncommon on the Swan Coastal Plain. Moderately common in the Darling

Range. Moderately common in the marginal zone of the Wandoo Woodland. *xanthogenys* is uncommon in the outer Wheatbelt areas and the Transitional Eucalypt Woodland. **Where to find:** *icterotis*, throughout the Karri Forest. Also from Dunsborough all the way along the southern coast to Bremer Bay. Most prolific between Dunsborough and Albany and the inner Wheatbelt from Jurien Bay across to Tuttaning NR down through Dryandra Woodland NR. Dongolocking NR and the Stirling Range NP. subspecies *xanthogenys* is found in the outer Wheatbelt and well past Norseman into the huge Dundas NR as far as Newman Rocks, also north to Southern Cross.

Australian Ringneck *Barnardius zonarius* subspecies *semitorquatus*

32–44 cm

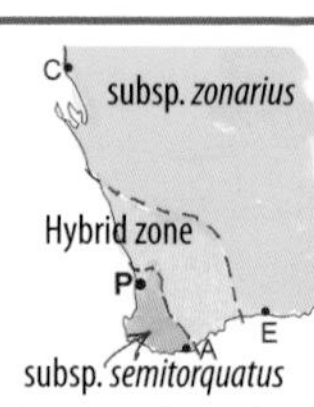

One of the most prolific birds to be found in the whole of the GSW. In Australia, authorities have split the Ringnecks into 3 subspecies groups (some argue for four). Here in Western Australia we have 2, *zonarius* and *semitorquatus,* with a hybrid zone between them. *zonarius* is a bird of the dry country, its southern boundary running roughly from Jurien in the far west through to Wyalkatchem, Hyden to Israelite Bay. It stretches north to the Great Sandy Desert and right across central Australia excluding the Nullarbor. In the northern parts *zonarius* is a markedly smaller and slimmer bird. As you move through the range of the Australian Ringneck, one will find that there are subtle differences in call. The main plumage variation is that there is no red dot above the bill on the forehead. There is a distinct contrasting break on the underbody from a green chest to a bright yellow belly. All the green plumage is paler, particularly on the back. *semitorquatus* has a distinct red patch just above the bill on the forehead, an all green underbody, darker on the breast, lighter on the underbody. The bird is much thicker set and longer bodied. When pairing or making contact with a group, will give a chattering call while shaking their tails from side to side; also will give a high pitched alarm call when disturbed, and the characteristic 'twenty eight-twenty eight' is the normal contact call. *semitorquatus* has certainly increased in numbers since European settlement and has become a major problem for orchardists. **Nest:** Nests in a variety of eucalypts throughout its range. Clutch size 3–5. **Similar species:** None. **Status.** Common in the South West. Very common in the Wheatbelt. Moderately common in the drier regions. **Where to find:** Any region. Not common in the Karri Forest and heathlands of the Esperance region. Both hybrids and the distinct subspecies can occur together in localities like Dryandra Woodland NR which is in their transitional zone.

Red-capped Parrot *Purpureicephalus spurius* 34–38 cm

Endemic bird to Western Australia

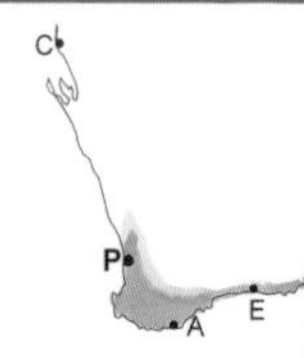

The male bird is one of Australia's most stunning parrots with a distinct red crown, lime-green cheeks, purple underbody, red vent, green back and wings, yellow rump and long green tail. Many birdwatchers presume the duller juveniles are the female of the species but in fact both the juvenile male and female have a duller and more subdued plumage, having a dull green not red crown, pale green cheeks, vent mottled lime-green and red, underbody pale grey tinged purple with no bright purple underbody. The difference in male and female juveniles is very difficult to see and too subtle to warrant inclusion here. They retain the duller plumage through the summer until the following breeding season. The female adult is very similar to the male but the crown is slightly duller, more dark maroon than red, the back is duller green and the vent has more yellow flecking in the red but all in all they are difficult to split the main difference is that the male's colours are more intense, particularly the red crown and lime-green cheek patch. The Red-capped Parrot's long down curved bill is designed expressly to remove the seed from eucalypt fruit capsules, particularly the fruit from the Marri tree. It grasps the large fruit capsule with one foot just like the larger Cockatoos but, unlike the Cockatoos whose bill has the ability to sever a hard nut in two, the Red-capped Parrot delicately probes with the long bill cutting free the internal seeds. They feed quietly, the only sign of their presence often being the sound of falling eucalypt fruits from high up in the canopy. They will feed with other parrots but generally are in very small groups of 2–6 birds or on their own. After the breeding season through the summer months, they can congregate in small groups of 10–15 birds. Besides the fruits of Marri, Jarrah and Tuart, they will also eat the fruits of Dryandras and Hakeas. Their range in the north almost follows the limit of the Marri tree from Hill River, then south east to Dumbleyung and across to Esperance where it is very common. **Nest:** Nests in Marri, Jarrah, Flooded Gum and Wandoo. Clutch size 3–5. **Similar species:** None. **Status:** Moderately common in the wetter forests of the South West and along the southern coast. Moderately common in the inner Wandoo belt, uncommon in the outer Wheatbelt. **Where to find:** Throughout the Swan Coastal Plain and particularly the Darling Range to the south coast. Highest numbers occur from Margaret River down to Pemberton and then along the coast to Esperance. Particularly abundant in the Walpole to Albany region and the Esperance Region.

Mulga Parrot *Psephotus varius* 27–32 cm

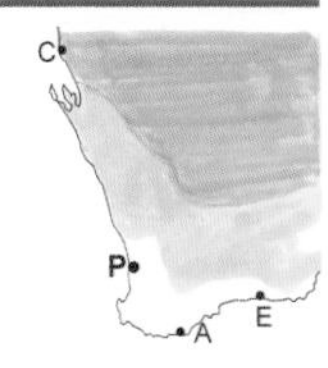

Well named, as its range follows almost entirely the extent of the Mulga (*Acacia aneura*) and other acacia trees. In the context of this book it covers the northern, north eastern and east range of the GSW Region. It does come into the Wheatbelt region, but in the main its primary habitat is north and north east of the Transitional Woodland line. The male is brightly coloured with a turquoise head, underbody and mantle and wings. On the very top of the crown is a small patch of red. On the forehead is a small patch of yellow. The shoulder is bright yellow and stands out from the turquoise wing. The belly is bright red bleeding into a yellow vent. In flight, the blue in the wings becomes prominent and the red rump shows well. The female is much duller. The main body and wings are shades of olive-green. The shoulder is a dull red unlike the bright red of the male. The crown and the nape have a red patch more extensive than the male but a dull red-brown, also on the forehead there is a small yellow patch above the bill. It feeds on seeds on the ground, mostly on native grasses, hence in the Wheatbelt it is invariably found along roadside verges. In the semi-arid zone it starts feeding soon after sunrise and then rests for much of the day. Comes to cattle troughs and waterholes in the morning and late in the evening particularly in the summer months. Often missed at midday as it sits quietly in mulga foliage like Scarlet-chested Parrots and Bourke's Parrots. Has a pleasant soft whistle but does not call much out of the breeding season except in flight to keep contact. **Nest:** Nests in a variety of eucalypts as well as mulga trees. Clutch size 4–6. **Similar species:** Red-rumped Parrot, not found in this state. **Status:** Uncommon in the central and northern Wheatbelt. Scarce in the Transitional Woodland. Common in the Mulga Woodland. **Where to find:** Throughout the sheep station country in the Mulga Region.

Male

Female

Budgerigar *Melopsittacus undulates* 18 cm

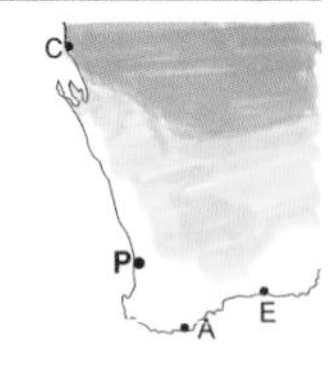

A quintessential Australian bird, found throughout the arid regions of Australia. Highly nomadic, its movements are related to rainfall which governs the growth of native and introduced grasses. It occasionally comes into the South West Region when the arid regions are experiencing drought and is likely to occur in the Gascoyne River region; however the Pilbara is far more reliable having permanent water and profuse grasses. Budgerigars can be occasionally found in any part of the northern, central and eastern part of the Wheatbelt in summer but never in the numbers that can be found in the Pilbara and the Mulga Region and the Gascoyne catchment. When conditions are good, river systems with Red River Gum (*E. camaldulensis*) can be alive with birds all chattering and quite approachable near their nest sites, with every tree and nest hollow being taken up with resident pairs. To witness great flocks circling over waterholes is a wondrous sight, with the swirling mass of 3–4 thousand birds making turns in total unison; the sound of the swirling wing feathers is also unforgettable as the flock twists and turns and then breaks up and falls like confetti above the waterholes to drink. **Nest:** Nests in a variety of eucalypts, particularly River Red Gum and Coolibah. Clutch size 4–6. **Similar species:** None. **Status:** Scarce to uncommon in the Wheatbelt (never in large numbers). In the mulga can be abundant or scarce, depending on the season. Gascoyne catchment, scarce or abundant. **Where to find:** Gascoyne catchment: north of the Murchison Settlement,

Mt Magnet and north and east of Leonora. Seen mainly in the lower Mulga Region when the Pilbara and deserts are drier and the season is exceptional in the southern Mulga. Out of the GSW Region seen best in the Ashburton and Pilbara regions

Bourke's Parrot *Neopsephotus bourkii* 20–23 cm

The Bourke's Parrot can be found in a similar range to the Mulga Parrot, sharing the same habitat. Unlike the nomadic Budgerigar, the Bourke's Parrot is basically sedentary and unless there is severe drought in the area, will remain in the same region providing permanent water is available. They come to drink just before first light and after sunset, perhaps as a precaution against raptors such as Collared Sparrowhawk and Brown Goshawk, making soft twittering calls as they come to drink in the semi-darkness, one group after another slowly walking to the edge of the water. The female differs slightly from the male, mainly in having a lighter grey-brown back with stronger pink colouring on vent. The main distinct difference, and one that requires a good view of the bird, is that the male has a fine light blue supercilium stripe that passes around the forehead. The female has no such stripe. Like all the Neophema group, Bourke's Parrots sit for hours resting at midday, particularly when hot, so can easily be missed. Most active early morning. **Nest:** Nests in a variety of eucalypts and also in Callitris pines. Clutch size 4–5. **Similar species:** None. **Status:**

Uncommon to common in the Mulga Woodland but moderately common from Muggon in the west through to Laverton in the east, and Mt Magnet in the south to Kumarina in the north. Also moderately common in parts of the Pilbara that have extensive stands of mulga. **Where to find:** Wooleen Station. Austin Downs. Nallan Station. Erong Springs. Doolgunna and Mooloogool Stations. Laverton Downs Station.

Elegant Parrot *Neophema elegans* subspecies *carteri* 22–25 cm

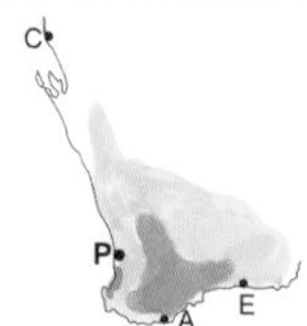

There are two subspecies of Elegant Parrot in Australia, over 1000 kilometres apart. The eastern states subspecies is the nominate race *elegans*, in Western Australia the subspecies is *carteri*. There are no differences in plumage, only size, *carteri* being smaller with a shorter tail. Elegant Parrots inhabit open woodlands with grasslands. Since European settlement, it has extended its range into the south east. Although not common, it can now be found as far south as the Albany region, in fact only reaching Albany and the Swan Coastal Plain in the late 1960s. Its main northern limit is approximately to Morawa, although has be been seen further north. It avoids the coast until just south of Perth. Found inland to Wubin and across to Merredin and then past Salmon Gums down to Condingup. Elegant Parrots feed almost entirely on the ground on seed, small fruits and occasionally insects. Often found on roadside verges in the inner Wheatbelt or amongst native grasses in the Wandoo Woodland. The female is very similar to the male except the back is duller, it has a blue and yellow band to forehead and is thinner and duller. The male has more blue in the tail. The female looks overall duller, almost the colours and hue of a Rock Parrot. **Nest:** Mostly in Wandoo trees in the South West. Clutch size 4–5. **Similar species:** Rock Parrot, which is a generally duller bird, more so than even the female Elegant and closer to the immature Elegant Parrots' colouring. The Elegant adult bird is a brighter green overall. The specific difference is that the Rock Parrot has no yellow on the lores but a two-coloured blue band that goes from the eye to the forehead and is less contrasting in blue tones than the Elegant. The Elegant has a distinct light blue and dark blue band. The Rock Parrot has a dull blue eye ring whereas the Elegant has a faint yellow eye ring; the Elegant has yellow in the outer tail feathers whereas the Rock Parrot has green. The Elegant certainly does not feed on succulent plants on beaches and sand dunes, as does the Rock Parrot. The Rock Parrot nests in or under rock crevices on offshore islands whereas Elegant Parrots nest in tree hollows. **Status:** Uncommon in open woodlands with grassed understorey. Scarce on the periphery of the Wheatbelt. **Where to find:** Boyagin Rock NR. Dryandra Woodland NR. Stirling Range NP and particularly the surrounding farmland abutting the Stirling Range. Locally common from Tenderden down to Albany.

Elegant Parrot

Rock Parrot

Rock parrot *Neophema petrophila* 22–24 cm

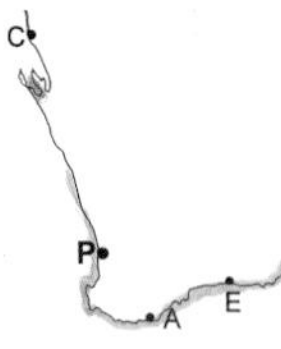

There are two subspecies of Rock Parrot: the nominate race in Western Australia *petrophila* and subspecies *zietzi* in South Australia. A bird of the seashores and islands along the South West Region coastline, does not venture far from coastal shores. Feeds on succulent plants like pigface as well as other seeding plants like beach spinifex and dune arctotheca. Found along beaches and on sand dunes running from one clump to another; normally one or two birds, or in small groups of up to 6–10 at most. Will also feed on low bushes that are close to the sea. On Rottnest, comes to the centre of the island to feed on samphire seed adjacent to the salt lakes. **Nest:** Nests under rock overhangs and crevices on offshore islands, flying to the mainland to feed. Clutch size 3–4. **Similar species:** Elegant Parrot. Refer to notes on Elegant Parrot. To confirm sighting of Rock Parrot look at the lores. If you know the colouring of the Elegant, note how dull the overall plumage of the Rock Parrot is, being more olive-green than the brighter lime-green of the Elegant Parrot. **Status:** Scarce in the Shark Bay Region on small islands in Freycinet Reach between Useless Loop and Peron Peninsula. Uncommon from Jurien Bay to Lancelin. Moderately common between Cape Naturaliste and Cape Leeuwin. Moderately common from Walpole to Esperance. **Where to find:** Lancelin. Rottnest (not so easy nowadays but they are there). Carnac Island. Easiest to find on south coast: Torbay Beach and beaches opposite Shelter Island. In Albany walking along Middleton Beach to Emu Point or on grassed lawns adjacent to Oyster Harbour. Two Peoples Bay at Little Beach. Bremer Bay at the inlet at John Cove and Short Beach and Fisheries Beach. In Esperance along coast and very good chances on Woody Island.

Scarlet-chested Parrot *Neophema splendida* 19–21 cm Vagrant

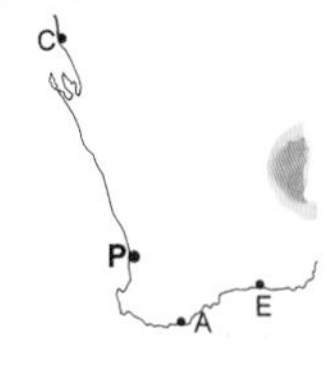

This bird rarely comes into the GSW, although sightings have been made near Mt Jackson and Paynes Find. The author has only seen this bird in the Great Victoria Desert and west of Warburton and in spite of numerous re-visits, attempts to find it have been unsuccessful, such is the scarcity of this species in Western Australia. Its stronghold seems to be centred on the Western Australian and South Australian border and across into Maralinga and Yellabinna Regional Reserve in South Australia, although has been seen several times in the Plumridge Lakes region. It is an irruptive species and will move to better feeding areas out of its normal range and it is often sighted a long way from its central range. The male is a stunning little bird with its bright red chest, blue face and yellow belly. Feeds on seeds from native grasses and herbaceous plants. Sits in bushes and trees for long periods through the day so can be easily missed; often flushed from the side of desert tracks by vehicles. Their call is a soft whistle. **Nest:** Nests in eucalypts mainly in the Victoria Desert. Clutch size 3–5. **Similar species:** None in their habitat. **Where to find:** Out of this region. In localities like Plumridge Lakes. Northern end of Connie Sue. Warburton. Along the Anne Beadell Highway into South Australia. On a tour all the way from Yeo Lakes to Volkes Hill Corner in South Australia not one was seen, even though a few years previously the largest flock was sighted with over 200 birds just south of Volkes Hill Corner where we travelled, such is the nature of this elusive bird.

Captive bird

Ground Parrot *Pezoporus wallicus* subspecies *flaviventris* 30 cm

There are two subspecies in Australia: *wallicus* in the eastern states and *flaviventris* in Western Australia and possibly in the future the Tasmanian birds may be split, as they are certainly darker than the mainland birds. The Western Australian birds have lighter yellow-green underparts and fainter barring on belly and are generally lighter green all over. The Ground Parrot is basically an all green plumaged bird, with black and yellow flecking covering much of its body. Has a relatively long tail with a distinct red dot above the bill at the base of the forehead. The Ground Parrot is perhaps Western Australia's most endangered land bird (excluding the

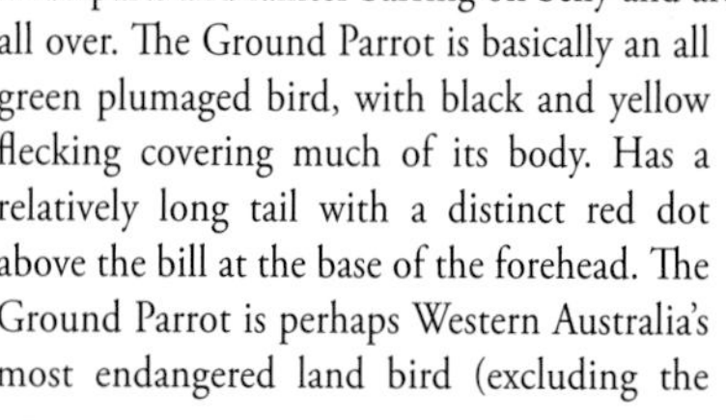

Western Ground Parrot young are greyer green than the eastern states birds
Photos: Brent Barrett

Night Parrot). Its population since European settlement has drastically declined, primarily due to the introduction of the fox and even more so the feral cat which has had a devastating impact on all ground dwelling birds. Also in some of their last remaining strongholds, fires have greatly affected their population. The Ground Parrot feed almost entirely on the ground, bending grasses and sedges down to beak height to eat the seeds. They feed on buds, green seeds and heath plants (*Epacridaceae*). They apparently derive enough moisture from the plants they feed off and do not need to go to water to drink like most parrots. They will climb into low bushes to feed but more commonly walk through the undergrowth selecting seed. It has a plaintive call reminiscent of a Tawny-crowned Honeyeater which also calls in the same region, but it is a stronger and longer lasting call and once heard is easily remembered. It calls mostly 20 minutes or so after sunset before flying to its roosting site. It calls well before sunrise as much as 90 minutes and will then fly to its feeding area, so chances of seeing flying birds are remote and finding them in the bush even harder; throughout their range Ground Parrots in Australia requiring dense low heath which often make it hard to walk through. **Nest:** Nest a shallow scrape on the ground below dense bushes or clumps of grass, lined with short lengths of grass. Clutch size 2–3. **Similar species:** None. **Status:** Extremely rare. **Where to find:** Four known populations: Waychinicup (population tenuous). Fitzgerald River NP. Cape Arid NP. Nuytsland NP. Looking for Ground Parrots is discouraged due to the fragile nature of their population. However, volunteers from time to time are welcomed to assist with surveys but must be reasonably fit. Organised under the guidance of the government agency the Department of Environment and Conservation and mostly coordinated through the agency's office in Albany.

Pallid Cuckoo *Cuculus pallidus* 31 cm

The movements of many cuckoo species are still not well known, mainly due to the fact that some birds stay longer in the south, and some remain in the north and do not migrate south during the spring and early summer breeding season. There is however a marked movement after the breeding season of Pallid Cuckoos moving north in the months of October to January and then arriving again in the south mostly between May and July. Pallid Cuckoos prefer open country that is lightly wooded or open acacia woodland. The Mulga Region is one of their preferred habitats. They also can be found along creek and river systems in dry country and throughout the desert regions. They do however come to northern and central parts of the Wheatbelt Region. The male has an all grey plumaged head with a dark line running through the eye to the shoulder. The female differs in having a brown

stripe along the crown to the nape with a white spot on the nape. Generally, the male is greyer with no brown on the crown. Their call is a single whistle that is rapidly repeated in an ascending scale. Most often seen in a dead tree or on an exposed limb either calling or looking for food in open areas. They not only call for long periods during the day but also at night even when there is no moon. They call soon after arriving in areas in the mid west, typically in late winter and early spring. Several species are parasitised by the Pallid Cuckoo, the majority have open nests and must be insect feeding birds. The biggest percentage are honeyeaters, others include flycatchers, robins and woodswallows, all well represented in the semi-arid regions. Pallid Cuckoos lay through much of the year but the high point is August through to September when breeding by other species is at its maximum peak. All cuckoos in Australia will lay only one egg in the host species nest, and laying in a number of other nests allows them to maximise their prodigies' chances of survival. How many they lay throughout the year is still not well known but one would presume it to be between 3 and 5 eggs per season. The Pallid Cuckoo is the largest cuckoo found in the GSW. Like many cuckoos it feeds on caterpillars, removing the guts and toxins by hitting the caterpillar against a branch or rock. It supplements its diet with other insects but caterpillars certainly make up the largest percentage of its food. **Similar species:** Oriental Cuckoo, not found in this region. No other cuckoos similar. **Status:** Scarce in the lower South West. Uncommon in the central and eastern Wheatbelt. Moderately common in the northern Wheatbelt. Common in the Mulga Region. **Where to find:** Dryandra Woodland NR. Tutanning NR. Wongan Hills. Lake Magenta NR. All northern and most of the eastern Wheatbelt reserves. Anywhere north and north east of the Transitional Woodland zone.

Fan-tailed Cuckoo *Cacomantis flabelliformis* 24–28 cm

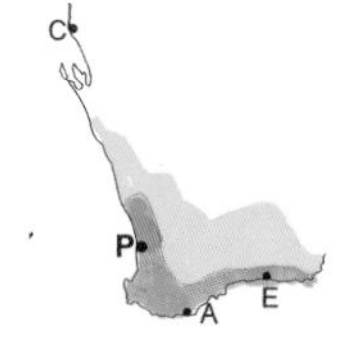

Unlike the Pallid Cuckoo that prefers semi-arid open woodland, the Fan-tailed Cuckoo prefers the taller wetter forests of the South West Region, often in areas with a thicker understorey. Perches at the mid canopy level, rarely in the high canopy. It has a distinct call very different to the Pallid Cuckoo. It has several calls but its primary contact call is a whistle with descending notes that are rather plaintive and mournful. It is found in a variety of habitats including the tall Karri Forest, Jarrah Forest, and Wandoo Woodland. Thick riparian gullies. In trees adjacent to heath. Its main breeding area is the deep South West Region and Southern Coastal Belt where it arrives in August to October; after breeding, it stays in the Lower South West, leaving the region in April or May and moving northwards to the northern Wheatbelt and beyond through the winter months. In the Wheatbelt, the birds breed earlier, normally in August to early September. Most female cuckoos will watch birds building a nest and will remain in the same locality feeding until the host species is ready to lay. They parasitise mostly domed nests such as those of the thornbills, fieldwrens, scrubwrens, even fairy-wrens. They

will parasitise some open nests but have a preference for domed nests. They feed on caterpillars, beetles, moths and any other form of insect. Their breeding range extends from the Lower South West to Kalbarri in the north, down to Koorda and east to Norseman and down to Cape Arid and all areas south of this line. There are 4 subspecies in the world with one in Australia *flabelliformis*. **Similar species:** None. **Status:** Moderately common in the Lower South West and uncommon in the Wheatbelt particularly furthest away from the Lower South West. **Where to find:** Pemberton region, all along the southern coast from Augusta to Esperance. Stirling Range NP. Dryandra Woodland NR. Throughout the Darling Range.

Black-eared Cuckoo *Chrysococcyx osculans* 19 cm

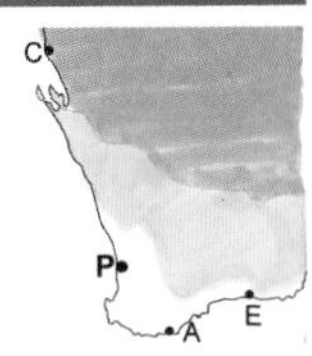

Found in the central semi-arid and arid regions and also the Kimberley. In the GSW found predominately in the Mulga Region. There is still much to learn about this species; we know they breed in the central arid region particularly between Billabong in the west and Ashburton Downs in the north, to Laverton and beyond in the east and to Bimbidji in the south. They do occur in other areas particularly the Pilbara, but between these locations would be their main breeding range in Western Australia. They come to the central arid regions in April to July and, after the breeding season, leave to travel north in October to December. Black-eared Cuckoos parasitise mainly domed nesting birds such as Southern Whiteface, Western Gerygone, Redthroat and Slaty-backed Thornbill. Occasionally Grey-crowned Babbler and White-browed Babbler. They have been recorded nesting in open nests such as the Red-capped Robin's. Feed entirely on insects particularly caterpillars. Are mobbed instinctively by birds such as thornbills even if not near the thornbill's nest. Feed from perches low down, pouncing on prey or hopping on the ground in search of insects. Their call is very similar to the Horsfield's Bronze-Cuckoo with which it often shares the same territory. There are several calls but the most common contact call of both species can be described as follows: the Black-eared Cuckoo's call is stronger than the Horsfield's, a longer drawn out 'seeeeuu...seeeeuu…seeeeu' that goes up and then down. The Horsfield's call is a shorter, softer and more rapid 'seeu seeu seeu'. **Similar species:** None, although confusion can occur with Horsfield's Bronze-Cuckoo which has barring on the underbody and a green metallic tinge to the upperbody, rust-brown in the outer tail feathers, eye stripe faint. Black-eared Cuckoo has plain olive-grey back, strong unmistakable eye stripe, no barring on underbody just plain cream coloured plumage. It also is a slightly larger bird. **Status:** Uncommon throughout range unless in country that has received above average rains and then can be moderately common. **Where to find:** In the north and north east of the GSW. Within this region, stations like

Wooleen (visitors can stay on the property). Thundelarra (although better chances further north). Nallan (can stay at property). Gascoyne Junction particularly around Yalbalgo Station. Sandstone region. Between Kalgoorlie and Leinster. Uncommon in northern Wheatbelt but rarely comes down to a line from Wongan Hills across to Kellerberrin and Southern Cross. Scarce below this line.

Horsfield's Bronze-Cuckoo *Chrysococcyx basalis* 16 cm

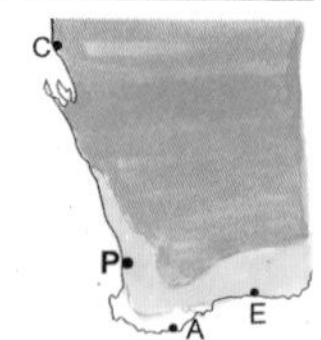

Comes down from the north particularly the Kimberley from March to May, although some do over-winter in the north. Breeds throughout the central regions as far north as the Great Sandy Desert and as far south as the edge of the wetter South West Region, virtually taking the place of the Shining Bronze-Cuckoo which only occurs in the wetter South West Region; however there is an overlap with some birds sharing the marginal zones. Horsfield's return to the Kimberley and some even go further north to New Guinea and Lesser Sundas Islands between October to January. The Horsfield's Bronze-Cuckoo is more widespread in choice of habitat than the Black-eared Cuckoo and also more common and, like the Black-eared Cuckoo, parasitises birds that build domed nests but more so the fairy-wrens, being a smaller cuckoo. The range of nests varies from habitat to habitat. In the north grasswrens, emu-wrens, Redthroats and thornbills are often selected. In the south, fieldwrens, fairy-wrens and thornbills are parasitised. In the Fitzgerald River National Park the author watched for a full hour or so, a poor Southern Emu-wren battling to keep pace with the demands of a well developed Horsfield's Bronze-Cuckoo four to five times its own weight. **Similar species:** Shining Bronze-Cuckoo, which has a more lustrous metallic green back. The important difference is that the Shining has no prominent eye stripe, and barring on underbody is stronger. The Horsfield's has a duller green-bronzed back and the barring is incomplete in the centre of underbody with bars tapering and fading to points. Has a distinct black line running from the eye, broadening on the ear coverts to the shoulder. Calls are totally different; refer to Shining Bronze-Cuckoo. The Horsefield's is a long drawn out 'seeeuu…seeeuu…seeeu' that goes up and then down with each call. **Status:** Uncommon throughout parts of the Wheatbelt and southern coast from Bremer Bay to Cape Arid. Moderately common in the northern Wheatbelt into the Mulga Region. **Where to find:** Best chances north from Wongan Hills to Kellerberrin. East from Kondinin to Norseman. Fitzgerald River NP to Cape Arid. Most prolific in the lower regions of the Mulga Region.

Shining Bronze-Cuckoo *Chrysococcyx lucidus* subspecies *plagosus*

14–18 cm

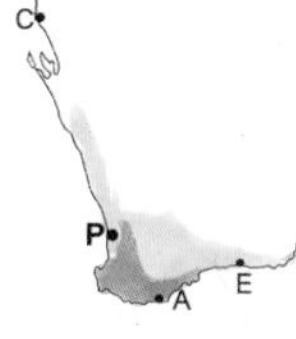

The Shining Bronze-Cuckoo arrives in the deep South West Region mainly from July to August and leaves after the breeding season between December and March. Their preference is for heavier forested areas but unlike the Horsfield's Bronze-Cuckoo that does not come into the thicker wetter forests and into the Wandoo only rarely, the Shining Bronze-Cuckoo breeds not only in the wetter South West but is found in open woodlands which are semi-dry such in the New Norcia region and even further north. It still is the dominant Bronze-Cuckoo nesting in Dryandra Woodland Reserve even though one would not class the area as a wetter South West reserve. Inner Wheatbelt reserves like Dryandra Woodland Reserve are a fascinating transitional zone, as all four cuckoos that enter the South West Region, namely Fantail Cuckoo, Pallid Cuckoo, Shining Bronze-Cuckoo and Horsfield's Bronze-Cuckoo, can be seen in that reserve, showing how transition zones allow overlap of all known cuckoos that enter the South West Region. Shining Bronze-Cuckoo is more selective than the Horsfield's Bronze-Cuckoo on what type of nest it will parasitise. They almost exclusively parasitise enclosed domed nests such as those of White-browed Scrubwren, Yellow-rumped Thornbill, Western Gerygone, Southern Emu-wren, Inland Thornbill, Splendid Fairy-wren and Red-winged Fairy-wren. Rarely will they use open nests. The call is unmistakable and is sometimes given the nickname 'walking the dog' call. A repetitive, rapid whistle with each note descending 'seee seee seee' finishing with an extended 'seeeeeuu' which has an undulating whistle-warbling tone. All bronzewing cuckoos share the occasional habit of stretching their wings out while singing their contact/breeding call. There are 4 subspecies of Shining Bronze-Cuckoo in the world, only two migrate and breed in Australia, *plagosus* and *lucidus* the other two are sedentary, *layardi* on New Caledonia and New Hebrides and *harterti,* on Renell and Bellona Islands. In the west, *plagosus* migrates south from either northern Australia or from New Guinea or the Lesser Sundas Islands, most probably the west coast birds come from the Lesser Sundas. Some come south from the Kimberley and Northern Territory. **Similar species:** Horsfield's Bronze Cuckoo. Calls totally different. Horsfield's has barring on underbody broken at centre, strong eye stripe, duller bronzing on upperbody. Shining Bronze's barring on underbody is complete although thinning near centre, broader and bolder on flanks. No eye stripe. Brighter green-bronzed upperbody. **Status:** Moderately common in South West. **Where to find:** Any Karri Forest in the South West. The Jarrah Forest. The inner Wandoo Woodlands. All along the southern coast.

Barking Owl *Ninox connivens* subspecies *connivens* 39–44 cm

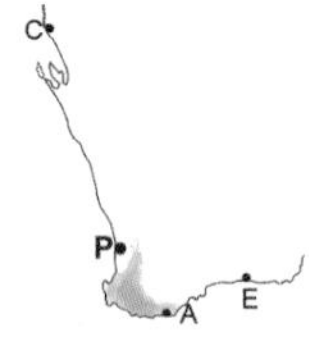

There are 4 subspecies of Barking Owl with two being found in Western Australia. The South West birds *connivens* are found in the deep South West Region of the state and are very scarce. They are bigger than the common Boobook Owl and can tackle much larger prey. Not a lot is known about the South West birds as their numbers are few and far between, being far more common in the Kimberley and to a lesser degree the Pilbara. Their call is very distinct reminiscent of a barking dog, a rapid 'woof woof.....woof woof......woof woof', hence the name Barking Owl. If you get a duelling pair calling, it can last for at least 15 minutes, rising in pitch and speed as they call. It is by far the most vocal of the owls. They also will start hunting earlier than most owls, often just after sunset when reasonable light is still available. **Similar species:** Boobook Owl, which is similar in shape but smaller and the head looks larger in proportion to the body. The Boobook subspecies *ocellata* is lighter brown and the Barking is more grey-brown. The Boobook has dark patches around the eye like eye patches whereas the Barking has a light whitish ring around the eye. The barring is heavier and bolder on the underbody of the Barking. It is not easy identifying owls by colour alone at night and it is the jizz of the bird that gives them away. **Nest:** In hollow from 5–20 metres high. Clutch size 2–3. **Status:** Scarce to rare in South West. Putting it into perspective re populations in other parts of Western Australia, in the Pilbara uncommon, in the Kimberley (different subspecies) common. **Where to find:** Has been seen in the Busselton region, Augusta region and Esperance region. Also in the Katanning to Cranbrook area.

Captive bird

Southern Boobook *Ninox novaeseelandiae* subspecies *ocellata* 30–35 cm

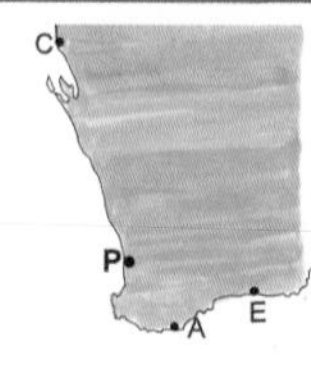

A very variable owl in terms of plumage colour. It is Australia's smallest owl and by far the most common, covering most regions in this state and throughout the GSW. Found in thick forests, open woodland, river systems and heath with woodland. In the South West mainly sedentary but with some movement north. Feeds on reptiles and invertebrates but mostly small mammals and birds. It is a stocky owl with a large head for its size and rounded wings and short tail. Birds in the deep South West tend to be darker than those in the drier regions. The well known 'boobook' call is its main contact and territory call, which it uses mostly in the first hour of darkness. It has a variety of other calls, one of which is an extended 'brrrrrrrrr' call which it uses in defence of its territory. Will take advantage of floodlights and remain in that area, then swoop on anything that passes on the ground. **Nest:** In hollows from 5–15 metres high. Clutch size 2–3. **Similar species:** Barking Owl which is larger and with a smaller head in proportion to body; refer to Barking Owl. **Status:** Common throughout most of the GSW. Resident in Perth and many other towns. **Where to find:** Any extensive woodland in the Wheatbelt. The Jarrah Forest and the Karri and Tingle Forests of the South West.

Masked Owl *Tyto novaehollandiae* subspecies *novaehollandiae*

33–41 cm

There are 8 subspecies in Australasia with 4 on the mainland of Australia. The South Western subspecies *novaehollandiae* may one day become a separate species from the eastern states birds as it is larger and also has longer wings and thicker tarsus. It is the largest owl found in the GSW, restricted to the thicker humid forests of the South West Region, particularly in the Pemberton and Manjimup area and along the Murray River in the Lane Poole area. One of their favoured prey is the Ring-tailed Possum and their heavier tarsus and feet are well able to tackle bigger prey than their close relative the Barn Owl. They prey on mammals and some birds taken mostly from the ground. The declining population of many of the South West mammals may have greatly affected the Masked Owl population. In Tasmania where mammals are more prolific the population of Masked Owl is greater and more stable. They roost mostly in large hollowed trees, coming to the entry while there is still light. The owl's call, or one should say screech, is stronger than the Barn Owl with a richer quality and more extended. The Barn Owl a more rapid, sharper and shorter screech. **Similar species:** Barn Owl, which is smaller, sits more upright. Facial disc is more heart shaped, coming to a point at base. Tarsus

Captive bird

much thinner and slightly longer in proportion and feet smaller. Crown has lighter coloured flecking not contrasting so much with white facial disc. Flecking on underbody, smaller dots and not so dark. Female Barn Owl is darker on the back than the male, so is closer in colour to the Masked Owl. The Masked Owl has a distinct hunched rounded shoulder look as if leaning forward. The facial disc is more circular even though it comes to a point at the base. The back is darker even in the lighter phased birds. The crown has darker flecking that makes the white facial disc stand out. The legs are decidedly thicker; you can imagine this bird tackling Ring-tailed Possums whereas the Barn Owl tarsus only looks fit for what it does most, tackling small rodents. **Nest:** In large Marri, Jarrah and Karri trees, almost always hollows at a great height. Clutch size 2–3. **Status:** Scarce in the lower South West forests but most probably under recorded. Masked Owls are never common and with the demise of many of our larger marsupials, particularly the Ring-tailed Possum, its population may be on the decline. **Where to find:** Pemberton, Manjimup area and Lane Poole area.

Eastern Barn Owl *Tyto alba* subspecies *delicatula* 29–38 cm

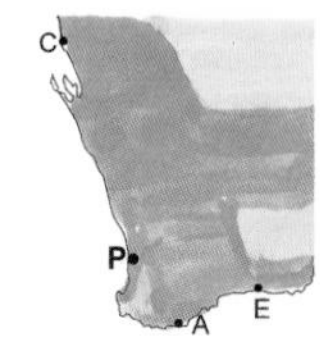

An owl that is found in every continent of the world, except the Antarctic, there being about 31 subspecies in total. After the Boobook Owl, the Barn Owl would be the second most common owl in the GSW. Smaller than the scarce Masked Owl, it feeds almost entirely on rodents particularly the introduced European House Mouse (*Mus musculus*). With land clearing and the introduction of vermin like the House Mouse, the population of Barn Owls in the Wheatbelt Region has increased. Some small reserves like Dongolocking Nature Reserve have high numbers of Barn Owl and there would be more if it were not for the lack of suitable nesting sites. The Barn Owl is a tall slim owl, rather pale particularly the male which is always lighter. Its preferred habitat is open grasslands but it requires woodland to both nest and roost in. In the drier arid regions outside the Wheatbelt it nests along creek and river systems, particularly in Red River Gums, although has been recorded nesting in caves. It is a silent bird when hunting, just gliding over crops or grasslands ;when it hears movement it hovers and drops to take prey. Calls just after sunset for a good 20 minutes in the breeding season. Its hissing screech shorter and more rapid than the bigger Masked Owl. **Nest**: Is often located in Wandoo trees but also most large eucalypts throughout the GSW Region. Clutch size 3–4. **Similar species:** Masked Owl, refer to notes on Masked Owl. **Status:** Moderately common throughout most of the GSW. Scarce in

Captive bird

thick Jarrah Forest. Dependent on mouse populations, will move from areas when mouse populations collapse. **Where to find:** Darling Range on the edge of farming country. Most Wheatbelt reserves like Dryandra Woodland NR.

Tawny Frogmouth *Podargus strigoides* subspecies *brachypterus*

35–40 cm

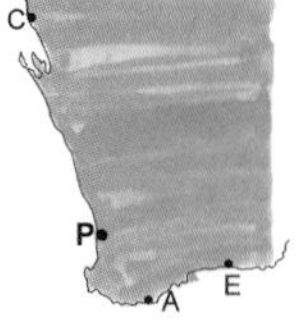

There are 4 subspecies of Tawny Frogmouth in Australia. Unlike the other 3, the one found in the GSW, *brachypterus*, is the only subspecies that is always a grey morph; the other subspecies are variable from grey right through to chestnut-brown plumage. The South West birds are larger than the eastern states birds. Unlike many bird species, the male is a larger heavier bird with a wider bill. Frogmouths have exceptionally wide bills adapted to catching moths and other insects. They often roost in sheoak woodland that has dense covering during the day. It is not unusual to see a pair or even a family group sitting side by side. When approached both day and night, they will develop the vertical stick posture with bill held high, looking like a broken off trunk. If you walk around them slowly you will notice the head moving with you almost rotating 180 degrees. The plumage, although overall fawn-grey, is exquisitely marked with mottled coverts to the wings and back and black streaking on the underbody. If you find a bird during the day; in the breeding season, there is a good chance it is a female as the male is the one that incubates the eggs during the day at night both sexes take turns, as that obviously is their feeding period. Tawny Frogmouths are found throughout the GSW in every type of habitat from rocky gullies in breakaway country to the thick forests of the South West. They not only feed on large moths and other insects but also will take small mammals, pounding them to a pulp before digesting. Their call is a distinct deep resonant call as if coming from the depths of the throat, slow 'ummm….ummm…..ummm', repeated rapidly for at least a minute then repeated again after a short break. **Nest**: Unlike the owls and Owlet-nightjar, the frogmouths build a stick nest, a loose collection of short twigs occasionally with a few fresh leaves on the top, placed on a horizontal branch or a vertical fork often in sheoak trees. Clutch size 2–3. **Similar species:** The two other frogmouth species but not found in this region. **Status:** Common throughout the region and in some areas densities possibly higher than many people realise. **Where to find:** Found in a variety of habitat but if sheoak woodland is nearby, your chances will increase of finding them. Spotlighting in vehicles will normally find them in the right type of woodland like Wandoo, either seen gliding or perched. Common in all Wheatbelt reserves.

Spotted Nightjar *Eurostopodus argus* 27–35 cm

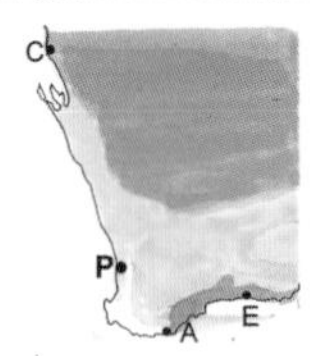

Nightjars are found throughout the world and have adapted well to taking insects in flight. In Australia we have 3 nightjars with only one occurring in the GSW. All Australian nightjars have spotting on the body as well as the classic 'bullseye' on the wings except the White-throated Nightjar found on the east coast. The Spotted Nightjar's white bullseyes are clearly visible at night when seen in headlights or spotlights. The wings are very long and broad, its flight very manoeuvrable; it catches insects particularly moths on the wing with its wide mouth. Often seen in the middle of gravel roads waiting for large flying insects to move. The birds are well camouflaged with their mottled markings; the author has walked only two metres away from a Spotted Nightjar on the side of a gravel track and not seen it, only to turn back a few metres past it and it has finally taken flight, such is their ability to blend in with foliage. You will always know when they are near you at night as their characteristic laughing chuckle call will give them away, hence one of its common names is 'laughing owl'. It has 3 distinct calls; the main contact/territorial call starts as a slow laughing 'whoo- whoo-whoo-whoo, whoo,whoo' ending in a fast gobbling set of notes, hard to describe but very distinct. It calls before the sun has set, mainly in breeding season; it will however call during the day particularly on overcast days but the call is very brief. On the southern coast, it has a preference for open heathlands with gravelly soils where it sallies for insects on the wing, flying only a few metres above the vegetation tops or just sitting on gravel ridges and roads waiting for moving insects. It can also be found in thick mallee, which abuts open farming country. In the Mulga and Gascoyne region, has a preference for stony ridges in breakaway country. **Nest:** No nest is made, just a scrape on the ground and the one egg laid directly on leaf litter or between stones. Clutch size just 1. **Status:** Moderately common in the southern coastal heaths from Waychinicup to Cape Arid. Rare in the heavy forested region of the South West. Uncommon in the inner Wheatbelt. More common in the outer Wheatbelt. Moderately common in the Mulga and stony regions past the Transitional Woodland zone. **Where to find:** Locally common in the Fitzgerald River NP. All the national parks containing heath habitat, from Hopetoun to Cape Arid. All stony ridges throughout the Mulga Region.

Australian Owlet-nightjar *Aegothleles cristatus* 19–25 cm

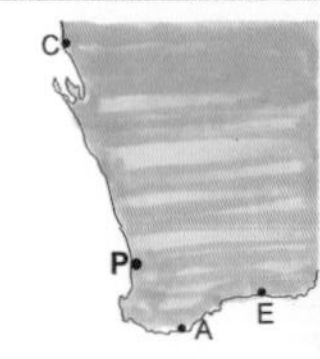

Smallest of all the Australian nocturnal birds, looks like a combination of a small owl and a nightjar. Feeds on much smaller insects than nightjars or frogmouths. Uses the same technique as nightjars of hunting on the wing for insects but flies less than a nightjar and pounces more like frogmouths, taking small insects from the ground. It has 3 distinct calls but the territorial call from a nest or roosting hollow is the most common; it has a funny laughing quality totally different to the nightjar's. A three noted bubbling call that starts on an extended note followed quickly by 2 short notes. It will give this call 4 or 5 times during the day either from the entrance of the nest or roosting hollow or within the nesting hollow. While taking bird groups, the author would often hear the call, find the appropriate hollow, and get people to look at the hollow with binoculars, while the author scratched the side of the trunk with a branch to imitate a crawling monitor lizard climbing up the trunk. Often out would pop the Owlet Nightjar's head, checking who was there, much to the amazement of the group, nothing special, just knowing the call certainly helps. Owlet Nightjars pair for life and will use the same hollow year after year. They are not always easily recognised if you are looking at the face in a tree hollow, with its dark black-brown stripes passing from the base of the eye over the top of the crown as well as a less visible stripe in the centre of the crown making it quite camouflaged against the tree trunk colours. **Nest:** Mostly in hollows of Wandoo and Karri trees in the South West. Clutch size 2–3. **Similar species:** None. **Status:** Scarce in deep South West. Moderately common throughout open woodland and river systems with adequate small nest and roosting hollows. **Where to find:** Locally common in mature Wandoo Woodland around the Stirling Range. Most Wheatbelt reserves with adequate woodland. Salmon Gum Woodland due east of Hyden. York Gum Woodland near Wubin and north of the Murchison Bridge. Any large river system in the arid region.

Fork-tailed Swift *Apus pacificus* 18–21 cm Vagrant

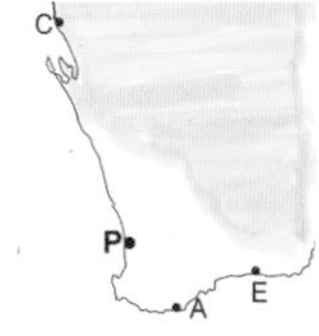

A fascinating bird that breeds from Siberia in the north, to Japan in the east and Thailand in the south. A migrant to Australia. A very large swift with long curved scythe-like wings and a distinct white rump seen well in flight, and a small white throat not so easily seen. If ever a body was designed for living much of its life on the wing, flying at times at great speed, it is the larger swift's. Fork-tailed Swifts spend most of their life on the wing, they feed, drink, rest, sleep and even mate on the wing. The Fork-tailed Swift is a gregarious bird that flies as high as 1000 metres to gain food but mostly between 50 and 200 metres where most of the insect life occurs. They call constantly, keeping the group together even though they zoom in from all angles and directions while feeding, and it's amazing they don't collide head on with the speeds they attain flying often in opposite directions. The call is a single high-pitched metallic note 'zit…zit…zit' made with long gaps between each 'zit'. Records of actually roosting in trees are extremely rare, so it is presumed to roost almost entirely on the wing. This bird is scarce in the GSW; the author has only seen these birds a few times in this region, once coming very low over Boyagin Rock Reserve in late summer. It was not cyclonic weather which is unusual as they normally take advantage of the cyclonic turbulent winds which aid rapid flight without requiring much effort. More importantly, at the head of the storm and away from the epicentre, thousands of insects are whisked up in the massive thermal drafts. The picture shows a storm on the highway near Eighty Mile Beach in December. Driving through the eye of the storm to the north side, the author was confronted by hundreds of swifts in the grey stormy sky hawking for insects. **Similar species:** On the east coast White-throated Needletail, often flies with Fork-tailed Swifts and are similar looking birds being larger with thicker set body, longer but less curved wings and no white on rump but on vent. Chance of seeing them in the GSW is scarce but they do visit. **Status:** Rare in South West. Scarce in northern region of GSW. Mainly seen between late November through to April.

Typical storm where Fork-tail can be sighted

Laughing Kookaburra *Daceelo novaeguineae* 40–48 cm Introduced

One of the 'tree' kookaburras of the world and also one of the largest. Many people forget that this bird was introduced in the South West, similar to those introduced into Tasmania. The Western Australian birds were released from the Perth Zoo between the years 1897 and 1912, often in the vain hope of removing snakes from many areas of the city. It did not take long for the bird to become established in Perth and by 1927 they had expanded their range to Denmark on the south coast. They now cover a range as far north as Dongara and then follow a line through Moora and across the southern Wheatbelt to Ravensthorpe. Sadly, many of the native birds have not adapted to the hunting skills of a kookaburra, which can sit motionless save for the occasional movement of the head for long periods of time, their eyes scanning for the slightest movement. Often it's a robin or flycatcher returning to the nest and exposing the chicks as prey. Also the reptilian world has been greatly affected, as a high percentage of their prey is snakes and other reptiles. They are a bird primarily of the wetter South West, preferring heavily forested areas and open woodland. The call needs

no introduction. The female has almost the same colouring as the male but lacks the blue patch on the rump of the male seen well in flight, and tail is not as long. **Nest:** They nest in hollows of both dead and live trees. Clutch size 2–4 mostly 3. **Similar species:** Blue-winged Kookaburra, the subspecies *clifftoni* in the Gascoyne and Pilbara region. Slightly smaller but has longer bill. Light blue shoulders. Light blue rump on both sexes. Male has strong dark blue tail. Head and crown are white with small black streaking from forehead to nape. No black-brown eye stripe or medial crown band. Call is different. **Status:** Common in much of the South West, particularly the Karri and Jarrah Forests and less so the inner Wandoo Woodland. **Where to find:** Most metropolitan parks with extensive woodland and grassed areas particularly on the base of the Darling Range scarp. Most picnic grounds throughout the Jarrah Forest in the lower South West.

Blue-winged Kookaburra *Dacelo leachii* subspecies *cliftoni* 39 cm

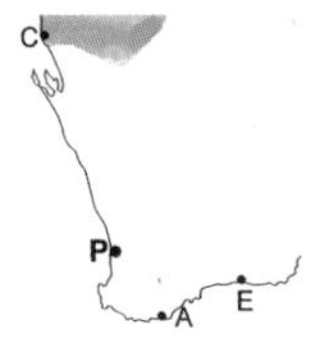

A kookaburra of the tropics and dry regions of northern Australia. In the GSW Region only found along the Gascoyne River. Slightly smaller than the Laughing Kookaburra, the subspecies *cliftoni* is restricted to the Gascoyne River system north to the De Grey River system, cut off from the Kimberley and Northern Territory birds by the Great Sandy Desert. The subspecies *cliftoni* differs from its nearest subspecies *leachii* of the Kimberley and northern Australia, by having finer black streaks in the crown making the head look whiter, and a buffy underbody and tail marginally longer. Its cacophonous call is certainly different from that of the Laughing Kookaburra but, once heard, one can detect the similarities in tone and noise, almost like a series of loud gurgling laughs, very hard to describe but dominating any other birds that call in the area. They behave in the same manner as Laughing Kookaburra having strong family and territorial bonding, the group often coming together on one branch with maybe 3–4 birds all calling with bills held upwards giving a raucous song. This is normally done after sunset and even into the first hour of darkness; it is also one of the first calls heard before the first dawn light. **Nest**: Location and clutch size same as Laughing Kookaburra, 2–3. **Similar species:** Laughing Kookaburra, refer to notes on Laughing Kookaburra. **Status:** Moderately common along lower Gascoyne River

Red-backed Kingfisher *Todiramphus pyrrhopygia* 23 cm

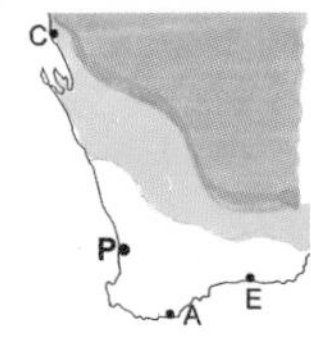

Found in the drier regions of the GSW, in open woodland in the Mulga Region but even more so along river systems like the Gascoyne and upper Murchison Rivers. Basically sedentary, although some movement in species breeding in the southern areas. They require a feeding location that is near a sand bank where they can excavate a nest hollow and have trees nearby from which to hunt for prey. Requires nest sites where firm soils occur. Feeds on insects, grasshoppers and reptiles, by sitting on branches for short periods before moving to new areas to check prey and waiting for movement so they can then pounce. Will whack prey against a branch to make sure it is killed before digesting. Red-backed Kingfishers don't have a red back but have a rust red rump seen well in flight. The crown is white with heavy black streaking (male) with a prominent black eye stripe. Wing coverts are light royal blue; it has a blue-green upperbody and blue tail. Female has a duller green back and the crown streaks are dark green; it's not easy to split the sexes in the field. **Nest:** In earth banks, placed at the base of an excavated tunnel, nest chamber being from 50–120 cm into the bank but never close to water levels, always higher up on cliffs or lower down on sandy embankments away from water. Clutch size 3–4. **Similar species:** Sacred Kingfisher has green crown with no streaking. Buff-white dot between bill and eye. Collar narrower. Back greener. Flanks buff coloured. No rust red rump. Nests in tree hollows. Calls quite different. **Status:** Common along major rivers of the north. Uncommon in open stony country where breakaways occur with some trees. Uncommon in northern Wheatbelt and north eastern Wheatbelt. **Where to find:** Middle and upper Murchison and most of the Gascoyne River and Lyons River. Found on stations where no rivers occur such as Wooleen and Nallan Stations.

Sacred Kingfisher *Todiramphus sanctus* 21 cm

C P A E

Found throughout much of the GSW, the Sacred Kingfisher lives in a variety of habitats but in the South West it mostly lives in open woodland or along river courses, where there is not too much undergrowth but open areas with grasses. It is not a bird of the inland arid regions; that environment is taken over more by the Red-backed Kingfisher. Sacred Kingfishers migrate north from the South West from early December through until January and do not return till August or September. They feed on a variety of prey from insects through to small rodents, reptiles and even young birds. Sacred Kingfishers have a blue-green crown and buff spot on the base of forehead. Strong black eye stripe that passes around the nape of the neck, green back and blue-green wings, blue rump and blue tail, white underbody with buff flanks. **Nest:** They nest in tree hollows often returning to the same location to nest. Clutch size 3–5. **Similar species:** Collared Kingfisher, does not occur in this region. Red-backed Kingfisher, refer to notes on that species. **Status:** Uncommon to moderately common in the South West during spring and early summer. **Where to find:** Any of the larger Wheatbelt

reserves with woodland as far east as Dumbleyung. Found in parts of the eastern Darling Range and Swan Coastal Plain including Rottnest Island. **Where to Find:** Throughout much of the South West including Tutanning NR. Boyagin NR. Dryandra Woodland NR. Bungendore State Forest and Rottnest Island.

Rainbow Bee-eater *Merops ornatus* 25 cm

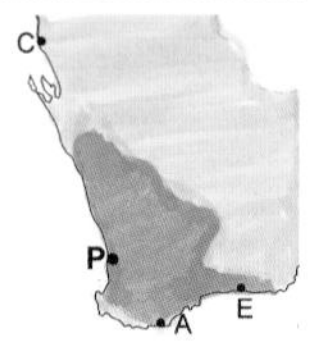

A breeding migratory bird to the South West arriving mainly in September to October and departing the South West January to March, sometimes as late as April. They often return to the same area the following year digging out nests in open areas where there is relatively soft earth. The angled nest is either on flat ground or in the side of a sandy bank. They feed on insects particularly large flies, dragon flies and bees, sitting on exposed branches and darting out to take prey on the wing, then returning to whack the insects hard against the branch, killing them before swallowing. Their pleasant trill when walking through woodland often leads one to where they are nesting. After the breeding season around February to March, the adult and immature birds congregate in small groups, normally between 8–10 birds, still feeding in the same locality getting ready for their migration north. When they finally depart, they often meet other groups heading north and the group's size can increase to 30–40 birds as they move through the northern regions of the GSW. They over-winter as far south as the Gascoyne but most travel to the Kimberley and many fly on to Indonesia, not to return until September and October. **Nest:** Excavated tunnel is from 50–120 cm long with large chamber at base, the nest lined with soft grasses. Both sexes excavate nest tunnel. Nest location is almost invariably close to trees with exposed dead limbs from which they can hawk for insects and also drop down to nest. **Similar species:** None. **Status:** Common throughout the South West. **Where to find:** Any clearing with loose soils in wooded areas or open areas near trees. Common on the eastern side of the Darling Range. On the Swan Coastal Plain including Perth in gardens and playing fields. Throughout the Wheatbelt and into the Transitional Woodland.

Noisy Scrub-bird *Atrichornis clamosus* 23 cm Endemic to Western Australia

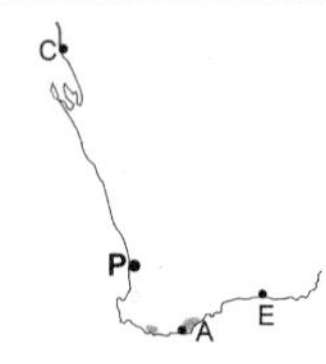

The Noisy Scrub-bird is a fascinating bird with its evolutionary development going back to connections with species like the lyrebird which have no wishbone, which is the main bone structure that flight muscles are attached to and is required by most flying birds. That's why you will not see a Scrub-bird fly far; it will make a short flight burst and semi-glide as it does so. Most of the time they will run and that they do extremely well, having very strong thighs just like their distant relative the lyrebird, which also does not like flying and only does so to roost in trees or glide a short distance down steep hillsides. The story of the Noisy Scrub-bird and its rediscovery and recovery in Western Australia is a credit to all the hard working research workers and volunteers who were involved in its recovery program, for it was thought that the Scrub-bird was extinct. In 1961 the amateur birdwatcher Harley Webster of Albany found the bird on Mount Gardner at Two Peoples Bay. By a systematic program of translocating captured birds and releasing them in varying sites like

Mount Many Peaks, Cheynes Beach and Bold Island, the population has gone from at the most 100 birds prior to the 1970s to over 2000. With two major fires over the last ten years, the author is not sure of the estimated population now but it will always be far greater than the fragile population before discovery. Its population has now well surpassed the rare Western Ground Parrot which is found over a greater range but its status is very tenuous and researchers and volunteers are working hard to get to grips with its needs and habitat. Well, we know its needs but what to do to protect it is the big question. The Noisy Scrub-bird is one of the hardest birds to see, even more so than its east coast relative the Rufous Scrub-bird. Some birdwatchers get lucky at Cheynes Beach and see the bird in the open but generally it is extremely difficult to see. The author has had groups of birdwatchers only metres away from where the birds have been calling, only to have the bird run behind us or through us, such is its ability to run through thick undergrowth and still avoid detection. Its call is amazingly powerful for such a small bird and can carry several hundred metres. The call starts slowly and builds up rapidly, finishing in a crescendo burst. It also has a warning call, a sharp grating 'chip' similar to the Western Bristlebird's warning note, using it normally when it sees you first. First year males try to develop the power and coordination of the full adult call but it lacks the full volume and tends to be broken in parts. They will call away from the main occupied gully territories. Males will call in summer on overcast days, even at midday but with nothing like the quantity of calls in the pre-breeding and breeding season. The dominant males tend to select and dominate the lushest, thickest gullies. The feeding path often follows the line of a very small creek or runoff where the riverine vegetation has a taller canopy and the understorey is incredibly dense with thick areas of sedge. Other less dominant males have to occupy territories with less of an overstorey but the species always requires thick undergrowth, more so than the bristlebird. They feed on small macro-insects in the leaf litter, turning over the soil to get to insects etc. The male is a much bigger bird, has a stronger white throat with strong scalloping on the centre of the throat and upper breast, pale underbody. **Nest:** The nest is an oval dome structure made from rushes with a side entrance often with a platform entry. The base of the nest has a hard pulp consistency made from masticated rushes. The female builds the nest and she will often use the same nest or build another in close proximity to the old one. She lays just one egg. Surprisingly for such a wet cool region it lays in the middle of winter mainly July, just like its ancient ancestor the lyrebird; however, there maybe replacement clutches in late spring into October. **Similar species:** Western Bristlebird which is smaller. Has longer tail but body looks and is slimmer. Distinct scalloping on underbody and mantle. Call totally different being more musical and is a shorter four noted call, first two notes extended, last two very rapid. **Status:** Overall rare but locally common in a restricted area. **Where to find:** Two Peoples Bay. Mount Many Peaks. Waychinicup. Cheynes Beach. Has been released in a few other locations many kilometres away in former territories known in the mid to late 1800s. Note: Please do not use tapes to attract these birds as they have been overplayed in many areas creating disturbance and stress for the birds. At Cheynes Beach or Two Peoples Bay there is a reasonable chance of seeing the bird without the need for tapes.

Noisy Scrub-bird female Photo: Graeme Chapman

Rufous Treecreeper *Climacteris rufa* 17 cm

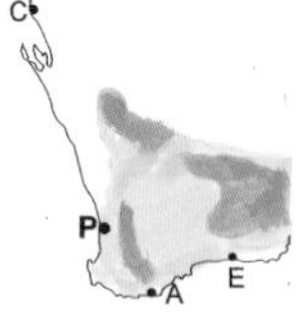

An attractive, all rufous-coloured Treecreeper, found in the South West and in the Great Victoria Desert in Western Australia with another population in lower south east of South Australia. It is a sedentary bird, requiring much fallen timber and mature large eucalypts. Found in varying eucalypt woodlands in the GSW including Wandoo, Karri, York Gum and Salmon Gum Woodlands, to a lesser extent Jarrah Woodlands. Some of the highest population densities occur in the Wandoo Woodland. Feeds both on the ground and on tree trunks. Their rasping call often warns other birds of ones presence. Both sexes similar but the male has distinct vertical white flecking with black edges to the margins located on the chest. The female has just white flecking and lacks the strong black edging. In flight they show the prominent cream band on the centre of the wings. **Nest**: Like all treecreepers nests in tree hollows, normally placed between 2–10 metres up in a tree, often in an angled spout. A nest is built at the base of the hollow and a mat of grasses and bark is used. Clutch size 2–3. **Similar species:** None. **Status**: Locally common in the larger remnant Wandoo Woodlands and in the Transitional Woodland belt on the east and north of the Wheatbelt. Now scarce on the Swan Coastal Plain where it was once common before European settlement. **Where to find:** Boyagin Rock. Dryandra NR. Dongolocking NR. Stirling Range NR. Bungendore NR. All along the eastern boundary of the Jarrah Forest where it blends with Wandoo Woodland. East of Perenjori and north east of Wubin, in the Transitional Woodland.

White-browed Treecreeper *Climacteris affinis* subspecies *superciliosa* 14–16 cm

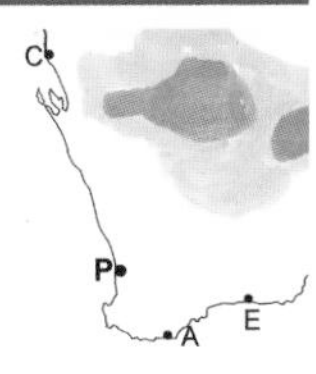

A bird of the semi-arid to arid regions, its distribution is fragmented over its range. In the GSW Region, it is found in the Mulga Woodland Region and has a preference for areas where the native pine (*Callitris glaucophylla*) grows, for two reasons: one is that it is one of its favoured trees to feed on, having deep fissures in the bark where it gathers insects; the other is that it is one of the primary trees in which it nests requiring suitable hollows which most of the long standing but now dead Callitris trunks have but the Mulga trees do not have. They also feed on the trunks and branches of acacias, principally the broad and narrow leaved Mulga. They are locally common in certain locations but never in large groups, there normally being only 4–8 birds in each feeding group, and are patchily distributed throughout the mulga. Their call often gives them away, a high-pitched rapid trill slowing at the end 'stzz stzz stzz stzz–stizzz–stizzz' often uttered from the top of dead exposed branch. Has an undulating flight as it flies from tree to tree. Feeds on insects from crevices in the bark starting at the base of a tree and working up to the mid level before dropping down to the next tree trunk. There are two subspecies in Australia, the nominate subspecies *affinis* in eastern Australia and subspecies *superciliosa* in central and western Australia. The Western Australian birds have a browner back and rump not grey-brown as in *affinis*. There are other small colour variances with the scapulars and throat but very subtle differences. **Nest**: As mentioned, placed in a tree hollow; sometimes the bird enters a hollow in the middle of a trunk and exits through the top of the hollow trunk. Clutch size 2–3. **Similar species:** Brown Treecreeper, not found in this region. **Status:** Uncommon in Western Australia. **Where to find:** Pindabunna Station (no tourist facilities – working station). Maranalgo station Wooleen Station. Nallan Station. Billabalong Station (no tourist facilities – working station). North of the Mt Jackson area. Goongarrie NR.

Black-tailed Treecreeper *Climacteris melanura* subspecies *wellsi*

16–19 cm

A bird of the Kimberley and northern Australia, subspecies *melanura* and the Pilbara subspecies *wellsi,* with a small restricted population along the middle Gascoyne River just within the boundary of the GSW. It has the same feeding habits as the other two Western Australian treecreepers. On the Gascoyne it frequents the Red River Gums that run in a broad band along much of the central Gascoyne River. It is said to be found between Rocky Pool and Bigemia Station. The author has birded the Rocky Pool area but never seen it there, only further north in the Pilbara and the Kimberley. The male differs from the female by having a white throat with black vertical streaks and darker rust red underbody. The female has a white throat with no black streaks. The subspecies *wellsi* in this region has smaller wings and tail but body size is the same. Also the underbody is much lighter than the Kimberley birds being rufous rather than black-brown. In flight both sexes show a light cream band when flying that spreads across the centre of the wings. **Nest:** In tree hollows, sometimes in a horizontal hollow branch. Clutch size 2–3. **Similar species:** None. **Status:** Uncommon throughout its range. **Where to find:** In the GSW, apparently between Rocky Pool and Bigemia on the Gascoyne River.

Splendid Fairy-wren *Malurus splendens* subspecies *splendens* 11–13.5 cm

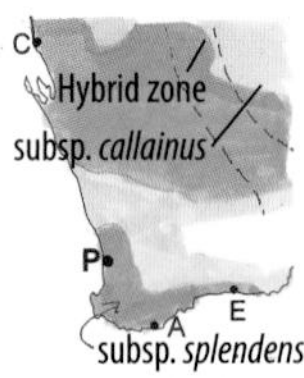

There are 2 subspecies of Splendid Wren within this region *splendens* occurs throughout most of the GSW but above Kalgoorlie and up to Wiluna and east of that line, hybrids start to occur between *splendens* and the desert subspecies *callainus* which used to be known as the Turquoise Wren. If you see it in the central deserts set against the rust red sand dunes, it certainly is a stunning subspecies, showing its distinct turquoise back. In the South West Region *splendens* occupies relatively thick undergrowth often overlapping the territories of the larger Red-winged Fairy-wren. Both have their food niches. Away from the lower South West, the Splendid Fairy-wren is found throughout most of the GSW into the Mulga Woodland and into the Pilbara. It can be seen scurrying around the bases of mulga trees with no groundcover unlike the habitat of the deep South West. They feed mostly on the ground or within low bushes but will occasionally feed higher up in low trees. In the Wandoo Woodland it occupies a different habitat to the Blue-breasted. The male plumage varies with age; an older dominant bird often holds its breeding plumage longer and the moulting period is often only short. In full breeding it is unmistakable as in the photograph below; in non breeding it retains its blue tail which is a stronger brighter blue than the female. Also on the wings it retains a blueish tinge which the females do not have. It also lacks the orange-brown orbital eye ring that the female possesses. The female has a dull blue-green tail. No blue on the wings at any period. The main diagnostic feature is the orange-brown orbital ring that goes around the eye and extends to the bill. **Nest:** They build the typical Fairy-wren dense ball nest low to the ground with topside entrance. In the South West they nest from September through to December but the more inland birds will nest as early as late July and August. They will breed twice and the author has seen nests with young in April after good rains in the Mulga Region. The inner nest is lined with soft grasses or wool. Clutch size 2 to 4. **Similar species:** None. **Status:** Common in the lower South West. Uncommon in the Wheatbelt. Moderately common past the Vermin Fence and to the desert regions. **Where to find:** Prolific in the South West and all along the coast to Cheynes Beach then a distinct drop in numbers as one goes east into a less humid region. Common in parts of the Swan Coastal Plain all the way to Carnarvon but after Carnarvon becomes very uncommon. In Perth and surrounding country found in larger bush areas particularly at the base of the Darling Range and right into the Jarrah Forest.

Variegated Fairy-wren *Malurus lamberti* subspecies *assimilis* 12–15 cm

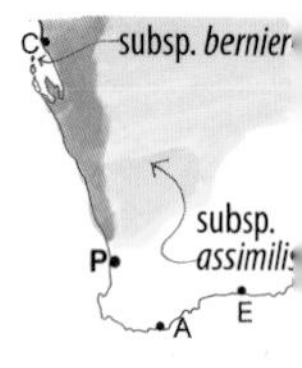

There is great variation in plumage throughout Australia from one subspecies to another, as well a clinal change within the subspecies themselves. *assimilis* on the east coast is darker overall than the Western Australian birds. Also within Western Australia the bird's colour gets paler the further north they occur. Where the Red-winged Fairy-wren requires moist gullies of the lower South West, the Variegated is the opposite and in Western Australia it survives in far drier habitats. Most common on the coastal belt as far south as Perth. It is one of the common fairy-wrens of thick coastal heath, particularly north of Jurien all the way to Kalbarri. It is often asked how long do these little fairy-wrens live; well it's not unusual for a fairy-wren to live for about 6–7 years. In the non-breeding plumage the male differs from the female by having a dark bill. Lacks the orange orbital eye ring, instead has a smaller pale eye ring. Has a light blue tail, female has a dull grey-blue tail and orange bill and orange orbital eye ring. **Nest**: Is similar to the Splendid Fairy-wren but slightly bulkier. **Similar species:** Blue-breasted Fairy-wren, which has black-blue breast seen in sunlight only. An even violet-blue crown and ear coverts although there is a slight change to lighter coverts. With Variegated the contrast is greater and the crown is lighter blue and the coverts even lighter still. The breast is black on the Variegated, even in full sunlight. There are only subtle differences between females. The Blue-breasted female has a brighter orange orbital eye ring than the darker brown-orange of the Variegated. The bill on the female Variegated is bright orange whereas the female Blue-breasted's is a brown-orange colour. **Status:** Common on the coastal belt. Uncommon through the arid regions. **Where to find:** Kalbarri National Park particularly near the coast. From Lancelin to Dongara and parts of the northern Wheatbelt past Moora to the Mulga Woodland. Moderately common in the Shark Bay region, particularly near Monkey Mia.

Photo: Graeme Chapman

Blue-breasted Fairy wren *Malurus pulcherrimus* 12.5–14 cm

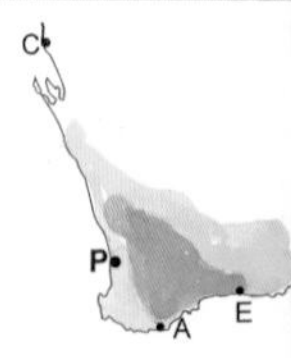

Sadly much of the territory that the Blue-breasted occurred in has been cleared for farming and some of their populations in the Wheatbelt remain tenuous. It has a particular preference for sandplain heaths, known as Kwongan Heath, and also for open Wandoo Woodland where the Sandplain Poison (*Gastrolobium microcarpum*) occurs. It does not occur in the lower wetter South West, so there is never any confusion with

Red-winged Fairy-wren except at a crossover region around Cheynes Beach and east. The difficulty with identification is between Variegated and the Blue-breasted; on the coast north of Perth and the northern Wheatbelt there is an overlap particularly in the Badgingarra area. Most of their territory starts where the Red-winged Fairy-wren's range finishes and goes through the Wheatbelt and Transitional Woodland to where the mulga starts and the Variegated Fairy-wrens occur. Its distribution also spreads as a narrow band at the base of the Nullarbor Plain and then its population recommences on the Eyre Peninsula in South Australia. The non-breeding Blue-breasted male has similar plumage colours to the female but the bill is black not brown-orange and there is no orange orbital eye ring or lores. **Nest**: Similar to Variegated Fairy-wren but often built very close to the ground, often in one of the prostrate dryandra bushes. **Similar species:** Refer to the notes on Variegated Fairy-wren. Red-winged Fairy-wren is slightly larger and slightly heavier bodied. The crown on the male is a lighter silvery blue and the ear coverts even lighter again. The lores on the female are larger and more chestnut in colour. The mantle seen best in flight is a much lighter blue. The chestnut shoulder patch slightly narrower than on the Blue-breasted. **Status:** Locally common in some reserves but overall throughout its range uncommon. **Where to find:** Wongan Hills. Watheroo NR. Tutanning NR. Dryandra Woodland NR. Dongolocking NR. East Yorkrakine NR. Magenta NR. Dragon Rocks NR. Much of the Wheatbelt population now diminished.

Red-winged Fairy-wren *Malurus elegans* 14.5 cm Endemic to Western Australia

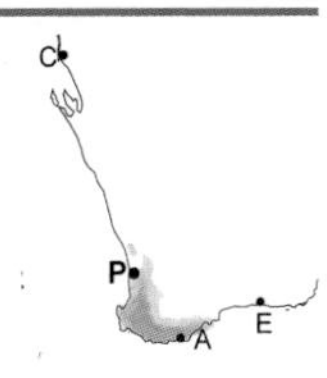

Found in the wetter parts of the South West. It is the largest of the fairy-wrens found in the GSW and also the largest of all the Australian chestnut-shouldered fairy-wrens. Its preferred habitat is lush riverine vegetation or thick undergrowth of the heavily forested Jarrah, Karri and Tingle Forests of the lower South West. They range as far north as the remnant population on the Moore River, then a break to the northern part of the Darling Range broadening their range in the South West corner. They extend to Waychinicup National Park and inland to the Porongurups. The male has a pale silvery blue crown and the ear coverts are even lighter. The mantle is the same light silvery blue, seen best in flight. The lores on the female are larger and more orange-chestnut in colour than Blue-breasted Fairy-wren's. Red-winged Fairy-wrens were found on the Swan Coastal Plain when settlers first arrived but the clearing of land along the river systems has almost removed all populations except on rivers like the Harvey River. **Nest**: Similar to Variegated but often placed higher in a bush. **Similar species:** Refer to the notes on Blue-breasted Fairy-wren. **Status:** Moderately common throughout its range. **Where to find:** Most rivers and creeks that run down the scarp of the Darling Range such as Serpentine, Wungong, Dandalup Rivers, Piesse, Bickley and

Churchman Brook. Throughout the lower South West, from Dunsborough to Albany. Particularly common from Walpole to Elleker. Common in the gullies of the Porongurup Range.

White-winged Fairy-wren *Malurus leucopteris* subspecies *leuconotus* 11–13 cm

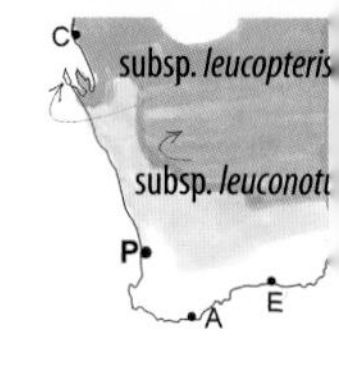

There are 3 subspecies of the White-winged Fairy-wren, all occur in Western Australia. It is interesting that the nominate subspecies *leucopteris* was collected first on Dirk Hartog Island where there is an unusual relic population which instead of having the normal cobalt blue body and head is in fact all black, quite a stunning little bird. The other restricted subspecies *edouardi* occurs on Barrow Island and is very close to the black and white birds of Dirk Hartog with very subtle differences that this book does not need to cover. The bird that covers much of the northern part of the GSW in the semi-arid zone is the subspecies *leuconotus*. It is a blue and white fairy-wren. In the GSW, it comes as far south as Perth although is losing its coastal territory each year. It can be found throughout the GSW except the lower South West but is found in parts of the northern Wheatbelt region. It is a fairy-wren of the semi-arid regions. Calls of the other fairy-wrens have not been discussed, as they are so similar and hard to split unless you know the calls exceptionally well. However, whereas the other fairy-wrens have soft but very high pitched short whistles that some people can not even hear, the White-winged Fairy-wren is easier to pick, as its call is far louder and instead of being soft short whistles with breaks in between, it is a strong rolling reel that is extended for several seconds 'treeeeeeeit' then a break 'treeeeeeeit'. They have a particular preference for chenopod vegetation, samphires and blue bush, also dense coastal low heaths and margins of ephemeral inland lakes that have lignum growth. The female is very similar to non-breeding male and one has to see them well to split them. The non-breeding male has a black bill not pale pink and the central tail feathers are slightly tinged blue not easily seen; best to check the bill. Luckily the dominant male normally remains in moult for only a short period. **Nest:** The dome nest is built by the female and situated low only 20–40 cm off the ground. **Similar species:** None, although the females are similar to other female fairy-wrens. **Status:** Subspecies *leuconotus* moderately common on coastal heaths to Dongara. Common north of Geraldton to Kalbarri. Common in Shark Bay region. Uncommon but locally common on preferred habitat in the drier inland regions. **Where to find:** Guilderton to Green Head. Kalbarri coastal heath. Throughout the Shark Bay region, mainly on Peron Peninsula. From Gladstone to Carnarvon all along the coastal belt. Inland anywhere there are extensive stands of samphire.

Southern Emu-wren *Stipiturus malachurus* subspecies *westernensis*

14–18 cm

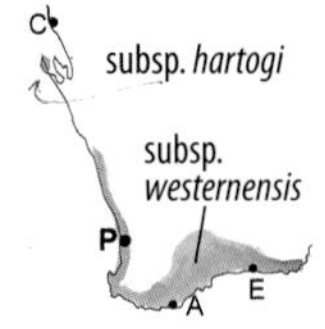

Eight subspecies throughout Australia and 2 within this region, *westernensis* in the lower South West and *hartogi* on Dirk Hartog Island. The Southern Emu-wren requires thick low heath, where it manoeuvres through the densest vegetation only occasionally popping up to check territory. A very small-bodied wren, the male having a distinct pale blue throat and chest as well as a pale blue supercilium eye stripe. The subspecies on Dirk Hartog Island has a much paler blue chest and the flanks are a lighter orange-cream, black streaking on the crown not as bold. Their call is so high pitched that people who cannot hear high pitches just do not hear them. Their range follows much of the coast from as far north as Jurien Bay all the way down to the capes and along the southern coast to Cape Arid. They are not found in the main Darling Range except in the very south of their range. From Albany north they can be found in several of the lower Wheatbelt reserves. **Nest**: Is a small round dome with topside entry often woven into grasses or small plants growing alongside. Always well concealed and the inner nest lined with grasses or fur as a soft internal lining. **Similar species:** Rufous-crowned Emu-wren, not found in this region and territory does not overlap (furthest southern population on the top of the Kennedy Ranges). **Status:** Moderately common in closed heath throughout its range except the lower Wheatbelt where it is scarce. **Where to find:** Heaths near Cervantes and Lancelin. Remnant population near Ellis Brook on the Darling scarp. Locally common between Cape Naturaliste and Cape Leeuwin and all along the southern coast to Esperance and Cape Arid. Locally common in the following parks: the Leeuwin-Naturaliste NP, Walpole-Nornalup NP, West Cape Howe NP, Waychinicup NP and Fitzgerald River NP.

Thick-billed Grasswren *Amytornis textiles textiles* 17 cm

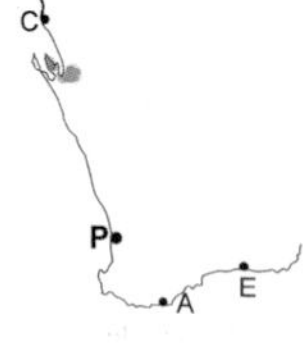

Most grasswrens are associated with spinifex (genus *Triodia*) but the Thick-billed Grasswren can be found in saltbush and bluebush country as well as acacia thickets on sand dunes. The Thick-billed Grasswren is one of the smaller grasswrens with a shorter tail than most and as the name implies has a stout bill. The sexes are almost identical, the female showing a small but distinct rufous patch on the flanks. Thick-billed Grasswren are no longer found throughout much of their former territory, which included a large area on the Nullarbor and into the Great Victoria Desert. It is believed that with the introduction of the rabbit, the impact on bluebush country greatly affected their survival and now the subspecies *textiles* can only be found on the Peron Peninsula and east of Hamelin Pool and parts of Woodleigh Station. They are omnivorous not only taking insects but feeding on fruits and seed. They have two basic calls, a contact call which is just a single high pitched 'zsit zsit zsit' and strange mewing call. **Nest:** One of the few grasswrens that does not always nest in spinifex, nesting mainly in bluebush and samphire. In the Monkey Mia region there are several other low shrub species that it also nests in. The nest can be a deep cup of dense matted grasses and twigs without a hood, or with a partial hood or a complete hood with side entry. Clutch size mostly 2 sometimes 3. **Similar species:** Dusky Grasswren which is a long way from both subspecies. **Status:** Uncommon throughout most of its range. Locally common at Monkey Mia and adjacent dunes. **Where to find:** Easiest location is in the parking area and adjacent dunes opposite the resort and camping area as they have become accustomed to people.

Western Bristlebird *Dasyornis longirostris* 17 cm Endemic to Western Australia

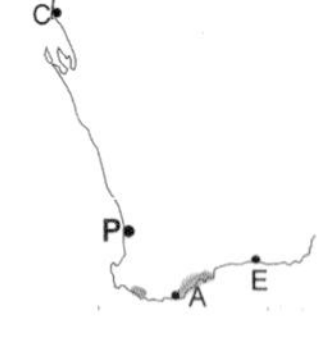

Now restricted to some of the dense low heaths from Two Peoples Bay to Hopetoun, although there are some translocated birds in the Walpole area. A little more widespread than the Noisy Scrub-bird in its distribution with pockets of populations throughout the Fitzgerald River NP. Cheynes Beach area. Mt Manypeaks. Betty's Beach and Two Peoples Bay area. This is a scarce bird even more so than its eastern states counterpart the Eastern Bristlebird. Increased protection of the Noisy Scrub-bird has certainly helped the Two Peoples Bay Bristlebird population. For years, the author has seen populations of bristlebirds come and go in the Fitzgerald River NP. Western Bristlebirds require low heath mostly very dense, occasionally more open in stands of Baxter's Banksia (*Banksia baxteri*) and Southern Plains Banksia (*Banksia media*) heath on the eastern side of the Fitzgerald. Wild fires particularly in the Fitzgerald and Mt Manypeaks area have affected many small populations. However, its status is nowhere near as tenuous as the Western Ground Parrot's. It spends most of its time on or near the ground, taking insects from low shrubs or in leaf litter. If approached will sometimes give a warning 'click' call similar to a Noisy Scrub-bird. It has a plaintive but strong 'deeeeee..da...diditdit........deeeeee..da...diditdit'. In the Fitzgerald River NP, it often gives after the main call a rolling trill hard to put into words. The Western Bristlebird is a plain brown ground dwelling bird with short dark chestnut wings and a long tail. Slight scalloping on the mantle and crown. Light off white throat, not as extensive as Rufous Bristlebird or Noisy Scrub-bird but very similar to the Eastern Bristlebird. Has a small white eye stripe above the lores. Pale grey-brown underbody with scalloping far more pronounced than in the Eastern Bristlebird. Its species name *longirostris* comes from the Latin '*longus*' meaning long and '*rostrum*' meaning billed. However, its bill is slightly longer than the Eastern Bristlebird's. **Nest:** The nest is a large oval ball constructed of dry grass or sedge stems placed close to the ground at the base of a tuft of sedge or other low shrub. There is a large entry hole at the top side of the oval. Inside it is lined with finer grasses. Clutch size 2. **Similar species:** The jizz and colouring has some similarities to Noisy Scrub-bird but even though they share the same general area, their territory is different. The Scrub-bird inhabits dense riverine gullies or taller dense scrub with an understorey of thick sedges whereas the Bristlebird inhabits mostly low vegetation with no tall over storey as it prefers thick low heath. The Noisy Scrub-bird has a bulkier body being a heavier slightly larger bird. Its back is darker and tail is shorter in relation to body. Bill more down curved. Throat on male very white, contrasting with the dark crown. White on underbelly. Female less white on throat and no white on underbelly. Calls are totally different, the Bristlebird sounding plaintive, the Noisy Scrub-bird being just that, with a powerful strong resounding and far carrying call. **Status:** Scarce to rare. **Where to find:** Mount Manypeaks. Two Peoples Bay. Waychinicup. Cheynes Beach. Fitzgerald River NP.

White-browed Scrubwren *Sericornis frontalis* 11–15 cm

subsp. *balstoni* · subsp. *mellori* · subsp. *maculatus*

Spread right across Southern Australia, this species has been split into a diverse range of subspecies, nine in all. In this region, three subspecies occur. *maculatus* occurs in the lower South West and is illustrated here with slightly more yellow on the flanks and belly. *mellori* is found along the southern coast to Bremer Bay and partly into the Wheatbelt; it has a white underbody with only pale yellow on the lower flanks and vent, strong black streaks on the chest. *balstoni* occurs from Jurien all the way up to Shark Bay, has less bold streaking on a plain white chest and white flanks and only the vent and lower flank have slight pale yellow. The White-browed Scrub-wren is a bold bird that will defend territory and scold intruders with its rasping chatter. Spends most of its feeding time within the foliage but will go into the lower strata of small trees, rarely in the canopy of tall trees. **Nest:** The nest is a loosely woven dome structure built in the centre of a low dense bush, with a side entry hole mostly low to the ground. It is made from grasses or strips of bark and lined with soft materials like fine grasses, leaves or feathers. Clutch size 2–3. **Similar species:** None really. The only possibility is the Shy Heathwren, as both often occur in the same area. The Heathwren does have a white supercilium eye stripe and also chevrons on the wing but does not have the dark facial patch. Has a bright rust coloured rump. Streaking on the underbody is far more extensive and bolder than on the Scrubwren. The Heathwren is a slightly larger bird and has a different call and as the name implies does not readily show itself nearly as much as a White-browed Scrubwren will. **Status:** Common throughout range, *balsoni* less so in the north. **Where to find**: Not in the inner part of Perth but in the surrounding country and foothills and throughout the rest of the South West wherever there is uncleared thick undergrowth.

Shy Heathwren *Hylacola cauta* subspecies *whitlocki* 13 cm

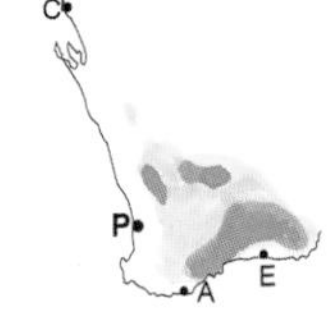

There are four subspecies in Australia and only one in this state, subspecies *whitlocki.* Their range is very habitat based, requiring semi-dense shrub-heath but not as dense as the low heath that Bristlebirds require. Mostly it occurs wherever there are shrubs under mallee such as Broom Bush (*Melaleuca uncinata*). Most of their range is confined to the GSW basically a region from Bullfinch in the north, across to Buntine Reserve near Wubin and down to Dongolocking Reserve and the Stirling Range. East along the coast to the Fitzgerald River NP then Grass Patch and east to Eyre, its limit in WA. Then from Dundas NR and north to Mt Jckson. It is a ground dwelling bird getting nearly all its food needs from the vegetation litter. Shy by name and shy by nature, this is not an easy bird to approach and typically will run away rather than fly. The male has a distinct white supercilium eye stripe with black line through the eye from lores to rear of head. Very strong black streaking on the throat and underbody. Has black and white chevrons on the wings. Rust coloured rump seen clearly. Female is very similar but lacks the intensity of facial colours, the eye stripe is brown not black. The streaking on the throat not so bold and underbody streaks narrower. Call is very musical, a rapid series of up and down notes. When on the ground always cocks its tail at a steep angle. **Similar species:** Rufous Fieldwren which can occur in close proximity to the Heathwren. It lacks the black eye stripe. Streaking marks not quite as broad. All subspecies have a rufous crown not dark brown as in the Shy Heathwren. No white chevrons on the wings. Rump colour is a more subdued chestnut colour. Has mottled dark brown streaking on the brown back. White-browed Scrubwren, but has no rust colouring on rump and rarely cocks tail. Chevrons are smaller, black eye stripe broader. **Nest:** Is a loosely structured dome nest, flattened at the base with a low side entry, invariably placed directly on the ground and normally at the base of a mallee or casuarina bush or under a dense shrub. Clutch 2–3. **Status:** Locally moderately common. Throughout much of the range uncommon. Western Wheatbelt populations threatened with inadequate areas to inhabit. **Where to find:** Dongolocking

Reserve. Wongan Hills. Buntine Reserve. Milton McNeil Reserve. Stirling Range NP. Corakerup NR. Fitzgerald NP. Hyden NR. Throughout much of the Transitional Woodland from the Vermin Fence east of Lake Cronin, all the way across to Dundas Reserve. Some small and rarely visited reserves like North Tarrin Rock have amazingly high densities of Heathwren showing their tenacity to survive in the most drastically changed environment.

Rufous Fieldwren *Calamanthus campestris* 12–13.5 cm

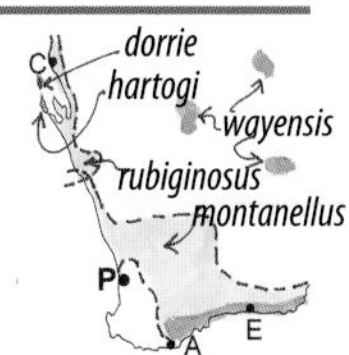

Note: all above are subspecies

A complex group with eight recognised subspecies, one that was considered a separate species in Western Australia, the Western Fieldwren subspecies *montanellus*. Six subspecies occur in WA and five in the GSW, the nominate race *campestris* stopping just short of the eastern boundary of this region. The five included in the GSW are *rubiginosus* along the central west coast from Kalbarri to Exmouth; *wayensis* on salt lakes from Lake Austin in the west to Yeo Lakes in the east and Lake Disappointment in the north and Lake Barlee in the south; *montanellus* south of line from the lower Nullarbor across to Geraldton but not in the very deep wetter South West; *hartogi* on Dirk Hartog Island; and *dorrie* on Dorre Island. Like the Shy Heathwren, this is a shy ground dwelling bird that occurs in low dense heaths feeding mainly on insects gleaned from the ground. When disturbed it will run along the ground with tail cocked high moving fast away from intruders. In the breeding season it will perch on a low bush singing its lovely melodious song. The South West subspecies *montanellus* is normally found in low Kwongan Heath, sometimes in adjacent samphire. The west coastal bird *rubiginosus* has a preference for samphire and low bushes in low dunes that hug the coastline. The inland birds *wayensis* are only found around the perimeters of salt lakes with samphire and adjacent low shrubs. The sexes are almost impossible to split by viewing, if anything the female's facial markings and black streaks are less prominent than the males. The male has a rufous crown, most rufous in the inland birds and darkest on the central west coast birds and least rufous in the South West birds. All have a pale rufous rump not as pronounced or bright as Shy Heathwren. Mantle and lower back varies from pale rufous-brown with pale dark rufous-brown streaking in inland and west coast birds, to plain olive-brown with darker streaking. Call is a plaintive series of notes, not as rapid as Shy Heathrwen and softer. **Nest:** The nest is a round dome structure with finer strands of grasses than Shy Heathwren's and is lined inside with soft fine grasses and leaves. Sometimes built in a depression made by the bird, occasionally built off the ground in the centre of a very dense bush. Clutch size 2–3. **Similar species:** Refer to Shy Heathwren. **Status:** Inland subspecies *wayensis* locally moderately common, west coast subspecies *rubiginosus* locally common, south west subspecies *montanellus* is threatened according to some authorities, but the author believes is vulnerable if any more habitat is lost though where they occur locally they can be moderately common. **Where to find:** West coast species at New Beach. Red Bluff at Kalbarri. Coral Bay. Many coastal heathlands from Jurien Bay all the way to Exmouth. Inland species: Lake Anneen. Lake Disappointment. Lake Carnegie. Yeo Lakes and possibly Plumridge Lakes. South West species: Dongolocking NR. Coblinine NR. Tarrin Rock and North Tarrin Rock NR. Fitzgerald River NP particularly on coastal heath.

Above: Subspecies *montanellus*
Left: Subspecies *rubiginosus* – note the rich chestnut crown and lores

Redthroat *Pyrrholaemus brunneus* 10.5–12.5 cm

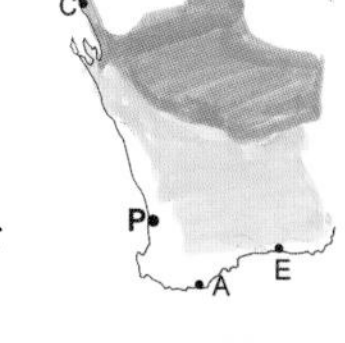

A bird of the semi-arid regions of Australia. Found from as far north as the Ashburton River in the Pilbara right across into the eastern deserts, then south east to the northern part of the Great Victoria Desert and south to the Transitional Woodland Line and most of the drier areas of the Wheatbelt. Its habitat requirements are varied and although common in much of the Mulga Woodland and Transitional Woodland belt it is patchily distributed and found in distinct locations like thick acacia scrub along creek lines in stony country or thick acacia in open mulga. In the Transitional Woodland zone particularly south

Right: female

of Coolgardie, they are found in the understorey bushes of the Salmon Gum Woodland, mostly medium height bushes of the melaleuca group. Its call is well known to many and is an absolute joy to listen to. It is also a great mimic bringing other bird calls into its repertoire, particularly scolding calls of thornbills, or parts of the Pied Butcherbird call. It is a plain brown bird bigger than thornbills or gerygones, the male having a small orange-brown circular throat patch not always easily seen. The young juvenile males do not have this coloured patch but look very similar to the female. Both sexes have a grey-brown back, grey breast and white belly with buff flanks, the female having no orange-brown throat patch. **Nest:** The nest is a dome structure made from bark, fine twigs or grasses; it is quite a compact ball not a loose structure, with a side entry, rarely on the ground like Shy Heathwren's but placed in thick bush above ground usually not more than a metre high and placed in the centre of the dense shrub. It is a sedentary bird. Clutch size normally 3. **Similar species:** None, possible confusion with Gilbert Whistler as they share the same habitat in the southern Transitional Woodland. The Gilbert Whistler is larger with a more upright stance except when alert or agitated and it bobs up and down. Has a larger throat patch, distinct black lores and a thicker whistler type bill. Calls totally different. **Status:** Moderately common throughout range. Now scarce to rare in the inner Wheatbelt. **Where to find:** Nearest to Perth, Wongan Hills area. Some northern Wheatbelt reserves like Billyacatting. Chiddarcooping NR. Buntine NR. Reserves east of Dalwallinu. Low coastal dunes along Gladstone coastline. Throughout the Mulga Region down to the eastern Wheatbelt in reserves like Lake Gaunter near Hyden.

Weebill *Smicronis brevirostris* subspecies *occidentalis* 8.5 cm

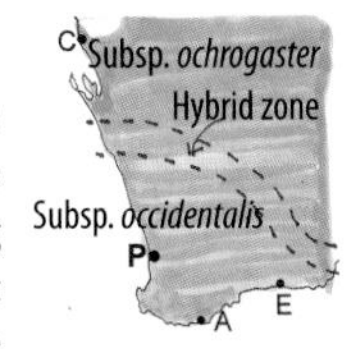

Australia's smallest bird, although if the emu-wren did not have such a long tail it would be the smallest. Weebills are found throughout the GSW in varied habitats. There are four subspecies with three occurring in Western Australia and two within the GSW region. The South West birds *occidentalis* have a darker upperbody, slight faint streaking on the throat and upper breast and overall are darker than the subspecies *ochrogaster* of the Pilbara and the upper Murchison. The Pilbara birds have no faint streaking at all on the throat and upper chest. Further north into the Kimberley, the subspecies *flavescens* are very different having a bright yellow underbody. All Weebills have an orange-chestnut tinge to the lores. When feeding, Weebills spend nearly all their time gleaning lurps and insects off leaves. You can actually hear them peck at lurps on leaves as they make their way through the foliage. Weebills chatter as they communicate with other members of the group as they feed with their call often described as 'I'm a weebill' with the first notes starting high and dropping down. Their preferred habitat in the South West is areas with taller eucalypts and middle

storey shrubs. In the Mulga Woodland they can be anywhere working creek lines or moving through open mulga. **Nest:** They build a suspended nest, normally from the upper branches of eucalypts or acacias. Is a pear shaped domed nest with a top side entry, neatly woven from fine grasses and held to the branches by spiders webbing. Is a more dense structure than the gerygone's or thornbill's nests. Located in the dropping outer branches of eucalypts, similar location to Yellow-rumped Thornbill but harder to find and much smaller. The inside is lined with fine grasses and feathers. Clutch size 1–3. **Similar species:** Possibly Western Thornbill which has longer tail and a more dumpy body than the Weebill. Slight flecking on forehead. No orange flush to lores and no yellow tinge on flanks but buffy colour. Bill slimmer and longer. Call different. **Status:** Common throughout range. **Where to find:** All tall woodlands throughout the GSW as well as the Mulga Region.

Dusky Gerygone *Gerygone tenebrosa* subspecies *christophori* 11.5 cm

Endemic to Western Australia

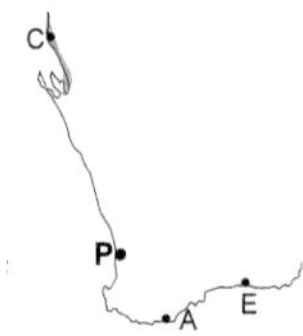

There are two subspecies in Western Australia and the differences are very slight, mainly based on wing and tarsus size. Dusky Gerygones just come within the range of the GSW from Miaboolia Beach near Carnarvon down the mangrove-lined coast to just north of Gladstone. Where the White Mangrove (*Avicennia marina*) is the dominant mangrove, the Dusky Gerygone only inhabits those areas. It is a grey-brown backed gerygone, with a split white eye ring and importantly, a white eye. Slight buff colouring to flanks. Plaintive whistle 'de..dude.. de'. **Nest:** Nests within mangroves; the typical gerygone nest is a neatly woven suspended structure with trailing beard at base, bound to a mangrove branch with spiders webbing and woven bark or plant strips. Lined internally with feathers and soft grasses. Clutch size 2–3. **Similar species:** None in its habitat. Western Gerygone has far more white in the tail and a red eye not white. Bill is slimmer and smaller not as robust as the Dusky Gerygone's. Totally different call. **Status:** Common all along a mangrove band from Carnarvon down to Gladstone and parts of the Shark Bay region. **Where to find:** New Beach. Miaboolia Beach and throughout the mangroves at Carnarvon.

Western Gerygone *Gerygone fusca* subspecies *fusca* 10.5 cm

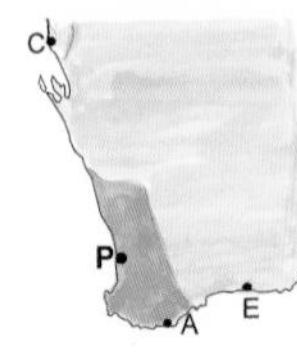

Three subspecies occur in Australia and one in this region, *fusca*. A very common bird found in a variety of woodland and forest habitats. Is considered partly a passage migrant, leaving the deeper colder South West region in autumn and winter and returning in spring to breed. Found in the Jarrah and Karri Forests and Wandoo Woodland and peppermint groves along the south coast. When attending nest to feed young, does varying twists and turns as if chasing insects, never flying straight to the nest. Adult bird has slightly white supercilium eye stripe. Dark red eye and a split orbital eye ring. White to the outer tail feathers, seen well in flight from underneath particularly if it is fanning its tail. Plain grey-brown upperbody and off white underbody. Call melodious, starting high pitched continuing in a descending scale which sounds as if it is not finished, 'ceeeeee…ce..ce..ce. **Nest:** A suspended dome nest typical of gerygones is placed in outer foliage of a eucalypt or mulga tree. Made with fine grasses bound by spiders webbing and lined with plant down or feathers. Clutch size 2–3. **Similar species:** None really; possibly Western Thornbill which is smaller and has no white eye ring or white in the tail. Buff-fawn underbody while the Western Gerygone's is off white. Shorter tail. **Status:** Common throughout the South West. Uncommon to moderately common in the arid regions, particularly in winter. **Where to find:** Anywhere in the Jarrah or Karri Forests or Wandoo Woodland, also in mallee and mulga.

Inland Thornbill *Acanthiza apicalis* 10.5 cm

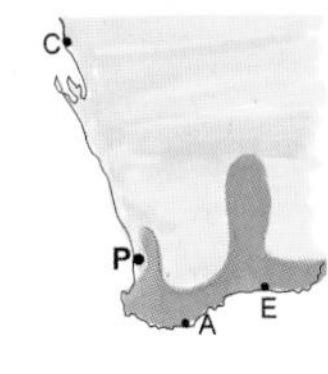

Named 'Inland' because the eastern states birds are found on the eastern side of the great divide while the Brown Thornbill occupies the more humid habitats, but the name is a little misleading for the South West birds which frequent the wettest areas as well as the semi-arid regions of Western Australia. The lower South West birds are the subspecies *apicalis* and their range goes as far north as the central Wheatbelt; the subspecies *whitlocki* covers the mulga and Pilbara region and like most subspecies hybridisation occurs where the ranges overlap. The South West subspecies *apicalis* are the darkest of all the Inland Thornbills and the scalloping on the head is heavier, also the streaking on the breast is much bolder. The subspecies *whitlocki* have paler backs, finer scalloping on the forehead and streaking on the breast. Throat streaking not as contrasting or bold, also the flanks have a paler buff colouring. In the South West, the birds feed in the thick understorey of the forests as well as working the canopies of taller trees. The drier country subspecies *whitlocki* frequent the mulga woodland and will feed in mixed flocks with Chestnut-rumped and Slaty-backed Thornbills, although Inland Thornbills tend to be less gregarious than some of the other thornbills like Western Thornbill and Chestnut-rumped Thornbill. Inland Thornbills in the lower South West tend to cock their tails most of the time, a characteristic that does not occur with Brown Thornbills on the east coast. The calls are pleasant soft whistles with occasional grating notes. Surprisingly it is a good mimic and combines calls of other birds in its repertoire. The adult bird has heavy streaking on the throat and chest. A red eye. Faint horizontal flecking on the forehead. Distinct chestnut rump. Buff flanks. Diffused dark band on tail. **Nest:** Is a loosely structured dome nest with a slightly hooded entry woven to vertical branches or placed in the centre of a prostrate bush. Nests are mostly from 50–120 cm off the ground. Lined with plant down, fine grasses or feathers. Clutch size 2–4. **Similar species:** Chestnut-rumped Thornbill has no streaking on the throat and chest and has a white eye not red. Does overlap territory with deep South West population so be careful. Slaty-backed does have a dark red eye but no streaking on throat or chest and has lateral small streaks on crown. All species have distinctly different calls although Slaty-backed and Chestnut-rumped Thornbills have similarities. **Status:** Common in South West. Moderately common in the arid region of the GSW. **Where to find:** *apicalis* anywhere in the heavier forested region, less so in the Wheatbelt. *whitlocki* along creek lines and in the denser parts of the Mulga Woodland.

Chestnut-rumped Thornbill *Acanthiza uropygialis* 9.8 cm

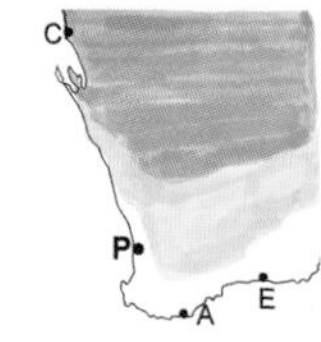

A thornbill of the inland regions of Australia not the lower South West. It ranges from the central Wheatbelt from Corrigin avoiding the west coast until just north of Geraldton up to Manilya and across to central Australia. In the south from Corrigin, sometimes lower, its range runs north east into the desert regions across to the centre. It is the most common specie of thornbill in the Mulga egion, sometimes occurring in mixed flocks with Southern Whiteface and occasionally Slaty-backed Thornbill. Out of the breeding season, feeding parties of thornbills

move through the bush accompanied by different species like Rufous Whistler and Red-capped Robin. Adult birds have a grey-brown upperbody, red eye, chestnut rump, black-brown tail with a white tip, horizontal black and white flecking on the forehead, and plain off white underbody. Feeds in trees but also on the ground. **Nest:** Mostly in hollows in trees, often in larger mulga trees or dead stumps. The nest is still a typical dome structure but the entrance is placed where the hole in the tree is located. Clutch size 2–4. **Similar species:** Slaty-backed Thornbill, which is very similar and requires clear observation but once you know the Slaty-backed you can pick up the pure grey back rather than grey-brown back. The Slaty-backed has a distinct plain dark grey back, no hint of brown. Very fine lateral black streaks are set against the grey crown, unlike the Chestnut Thornbill that has fine horizontal black and white mottling on the forehead, which could be described as scalloping rather than streaks. The eye of the Slaty-backed Thornbill almost looks black, in fact it is a dark red whereas the Chestnut-rumped is white. Slaty-backed has two sets of calls, one is soft and high pitched not dissimilar to Chestnut-rumped so one must be careful if relying on calls. **Status:** Common to very common in the Mulga. Moderately common in other desert regions. **Where to find**: Any of the lower sheep stations once you enter the Mulga Region and much of the drier part of the Wheatbelt Region.

Slaty-backed Thornbill *Acanthiza robustirostris* 10.5 cm

C
P
A
E

Slaty-backed Thornbill virtually covers the same range as the Chestnut-rumped Thornbill but is far less common. Tends to feed less on the ground than Chestnut-rumped but still accompanies them through mulga woodland. It's said that they are not easy to pick from Chestnut-rumped but once you have become familiar with them, the plain slate grey back stands out from the lighter brown grey of the Chestnut-rumped, and the darker head and red eye confirm the difference. Has a slightly thicker bill than the Chestnut-rumped. It has two types of call, one a high pitched soft twittering similar to the Chestnut-rumped and the other stronger more agitated grating call, that is uttered rapidly 'chirp chirp chirp chirp'. The nest location is also different to Chestnut-rumpeds not built in a tree hollow but a dome nest built in a low bush such as an eremophila bush or sometimes in a dense mulga tree. **Status:** Can be moderately common locally but generally uncommon throughout its range. **Where to find:** Particularly stations in the southern Mulga Region from Tallering Station in the west right across to Yeo Lakes in the east. Does not favour dune country with acacia. Specific stations. In the Paynes Find – Yalgoo region the following stations: Maranalgo. Thundelarra. Muralgarra. Gabyon. Carlaminda. In the Cue region: Nallan and Austin Downs stations. Found also in mulga country in the Pilbara region.

Slaty-backed Thronbill Photo above: Graeme Chapman

Western Thornbill *Acanthiza inornata* 9 cm Endemic to Western Australia

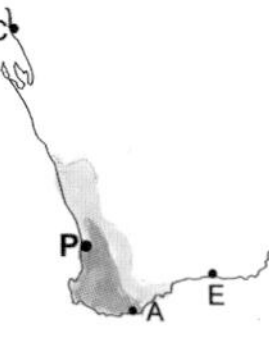

Found in the heavily forested regions of the South West. Feeds in the middle strata of tall eucalypts and occasionally in lower shrubs. Has an olive-brown back, slightly darker brown on wings, white eye, fine flecking on the forehead not always clear, orange-brown tinge on the lores, underbody cream-olive, short tail. Call varies and is generally softer than most thornbills with also a rapid 'seep..seep..seep..seep'. Its range extends from Hill River in the north and follows the edge of the Jarrah Forest and inner Wandoo Woodland through to Boyagin Rock, down to the Stirling Range and across to Pallinup River as its furthest east location. Often not as easy to get as many of the other smaller passerines, many visitors on brief trips miss out or overlook this small endemic. **Nest:** Is a dome structure with top side entry, lined with soft bark or fur or feathers, placed in various locations, within drooping foliage on eucalypts but more often wedged behind loose bark or in a crevice between vertical limbs which is a common location in the Darling Range. Clutch size 2–3. **Similar species:** None. **Status:** Generally uncommon but can be moderately common in some areas. **Where to find:** Darling Scarp within the Jarrah Forest, Karri Forest and Wandoo Woodland.

Slender-billed Thornbill *Acanthiza iredalei iredalei* 10 cm

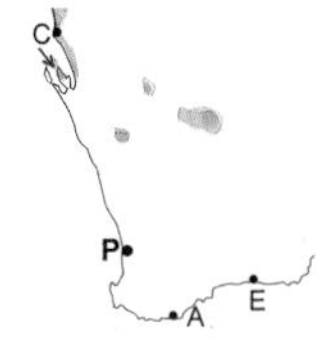

There are three subspecies in Australia and only one in the GSW, namely *iredalei*. This thornbill lives its life entirely in samphire and bluebush habitats. In the Nullarbor it is found throughout the region where bluebush has not been heavily grazed but alas much of its habitat on the West Australian side of the Nullarbor has been greatly affected by the grazing of sheep. The other populations in Western Australia are confined to some of the larger ephemeral salt lakes and a band of costal samphire on the mid west coast. The range is fragmented, with populations on the west central coast from Lake MacLeod down to Hamelin Bay and a population on Peron Peninsula. Other populations occur on Lake Anneen and Lake Austin. Also Lake Barlee, Lake Ballard, Lake Way and Lake Throssell. Also in the Yalgoo area. None of these however match the numbers that can be found on the central eastern Nullarbor, particularly on the South Australian side. The Slender-billed Thornbill is one of the smallest thornbills. It has a longish bill for its size, pale underbody tinged buff-lemon yellow on the flanks, strongest on the rump but far paler yellow than Yellow-rumped Thornbill. Pale grey-brown back with faint mottled throat almost not visible. Black and white mottling on forehead and lores is the most distinct feature. Has a white eye. Out of the breeding season forms small feeding parties moving through the bluebush or samphire. The Slender-billed Thornbill found in mid western Australia has a yellower underbody and a greener rump. The upperbody is pale olive-grey rather than dark olive as in eastern subspecies *rosiinae*. **Nest:** Is a round dome structure of very loose grasses sometimes seaweed when near the coast, placed near the top of a samphire or bluebush shrub. Clutch size normally 3. **Similar species:** Buff-rumped Thornbill subspecies *reguloides*, but that does not occur in this state. **Status:** Moderately common south of Carnarvon. Uncommon in all other Western Australian locations. Moderately common on the central and eastern Nullarbor.

Photo Graeme Chapman

Yellow-rumped Thornbill *Acanthiza chrysorrhoa chrysorrhoa* 11 cm

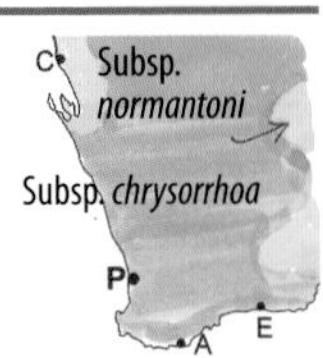

Mainly a ground dwelling thornbill although rarely found on open plains; requires open woodland where it will occasionally forage in trees but most of its time is spent feeding on the ground. One of the easiest thornbills to identify with its bright yellow rump, black crown with white spotting, diffused supercilium stripe and black eye stripe with white spotting on ear coverts, slight buff flanks, olive-brown back. When in flight yellow rump stands out clearly against dark black-brown tail and brown back. It is the largest of the thornbills, and is a sedentary species rarely moving far from its territory except in arid zones where it will move after bad seasons. Often its tinkling contact call leads one to the birds and, out of the breeding season, one can see the small feeding parties hopping across the ground, they don't walk. Found throughout the GSW from the tall forests of the lower South West, through the Wheatbelt and into the Mulga Region. Their range stretches to the Pilbara and across central Australia but avoids the Nullarbor. There are four subspecies in Australia with two in Western Australia, subspecies *chrysorrhoa* in the South West and mid west WA and

normantoni in the eastern parts of central Western Australia. The western birds tend to be pale olive-brown rather than olive-brown and the rump is paler yellow but they have more buff colouring on the underbody than the eastern birds *leighi* and *leachi*. **Nest:** The nest is extremely large for a thornbill, unlike any other and perhaps one of the easiest nests to find. Various trees are used in the South West especially Marri trees, and in the Wheatbelt the sheoak trees are a common location. In the Mulga Region often in Kurrajong trees; the common denominator with all these trees is that they have dense foliage that often droops down in thick clusters of leaves. The Yellow-rumped Thornbill builds at least one but often two false entry holes and false nesting chambers. The main chamber is at the base of the structure. They may work on the nest in the pre-breeding season taking up to 2–3 weeks to complete it. Clutch size 3–4. **Similar species:** None. **Status:** Common in the South West. Moderately common in parts of the Wheatbelt and Mulga Region. **Where to find:** Throughout the GSW except a narrow coastal band south of Carnarvon which is dominated by samphire.

Southern Whiteface *Aphelocephala leucopsis* 11.5 cm

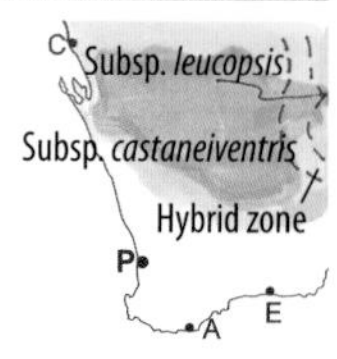

The most common of all the whitefaces, found in the semi-arid and arid areas of the GSW Region. There are two subspecies both occurring in Western Australia, *castaneiventris* and *leucopsis*, there being a hybrid zone between the two subspecies. *castaneiventris* is found from Carnarvon across to the edge of the Victoria Desert and the Nullarbor and *leucopsis* is found through the rest of central Australia. The subspecies *castaneiventris* that covers the bulk of the Mulga Region in the GSW is the more attractive of the two subspecies, having a distinct chestnut flank and the head markings are cleaner with more demarcation around the head with its pure white throat, forehead and underbody, whereas *leucopsis* has pale grey-buff underparts. Feeds almost entirely on the ground, hopping all the time and picking insects as it goes although seeds make up a reasonable part of their diet, hence the finch-like bill which can crack small seed. **Nest:** They nest in a variety of locations but the vast majority of nests in Western Australia are placed in a hollow or a crevice between trunks, mostly in mulga trees. Close to the entry hole they wedge grasses and twigs to form a base for the nest, and line it with feathers. Clutch size 3–4. **Similar species:** Banded Whiteface, refer to text on Banded Whiteface. **Status:** One of the most common birds of the Mulga Region. **Where to find:** All stations from north and east of the Transitional Woodland line to the Gascoyne catchment across to Warburton and south to the Nullarbor.

Banded Whiteface *Aphelocephala nigricincta* 10 cm

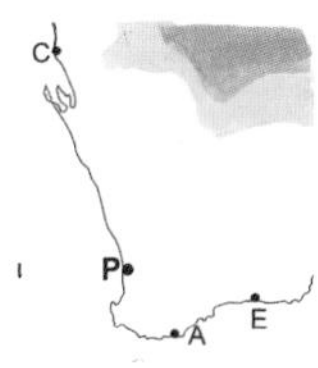

The Banded Whiteface has, as its name implies, a black band running through the centre of the breast. It also has a chestnut mantle, which is clearly seen in flight. On the flanks there is also a diffused area of chestnut. The head is similar to Southern Whiteface having the white forehead and grey-brown crown, but the colour is lighter and bleeds into chestnut on the nape. The tips of the tail feathers are white. The type of habitat where certain species of a genus live can be intriguing, no less so than with the Banded Whiteface and Chestnut-breasted Whiteface. We will just concentrate on Banded Whiteface as the other specie occurs in South Australia. Banded Whiteface can be found in various habitats. Over the years the author has found them in three types of habitat in Western Australia. One is open stony country with little shrub growth mainly north and south of Meekatharra. Another is open country often where chenopod plants (samphire etc.) are growing with scant vegetation; sometimes it only needs to be a small area such as on the southern boundary of Nallan Station; others are more extensive such as on the northern part of the David Carnegie track in the northern Victoria Desert. The third type of habitat is in recently burnt country particularly in desert regions, for example on the Canning Stock Route and also the Gary Highway. However in this state they are not as prevalent as in the Simpson and Strzelecki Deserts. **Nest:** The nest is a bulky dome structure with a wide entry hole on the side, placed in thick foliage, typically the thorny Kurara bush. The nest is lined with soft feathers. Clutch size 2–3. **Similar species:** Southern Whiteface, which has a plain grey-brown back not a chestnut back. This is often all you see of the Banded Whiteface as it flies away from you but its back shows up clearly as different from the more common Southern Whiteface. The Southern Whiteface has no black band on the breast. However their territories can overlap so one must be aware of that. **Status:** Uncommon throughout the north eastern part of the GSW. **Where to find:** In the GSW around the Cue area and due south east of Gascoyne Junction.

Photo Graeme Chapman

Spotted Pardalote *Pardalotus punctatus* subspecies *punctatus* and *xanthopyge* 9 cm

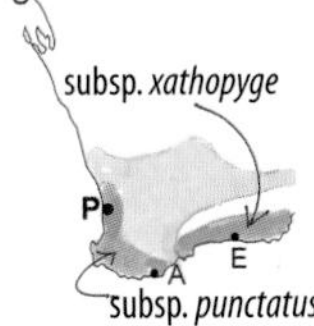

There are three subspecies in Australia and two occur in the west, although there is hybridisation in the south east region. The two subspecies were once separated as two distinct species, one being a bird of the wetter forests of the South West and one a bird of the mallee. Spotted Pardalote can be found in the heavier wooded regions of the South West as far north as Badgingarra and then east across to Coolgardie and down to the coast at Esperance, in all areas within this boundary line. The subspecies *xanthopyge* has a preference for the mallee regions. The birds in the far eastern mallee of WA call differently than the South West forest birds *punctatus* and have a slight variation in their call, whereas the mallee bird *xanthopyge*

has a single high pitched but soft call repeated several times and easy to imitate to call up the bird. Both subspecies nest in hollows in the ground unlike Striated Pardalotes that nest in tree hollows, although the author has seen Striated nest in a hole in a limestone wall in Perth. Both sexes play an active role in building the nest but the female does the final nest chamber structure and lining. Their nest site often gives them away as one is walking or driving slowly down a track; they will fly out of the nest hollow when there is imminent danger. The female has a more subdued black-grey crown and spotting does not stand out as much. The throat is not as bright yellow as the male. Overall colouring very similar but colours less contrasting nor as bright. **Nest**: Is built at the end of an excavated tunnel, normally 30–80 cm long. The end nest chamber consists of a ball of dry grasses or narrow strands of bark woven into a tight ball. Clutch size 3–4. **Similar species:** Striated Pardalote, which has no spots on the black crown just faint white streaking mostly at rear of crown. No white spotting on wing but shows a single red dot at the top of the white edging on the wing. No red or yellow on rump, just beige colouring. Larger supercilium white eye stripe with frontal part near the bill yellow. Mantle is plain grey-brown not scalloped brown. **Status:** Moderately common throughout range, more common in the heavier forested areas. **Where to find:** Subspecies *punctatus*: within the Jarrah Forest but more so in the Wheatbelt and Wandoo Woodland. Found in Dongolocking NR Dryandra Woodland NR Subspecies *xanthopyge*: common in the mallee in Fitzgerald River NP Lake Magenta. Cape Arid. Eastern Wheatbelt reserves and within the eastern Transitional Woodland.

Striated Pardalote *Pardalotus striatus* subspecies *substriatus* 9–12 cm

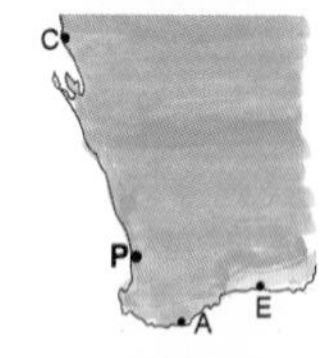

There are six subspecies in Australia. In Western Australia there are two but only one occurs in the GSW, subspecies *substriatus*. The Striated Pardalote is slightly larger than the Spotted Pardalote and nests mostly in tree hollows. It breeds not only in spring but can breed in middle and late summer, one of the few passerines to do so. Often seen calling

at the very top of a tree when holding territory. It feeds on lurps and other insects gleaning them off leaves and bark. Often feeding high in the canopy which makes them hard to see but they do come down to lower shrubs. Throughout their range they are mainly associated with eucalypts and in the drier regions are more common along river systems. The calls of each of the subspecies throughout Australia vary quite a lot, so anyone visiting this state will hear slightly different calls to the eastern states birds or birds from the tropics. The female is hard to split from the male and the only feature is that the crown is black-grey rather pure black and slightly blotched. **Nest**: Is placed in a hollow in a tree. Prefers to use hollows that are only just wide enough for pardalotes to enter. The actual nest is a mass of dry grasses placed at the base of the hollow. Clutch size 3–4. **Similar species:** Refer to Spotted Pardalote. **Status:** Common throughout most of the range except ephemeral lakes. **Where to find:** Perth region. The Darling Range. In the Jarrah Forest and Karri Forest. Throughout the Wheatbelt. Along the Murchison and Gascoyne Rivers.

Red-browed Pardalote *Pardolotus rubricatus rubricatus* 9–11 cm

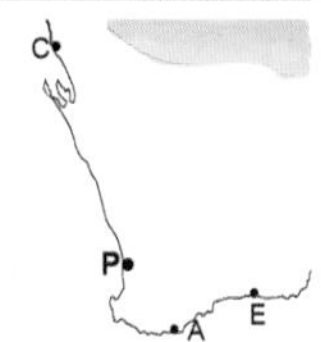

A pardalote of the arid regions, particularly along river and creek systems where it builds its nest and feeds in the eucalypts and other trees that line the river; it can be found away from rivers but that is the common location for this species. There are two subspecies and only one comes into this region, the nominate race *rubricatus*. It only just comes into the GSW Region in the far north in the Gascoyne and across to Laverton and east through the Yeo Lakes area. It has a plaintive call 'daaa de de dit….daa de de dit….daa de de dit', the calls are softer in the west and the centre than those of the east coast birds. It will call even when the temperatures are very high. Red-browed Pardalote have a black crown with small white spots. The yellow supercilium eye stripe has an orange-red dot near the bill. Its back is olive-brown with mottling in the feathers. The rump and upper tail is olive-yellow and there is a small faint patch of yellow on the breast. **Nest**: Is similar to Spotted Pardolote but often on higher banks alongside dry river beds. **Similar species:** Striated Pardalote, which has a black crown but no white spots just a few faint white streaks. Has a red dot on the side of the wings and clear white band on the primaries. Red-browed does not have but has yellow tingeing in the centre of the wings. Lacks the bright yellow throat and has a small red patch on the front of the eyebrow. Spotted Pardalote is not found in the same region as the Red-browed. **Status:** Uncommon in the Gascoyne, becoming more common further north and in the central desert regions. **Where to find:** In this region, the Gascoyne and part of the upper Murchison.

Photo Graeme Chapman

Red Wattlebird *Anthochaera carunculata* subspecies *woodwardi* 35 cm

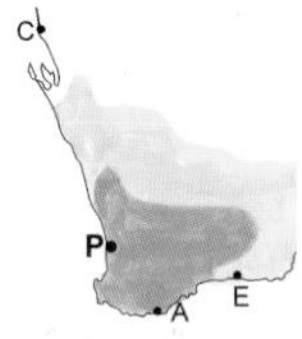

The Red Wattlebird is the largest honeyeater in the GSW, and has two distinct red wattles protruding from the base of the lores and a yellow belly and vent. Feeds mostly on flowering plants for nectar but also eats invertebrates. The range of flowering plants is diverse including banksias, bottlebrush, flowering eucalypts and grasstrees. Found throughout much of the GSW, its northern limit basically following the outer limits of the Transitional Woodland and the limit of most banksias. There are records as far as Goongarrie north of Kalgoorlie and beyond, in the east of their range and as far north as Billabong Roadhouse. Red Wattlebirds are pugnacious, driving off smaller honeyeaters from their feeding territory. Some remain sedentary but with many there is partial migration to the north leaving the South West Region in April and May when the greatest number of banksias are flowering, and then move south in early spring in August and September when a greater range of flowering plants are in bloom in the south. Their calls vary from noisy, harsh and grating calls to loud squeaks uttered regularly. They occur in heavy forested areas as well as open heaths. There are 3 subspecies in Australia; *woodwardi* in South West Australia is smaller than the other subspecies, has a smaller wing length and the yellow underbelly is brighter. **Nest**: Is a shallow cup of larger twigs on the outside and smaller twigs on the inner lining, being finally lined with soft grasses or wool or feathers. Located in various bush or tree species, often in banksias and dryandras. Clutch size 2–3. **Similar species:** Western Wattlebird, which is smaller. No red wattles. Finer and longer curved bill. No yellow on the belly. Has chestnut in the wings, seen very well in flight. Eye brown not red. Longer down curved facial patch. Call similar but certainly not as rasping or harsh, more like gurgling chatter that continues for a longer period. **Status:** Common throughout the lower South West Region, not so common in the outer regions to the Transitional Woodland. **Where to find:** Found throughout Perth in gardens and parks, particularly the hills. In the Jarrah Forest. All along the southern coast to Cape Arid and beyond, although nowhere near as plentiful in the Esperance region as Western Wattlebird. Range passes east of Kalgoorlie.

Western Wattlebird *Anthochaera lunulate* 30–33 cm

Endemic to Western Australia

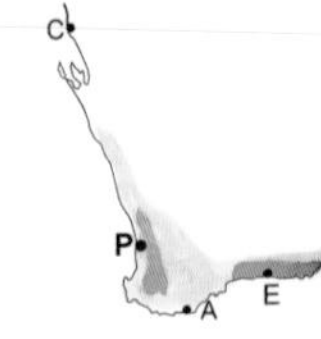

Now classed as a separate species from the Little Wattlebird of the east coast. The Western Wattlebird has a longer stouter bill, much darker and less streaked crown and back, the eye is distinctly red not brown. Has a slightly larger cheek patch that contrasts with the dark crown, more so than the eastern Little Wattlebird. Feeds on nectar and insects. Can share the same territory as Red Wattlebirds but generally avoids flowering areas where Red Wattlebirds occur, as they

are the dominant bird and extremely pugnacious. Does not travel to the drier areas in the north or the north east as does the Red Wattlebird; its limit is restricted to the wetter zone which follows the eastern edge of the Jarrah-Marri Forest and most of the dense dryandra heaths to Eneabba, down to Tutanning and further down to the Stirling Range and across to Cape Arid and beyond. Throughout most of their range they are not a common bird. In the Darling Range they have a preference for *Dryandra sessilis* and can be locally common where it grows. However, Western Wattlebirds can be common from the Fitzgerald River National Park through to Esperance and Cape Arid where they are the dominant large honeyeater and extremely common in the township of Esperance. One of the major plant species that attracts them to this region is the Showy Banksia (*Banksia speciosa*), which has an extensive flowering period. There are of course many other flowering plants that they feed off, particularly the dryandras (now grouped under Banksia). **Nest:** Mostly in dryandra and banksia bushes. Nest is similar in construction to Red Wattlebird but smaller. Clutch size 1–3. **Similar species:** Refer to Red Wattlebird. **Status:** Uncommon throughout most of its range except the southern coast from Bremer Bay to Cape Arid. **Where to find:** Kings Park occasionally in the botanic gardens section. Yanchep NR. Bungendore NR. in late spring. Heathlands in Dryandra NR in late spring. The Fitzgerald River NP. The town of Esperance where it is very common.

Spiny-cheeked Honeyeater *Acanthagenys rufogularis* 23–26 cm

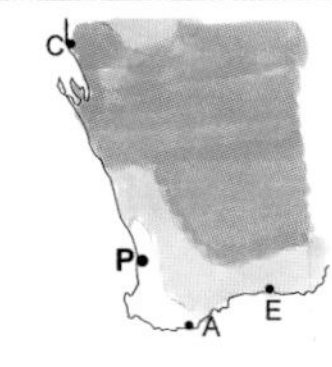

A large honeyeater of the semi-arid regions within the GSW. Found in a variety of habitats including Mulga Woodland, dry river creek lines, breakaway country, and heath. However it is most common throughout the Mulga Region feeding on a variety of flowering plants particularly the erymophilas, amyemas (mistletoes) and grevilleas. It is a semi-nomadic species moving to areas where plants are flowering. There are also some movements north and south; little is known about their partial migrations but flocks can be seen moving in late November south through the northern Wheatbelt from the drier regions north. They do not occur in the wetter South West. The Spiny-cheeked Honeyeater's name relates to the small feathers that grow from the side of the neck, not easily seen. The important features are the distinct bi-coloured bill, black at the tip and pink at the base, orange-pink throat, pink eye ring, strong bare pink coloured gape, white spines on side of neck, crown and mantle olive-brown with black scalloping. Black flecking on the white lower breast and belly. Long tail with white tip. The call is a pleasant series of gurgling and bubbling notes normally given perched on bare branches at the top of a tree. **Nest:** Is a deep thin walled cup suspended from branches. Constructed with long dry grasses and fine twigs bound with spiders webbing and lined with any soft material available. Clutch size 2–3. **Similar species:** None. **Status:** Uncommon in the Wandoo section of the Wheatbelt. Moderately common in the central, eastern and northern Wheatbelt. Moderately common in the Transitional Woodland. Locally common in the Mulga Woodland particularly along creek lines. **Where to find:** Northern Wheatbelt reserves like: Buntine NR. Billyacatting NR. Mollerin NR. Chiddarcooping NR. Wallyahmoning NR. Goongarrie NR. Most stations north of the Transitional Woodland line right past the boundaries of the GSW.

Yellow-throated Miner *Manorina flavigula* subspecies *wayensis* 28 cm

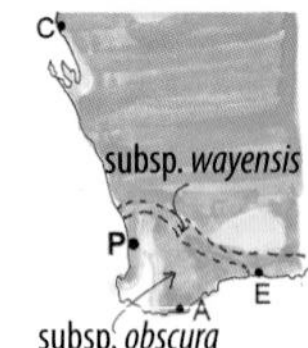

There are 5 subspecies of Yellow-throated Miner in Australia. In the GSW there are two, *obscura* and *wayensis*. *obscura* occurs as a line from Moora across the central northern Wheatbelt through Kellerberrin across to the Australian Bight basically all areas below this line in the South West but it's a subjective line and obviously hybrids occur. The differences involve subtle changes in the colour of the back and upper breast but in the context of this book it really is not important; suffice to say that *obscura* occurs in the lower part of the Wheatbelt to Esperance and *wayensis* north of this region into the semi-arid and arid zone. We will discuss the range as combined. On the Swan Coastal Plain before European settlement Yellow-throated Miners were more common but numbers have reduced greatly. They are found as far south as Bunbury. They avoid the heavy Jarrah Forest area but come around its eastern boundary where it abuts the Wheatbelt, down to the coast just west of Albany and throughout the rest of the GSW Region. Its distribution stretches all the way north to the Kimberley where the subspecies *lutea* occurs. Yellow-throated Miners are gregarious birds rarely found alone. They have little colour save the bright yellow bill and distinct yellow eye ring which extends to the rear of the eye. They have a dark cheek patch that contrasts with the yellow eye patch. In flight the lighter grey back and rump contrasts with the darker wings and dark tail. They are highly aggressive to intruding birds and group together in defence of territories, giving their raucous calls. **Nest**: Is a thin walled cup suspended on a horizontal fork, consisting of dry grasses and fine twigs bound with spiders webbing and lined with soft materials.

Clutch size 2. **Similar species:** None. **Status:** Uncommon in the Swan Coastal Plain. Uncommon in the Mulga (subspecies *wayensis*), occasionally locally common. Common in the northern, central and eastern Wheatbelt. Extremely common in the Esperance to Cape Arid area and would be the most common bird of that region. **Where to find:** In the Perth region locally common in parts of Pinjarra. Occasionally in the Armadale Golf Course and Whiteman Park. Found throughout the Wheatbelt particularly moving along roadside verges. Easily seen in Esperance (subspecies *obscura*).

Singing Honeyeater *Lichenostomus virescens virescens* 19 cm

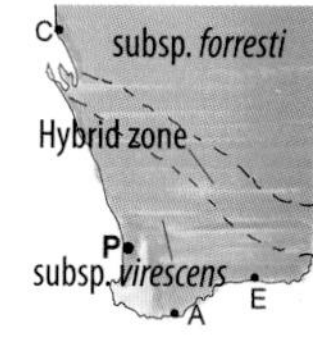

The Singing Honeyeater can be found throughout most of the semi-arid and arid parts of Australia. There are 4 subspecies in Australia all with small subtle differences; subspecies *virescens* covers much of the GSW, hybridising with *forresti* from a line roughly from Shark Bay across through the Wheatbelt and across and down to Eyre. They are very common in Perth and have adapted well to the urban environment. They rarely enter the central parts of the Jarrah and Karri Forests, preferring more open woodland. They are at

home on the Swan Coastal Plain as they are in our driest desert regions. In the South West there is little movement, with this species being mainly sedentary. Like most honeyeaters, they feed on both nectar and insects but their percentage of insect intake is much higher than nectar, which is a reversal of many of the honeyeaters. **Nest**: Is a shallow cup of twined bark and grasses with spiders webbing bound from the rim to a fork. Clutch size 2–3. **Similar species:** In this state none. On the east coast both Mangrove and Varied Honeyeater are very similar. **Status:** Common to very common throughout most of the GSW. Uncommon along the southern coast. **Where to find:** Throughout Perth and most of the Swan Coastal Plain. Most of the Wheatbelt and any region in the Mulga Region and coastal belt.

White-eared Honeyeater *Lichenostomus leucotis* subspecies *novaenorciae* 17–20 cm

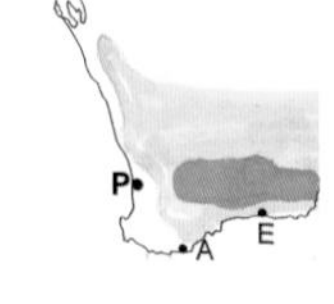

Three subspecies in Australia; only one in the GSW, subspecies *novaenorciae* . The differences are minor with the western birds having shorter wings and smaller ear patch. On the east coast White-eared Honeyeaters not only occur in dry areas but also in wet-sclerophyll forests, which they certainly do not in Western Australia. In the GSW they are found in distinct habitats. In the Wandoo Woodland region they occur in patches of heath but less so within pure stands of open Wandoo and Powder-bark Wandoo. Also in the Wandoo Woodland they occur in sheoak woodland but not exclusively they are also common in areas of mallee and heath. Its strong scolding 'cheeew…cheeew…cheeew'; is often the first sign they are in the area. The Western Australian birds are nervous and will skulk and hide when pursued. They are a medium sized honeyeater bigger than, say the Yellow-plumed Honeyeater. Their range extends from inland of Geraldton south to Broomehill and across to Twilight Cove, and then north and east of these areas to the edge of the main eucalypt belt. **Nest**: Is thicker walled than those of many honeyeaters and quite deep, often not far from the ground in either shrubs growing in open heath or taller shrubs in mallee. Clutch size 2–3. **Similar species:** None. **Status:** Common in some southern central Wheatbelt reserves but not on the coast. Moderately common in the Transitional Woodland east of the Vermin Fence east of Hyden and Lake King. **Where to find:** Wongan Hills. Buntine NR. Billyacatting NR. Tutanning NR. Boyagin NR. Dryandra NR. Tarrin Rock NR both north and south blocks. Dragon Rocks NR. Lake Magenta NR. Dunn NR.

Purple-gaped Honeyeater *Lichenostomus cratitius* subspecies *occidentalis* 16–19 cm

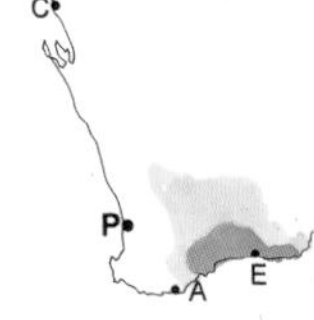

Two subspecies, one in South Australia *cratitius* on Kangaroo Island, the other in Western Australia, Victoria and south west NSW. In the GSW their preferred habitat is mallee. They also have a close association with granite outcrops, feeding on the mallees that surround the bases of many of the larger granite rocks, particularly those within the Transitional Woodland belt between Hyden and Norseman and up to Coolgardie. The purple gape that their common name is derived from is not easy to see but it contrasts well with their plumed lores and yellow throat streak. They are a very active bird and their rapid chatter around flowering mallees, particularly in the breeding season when defending territories, fills the air. Their range is now quite fragmented as much of the mallee has been cleared but even in small patches of about 600 acres they can still survive and remain there as sedentary birds. Their range has now been reduced; a few birds remain in the northern Wheatbelt mostly centred in the mid and southern zone of the Wheatbelt. **Nest:** The nest is a small delicate deep cup made of woven grasses and fine bark held together with spiders webbing with egg sacks often surrounding the cup. Lined with any available soft material such as plant down or wool. Normally suspended between two vertical branches in a dense bush, mainly from 1 to 2 metres above ground. Clutch size 2–3. **Similar species:** None although for those starting birding maybe Yellow-plumed which has no grey crown, has black streaking on a fawn breast not yellow throat and breast, no dark lores. **Status:** Common throughout its range. **Where to find:** The following Wheatbelt reserves: Chinocup NR. Corackerup NR. Northern Stirling Range NP. Fitzgerald River NP. Lake Magenta NR. Dragon Rocks. NR. Dunn Rock NR. Tarin Rock NP. Also from Hyden all the way across to Dundas NR mainly at the base of granite outcrops like McDermid Rock and Disappointment Rock on the Hyden – Norseman road. Along Salt River road to the northern Stirling Range boundary.

Grey-headed Honeyeater *Lichenostomus keartlandi* 13–16 cm

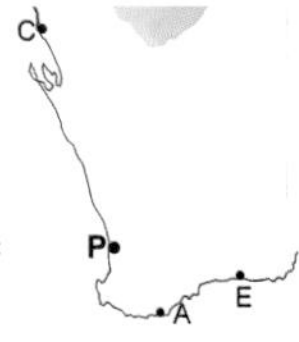

Rarely enters the GSW Region as this is a bird of the arid regions of Australia, coming to the coast only in Western Australia. A nomadic species of the deserts and more sedentary in the Pilbara region. In the deserts, moving to areas where there has been abundant rain. Very common in the Pilbara particularly along creek lines. Found in the desert regions when Holly-leaved Grevillea (*Grevillea wickhamii*) is in full flower, then hundreds will congregate in those areas. An attractively plumaged honeyeater with its blue-grey head, black lores with bright yellow submoustachial stripe at the base of the lores. Yellow throat and upper breast and grey mantle. Pugnacious around flowering plants, chasing off rival feeders. It does occasionally come to the far north corner of the GSW. **Nest**: Is a fine thin walled, deep, suspended nest normally placed between two horizontal branches. Clutch size 2. **Similar species:** Possibly Grey-fronted that overlaps the territory but has no grey on the crown, but olive-green. No dark facial patch the most obvious difference. No yellow on throat but beige with pale yellow streaks. **Status:** Common north of this region. **Where to find**: The Pilbara and desert regions, occasionally north of the Gascoyne River catchment.

Grey-fronted Honeyeater *Lichenostomus plumulus plumulus* 14–16 cm

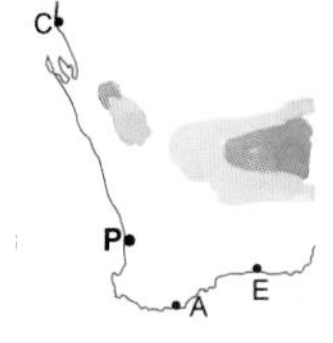

The subspecies *plumulus* occationally comes into the GSW in the north and north eastern areas, from Hamelin Pool down through a narrow band following the Transitional Woodland down to Ninghan Station and White Wells; then a gap until its primary range which is far more extensive from Sandstone east right across the Victoria Desert and south to the Trans Line at Zanthus, north to Warburton. Their habitat is diverse in the west from flowering tall eucalypts to mallee as well as hakeas, eremophilas and grevilleas. **Nest**: Is similar to Grey-headed Honeyeater. Clutch size 2. **Similar species:** Yellow-plumed Honeyeater. Now these 2 species can be tricky as too their territoryies which in the north and north east part of the Wheatbelt region almost connects, although few Yellow-plumed get to the northern Wheatbelt or beyond. The Yellow-plumed Honeyeater's plume turns to a point and is more raised from the neck and longer. The black border shows clean and contrasting against the yellow plume. Yellow-plumed has stronger darker black-grey streaking on a white underbody. The Grey-fronted has weak grey-brown streaking to a grey-white underbody, not always yellow tinged as described in many books. The calls are different but both have a range of calls, the dawn call is clearly different. To describe them in detail is too difficult, however the Yellow-plumed is more melodic but still has harsh calls at times like the Grey-fronted. **Status:** The western populations from Hamelin Pool south are

far less common than the northern Goldfields and become more numerous as one travels into the Great Victoria Desert. **Where to find:** Between the 40 km and 80 km range north of the Murchison Bridge but scarce. From Yalgoo to White Wells scarce. Further west, better chances along the Leonora to Laverton road and then very common on the Warburton road.

Yellow-plumed Honeyeater *Litchenostomus ornatus* 15–18 cm

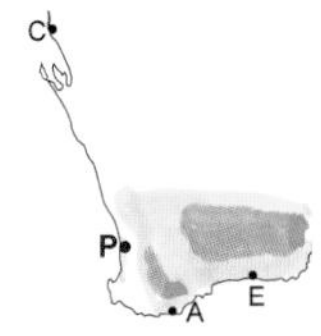

In the South West Region the Yellow-plumed Honeyeater has lost much of its former territory. It was known to be common in the Wongan Hills region and the northern central Wheatbelt particularly around Kellerberrin but now it frequents the central Wheatbelt reserves. One of its favoured habitats is the Wandoo Woodland, also reserves like Dryandra Woodland Nature Reserve. It is by far the most common honeyeater in this area with high population densities. It also ranges across the eastern Wheatbelt through the Transitional Woodland to Dundas NR where it is common throughout much of that range. In the Wandoo Woodland it feeds both in the canopy of the Wandoo and on the low understorey like the Sandplain Poison, although interestingly it feeds less in the heath where other honeyeaters are dominant like New Holland, White-eared, Tawny-crowned and White–cheeked Honeyeaters. Yellow-plumed Honeyeater's calls are varied and territorial disputes are common, with family groups defending breeding and feeding territories strongly. Like New Holland Honeyeaters and other honeyeaters, they will warn all birds of their kind when hawks or falcons are flying into their territory, the fast staccato sound spreading across the woodland from one bird to another. Warning calls vary and a snake alarm call is different again, not so high pitched, a slower harsh pitching. **Nest**: Is a small shallow cup of matted dry grasses and fine twigs lined with soft plant down and bound with spiders webbing. The nest is suspended from thin branches. Height can vary markedly even in the same area; one nest can be in a low gastrolobium bush and then another nest a few metres away can be on the outer suspended branches of a tall Wandoo tree some 8 metres high. Clutch size 2–3 . **Similar species:** None in the central and eastern Wheatbelt. On the north and eastern periphery of their range the very similar Grey-fronted Honeyeater occurs, refer to that species for details. **Status:** Overall moderately common. Locally very common. **Where to find:** Throughout the eastern boundary of the Darling Range where the Wandoo and Powder-bark Wandoo abut the Jarrah Forest. Found in Boyagin Rock NR. Dryandra Woodland NR. Dongolocking NR. Mission Road NR. Kojonup. Northern Stirling Range along Salt River road where there are patches of Wandoo.

White-plumed Honeyeater *Litchenostomus penicillatus* subspecies *carteri* 14–18 cm

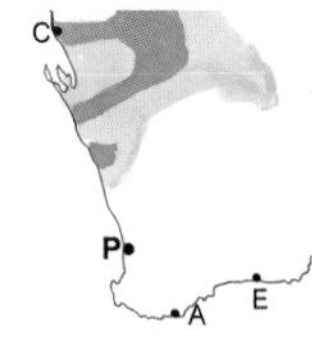

Found in the northern regions of the GSW. When one looks at distribution maps particularly for honeyeaters, one could easily think that they all occur in the same habitat but that is not always the case. White-plumed are an example, you rarely find them in open dry mulga where other honeyeaters occur. White-plumed are found wherever there are tall eucalypts normally along watercourses and wherever there is a body of permanent water. Their favoured habitat is riparian vegetation where the Red River Gum (*E. camaldulensis*) is the principal tree, in fact so much so that its distribution throughout much of western and central Australia is governed by the distribution of this tree and also the Coolabah tree (*E. victrix*). The subspecies *carteri* is found as far south as Mingenew. It is the common town bird of Geraldton and is very common along the Murchison and Gascoyne River systems. It is not noted as being a migratory bird but remains fairly sedentary along the watercourses and Coolabah (*E. victrix*) flats that it inhabits. Their pleasant calls of 'wheat-a-wit….wheat-a-wit' greet you whenever walking along the mid west rivers. It must be remembered that eastern states birds have different tones and timing in their calls, so an eastern states White-plumed Honeyeater does not have the same melody. Only the alarm call seems to remain a constant. **Nest:** Can be located in a variety of plants at varying heights, also the materials to make the suspended nest vary from plant stems to dry grasses bound with spiders webbing and lined often with hair, feathers or wool. Clutch size 2–3. **Similar species:** None, if good views are obtained, as it is the only honeyeater with a white plume contrasting with the black moustachial stripe. **Status:** Very common along river systems, uncommon away from rivers. **Where to find:** Murchison River. Gascoyne River. Permanent water tanks and dams near woodland in the Mulga Region.

Brown-headed Honeyeater *Melithreptus brevirostris* subspecies *magnirostris* 12–14 cm

There are 5 subspecies throughout Australia, only one in this region, subspecies *magnirostris*. It is less common than the similar plumaged White-naped Honeyeater. It often reminds one of a bird which has not come out of the immature plumage stage, having no strong contrasting colours and being overall dull in coloration. Often seen in small flocks passing over the canopy to new feeding areas, keeping in contact with a continuous clicking rasping call not unlike their territorial call but more rapid. More arboreal than most honeyeaters, feeding mostly in the higher strata of eucalypts, although will come down to heath plants to feed. Found in a variety of habitats especially heath with extensive stands of mallee, Salmon Gum Woodland

and Wandoo Woodland, far less so in the thicker Jarrah Forest. Particularly common in stands of Mallet (*E. astrigens*) which occurs on stony breakaways in the inner and central Wheatbelt. Common in parts of the Transitional Woodland. **Nest:** The nest is nearly always located on the outer edge of a eucalypt where the outer branches droop down. It is a neat heavily woven structure made from flexible grasses and lined with soft plant down and bound with spiders webbing interwoven around the stems of suspended branches. Clutch size can be 1–2 . **Similar species:** White-naped Honeyeater, which is larger and has a black head not brown. Important feature is the eye ring, which is a distinct cream colour whereas on the White-naped is pale white-blue. The white band on the White-plumed passes from the nape to centre of head but stops before the eye leaving the black of the head showing, whereas on the Brown-headed it bleeds into a cream eye ring. Bill is finer and slightly longer on White-naped. Mantle is bright olive–green on White-naped but dull olive-green on the Brown-headed. The black collar goes down to shoulder on White-naped but on Brown-headed the brown head colouring passes around the neck leaving a thin white gap. Calls of White-naped less grating than Brown headed, more whistle-like, markedly different from the eastern states subspecies. The difference between juveniles is a little tricky as the head is brown and does not become black on the White-naped for a couple months after leaving the nest. However all the other features discussed above are still relevant. **Status:** Generally uncommon but can be locally common particularly east of Hyden. **Where to find:** Scarce in the Jarrah Forest. Best on the eastern edge of the Darling Range in the Wandoo Forest. Uncommon in its northern range as far as Hamelin Pool. Best to see in the central and southern Wheatbelt reserves Dryandra Woodland NR. Dongolocking NR. Southern coastal heaths such as the Fitzgerald River NP. Ravensthorpe region. Throughout the southern Transitional Woodland all the way east to Dundas NR.

White-naped Honeyeater *Melithreptus lunatus* subspecies *chloropsis* 13–15.5 cm

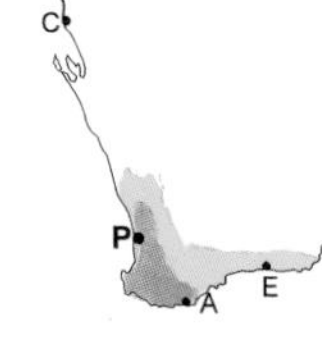

There are two subspecies in Australia; the Western Australian subspecies *chloropsis* is slightly larger and has a different coloured eye ring, pale cream instead of bright red as in subspecies *lunatus* on the east coast. The Western Australian birds prefer the wetter regions of the South West and are the dominant honeyeater in the Karri Forest and southern Jarrah Forest. Their range almost follows the distribution of Jarrah, stopping west of New Norcia and south west to Yanchep and covering all the Jarrah and inner Wandoo down to the Stirling Range and across to Esperance and all areas below this border line. Very common in the deep South West and southern coastal belt, less so past Two Peoples Bay. Far more common than the similar Brown-headed Honeyeater and is more sedentary in its feeding habits whereas Brown-headed tends to move through areas. Now uncommon on the Swan Coastal Plain and north of Moora. **Nest**: Is very similar to Brown-headed Honeyeater but not as thick walled. Clutch size 2–3.

Similar species: Brown-headed Honeyeater, refer to that species for similarities. **Status:** Very common in Karri, Jarrah and Wandoo Woodland. Moderately common in heathlands to Esperance. **Where to find:** Throughout the Darling Range. Lower Wheatbelt reserves particularly the Stirling Range. All the parks of the lower South West. Nowhere in the semi-arid and arid regions.

Brown Honeyeater *Lichmera indistincta* 12–15 cm

Three subspecies throughout Australasia but only one in Western Australia, the nominate race *indistincta*. The word 'indistinctus' in Latin means 'obscure' and relates to the plain colouring of this small honeyeater and it is certainly that; its only features besides its overall grey-brown colouring are the yellow gape and the yellow rear orbital eye ring. However, it certainly makes up for its drab plumage with a great array of chirping musical calls as well as its common scolding call. Found throughout the GSW except for part of the mid west coast, and outside this region in the desert regions. A small honeyeater, highly active and very common in the Perth region. Most diverse in its choice of feeding habitats including wet sclerophyll forests, mangroves, dry arid woodland and heath. Found in town gardens throughout the Wheatbelt and South West. Although its distribution covers much of the state, it is more common in the South West and the far north in the Kimberley, and far less common in the semi- arid and arid regions. This is understandable as

it requires a high intake of nectar and is very common in heath country particularly where flowering grevilleas occur. **Nest:** The nest is a relatively deep cup suspended from thin branches mostly in low bushes, particularly in calothamnus or dryandra bushes. Clutch size 2. **Similar species:** None that occur in this region. **Status:** Very common to uncommon throughout the region. **Where to find:** Anywhere there are flowering plants.

New Holland Honeyeater *Phylidonyris novaehollandiae* subspecies *longirostris* 16–20 cm

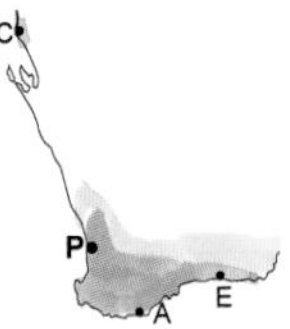

Five subspecies throughout Australasia with only one subspecies *longirostris* in Western Australia. Very similar to the eastern states birds but bill is finer and longer and there is minor plumage variation. A bird of the southern part of Western Australia, occurring in areas with blossoming plants. Certainly there are partial migratory movements in the state as it is not uncommon to see moving flocks of birds in autumn and early spring. Found throughout the Swan Coastal Plain, Jarrah Forest, Karri Forest and southern heaths. Moderately common in the southern Wheatbelt, in reserves that contain Kwongan heath. Can be found in all areas south of a line from Dongara through Northam, Corrigin and across to Pingrup, Ravensthorpe to Twilight Cove. **Nest**: Deep cup with an untidy outer structure of intertwined small twigs but internally is neater, often lined with the down from banksia cones. Nests often in dryandras or banksias. Clutch size 2–3. **Similar species:** White-cheeked Honeyeater which has much bigger white facial patch on the lores. Complete long eyebrow, which is not broken. Dark brown iris. Call distinctly different. **Status:** Common in Karri and Tingle Forest. Common on coastal heaths and wheatbelt heaths. Less common in the Jarrah Forest except on the scarp. **Where to find:** Throughout gardens in Perth and in suburbs on the Darling scarp. All inner Wheatbelt reserves with heath including Tutanning NR. Dryandra Woodland NR. Dongolocking NR and Stirling Range NP. Throughout the coastal heath from Dunsborough all the way to Albany and Esperance and Cape Arid.

White-cheeked Honeyeater *Phylidonyris nigra* subspecies *gouldi* 18 cm

There are two subspecies in Australia, *nigra* on the east coast and *gouldi* in the south west of Western Australian. The Western Australian birds are slightly larger but the white facial disc is not as large and narrower, quite evident for those who know both subspecies. The other features regarding the breast and forehead are so subtle they will confuse and are difficult to see. The western bird's call is louder and more intense, not as soft as that of the eastern subspecies. White-cheeked are not common overall but can be very numerous locally, particularly in the north of their range in the Eneabba area. Their distribution goes further north than New Holland. The distribution is unusual and slightly fragmented, mainly centred on areas with rich Kwongan heath or shrubland heath. They occur as far north as the Kalbarri coast then there is a break south until the flora species rich heaths of the Eneabba sandplain commence. Their range then continues down the coast through Perth to north of Mandurah and there are populations on the Cape Naturaliste to Cape Leeuwin coastal heaths. They do not frequent the Jarrah Forest as much as east and west of the range. On the eastern side of the Darling Range where there is heath in the Wandoo Woodlands, they occur all the way down to the coast at Denmark then along the coast to Cape Arid and inland to Hyden. **Nest**: Nest and clutch size as for the New Holland Honeyeater. **Similar species:** New Holland Honeyeater, refer to that species for details. **Status:** Uncommon to locally common throughout their range except in the Kalbarri sandplain. Eneabba and Badgingarra sandplain. **Where to find:** In Perth particularly the botanic gardens but seasonally more common in the northern Perth suburbs. Yanchep NP. Bungendore Reserve. Kalbarri NP. Eneabba NP. Badgingara. Lesueur NP. Tutanning NR and Dryandra Woodland NR. Heathland 65 km due east of Hyden on the Norseman road.

White-fronted Honeyeater *Phylidonyris albifrons* 14–18 cm

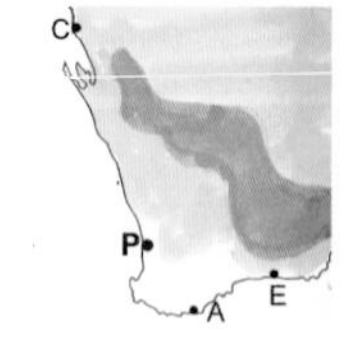

An unusual plumaged honeyeater, almost like a New Holland or White-cheeked Honeyeater without clear head markings. It has a huge range extending well out of this region into the deserts and across to inland New South Wales and Victoria. Found throughout the GSW except the lower South West along a line from Jurien south east to Ongerup and across to Esperance, past which they do not occur. However they are scarce in most of the southern Wheatbelt and do not reach reasonable numbers until the northern and eastern Wheatbelt. From the Transitional Woodland zone out to the mulga and deserts, they become more plentiful. They are highly nomadic and in summer may come deep into the heathlands to feed on banksias and other flowering plants in the northern Wheatbelt. In the mulga they feed on eremophilas, grevilleas, hakeas and mistletoe. They are common in the eastern Transitional Woodland east of Hyden and Lake King. Their calls are plaintive and varied with chuckles, whistles and the typical 'tuk..tuk' call. The important feature to note is an all white forehead running around the eye with a long white malar stripe. Black throat, lores and crown, the crown being faintly streaked with white. Pale lime-green on the wings. Strong black streaks to the white underbody giving way to an all white belly and vent.

They have an unusual bright red patch of bare skin just behind the eye but it is so small you can almost miss it. **Nest:** Can be either suspended from a horizontal branch or wedged in a vertical fork and bound to the stems with spiders webbing. Neat soft lining woven with plant down or wool. Clutch size 2. **Similar species:** None in this state. **Status:** Uncommon in the Wheatbelt, Moderately common in the Transitional Woodland and Mulga Woodland. **Where to find:** Heaths due east of Hyden. Within the Transitional Woodland from Eurady Station down to White Wells across to Mt Jackson, and particularly the extensive woodland between Coolgardie and Peak Charles in patches where flowering plants occur, particularly bottlebrushes. Any of the southern mulga stations where flowering plants occur.

Tawny-crowned Honeyeater *Phylidonyris melanops melanops*

15–18 cm

Two subspecies in Australia, *melanops* on the mainland both in the south west and south east and subspecies *chelidonia* in Tasmania. In Western Australia it virtually follows a line from the Transitional Woodland all the way to the lower South West. It is a bird primarily of the flora species rich heaths, and wherever there are flowering heaths occur Tawny-crowned will normally. Its range is the same as White-cheeked Honeyeater extending to the sandplain heaths of Kalbarri NP, then with a break to the Eneabba and Badgingarra sandplains the range becomes fragmented through the Wheatbelt down to the coast. It occurs between Cape Naturaliste and Cape Leeuwin and follows the southern coastal heaths all the way east to Cape Arid and north to Hyden. Will feed on eucalypts but primarily feeds in low heath where it also nests. **Nest:** The nest is mostly located very low sometimes only

20 cm off the ground, often placed in low heath shrub. The outside is an untidy meshed set of twigs but internally it is neatly woven with soft down. Clutch size 2–3. The bird will rarely fly directly to the nest but will perch on a nearby shrub then drop to the ground and run to the nest in a similar manner as the chats. **Similar species:** None. **Status:** Uncommon overall but locally common in species rich Kwongan heath. Now uncommon on the Swan Coastal Plain. Is not found in the dense Jarrah except in the few larger heaths that occur in the Darling Range. **Where to find:** Kalbarri NP. Eneabba sandplain. Mt Lesueur and Badgingarra sandplain. Various reserves in the Wheatbelt including Gardner NR. Boolanelling NR. Tutanning NR. Boyagin NR. Dryandra Woodland NR. Dongolocking NR. Tarrin Rock South and North NR. Stirling Range NP. Fitzgerald River NP. Sandplains east of Hyden and Lake King.

Western Spinebill *Acanthorhynchus superciliosus* 12.5–15 cm

Endemic bird to Western Australia

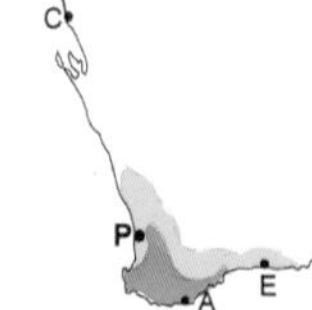

Requires areas with sufficient flowering plants to support its high nectar intake, so its range becomes restricted to wetter South Western Region and parts of the state that have extensive Banksia Woodland and Kwongan Heath. Found from Badgingarra south east through to the inner part of the Wheatbelt and across from Ravensthorpe to Esperance. On the south coast they may be sedentary only moving locally but the Jarrah Forest birds and Wheatbelt birds have seasonal movements. They occur along the Swan Coastal Plain including Perth and into the Jarrah Forest, feeding mainly on Bull Banksia (*Banksia grandis*) and lower storey plants like

Male

Hairy Jug Flower (*Adenanthos barbigerus*), Fuchsia Grevillea (*Grevillea bipinnatifida*), Wilson's Grevillea (*Grevillea wilsonii*) and One-sided Bottlebrush (*Calothamnus sanguineus*). In the Wheatbelt Region they are found where there are remnant patches of heath, which occur in the central and lower Wheatbelt. The sexes differ markedly when adults but when they are juveniles they are very similar. The female lacks the varied markings of the male particularly on the throat, having a plain brown back and white underbody like the male but the only colour is a chestnut rear collar band. **Nest**: Can vary in its location from higher in the outer foliage of tall banksias to low shrubs only 40–60 cm off the ground. The nest is a neatly made thick sided cup and always lined with soft materials from banksia down to fine bark or feathers. Clutch size 1–2. **Similar species:** None. **Status:** Moderately common on the Swan Coastal Plain and Jarrah Forest. Common in heath in the south west Wheatbelt Region and southern coast, less so east of Hopetoun. **Where to find:** In Perth at Whiteman Park. Seasonally Kings Park. Bungendore Reserve. Many suburban gardens on the Darling scarp. Jarrah Forest when Bull Banksias in full bloom. Wheatbelt reserves with heath including Tutanning NR. Boyagin NR. Dryandra Woodland NR. Dongolocking NR. Tarrin Rock NR. and Stirling Range NP and along the coast between Cape Naturaliste and Albany.

Black Honeyeater *Certhionyx niger* 11 cm

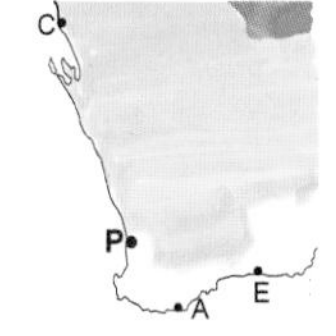

A nomadic species of the drier regions of Western Australia, can be found throughout the GSW except the lower South West. Its normal range when the inland region is not experiencing drought, is the Mulga Woodland and desert regions and less so the Pilbara and the Kimberley. Occasionally when the deserts and mulga are experiencing drought some birds will enter the Wheatbelt. The author has seen them in Boyagin Rock Reserve and Dryandra Woodland Reserve several times; in fact on a tour one gentleman found the nest in a calothamnus bush in Dryandra Nature Reserve. This is a long way from their normal range and so much is still not known about their movements, whether they are nomadic or irruptive. One interesting thing we do know is that Black Honeyeaters will move into regions after burns; the author witnessed this just east of the Vermin Fence east of Hyden, where the heath was burnt and only the grasstrees were sprouting and yet there were many pairs in the area. The two sexes are quite different, the male has the contrasting black and white markings with the black throat band passing down the underbody as a thin black band. The female has a plain brown back and white underbody with slight brown streaking on the throat and down the top of the breast. Both have a long fine down curved bill. The call is a single extended high pitched note, higher pitched than the Red-eared Firetail 'seeeee….. seeeee…..seeeee' and if you get the tone right, you can whistle them up. **Nest:** In a variety of locations but often in very exposed low shrubs, often in burnt bushes in the desert and yet not always easy to see as the nest is very small and placed between vertical branches, rarely suspended, and normally woven to the branches. Outside is a rough tangle of fine twigs and lined with even finer soft twigs and grasses. Clutch size 2. **Similar species:** None. Some similarity with the Pied Honeyeater, which is larger and bulkier and has white on the shoulder and down the wing at

rest. The black throat does not form a small band down the centre of the breast as with the Black Honeyeater. The Pied Honeyeater has a distinct blue crescent mark below the eye. Bill is bulkier and shorter in proportion. Call totally different. **Status:** Can be locally common but overall uncommon. **Where to find:** Best areas within the GSW in the Mulga Region particularly in good seasons.

Pied Honeyeater *Certhionyx variegates* 16–19 cm

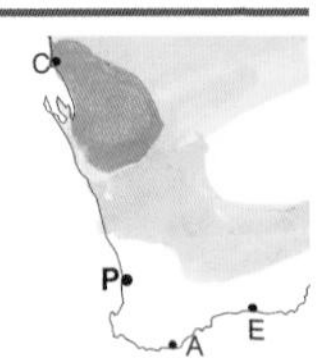

A bird of the semi-arid to arid regions of Australia. Found mostly in the GSW Region around the Shark Bay to Carnarvon area and throughout the Mulga Region. In the mulga it is very much reliant on rains and will move out of areas in severe drought, but most years can be found in the Carnarvon region and inland along the Gascoyne catchment. They rarely pass the Transitional Woodland zone into the Wheatbelt Region, occasionally into parts of the far northern Wheatbelt south of Mullewa. In the breeding season when the Mulga Region is ablaze with flowers the Pied Honeyeaters can be everywhere. The males fly up into the sky with their aerial displays while making their repeated high pitched whistle, confirming and holding their small territory with other males as close as one hundred metres away doing the same thing, flying up and down. Feed mostly on the eremophilas and grevilleas in the mulga. After good rains in late autumn through to winter and early spring they will gather in large groups and pair bonds may be established before nest sites are located. This occurred one year on Muggon Station when a concentration of maybe over 60 birds were connecting and then flying through. The female has a plain brown upperbody and hood with a off white throat and underbody with brown streaking on the throat and breast, with some diffused white in the brown wings. Her blue eye patch is more subdued in colour. **Nest:** Often placed in the centre of eremophila bushes, particularly the Turpentine Bush (*Eremophila fraseri*) or the thick Kurara bushes (*Acacia tetragonophylla*). The nest is a loose suspended nest with a rough outside of loose twigs bound with spiders webs but the cup is lined with finer dry grasses or very thin twigs. Clutch size 2–3. **Similar species:** None, refer to Black Honeyeater for possible similarities. **Status:** Locally very common in parts of the Mulga Region. **Where to find:** Any of the mid western and lower western sheep station properties.

Grey Honeyeater *Conopophila whitei* 11–13 cm

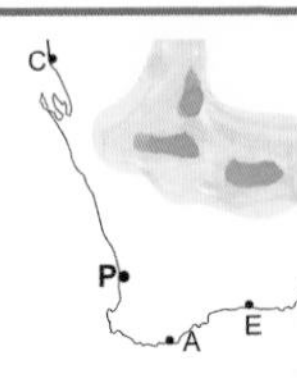

A fascinating scarce bird with still scant information on its behaviour. Found in a band of mulga country in Western Australia from west of Yalgoo through to Wiluna in the east and north into the Pilbara. Sightings are few and far between and most are from the Tom Price area and east into the Hamersley Range proper. The author has only seen it once in the Pilbara but several times in the mulga on Nallan Station and near Paynes Find area and north of Yalgoo. Ironically has seen it more times in the Northern Territory in the Macdonnell Ranges out of Alice at least once in every three to four tours there over the last 20 odd years. The bird is not only seen in mulga woodland but also in dry creek beds with scant acacia cover along the sides of rocky hillsides. They often frequent areas in the mulga that have a lot of mistletoe. One reason for many people overlooking this bird is the fact that it rarely calls, remains fairly unobtrusive and has bland colouring, which does not attract the observer but if it does birdwatchers often think it is a Western Gerygone or female Redthroat. It is most un-honeyeater-like in its behaviour choosing often to follow thornbills and gerygones through the mulga, gleaning insects more than feeding off nectar. When it does take nectar, its bill not being long and down curved like most honeyeaters it has to pierce the side flower heads, particularly eremophilas, to get at the pollen and nectar. There are some important features to note. Firstly the important word jizz applies to this bird. Its shape is closer to the birds of its genus *Conopophila*, being the Rufous-banded and Rufous-throated Honeyeaters, which do not occur in the Grey Honeyeater's territory. It does not have the jizz of gerygones, which are slimmer bodied and smaller and proportionally look to have a longer tail. One reason for confusion with gerygones is that the tail length is shorter than any other *conopophila* and most other honeyeaters, but it is still a longer and bigger bird than any gerygone. The upperbody is a plain grey with slight fawn tingeing in the wings. The bill is stout and short for a honeyeater but still larger than any thornbill or gerygone. It has white tips to the tail, which Western Gerygones also have. Around the eye is a small pale cream coloured split eye ring not easily observed. **Nest:** Is one of the frailest of all nests and it is a wonder that the eggs do not fall from the nest. The shallow cup is suspended from branches using spiders webbing. Clutch size 1–2. **Similar species:** Western Gerygone arid subspecies *mungi* which is a slightly smaller and slimmer bird, weighs 6 g the Grey Honeyeater weighs 10 g. Bill straight on the Western Gerygone, thicker and slightly down curved on Grey Honeyeater. White short supercilium stripe to eye plus dark loral band from bill to eye on Western Gerygone; white eye ring split front and rear of eye on the Grey Honeyeater. Eye distinct dark red in Western Gerygone, black in the Grey Honeyeater. More white in tail of Western Gerygone. **Status:** Scarce but not rare. **Where to find:** Yalgoo region including Gabyon, Carlaminda, and Thundallara Station. In the Paynes Find area

Maranalgo Station and Pindabunna. In the Cue region Nallan and Austin Downs Stations. Possible in any of the mulga areas in the Pilbara, particularly when mistletoe is in bloom. Can be found in the Tom Price region close to the townsite.

Crimson Chat *Epthanura tricolor* 11–13 cm

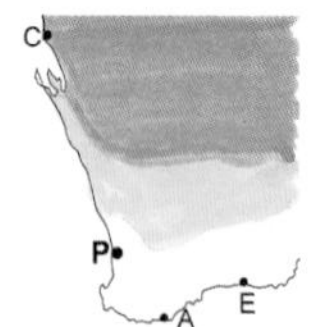

A brightly coloured ground bird of the semi-arid and arid regions of Australia, found throughout much of the GSW mainly north and north east of the Transitional Woodland belt. Its favoured habitat is the Mulga Woodland, particularly abundant after good rains have fallen in a region. When the low shrubs and everlastings are in full bloom in the Mulga Woodland, Crimson Chats can be one of the most common species and the nesting sites can be extremely close. The female is rather plain but in breeding develops small patches of crimson on lower breast and flanks and, like the male, has a bright red rump, seen well in flight. The male in non-breeding plumage lacks the intensity of the red on the crown and the breast is patchy and less intense. Being highly nomadic, they sometimes venture into the northern and north eastern Wheatbelt and even as far south as Ongerup. Most nests are only 20–50 cm off the ground sometimes in ephemeral plants that are short lived like Tall Mulla Mulla (*Ptilotus exaltatus*) or Cotton Bush (*Ptilotus obovatus*) but retain their dense foliage right through the brief breeding season. When approaching the nest, it will land on a nearby bush or dead twigs on low bushes and check surroundings before dropping to the ground and running to the nest site. **Nest:** The nest is a shallow neat cup made from grasses and twigs, lined with fine grasses and wool bound with spiders webbing. Clutch size 2–3. **Similar species:** None. **Status:** Locally common. **Where to find:** Remains fairly sedentary in the Gascoyne region unless extreme droughts occur in that region. Can be seen throughout the Mulga Woodland stations, but it's always best to check where there have been winter rains in the mid west before one travels, as the breeding birds will be in these areas.

Below: Male

Orange Chat *Epthianura aurifrons* 11–12 cm

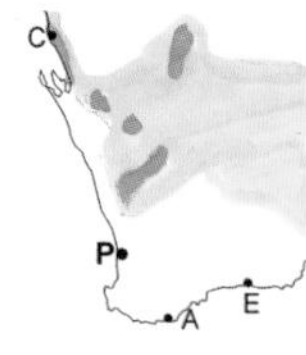

The Western Australian birds are almost exclusively found in samphire (*Halosarcia*), saltbush (*Atriplex*) and bluebush (*Maireana*) country, normally on low-lying areas often adjacent to ephemeral salt lakes. Easily overlooked as they feed, working one bush then running to another; but every now and then, they will sit on the top and survey the area and if the male does this, the bright orange contrasts really well against the dark greens of the samphire. The female is less colourful but when the female bird flies the bright yellow-orange rump can be clearly seen, similar to the brightness of the male. Like all chats they nest low to the ground, building an open nest. In the region of the GSW, they are found from Carnarvon to Hamelin Bay along the coast at various points in samphire flats. Inland their range is fragmented and the locations include Oyster Creek Road, Carnarvon. Also 9 km south east of Murchison Settlement on the Meeberrie – Wooleen road. On Wooleen Lake system. 4 km south east of Yalgoo. Lake Austin. Lake Anneen. Lake Barlee. 2 km south east of Mullewa (this is the furthest south west the author has seen them although they have been recorded at Lake Hinds near Wongan Hills). All areas mentioned require samphire that has received some rains through the year. **Nest:** The nest is a small neat cup lined with fine grasses and placed only 20–40 cm in samphire or bluebush on wide open flood plains of samphire or bluebush. Clutch size 2–4. **Similar species:** Yellow Chat, but not found in these localities as it requires different habitat with fresh water nearby. **Status:** Locally common. **Where to find:** The above ephemeral lake systems after good rains. Can often be found around the town of Carnarvon particularly on the dirt track to the racecourse and in good years around McNeill Claypan.

White-fronted Chat *Epthianura albifrons* 11–23 cm

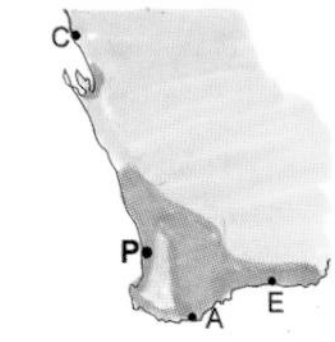

The distribution of the White-fronted Chat in Western Australia is almost a reversal of that of the Orange Chat, both requiring samphire and saltbush but the White-fronted Chat is found mostly further south than Orange Chats. It does range as far north as Coral Bay and then hugs the coast where samphire occurs, particularly south of Carnarvon to Gladstone. It is found throughout parts of the Shark Bay and Dirk Hartog region, particularly around Hamelin Bay. In the inland it then becomes fragmented, reaching as far north as Lake Moore area and as far east as Yeo Lakes on the edge of the Great Victoria Desert, south to the coast east of Cape Arid. However their greatest concentration of numbers is on the Swan Coastal Plain and Southern Coastal Belt all the way to Esperance. They would have been far commoner on the Swan Coastal Plain before much of their territory of samphire was cleared and land reclaimed. Like all chats and many other birds they do the typical broken wing distraction display if you approach a nest but it is often done well before the nest and this unfortunately gives the locality of the nest away far sooner than need be. **Nest**: Is a little more substantial than Orange Chat but still neatly bound with grasses and soft lining of tightly woven grasses, placed low in samphire or if in heath country in any of the many low Kwongan shrubs. Sometimes nests near water but other times at higher elevations such as the heaths in Tutanning NR. Clutch size 2–3. **Similar species:** None. **Status:** Moderately common on larger expanses of samphire and saltbush as well as Kwongan heath. **Where to find:** Common on Rottnest. Vasse Estuary. Peel Inlet. The coastal belt from Lancelin to Dongara. The coastal belt from Hopetoun to Esperance. Throughout the Wheatbelt around salt lakes and in heathland, often seen moving along roadside verges to new feeding areas.

Above: Male

Grey-crowned Babbler *Pomatostomus temporalis* subspecies *rubeculus* 25 cm

There are two subspecies in Australia and only one *rubeculus* in the GSW, which just comes into the northern area of the GSW on the Murchison and Gascoyne Rivers. A gregarious bird having 6-12 members in a family group. Like all babblers, they have a complex family structure with a dominant male and dominant female who have a lifelong pair bond. Then there are non-breeding support members, the young of previous years. In bigger groups there can be two dominant breeding pairs which share nesting and the raising of young. All support each other by mutual preening, or defending group members from danger. Will congregate together when agitated. They are highly active birds; when feeding they call regularly, keeping contact while turning over litter or pecking into bark removing insects. The sexes look alike. Found mostly along river systems but occur in semi-open acacia woodland. The similar White-browed Babblers occur in a large overlap range mainly in the Murchison and Gascoyne regions, for example Talisker and Muggon Stations inland from Overlander have both species. The Grey-crowned Babbler has a fine grey-brown lateral line running across the crown. A darker grey-brown eye stripe runs from the bill and broadens at the lores and into the upperbody. The southern subspecies *rubeculus* has a paler chestnut coloured chest and belly, hence the Kimberley birds are called the red-bellied form of the Grey-crowned Babbler. **Nest:** Their nests are bulky and there can be several in the one territory and the family group will roost in one or two of the non-breeding nests. One nest is solely used for breeding and is well lined with plant down and feathers. Clutch size usually 2–3. **Similar species:** White-browed Babbler which is noticeably smaller (length 19 cm whereas Grey-crowned is 25 cm). The White-browed has no chestnut on the chest or belly but white chest and belly with only the flanks having a grey brown tinge. The supercilium eye stripe is much narrower. Calls are different. **Status:** Moderately common throughout its range becoming more common out of the GSW. **Where to find:** All stations from the central Murchison north but not south and east of Mt Magnet.

White-browed Babbler *Pomatostomus superciliosus* 19.5 cm

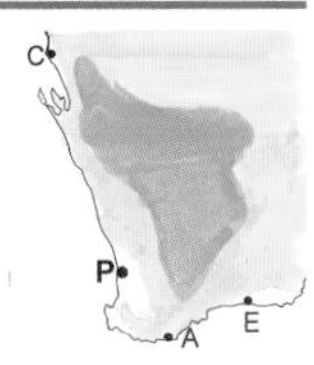

There are currently four subspecies in Australia and two occur in the GSW. *superciliosus* extends from the Victoria Desert down to Esperance and in areas north and north east of a line cutting across the south west from Ravensthorpe in the south to Geraldton on the coast and into the Pilbara. *ashbyi* can be found in all areas within that line, i.e. mainly the whole of the South West Region. The differences between the species are minor and unless you have the bird in the hand there is little variation that can be seen, which includes wing size etc. The range of the White-browed Babbler is extensive; the only area in the GSW it now no longer occurs in, is most of the Swan Coastal Plain. In the Wheatbelt even though the country has been largely cleared the White-browed survives in most areas, even in the most cleared farming areas. It is one of the few birds that can be seen working the fragmented roadside

verges, mainly out of the breeding season as it will use the remnant reserves and patches of uncleared bush as the main breeding territory. In the South West Region it occupies a more varied habitat than in the north being found in thick mallee woodlands adjacent to heath and throughout the Transitional Woodland. In the Mulga Region it occurs mostly in dense stands of mulga in the south. Like all babblers it is very gregarious and is Australia's smallest babbler foraging mostly on the ground but will go up into low trees picking at bark. **Nest:** The nest is similar to the Grey-crowned Babbler's but is smaller and the entrance hole can be more exposed and wider. The location tends to be more concealed in denser shrubbery. Clutch size 2–3. **Similar species:** Grey-crowned Babbler. For differences refer to Grey-crowned Babbler text. It will not be a problem misidentifying the babblers south of the Transitional Woodland or throughout most of the Goldfields, as the Grey-crowned does not occur there. **Status:** Moderately common throughout the Wheatbelt, Transitional Woodland and Mulga Region. **Where to find:** Most large Wheatbelt reserves mostly in northern, central and southern belt. Common in the larger reserves like Magenta NR and Dragon Rocks NR.

Western Whipbird *Psophodes nigrogularis* 23.5 cm

There is considerable debate as to the taxonomy of the Western Whipbird in Western Australia with some authorities splitting the birds from the wetter Two Peoples Bay population *nigrogularis* from the dryer mallee birds *oberon* of the Stirling Range, Chinicup NR and Fitzgerald River NP and the eastern mallee counterparts in South Australia. However in this book we will deal with them as a single entity. The Western Whipbird is a long ground dwelling bird that occurs in a variety of vegetation habitats including: peppermint (*Agonis flexuosa*) in the Two Peoples Bay region, dense stands of Tallerack (*Eucalyptus pleurocarpa*) and peppermint at Waychinicup NP. Amongst stands of Cayley's Banksia (*Banksia cayleyi*) and Southern Plains Banksia (*Banksia media*) and a variety of mallees in the north and eastern parts of the Fitzgerald River NP including Tallerack. In remnant reserves like Chinicup NR. in the dense stands of mallee. In the Stirling Range it's mostly found in Tallerack and a variety of mallees and stunted Jarrah. The Western Whipbird has an olive-brown back and head with a small crest, black throat with white submoustachial stripe. The underbody is light grey-brown with a tinge of olive on the flanks. A long tail with black and white bars to the outer tail feathers seen best in flight. It is not a strong flyer and rarely flies more than 10–15 metres and rarely over the canopy of trees. Very defensive of territory from other Whipbirds. If disturbed

will fly a short distance into a thick bush. Its call is totally different to the similar east coast species the Eastern Whipbird; the female of that species gives her loud whip cracking call at the end of the pair's duet. The Western Whipbird has a far more musical up and down scaled call, starting on a high note then dropping down to a fast extended note, Whatichee....... aawhiddiwit. Its call has a ventriloquial quality so it sometimes takes a while to get onto the location of the bird. If patient, you will see this bird in the breeding season come up to the top or near the top of low mallee to give its territory call and that is when you will get the best views. **Nest:** The nest is a broad bulky cup with fine weaving of dry grasses in the centre, placed in dense bushes often in banksias. Clutch 2. **Similar species:** Eastern Whipbird not in this region. **Status:** Scarce throughout its range except parts of the Fitzgerald River NP where it is locally common. Vulnerable in some of the small Wheatbelt reserves, some surviving on bush blocks no more than 250 hectares. **Where to find:** Best area without too much disturbance is the Fitzgerald River NP where they are moderately common near the north east entry to the park. Also the southern end of Hamersley Drive in the eastern section of the Fitzgerald River NP.

Chiming Wedgebill *Psophodes occidentalis* 20.5 cm

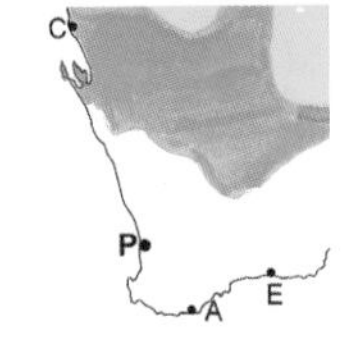

A bird of the same genus as the whipbirds but as the name implies has a very robust bill. Found in the semi-arid and arid regions of the northern part of the GSW Region, particularly the mulga country north and south of Carnarvon and just north of Meekatharra at Karalundi where high densities of this species occur. However, their range is well spread out through most of the central belt of mulga and way out into the remote central deserts along the Gary Highway; less common in the southern Mulga Region. It is a plain coloured bird having a plain fawn head and mantle, darker wings with white on part of the primaries. A long brown tail with white on the tip of the outer tail feathers. Underbody is a cream-brown. The main feature is a very long crest curving slightly forwards. The song is one of the first things you may encounter with this bird as it can skulk in thick thorny acacias. The call is a monotonous rapid undulating call which has been given the vernacular wording of 'did you get drunk-did you get drunk'. This song is repeated over and over again, starting faintly almost inaudible, and then reaching full strength minutes later. It has another call which it also sings late into the night and the notes go up then down 'did you-did you-did you-did you' repeatedly at some length. **Nest:** The nest is a neat open cup with finely woven grasses and plant stems, lined with finer soft twigs in the centre. Clutch size 2. **Similar species**: None, the very similar Chirruping Wedgebill is not found in this state. **Status:** Common in the central

Mulga. **Where to find:** Carnarvon region. Lower stations adjacent to Gascoyne River. Other stations Boolathana. Edagee. Callagiddy. Near Meekatharra, Yoothapina. Near Cue, Nallan and Austin Downs. One of the most southerly populations occurs along the Warne River on the Paynes Find–Sandstone dirt road.

Chestnut Quail-thrush *Cinclosoma castanotus* subspecies *fordianum* 24 cm

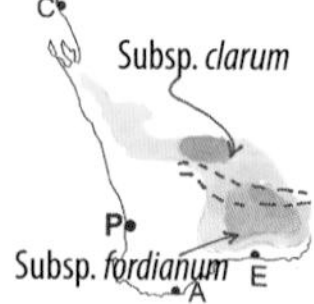

Three main subspecies occur in Australia, two of which are found in the GSW. *clarum* occurs from Shark Bay right across to central Australia to South Australia at its northern limits, and south via the Transitional Woodland and through the Mt Jackson to Goldfields region. It is found in varied habitats mostly under acacia woodland in sandy soil in the western areas south east of Shark Bay. In the Mt Jackson area under thick acacia and other dense shrubs, often in rocky terrain but not open stony country like the Chestnut-breasted Quail-thrush in north of this region. The subspecies *fordianum* occurs in the southern areas of the GSW in mallee and most now survive in the Transitional Woodland east of Lake Cronin across to Dundas NR and then in an outlying band along the southern Nullarbor coastline between Eyre and Eucla. From Coolgardie through to Balladonia is the main crossover where the subspecies intergrade. Chestnut Quail-thrush males have chestnut mantle and rump that varies from the Shark Bay area right through to Dundas NR. All males have a black throat, chest and

Above: Male

flanks with a white submoustachial stripe that borders the black throat. White scalloping on the shoulder. White supercilium stripe to almost the rear of the head. Grey-brown tail with white tips. Female quite different, having a blue-grey throat and chest not black, so the throat lacks the strong contrast between black and white as in the male. The male Chestnut Quail-thrush will sit 4–8 metres up in low branches of trees and give their territorial contact call particularly an hour or so after dawn, a very high pitched single piping note with an even scale repeated for about 10 seconds and then repeated again and again 'te..te..te..te..te..te te te'. Feeds entirely on the ground and only flies up into low branches to give its contact calls. **Nest:** The nest is an open cup nest sometimes in a depression scratched out by the bird, often placed alongside the base of a dense bush. The southern birds *fordianum* nest mainly near Blue Bush (*Mareana sedifolia*) or Grey Bush (*Cratystylis conocephala*). Clutch size 2–3. **Similar species**: Chestnut-breasted Quail-thrush. There are a few overlapping ranges, for example on the Butchers Track before the start of Toolonga Nature Reserve their habitats are close but the Chestnut-breasted Quail-thrush occurs where there are low breakaways with stony terrain. Also there is an overlapping area in the Mt Jackson region. The main differences are that the male Chestnut-breasted Quail-thrush has a complete orange-rust upperbody which goes down to the tail. It has a similar black throat and white submoustachial stripe but below the chest is a distinctive chestnut band running across the body splitting the black chest and black upper belly; also has orange-chestnut flanks. The main thing to register if you see it briefly, is that the bird appears all over orange-brown compared with the Chestnut Quail-thrush which is a greyer-brown bird overall. The female Chestnut-breasted Quail-thrush still has an orange-rust back but it is far paler with colours more subdued. The belly is all white with a pale beige band on the chest, and the head is lighter and greyer with cream throat not grey. **Status:** Uncommon in the northern parts. Locally common in the Mt Jackson area. Common in the Transitional Woodland from 20 km east of Lake Cronin all the way to the eastern boundary of Dundas NR **Where to find:** Easiest location is on the McDermid Rock to Coolgardie track and also even better the old track to Norseman that runs off the Coolgardie track and enters the Coolgardie-Norseman road about 20 km north of Norseman (be careful, this track is rarely used and requires 4WD). Of course, for best results, support Eyre Bird Observatory on the Nullarbor and stay there, it's a magic place and you can walk to see the birds.

Chestnut-breasted Quail-thrush *Cinclosoma castaneothorax*

subspecies *marginatum* 23 cm

There are two subspecies in Australia, *marginatum* (shorter wings, males only) in Western Australia and the nominate *castaneothorax* in central eastern Australia. Chestnut-breasted Quail-thrush are slightly smaller than Chestnut Quail-thrush with a slimmer body. Found mostly in stony country on stony hillsides and open stony plains with scant bushes, or along creek lines that run through stony country. This is a bird of the arid regions and in the GSW comes as far south as 40 km north of Mt Jackson and across to Thundelarra Station. They are common north of the Murchison Settlement region, Gascoyne Junction region and into the Ashburton catchment. The male can be recognised by his chestnut band between the black throat and the black on the lower breast. Has a complete chestnut crown, back and upper tail. In flight shows distinct white and black on the tips of the outer tail feathers. When surprised say by a vehicle, will fly low off the ground with an undulating flight and seek retreat under a

shaded bush, so register where it flies to. It has a few calls, one a high pitch piping not too dissimilar to the Chestnut Quail-thrush, but in the breeding season it has a soft and plaintive call almost mournful. This bird blends in very well with the stony country it inhabits where invariably the soils and stones are similar chestnut-orange colour, so seeing it is not always easy. Also it will remain motionless under a small shrub waiting for intruders to leave. **Nest:** Its nest is placed below a bush on the ground. A small depression is made by both the male and female and a shallow cup of loose mulga leaves is laid, often with twigs and leaves radiating out from the edge of the nest which makes it well concealed. **Similar species:** Refer to Chestnut Quail-thrush text. **Status:** Uncommon in the northern part of the GSW. Common in the central Gascoyne River area to the central Ashburton River. **Where to find:** In the GSW region. Common in a 100 km radius from Murchison Settlement including the following stations: Muggon, Mt Narryer, Wooleen, Murgoo, Twin Peaks. Specific locations: At the junction of the Gascoyne Junction-Mullewa road and the Butchers Track. On the Beringarra-Pindar road 3 km north of the turn-off to Twin Peaks. 16 km south east of Wooleen on the Mereberrie–Mt Wittenoom road. Also east in the Tukannara area north of Cue and 10 km east of Cue.

Varied Sittella *Daphoenositta chrysoptera* subspecies *pileata* 11.5 cm

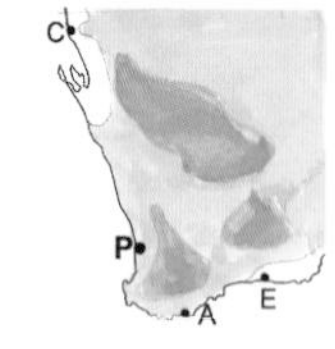

Five subspecies occur in Australia, the one in the GSW Region *pileata* being slightly larger than the others. The male has a black cap and a white face, forehead and underbody. The mantle is grey, wings black with small area of chestnut on the wing seen best in flight. Vent is barred black and white, tail short and black. Bill is fine and upturned with yellow at the base of the bill. Pale yellow legs. Female is similar but has black hood covering the eye and stopping at the throat and neck line. Sittellas are gregarious birds often in a family party of 4–8 birds with two primary breeding adults and 2–4 helpers who can be adult birds or the young of last season. They help with building the nest and feeding young. When they fly it is normally as a group constantly twittering to keep contact. Sittellas can be found in a variety of woodlands. In the South West they occur in all the well forested areas and open woodlands, including all the primary eucalypts of Jarrah, Marri, Karri, Tuart and Swamp Yate (*Eucalyptus occidentalis*). Their range extends from the lower South West up into the Pilbara and east through the central deserts avoiding the Nullarbor and Great Sandy Deserts. They do occur in the Mulga Woodland but more so in the Transitional Woodland. **Nest:** The nest is exquisitely made with loose bark placed on the outside in small patches to imitate the trunk and branches of the tree it is built in. Nearly all nests are at the junction of a steep fork, sometimes a three way junction of branches mostly well over 8 metres up. From the ground it's not easy to see the nest unless the bird leads one to it. The inner nest is lined with plant down and spiders webs and egg sacks. Clutch size 2–3. **Similar species:** None. **Status:** In the South West moderately common to uncommon. Uncommon in the outer Wheatbelt. Transitional Woodland and Mulga Woodland. Do not occur in open plains or lightly timbered country unless moving through. **Where to find:** Darling Range. Larger areas of Wandoo. Often in Yate woodland.

Crested Shrike-tit *Falcunculus frontatus* subspecies *leucogaster* 17 cm

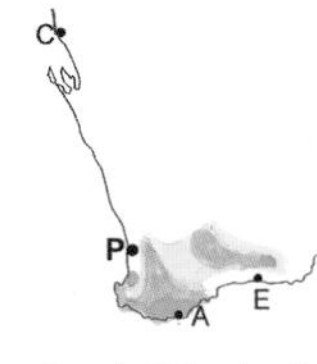

There are three subspecies of Crested Shrike-tit in Australia, *frontatus* from the east coast, *whitei* from northern Australia and *leucogaster* occurring in the South West. The eastern states birds are moderately common in most of their range but both the northern Australian and South West birds are not as common. The Kimberley and Northern Territory subspecies *whitei* most probably was always uncommon but the South West birds have certainly lost a large amount of their prime feeding habitat, the Wandoo Woodland, and they require adequate stands of mature Wandoo to support a pair's territory. In the main block of Dryandra Woodland Nature Reserve the author knows of five territories within an area of about 8000 acres of which few are exclusive stands of Wandoo. They do also favour Karri and that too, has been severely affected by land clearing and logging. The subspecies *leucogaster* in the South West has some minor variances with the nominate race mainly regarding bill size and wing size, but the main feature of the South West birds is that they have a white belly with a clear break with the yellow breast, whereas the northern and eastern subspecies have a complete yellow underbody with no white on the belly. The female only varies slightly from the male by having a dark olive throat rather than pure black, and crest length is shorter. Crested Shrike-tits have a mournful undulating territorial call 'suewit...sueweee...suewit...sueweee'. They also have a grating agitation call. Their strong bill allows them to lever off bark to get at insects, one of the few birds in the South West able to do this. They are totally arboreal in their feeding habits, often spending time in the canopy of trees, and can be easily overlooked as out of the breeding season they call infrequently and only the cracking of bark alerts one to their presence. **Nest:** The nest is placed in a fork normally above 6 metres. It is an exquisite construction made of thin woven strands of bark with copious amounts of spiders webbing holding the outside structure and woven around a fork in the branches. The inner cup is lined with finer bark strands or twigs and grasses. Clutch size 2–3. **Similar species:** Possibly male Golden Whistler which has a similar combination of colours. The Golden Whistler has no crest and has a white throat not black. Head markings totally different. **Status:** Uncommon in the Karri Forest. Vulnerable in the Wandoo Woodland. **Where to find:** Pemberton region particularly Warren National Park. Boranup forest in the Leeuwin-Naturaliste NP. Northern and central areas of Wandoo in the Stirling Range. Dryandra Reserve. Wandoo Conservation Park. Julimar Forest NR.

Crested Bellbird *Oreoica gutturalis gutturalis* 21 cm

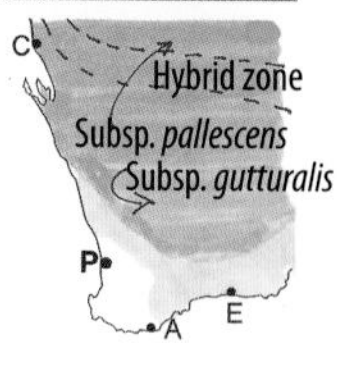

There are two subspecies in Australia. Both occur in Western Australia with *gutturalis* in southern Western Australia and *pallescens* in northern Western Australia through to the Northern Territory; the subspecies overlap in the Gascoyne River region. There is little variation save that the southern birds *gutturalis* are darker backed birds which is typical of a bird which is smaller and lighter the further north one goes. The Crested Bellbird has a distinct crest, white face with surrounding black border, bright orange eye, grey head with black crest and darker brown upperbody and pale underneath. Has a stout bill. The female lacks the white throat and black surrounding mask, does have a black crest but smaller. Has the well known bell-like call with a ventriloqual quality that makes it hard to place as it can sound close and then far away. If one is very close to the bird, you can actually hear the bill clatter when the call reaches its highest pitch. Birds in Western Australia have a marked difference in their call from the eastern birds. It is one of the few mulga species that remains sedentary even through the worst droughts when other nomadic species will move. Found in semi-arid and arid regions of the GSW mostly past the Transitional Woodland belt, having a preference for open mulga country. It also is found in the Wheatbelt region but has declined in the south west Wheatbelt. Dryandra Woodland Reserve lost its last male Crested Bellbird in about 1992, the same bird had been there for at least 5 years, calling for a mate that never came. In the late 1970s the author knew of at least 2 pairs. Even though scarce in the south west Wheatbelt, they do come down to the Stirling Range and Fitzgerald River National Park and some of the larger eastern Wheatbelt Reserves. Most of its feeding is done on the ground. **Nest:** It builds a bulky untidy nest, the outside twigs being fairly robust and loosely gathered; the centre cup is a little more finely woven with thin grasses and plant stems usually placed in the fork of a dense mulga bush only 1–2 metres off the ground. Clutch size 2–3. **Status:** Scarce in the inner Wheatbelt. Uncommon in the southern Wheatbelt. Moderately common in the eastern and northern Wheatbelt. Common in the Mulga Region. **Where to find:** Stirling Range. Central Fitzgerald River NP. Magenta NR. Dunn Rock NR. Chiddarcooping NR. Throughout the Mulga Region north and north east of the Transitional Woodland belt.

Gilbert Whistler *Pachycephala inornata* 19 cm

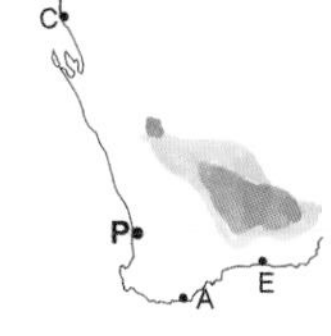

A whistler of the semi-arid regions of the GSW. Found mostly east of Lake Cronin 90 km east of Hyden to Balladonia in the east. It frequents the Salmon Gum Woodland and wherever the Goldfields Teatree (*Melaleuca pauperiflora*) occurs, that is where you will find them even if the dominant tree is not Salmon Gum. The Gilbert Whistler's call is one of the most powerful calls of all whistlers, in fact of any Australian passerine. The call starts off slowly and then finishes with the loudest penetrating 'chop chop' calls getting higher near the end 'soooee….soooee…soooee...chop…chop...chop...chop....chop…chop'. The male is recognised by its orange throat and dark lores. The rest of the body is a dull grey-brown with a lighter underbody. It has a robust bill just a bit shorter than White-breasted Whistler. The female lacks the orange throat patch. The crown is lighter and the lores much lighter. Gilbert Whistlers were once relatively common in the western Wheatbelt but by the 1930s were almost extinct in that region and only now survive on a few of the larger north eastern Wheatbelt reserves. There is a small outlying population on the Warne River east of Paynes Find, in a habitat not typical of most of their range in

Western Australia. **Nest:** The nest is a deep cup shape with twigs getting finer to the centre mixed with slivers of smooth bark all bound tightly together, placed only 1–3 metres high. Clutch size 2–3. **Similar species:** None for the male. Red-lored Whistler, not in Western Australia. The female can be confused with the female Golden Whistler. The Golden Whistler is a smaller bird with different jizz, tail not as long. Has an olive-grey look to the back. Bill is not as robust. The territory of the north western population is highly unlikely to have the Golden Whistler and they are not common in the Transitional Woodland east of Hyden although they tend to frequent denser vegetation, sometimes at the base of granite outcrops in that region where Gilbert Whistler do not occur. **Status:** Common from Jaurdi north east of Coolgardie south to Peak Charles and Lake Cronin in the east to Balladonia in the west. **Where to find**: Easiest anywhere just east of McDermid Rock. The Warne River population is just north of where the Warne River passes over the Paynes Find and Sandstone road.

Golden Whistler *Pachycephala pectoralis* subspecies *fuliginosa* 17.5 cm

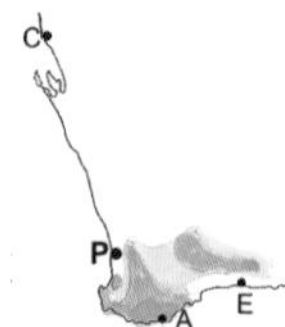

A medium sized whistler with a slim bill, stocky body and large head in relation to body. Sexes totally different in adult birds. The male has strong head markings with a white throat, black hood and yellow collar and yellow underbody. Olive back, black tail tinged dark green. The female of subspecies *fuliginosa* has no yellow tingeing on the vent unlike eastern states birds. The back is olive-brown. Slight supercilium stripe. Faint scalloping on pale brown throat. Buff underbody darkest on chest. The Golden Whistler is a bird of the wetter South West being commonest in the tall eucalypt forests and thick understorey of the lower South West, and common in the Karri Forest, and southern Jarrah and Tingle Forests. Found feeding in the middle and lower stratum and on the ground of forested areas. It occurs in the drier woodlands particularly Wandoo Woodland but mostly in sheoak thickets and mallee and dryandra over dense heath, less so in open Wandoo. Its range belies its population density as it occurs as far north as Shark Bay and south east to Kalgoorlie and down to Balladonia but generally past the northern Darling Range and lower wheatbelt it is not common; however it is more so in the lower Transitional Woodlands south of the Merredin to Kalgoorlie highway. Its pleasant whistling call is familiar to many 'choo…choo…choo…whip'. There are six subspecies throughout Australasia with only one occurring in Western Australia namely *fuliginosa*. **Nest:** The nest is shallower than most whistlers 'with the outside constructed of thin twigs which get finer and more compact in the centre often with the addition of leaves bound to the twigs with spiders webbing. The inner lining is of fine rootlets or

Above: Female

grasses. Clutch size mostly 2. **Similar species:** Mangrove Golden Whistler that does not occur in this region. **Status:** Very common in the lower South West. Common in the Darling Range and southern coast and Transitional Woodland. Uncommon past the Transitional Woodland belt. **Where to find:** Throughout the lower South West Region and Darling Range. Common in wetter gullies particularly in peppermint stands on the southern coast. Common on some islands like Woody Island off the Esperance coast. Most inner Wheatbelt reserves. Moderately common in the southern Transitional Woodland. Uncommon in northern Wheatbelt and northern Transitional Woodland.

Rufous Whistler *Pachycephala rufiventris rufiventris* 16 cm

C
P
A
E

Found throughout the GSW particularly the Wheatbelt, Transitional Woodland and Mulga Region. A common bird with a preference for semi-arid habitat although it is found in the South West, but less so in the wetter areas including the Karri Forest and heavier forested Darling Range. A master songster with one of the finest calls of any Australian bird given with so much power, particularly in the breeding season. Sexes very different, the male has a white throat, black surrounding mask, grey crown and back. Buff underbody. The female has no black or white on the head. Back grey-brown, underbody light buff with fine streaking on the throat and chest. There are four subspecies in Australia with two in Western Australia, *rufiventris* in the South West and *falcate* in the far north intergrading where they overlap. The South West birds typically are darker, with darker backs and richer buff underparts getting lighter in the northern regions where they are in greater numbers. **Nest:** The nest is slightly bulkier than the Golden Whistler with larger twigs spiralling into finer twigs in the centre, sometimes lined with a few feathers sometimes not. Built in the centre

Above: Female

of a dense bush mostly no more than 3 metres off the ground. Clutch 2–3. **Similar species:** Female Golden Whistler has a pale throat with slight mottling, grey-brown chest bleeding into a light beige belly. Grey-brown back. The Rufous Whistler female has pale cream underbody with long fine black streaks and grey back. **Status:** Common throughout the GSW including the Mulga Region. Uncommon in wetter forested areas of the lower South West. **Where to find**: Near Perth, Bungendore Reserve and Wandoo Conservation Park. Any of the larger Wheatbelt Reserves. Throughout the Mulga Region.

White-breasted Whistler *Pachycephala lanioides* subspecies *carnarvoni* 19 cm

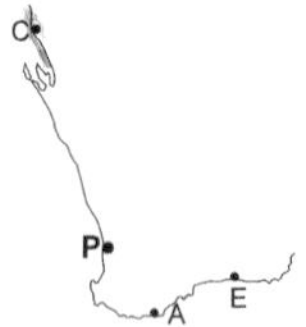

A whistler that only inhabits mangroves. Found in the far north coast of the GSW around the Carnarvon region and south to Long Point. Found mainly at Oyster Creek and south to Bush Bay, although not common there. Has the largest bill of any whistler, which is used to open small molluscs. Feeds in the mangrove trees but when the tide goes out will take food from the mud before returning to the mangrove trees with the high tide. The sexes are different. The male has a white throat, black crown and facial mask with a chestnut collar below. The back is pure grey with a black tail. Underbody white. Very robust bill with down curved tip. Female is a plain coloured bird with beige upperbody and pale cream underbody but with streaking from the throat to the lower belly. Grey tail. Same robust bill as male. Male has several whistling calls, the main territorial call is hard to put into words but is very varied undulating, not as robust a call as the Gilbert or Rufous Whistler's call, more a plaintive song but still carrying far through the mangroves. Has long pauses between bursts of song. There are three subspecies in Australia. All three occur in Western Australia but only *carnarvoni* in this region reaching just south of Carnarvon, then north in fragmented populations until Cape Keraudren where Eighty Mile Beach becomes the barrier to the next subspecies *lanioides* in the Kimberley. **Nest:** It is 2–3 metres up into the mangroves and both sexes build the nest. The nest is not dissimilar to the Rufous Whistler's nest but twigs are taken from mangroves or samphire bushes. It is placed near the tops of a large mangrove well above the high water mark. Clutch size 2. **Similar species:** None. The female is similar to the female Rufous Whistler but they do not share the same habitat.

Above: Female White-breasted Whistler

The White-breasted female is far larger than the Rufous Whistler with a more robust body. **Status:** Not common in the Carnarvon region. Becomes more common in the Exmouth Gulf region particularly in Gales Bay on Bullara Station and Giralia Bay on Giralia Station and further north. **Where to find:** In the GSW best place is Oyster Bay just south of Carnarvon townsite.

Grey Shrike-thrush *Colluricincla harmonica* subspecies *rufiventris* 25 cm

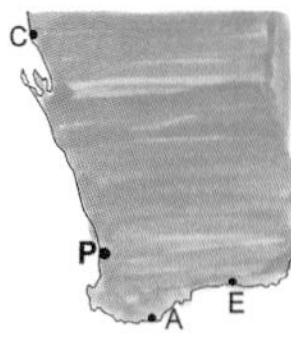

A large thrush-like bird, larger than whistlers. An overall grey bird with a grey head, dark grey back with only a slight chestnut tinge on the mantle and not as much as many books illustrate, being much greyer than eastern birds. The head is totally grey with a small white patch on the lores. Throat grey-white and underbody slightly darker. Tail long and dark grey. A long heavy bill with distinct hooked end. The female is similar in appearance but has fine streaking on the throat and belly. Feeds mostly on larger insects but will take small reptiles and also eggs and young birds, although not to the same degree as currawongs or ravens. Feeds both in trees and on the ground. The song is strong but very melodious with great variance throughout Australia, one of the master songsters. Found throughout the GSW, being very catholic in its choice of habitat. Found in the wetter forests of the South West, throughout the Wheatbelt, Transitional Woodland and Mulga Region. There are five subspecies in Australia and it is a complex taxonomy. Only one occurs in the GSW, subspecies *rufiventris*, but even within this subspecies group there are variants. The main feature and hence its Latin name *rufiventris*, relates to the slight rufous colouring on the vent; it also has one of the largest bills in the group. **Nests:** The location for Grey Shrike-thrush nests can vary greatly, mostly in the Mulga Region located in thick mulga in a three way fork, but in the lower South West forested areas, can often be found in tree hollows, not inside a trunk but where the trunk is broken or heavy bark pealed back, normally above 4 metres. The cup nest is a combination of woven twigs and strands of bark with an inner lining of fine rootlets and grasses. Clutch size mostly 3. **Similar species:** None. **Status:** Common throughout most of the GSW. **Where to find:** Anywhere there is woodland or thick mulga.

Restless Flycatcher *Myiagra inquieta inquieta* 19–21 cm

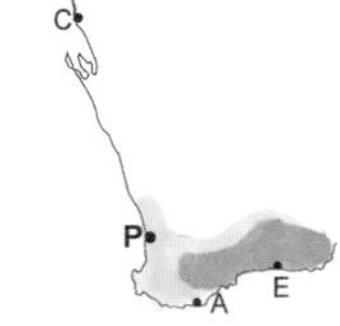

Well named, as this is certainly an active feeder frequently twisting and turning in flight to gather insects. It also has the unusual habit of hovering just 1–2 metres off the ground almost in Kestrel fashion, looking for movement of insects. It often does this while giving a continuous grating call hence its popular name 'scissor grinder bird', derived from its resemblance of sound to steel being ground on a stone grinder. Besides the grinding call, its contact call is a rapid 'chewe..chewe..cheweeee'. The male has dark blue-black head, nape, wings, upperbody and tail with a slight metallic sheen only seen in direct sunlight. The underbody and throat are all white. The male has a small crest and a long fine bill. The female is almost identical but has a slight buff on the side of the white shoulder. The crest is not as pronounced and the upperbody lacks the metallic sheen of the male. Found throughout the southern part of the GSW but is not a common bird and possibly declining. They are particularly at home in Wandoo Woodland, Salmon Gum Woodland and Mallee Woodland. Much of the Wandoo and Mallee has gone from the Wheatbelt, so they tend to occur in fragmented areas in the Wheatbelt Region. Their preference is for open woodland where they can forage in the foliage of trees but also they require large amounts of time searching for food in open areas. They rarely feed in the thicker Jarrah Forest but as soon as it mingles with the Wandoo, they start to occur. They do occur in Karri Forest but it seems only after burns for a few years, mainly due to the fact that the understorey is cleared giving them better feeding opportunities. The northern limit is basically a line from Lancelin in the west across to Zanthus on the eastern side of the Nullarbor down to the southern coast. There are two subspecies in Australia, *inquieta* found in the South West and *nana* which is found in northern Australia and is very similar but distinctly smaller with slightly smaller bill and the crest not so pronounced and calls slightly different. **Nest:** All flycatchers build exquisite nests and the Restless Flycatcher is no exception. A tight moulded mass of shredded bark and grasses all bound with spiders webbing and camouflaged on the outside with bits of bark or sometimes spiders egg sacks. The inside of the cup is made of fine woven dry grasses. Normally placed on a horizontal limb where it forks. Clutch size 2–3. **Similar species:** Willie Wagtail, which has a different jizz and a black throat not white. Has small white supercilium stripe. Tail slightly longer and broader when perching. Call different. **Status:** Uncommon throughout range. **Where to find:** Wandoo Conservation Park. Dryandra Woodland Reserve. Dongolocking Reserve. Stirling Range National Park. Magenta Reserve. Main stronghold is the eastern Transitional Woodland from Lake Cronin through to Balladonia.

Magpie-lark *Grallina cyanoleuca cyanoleuca* 26–28 cm

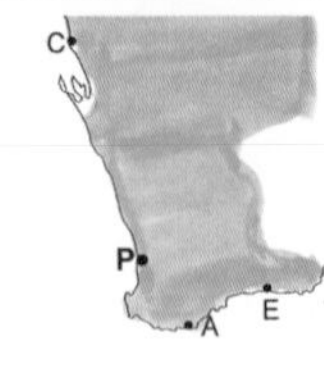

A common well known bird found throughout most towns in the South West. It is hard to imagine this is a member of the 'monarch flycatcher' group, it certainly is Australia's largest monarch flycatcher. The strong black and white markings make it a striking bird. The sexes have different head patterning. The male has a black face and throat, the female has white face and throat. The black band passing through the male's eye runs horizontally and in the female vertically. It is a ground dwelling bird and one of only three birds in Australia that builds a mud nest, hence one of its common names is 'Mud Lark'. The other two mud nest building birds are the Chough and the Apostle Bird. Magpie-larks occur throughout the GSW, mostly in open wooded country with open grassed areas as they are a ground feeding bird

and often found near lakes or dams as they require water for their nest building. Adult birds defend their territory strongly and remain in their territory permanently. When you see small moving flocks particularly through the Wheatbelt at the end of summer and autumn, these are mostly younger birds congregating to travel to other feeding areas for winter before returning to form territories themselves in spring. There are two subspecies in Australia, *cyanoleuca* basically south of the 20 degree latitude and *neglecta* north of 20 degree latitude. The tropical northern birds are smaller and typical of 'Bergman's Law' having shorter wings and tail and less weight. **Nest:** The mud nest is held together with dry grasses and the inner cup lined with finer grasses and sometimes feathers added. Mostly placed high in trees directly on top of a larger horizontal branch. **Similar species:** None. **Status:** Very common throughout its southern range. Moderately common north of the Wheatbelt. **Where to find:** Common in towns and throughout region.

Grey Fantail *Rhipidura fuliginosa* subspecies *preissi* 15–16.5 cm

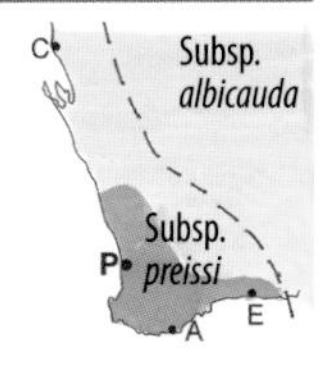

A small fantail, familiar to many as it is quite a confiding bird, in fact will take advantage of people walking by taking food as insects are disturbed. There is a great variance in colouring with this species. There are five subspecies on mainland Australia with two occurring in Western Australia, *preissi* in the lower South West and *albicauda* in the semi-arid and arid regions of central Western Australia. Besides subtle differences in tail length and tarsus length, which you are unlikely to see in the bush, what you may notice is that the inland birds *albicauda* have a distinct white tail and only the central tail feathers are dark grey,

also the body is distinctly paler. This is one bird that may become a separate species in the future, with the South West subspecies *preissi* moving through their territory travelling north in autumn and winter but *albicauda* remaining in the same territory. The calls are slightly different, the soft tinkering seems more grating with the inland birds. The calls of Grey Fantail are very soft with a high frequency, so people with hearing problems may not always pickup. The South West subspecies *preissi* is found in the wetter regions particularly along riverine habitat, also Karri Forest, Jarrah Forest and open Wandoo Woodland. When one enters the outer Wheatbelt regions particularly the sheoak areas, the white-tailed subspecies *albicauda* becomes common and is the dominant Grey Fantail in the central Mulga Region; it is nomadic moving to where weather conditions are favourable but may be sedentary in the Pilbara. **Nest:** They build the most exquisite nest which is moulded onto a thin branch of a horizontal limb with countless fine grass stems tapering to a point at the base of the nest giving it a wine glass appearance, the whole structure being bound by countless spiders webs. Clutch size 2–3. **Similar species:** None. **Status:** *preissi,* moderately common throughout the South West. *albicauda* moderately common locally, uncommon overall in the Mulga Region. Moderately common in the Pilbara. **Where to find:** Throughout the GSW, including many towns.

Mangrove Fantail *Rhipidura phasiana* 14–15 cm

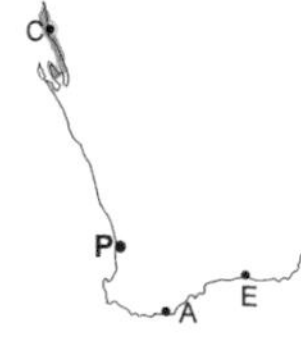

Very similar to the Grey Fantail but, as the name implies, a bird purely of the mangrove habitat. After the Yellow White-eye, it is the most common mangrove frequenting bird in the GSW Region. In this region it can be found from Lake MacLeod down to Gladstone and the northern tip of Peron Peninsula. Note that, particularly in winter, the Grey Faintail subspecies *preissi* can move through the coastal mulga belt but rarely feeds in mangroves. The Mangrove Fantail is much paler than the Grey Fantail especially *albicauda* which possibly does not reach the far west coast south of Carnarvon. The Mangrove Fantail has the palest upperbody and also a paler very narrow chest band (see photograph). When seeing the bird for the first time, you will notice that it is distinctly smaller than Grey Fantail. Feeds in the mangroves and on the mud or sand. Its technique of dislodging insects is often to twist and turn through foliage, disturbing insects and making them move. It occasionally will fly out over adjacent samphire, hawking for insects away from the mangroves. **Nest:** The nest is similar to the Grey Fantail, although the tail of the nest not as long, and it is built straight onto a horizontal mangrove branch above high water mark. Clutch size 2–3. **Similar species:** Grey Fantail, see notes above. **Status:** Common in mangroves between Lake MacLeod and Gladstone and Shark Bay region. **Where to find**: At Miaboolia Beach and Oyster Creek near Carnarvon and beaches north and south of Eundoo Creek and New Beach. Also northern Peron Point in Herald Bight.

Willie Wagtail *Rhipidura leucophrys leucophrys* 19–21 cm

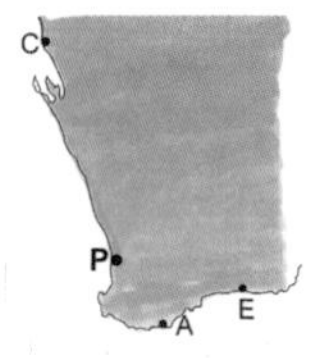

Well known to most people, this bird can be seen throughout Australia except in rainforests. Found in cities, towns, heath, woodland, desert dunes and rocky hillsides, it certainly has adapted well to all terrains and weather conditions. Found in the GSW throughout their range. This pied flycatcher is an active feeder constantly wagging its tail from side to side dislodging insects. As mentioned above can be found in all habitats but generally prefers areas where it can feed in the open and does not like enclosed thick woodland, as much of its feeding takes place on the ground. Its call is a sweet scratchy sound often given well into the night particularly on full moon nights. The Nyoongars of the South West aptly called them the 'Chitty Chitty Bird' which sums up their call exactly. There are three subspecies, *leucophrys* in southern Australia, *picata* in northern Australia and *melaleuca* on islands in the Torres Strait and Pacific. **Nest:** Builds a compact neatly woven nest, often on a dead exposed horizontal branch of a fallen tree and out in the open. When the chicks are fully developed it's amazing they never fall out of the small cup nest which seems built for a much smaller bird. The nest is similar to the Grey Fantail's but there is no suspended tail on the nest as it is moulded onto the horizontal branch, being constructed from dry grasses woven with copious amounts of spiders webbing and lined with fine grasses. Clutch size 3–4. **Similar species:** Refer to Restless Flycatcher. **Status:** Very common throughout the GSW. **Where to find:** Throughout the GSW including most towns.

Jacky Winter (Brown Flycatcher) *Microeca fascinans* subspecies *assimilis* 13 cm

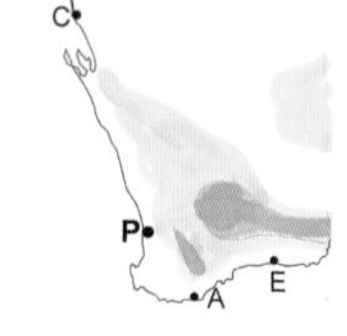

There are three subspecies in Australia and one in New Guinea. Only one occurs in the GSW, subspecies *assimilis*. Their range takes them from the Stirling Range in the south and in a line from the Wandoo Woodlands western boundary, all the way north to Billabong Roadhouse adjacent to Meadow Station, then south east down to Kalgoorlie and Dundas NR and west across the southern boundary of the Wheatbelt. However their main populations occur in the Transitional Woodland and some of the larger Wheatbelt reserves with heavier timbered woodland. They do not generally occur in the thicker Jarrah and Karri Forests or the Swan Coastal Plain or southern coastal districts. Jacky Winters require open areas to feed and hawk for insects but must have trees adjacent to the open areas and are particularly common in the Wandoo Woodland and Swamp Yate woodland (*E. occidentalis*), which is one of their preferred woodlands. They call

strongly in the breeding season from high up, normally on dead exposed branches, with their well known high pitched rapid 'peter, peter, peter' call. Regardless of what habitat they are in, Jacky Winters will always shake their tail on alighting after flight, revealing the white in their outer tail feathers. Often hovers for insects although flight is not as prolonged as say a Restless Flycatcher. The South West subspecies *assimilis* is slightly smaller than the nominate subspecies *fascinans* in eastern Australia and has darker bases to the outer tail feathers rather than all white. **Nest:** The Jacky Winter's nest is one of the smallest, shallowest cups of any passerine, placed mostly high up on a horizontal branch where it forks. The nest is constructed of fine grasses and decorated on the outside with slivers of bark all tightly bound with copious amounts of spiders webbing. Clutch size 2–3. **Similar species:** Possibly female Hooded Robin, a bulkier bird with no supercilium stripe and white on the tail only in the middle of the outer tail feathers; it has an all grey hood coming down the breast while the Jacky Winter has a white chest and throat. Hooded Robin never wags its tail like the Jacky Winter. Calls are very different. **Status:** Uncommon to moderately common in open woodland in the Wheatbelt and Transitional Woodlands. **Where to find:** Wandoo Woodland on the eastern boundary of the Darling Range. Dryandra NR. Stirling Range NP. Dongolocking NR. North Karlgarin NR. Throughout much of the Transitional Woodland east of Hyden all the way through to Dundas NR and north into the Goldfields. North between 40 and 60 km north east of Wubin.

Scarlet Robin *Petroica multicolour* subspecies *campbelli* 12.6 cm

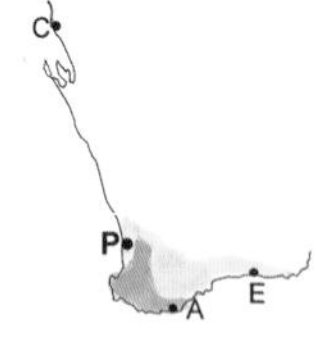

There are four subspecies in Australia and at least 13 on Pacific Islands. In Western Australia there is one *campbelli* which is slightly smaller than the eastern mainland subspecies *boodang* and the Tasmanian subspecies *leggii*, which has a longer bill. It is a robin of the wetter South West although can be found in the lower south west Wheatbelt. Most prolific in the larger trees of the Karri, Tingle and Jarrah Forests and along the southern coast. In Dryandra Woodland NR where the dominant tree is the Wandoo, it still selects those areas that mostly have Marri or Jarrah. When larger stands of Jam trees (*Acacia acuminata*) occur adjacent to Jarrah or Wandoo Red-capped Robins hold territory; in the Jarrah, Scarlet hold territory but the author has found that the Scarlet will dominate on the margins and confront the Red-capped Robin which retreats back into the Jam woodland. The Western Yellow Robins do not have the same conflict, as they prefer the Wandoo Woodland with open spaces often with little or no understorey, which is not the preferred site for Scarlet Robins. Like most robins, the male is a stunning bird with its distinct white forehead spot, set against the black hood. The breast is scarlet as the name implies, with white flanks and vent, white to the outer tail feathers and white on the shoulders on the black wings. The female breast lacks the intense scarlet, being a more subdued pale scarlet over a smaller area the scarlet only going to the lower chest. The hood and back is a dark grey-brown. Has a small white patch on the forehead above the bill and white eye ring broadest at the rear of the eye. The call is a delicate tinkling, often uttered high in a eucalypt. **Nest:** They can nest in low shrubs like sheoak but mostly higher in the mid strata of the taller eucalypts like Jarrah and Marri. The nest is a neat thick walled open cup lined with loose bark bound together with spiders webbing. The inner lining is woven with fine grasses and soft feathering woven into sides. Almost invariably placed in the fork of a horizontal branch. Clutch 2–3. **Similar species:** Red-capped Robin is smaller and has a red patch on the forehead rather than a white. Its call is totally different. The female Red-capped Robin has a pale scarlet patch on the forehead, the Scarlet has a smaller white patch above the bill. Red-capped nest lower down and in a fork. **Status:** Common in the Darling Range and Karri and Tingle Forest, less common in the Wandoo. **Where to find:** Throughout the Darling Range. Dryandra Woodland NR. Stirling Range. Throughout the Margaret River and Augusta region all the way along the coast to Esperance hugging the coastline.

Below: Male

Red-capped Robin *Petroica goodenovi* 11 cm

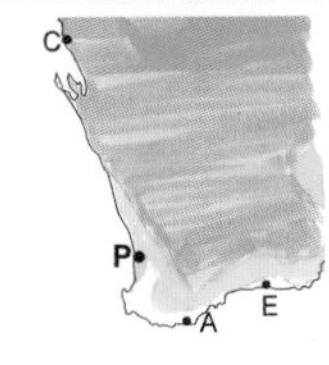

A small robin and one of the most stunningly coloured birds of Australia. It certainly is a jewel with its bright red forehead spot set against the jet black hood and the bright red breast to match. It prefers more semi-arid to arid areas of the GSW than the Scarlet Robin, avoiding much of the deeper lower South West. Its range almost mirrors the limit of the Scarlet Robin extending north of the Porongurups all the way to the Pilbara and lower Kimberley and east through all the desert regions except the central Nullarbor. There is a marked movement of some South West birds to over-winter in the north. They can be found throughout much of the Wheatbelt, preferring stands of sheoak woodland where they also nest. Further north they become the dominant robin as one enters the Mulga. They are not so common in the Transitional Woodland. On Rottnest there is a remnant population that is quite common on the island. They often give themselves away with their so called telephone call 'drrrrrit drrrrit.......drrrrit drrrrit........drrrrit drrrrit' reminiscent of a phone ringing. If you come too close to its nesting area it will give rasping clicks and flick its wings repeatedly.

Nest: The nest is a small compact cup of tightly woven grasses and bark heavily moulded with spiders webbing and the outside bark strands matching the branches it is attached to. Clutch size 2–3. **Similar species**: Refer to Scarlet Robin. **Status:** Moderately common in the Wheatbelt. Common in the Mulga. **Where to find:** Rottnest Island. Eastern side of the Darling Range. Most large Wheatbelt reserves particularly with good stands of sheoak. Found throughout the Mulga and desert regions and gullies in the stony country of the north.

Hooded Robin *Melanodryas cucullata* subspecies *westralensis* 16 cm

There are four subspecies in Australia with one occurring in the GSW, subspecies *westralensis*. Hooded Robins have an unusual distribution in the South West. They can be found quite low down in the South West in areas like Boyup Brook but then patchily through the Darling Range wherever small patches of Wandoo occur as in areas like North Bannister. They can be found on the eastern side of the Darling Range to the east of Yarra Road between Brookton Highway and Great Eastern Highway. The author feels that the population in the Wheatbelt may be declining. In the 1970s it was not difficult to see 5 to 6 pairs of Hooded Robin in the main block in Dryandra Woodland Reserve but by the early 1990s it was difficult to find two pairs. By 2000 only one pair, then for a while none and only recently has a pair returned. The male has a complete black hood with a white underbody, black wings with a white bar, and a black tail. The female has a dull grey hood and back with darker grey wings and the underbody is grey-white. Its call is a short series of semi-harsh notes 'churpede churpede churrrp' often uttered from a high dead branch. It feeds like many robins by sitting on lower branches of trees and waiting before pouncing on prey.

Below: Male

Nest: The nest is a larger version of the Red-capped Robin's nest but more loosely structured on the outside and in more diverse sites, sometimes placed behind pealing bark or wedged in the fork of a mulga tree. Clutch size 1–2. **Similar species:** None. **Status:** Uncommon in the South West. Moderately common in the mulga and common further north. **Where to find:** In some wheatbelt reserves like Tutanning and Dryandra. Near Perth in the Wandoo Conservation Park. Easiest in the southern sheep stations in the lower mulga country.

Western Yellow Robin *Eopsaltria griseogularis* 14.5 cm

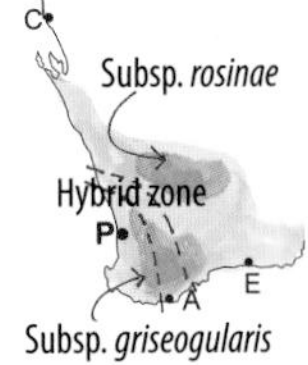

There are two subspecies in Australia and both occur within the GSW. The differences are not so much in terms of plumage variations but mainly in size of wing, bill and tarsus. The subspecies *griseogularis* can be found within a general line from Lancelin in the north down to Northam and to the coast near Albany. The subspecies *rosinae* can be found outside the lower South West beyond a line from Lancelin north to Tamala Station south of Shark Bay, then a line in a south easterly direction via Coolgardie and down to the Eucla coast. It has a longer wing and tail than the lower South West subspecies *griseogularis*. The Western Yellow Robin requires open woodland where it can perch and drop down to take insects. It can be found throughout the Wandoo Woodland often where a grove of young saplings are growing and will fly from trunk to trunk looking for insects. The sexes are alike. Has a lemon-yellow rump, vent and lower belly, white throat, grey crown and mantle with dark grey wings, faint white supercilium stripe and a stout bill. Has a great variety of calls from its agitation call, a rasping 'chip chip chipcheeeee', to the delicate high pitched 'pip... pip...pip...pip' of its contact call. **Nest:** It builds an exquisite well camouflaged cup nest with trailing bark that matches the trunk and branches where the nest is located. The internal nest is made of tightly woven fine grasses and lined at the base with feathers. Clutch size 3. **Similar species:** None. **Status:** Locally common in Wandoo. Less common through the Wheatbelt. Very common in the Transitional Woodland east of the Vermin Fence east of Hyden. **Where to find:** Darling scarp at Bungendore NR. Julimar Forest. Wandoo Conservation Park. Boyagin Rock NR. Dryandra Woodland NR. Stirling Range NP. Peak Charles NP. Dundas NR. Along the Lake King and Hyden roads to Norseman. Mt Jackson region.

White-breasted Robin *Eopsaltria georgiana* 15.5 cm

Endemic to Western Australia

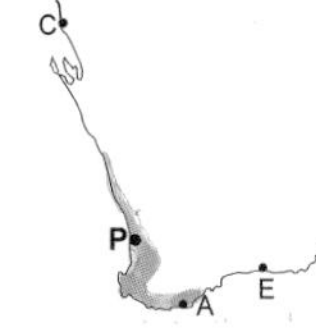

Found from Lake Indoon near Eneabba south to Lancelin. Then a break till the northern end of the Darling Range in Helena Valley and south to the heavily forested region of the lower South West and east to the Gairdner River on the eastern side of the Fitzgerald River National

Park. A bird that requires dense vegetation or a lush understorey as in the Karri Forest. Surprisingly, it still occurs in dense vegetation gullies in the semi-arid regions of Hill River area up to Lake Indoon; may be relic populations from when the coastal belt was wetter. Sexes alike, with a grey crown, back and lores, white supercilium stripe and white throat and underbody. In flight shows distinct white wing bars. Like most robins they have a variety of calls including a musical soft whistling call but the commonest call is a contact territory call of a series of single harsh notes 'cheuw.....cheuw..... cheuw'. **Nest:** The nest is similar to a Scarlet Robin's but has often ferns or other plant foliage woven into the sides disguising the nest. Placed in a fork often only a metre off the ground. Lined with fine grasses and soft bark. Clutch normally 2. **Similar species:** Jacky Winter, but territories do not overlap. **Status:** Common in the lower South West. Moderately common in riverine gullies along the Darling Range scarp. Uncommon in dense thickets between Jurien and Eneabba. **Where to find:** Near Perth. Wungong Valley. Upper Bickley Brook. Piesse Brook. Jarrahdale. Common in the Karri Forest and throughout the coastal scrub from Walpole NP to Waychinicup NP. Porongurup NP.

Southern Scrub-robin *Drymodes brunneopygia* 20.5 cm

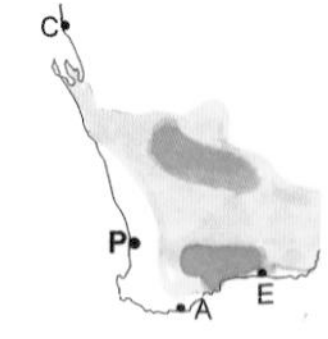

A ground dwelling thrush-like bird with a long tail that it will cock at times. Has a grey body with a chestnut rump and slight chestnut tinge in the tail feathers. Has a distinct white eye ring broken by a small black vertical stripe. Has white chevrons on the wing. Long legs. Has a soft contact call rising at the end of the two note call 'cheeeew... we...cheeeew....wee' also a warning scolding pitching call for intruders 'pipipitcheeee...... pipipitcheeee'. It is an inquisitive bird and it is not hard to imitate its contact call; if you sit quietly and just give a few extended 'picheeeee' calls, it will come and check you out. It ranges from Peron Peninsula down through the transitional Woodland to Coolgardie and south east to Dundas NR. Along parts of the southern coast through the Fitzgerald River NP and then north through to the Stirling Range. Wherever it occurs, it requires thicker vegetation to 2 metres high. In the southern region it is mainly in dense thickets of melaleuca under mallee. In the Wheatbelt say at North Tarrin Rock, it is not only in melaleuca thickets but also in low Kwongan heath as there is limited habitat for them to survive in. Below McDermid Rock east of Hyden it is found in broom bush (*Melaleuca uncinata*). Above the cliffs at Quoin Head in the Fitzgerald River NP it occurs in dense windswept thickets of Lemann's Banksia (*Banksia lemanniana*). In the north regions just north of the Murchison Bridge it occurs in heath with banksia woodland. In the Kalbarri NP in heath with an overstorey of mallee. **Nest:** The nest is always placed on the ground built into a depression excavated by the bird. It is a neat cup made of concentric fine twigs but with large twigs woven into the outside. Often placed at the roots of a mallee or mulga tree and invariably laid between a fallen branch or up against a tree root. Clutch size 1. **Similar species:** None. **Status:** Moderately common through most of its range. Scarce to extinct in many of the remaining small western Wheatbelt reserves. **Where to find:** All the locations mentioned above. Very common in the southern part of the Fitzgerald River NP.

Black-faced Cuckoo-shrike *Coracina novaehollandiae* subspecies *melanops* 30–38 cm

C
P
A
E

A medium sized cuckoo-shrike with a long tail and long wings found throughout the GSW. Generally prefers drier open woodlands but can be found in the lower South West although tends to avoid the dense Karri Forest and Jarrah Forest. Feeds mostly in the canopy of woodlands and rarely feeds on the ground, unlike the Ground Cuckoo-shrike. Feeds on a diverse range of insects, including caterpillars, beetles and grasshoppers but also will take fruit particularly in the semi-arid regions where native figs grow. The sexes are similar, only the immature birds can be recognised as different. They lack the full black facial mask but instead have a black broad eye stripe and the throat has not developed the pure black but has grey mottling that runs all the way down to the belly. Black-faced Cuckoo-shrikes have the interesting habit when landing after a flight, of always shuffling their wings. There is a distinct movement after the breeding season from the South West in mid January to March to the northern regions, mainly the immature birds. Call is rather cat-like rasping. **Nest:** They nest mostly above 5 metres on a horizontal branch where it forks, and build a shallow nest constructed of fine twigs and

grasses and on the outside bound together with spiders webbing. Clutch size 2–3. **Similar species:** In this region possibly Ground Cuckoo-shrike which is a bigger bird and deeper bodied. Has black wings that contrast with pale grey upperbody, barring on the underbody and rump. No facial mask. The Ground Cuckoo-shrike's flight is different as it is a direct flight that does not undulate, an important feature when seeing birds just flying. There are three subspecies in Australia and two in Western Australia: *subpalllida* in the Pilbara region has paler crown and upperbody, paler underbody than *melanops* which occurs throughout the rest of mainland Australia. **Status:** Common throughout range. Moderately common to uncommon in the Mulga Region. **Where to find:** Found near Perth on the Swan Coastal Plain and Darling scarp, mainly wherever there are open spaces near treed areas. Throughout parts of the Wheatbelt.

Ground Cuckoo-shrike *Coracina maxima* 32–36 cm

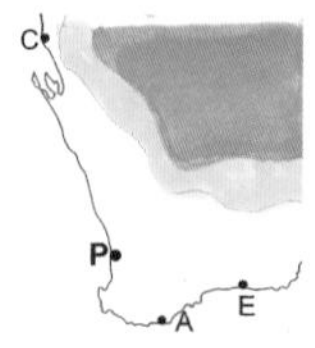

This is the largest of Australia's Cuckoo-shrikes, with a long tail, long pointed black wings, a grey head and upper back, distinct barring on the breast and rump. Yellow eye stands out from the grey head when close. A ground dwelling bird that walks on open ground with a jerky head movement searching for large insects, including spiders and caterpillars. Has a preference for feeding on stony ground often between spinifex or hummock grass. Normally a very nervous bird, when approached will fly off at a steep angle in the same manner and at the same speed as magpies, with a straight fast flight unlike other cuckoo-shrikes that are slower and undulate their flight. When it does fly, it shows the distinct contrast between its long black pointed wings and a very pale grey back, with paler white and black barred rump and long black tail making it easy to identify. It also utters its warning two noted contact call, a high pitched 'peep peep…peep peep' as it ascends. Often feeds in family groups of 5–6 birds, most probably the current and previous years non-breeding birds. Found throughout the Mulga Region, not a common bird but becomes more prevalent in the central Mulga Region centred on Meekatharra region and out to the desert regions and up to the Pilbara. The author has seen it a few times in the north eastern Wheatbelt near Chiddacooping NR and in ploughed fields north of Bonnie Rock and also north of Beacon. **Nests**: Normally 5–10 metres up in a fork not necessarily on a horizontal limb like Black-faced Cuckoo-shrikes. The nest is deeper and more substantial, made from fine grasses and strands of bark bound with lots of spiders webbing, often still with spiders egg sacks surrounding the outside. Clutch size 2–3. **Similar species:** Black-faced Cuckoo-shrike, which is smaller and has a black throat and face. No barring on the rump and underbody. Tail dark grey not black and distinctly shorter. Calls quite different. **Status:** Uncommon throughout the Mulga Region. Scarce in the Transitional Woodland and outer Wheatbelt. **Where to find:** Anywhere in the Mulga Region, can be seen as soon as one clears the Transitional Woodland areas such as around Ninghan Station.

White-winged Triller *Lalage sueurii* subspecies *tricolor* 17–19 cm

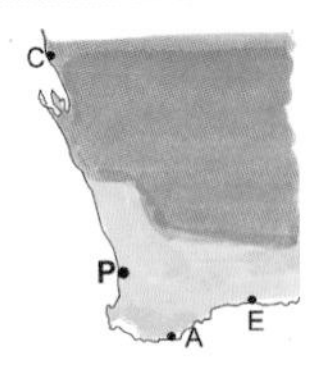

A small, slim black and white cuckoo-shrike. The male has a black cap, neck and mantle, a white throat and underbody and white shoulders on black wings. Female has a brown crown, neck and mantle, black and white in the wings and a slightly mottled fawn on white throat and under body. In non-breeding plumage, the male is almost identical to the female but rump is greyer and mantle darker brown with more black and white in wings but difficult to split. White-winged Trillers are a passage migrant moving into the South West Region in the spring to breed and more nomadic in the Mulga Region, travelling to areas that have had favourable rains where populations can be quite dense. When moving into areas to breed the male becomes really active calling loudly with low display flights between trees. The call is very powerful, a strong rapid 'chur chur chur chur chur' that can last a good 15 seconds or more. In the Mulga Region when an area has high densities of breeding birds after good rains, the triller may nest close to other birds and the calls of trillers, Pied Honeyeaters and Chiming Wedgebills asserting territories can be very noisy. Their nest is flimsy, normally only 1–2 metres off the ground in the mulga and higher up in trees in the South West. They prefer an open understorey below trees in the breeding season and do not enter the deeper south west in any reasonable numbers, having a preference for the Wheatbelt and eastern southern coastal areas. Feed mostly on the ground but will work through bushes, tending to alternate up and down to feed. Two subspecies occur in Australasia only one on the mainland *tricolor*. **Nest:** The nest is similar to a Black-faced Cuckoo-Shrike's nest, smaller in diameter but proportionally deeper. The outside is loosely bound with spiders webbing. Clutch size 2–3. **Similar species:** Pied Honeyeater, which is slightly smaller and has a complete black hood and mantle, black coming down to the middle of the chest. Distinct blue eye ring at base of eye. Much longer, finer, down curved bill. White rump not grey-white. Calls totally different. **Status:** Can be very common in the Mulga in the breeding season, disperses after breeding. Moderately common in the Wheatbelt. Uncommon on the Swan Coastal Plain south of Perth. Scarce in the heavy forested lower South West. **Where to find:** Wandoo Conservation Park (uncommon). All Wheatbelt reserves. Northern Stirling Range NP. Throughout the Mulga, less so in the Transitional Woodland.

White-breasted Woodswallow *Artamus leucorynchus* 16–18 cm

The largest of all the woodswallows, although only marginally so. Has a stocky body and short tail. Dark grey-black head and upperbody and wings. Distinct break from grey-black hood to white underbody. White rump seen well in flight, with grey-black tail. Grey-blue bill, small black tip. In the GSW found in the far north eastern coastal region around Carnarvon and the northern point of Peron Peninsula. Found along coastal beaches and has a preference for mangrove areas in much of Western Australia, although does not always feed over mangroves. Does not move inland as it does in the Kimberley and parts of the Pilbara region. Often perches in groups or singly on power lines when at rest, flying out to take prey on the wing. Will take prey from the ground. **Nest:** Nests in a variety of locations, mostly in mangroves or paperbarks near the coast. Can be in hollow tree trunks, broken off trunks, or a fork in branches. The nest is a broad cup shape of rough twined twigs getting finer to the centre with an inner lining of fine twigs and grasses. If in mangroves, placed in the fork of branches near the top of the tree. Clutch size 3–4. **Similar species**: Possibly Masked Woodswallow which occurs in the same area. They have a black mask and dark grey crown. Upperbody is grey not black-grey. Underbody pale grey not pure white. No black in tail. **Status:** Uncommon in Carnarvon region. Uncommon further south to New Beach. Far more common further north of Carnarvon to Exmouth and north. **Where to find:** Carnarvon area particularly Miaboolia Beach south to Gladstone.

Masked Woodswallow *Artamus personatus* 19 cm

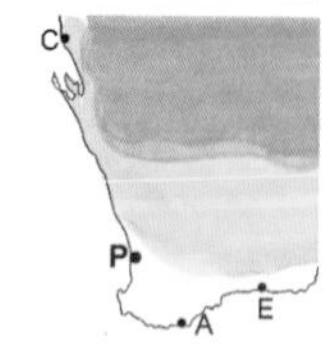

Similar size and shape as the White-browed Woodswallow, which it occasionally flocks with but in very low numbers in Western Australia and mostly in the desert regions only. As the name implies, has a mask on the face. The male has a black mask with a white border at rear of mask. Dark-grey crown, grey back and pale grey underbody. Fine down curved bill, longer than White-breasted Woodswallow. Female has similar markings but mask is grey not black and underbody more buff-grey than pale grey. Lacks the white border to the mask. Found in the semi-arid and arid regions of the GSW, mostly in open mulga. Occasionally comes into the northern and eastern Wheatbelt. Will fly over in flocks in the Transitional Woodland both east of Hyden and north east of Wubin. Forms large groups after the breeding season, in

some areas very large flocks that can be heard calling in the sky several hundred metres high, hawking for insects and constantly chattering keeping contact. They will also feed on nectar, descending in hundreds on the Honey Grevilleas (*Grevillea eriostachya*) and out of this region on the Holly Grevillea (*Grevillea wickhamii*). When near nests, pairs will give a more rasping harsh chatter. **Nest:** The nest is a shallow cup of twigs and bark quite frail at times, normally placed in the fork of a tree or end of a hollow, can be quite exposed. Clutch size 2–3. **Similar species:** None. **Status:** Can be locally very common. **Where to find:** Patchy distribution throughout the Mulga Region, can be on any of the stations where feeding conditions are good.

Right: Male Masked Woodswallow

White-browed Woodswallow *Artamus superciliosus* 18–20 cm

Can occasionally come into the Greater South Region but very rarely, mostly coming with large flocks of Masked Woodswallows from the eastern deserts and crossing into the Gibson and Great Sandy Deserts and occasionally into the Kimberley. The most colourful of all the woodswallows. The male has a rich chestnut-red underbody with blue-grey upperbody. Bold white supercilium stripe hence its species name. Grey tail with white tips. The female has a less rich coloured underbody being chestnut-brown. Back and head grey not blue-grey. Supercilium stripe diffused off grey-white. Easy to pick in flight with the Masked Woodswallow, having dark underbody and white wings whereas the Masked Woodswallow has a pale grey almost white underbody with pale grey wings, no dark colours at all. **Status:** Scarce in this region. Very uncommon further north and east, but can be locally common in Lake Gregory region. Moderately common to common in central eastern and south eastern Australia.

Captive bird

Black-faced Woodswallow *Artamus cinereus* 17–19 cm

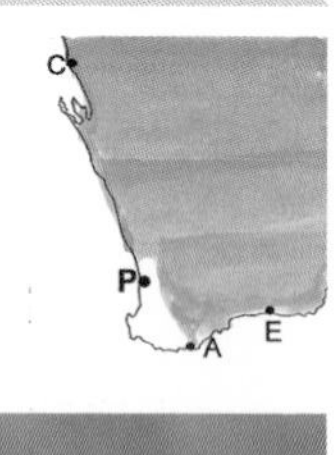

A medium sized woodswallow that covers most areas of Australia and all of the GSW, except the lower South West and denser parts of the Darling Range. Sexes alike with a small black facial mask on the lores and upper throat. Pale grey, slightly down curved bill with black tip. Grey back. Black tail with white tip. Like the Dusky Woodswallow, when birds alight on a branch they twist their tail in a figure eight movement before resting or after each time they call from a perch. A bird of varied habitat but not dense forests. Can be found on stony plains, in dry river courses, and mulga woodland, roadside verges alongside open fields, heathland. Does not like enclosed woodland even Wandoo Woodland. Before European settlement, the Black-faced Woodswallow did not occur in the lower South West but with land clearing the species spread into the agricultural region. To understand the preferences for certain habitats of species and specifically woodswallows, if you drive say to Dryandra Woodland Reserve in the inner Wheatbelt you will often pass the occasional Black-faced Woodswallow along the roadside verges but as soon as you enter the uncleared Wandoo Woodland of the reserve the populations of Black-faced Woodswallows cease and immediately Dusky Woodswallows become the dominant woodswallow. There are four subspecies in Australia and two occur in Western Australia: *melanops* that covers most of the arid part of Australia including the Kimberley down to the Transitional Woodland line, and *cinereus* that occurs in the South West. Differences are only slight and not easily visible in the field and integration occurs along the Transitional Woodland Line. **Nest:** Nests are a woven mesh bowl of twigs in varied locations from low shrubs, grasstrees in heath to the end of tree hollows. The nest is similar to a Masked Woodswallow's but not so exposed being placed in the centre of bushes or in vines or other thick foliage. Clutch size 3–4. **Similar species:** Dusky Woodswallow, same size and jizz but all dark chocolate-brown with no contrast between upperbody and underbody; also has white in the wings which can be seen at rest. **Status:** Very common in the Wheatbelt and common in the Mulga Woodland Region. Scarce in dense forest and the Transitional Woodland. **Where to find:** Swan Coastal Plain. The Darling Scarp. Throughout the Wheatbelt and Mulga Region.

Captive bird

Dusky Woodswallow *Artamus cyanopterus* subspecies *perthi* 16–19 cm

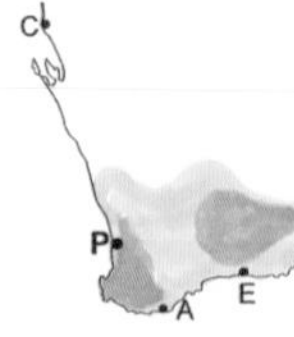

A medium sized woodswallow found in the forested South West. There is evidence of some movement in autumn and winter away from the lower South West. Dusky Woodswallows have an all dark chocolate coloured plumage and a gunmetal blue bill with a small black tip. The tail has a white tip and white on the primaries shown as a thin white line on the wings when at rest. In flight shows its light coloured grey underwing and from above an all dark brown body and upper wing, except the outer primaries which have white shafts. Dusky Woodswallows hawk from perches to gain insects, sometimes going to ground to feed. They are particularly prevalent in the Karri Forest and remnant Wandoo Woodland. There are two subspecies: *cyanopterus* in the east coast region and *perthi* in the South West. **Nest:** They nest mostly against the trunk of trees where bark is dislodged, a small sapling juts out from the trunk or a small trunk is broken off, but rarely build at the end of a horizontal branch as do many birds. A frail bundle of twigs is constructed with little or no lining, placed 3–8 metres high. Clutch size 3–4. **Similar species:** Refer to Black-faced Woodswallow. **Status:** Moderately common in Karri and Wandoo and some Jarrah woodland. Scarce in the open Wheatbelt. Common in the eastern part of the Transitional Woodland but not the northern part. Rarely in the mulga although there is a small amount of movement by some birds leaving the south at the end of autumn and through winter. **Where to find:** Julimar Forest. Wandoo Conservation Park. Boyagin Rock Reserve. Dryandra Reserve. Dongolocking. Cherry Pool Reserve. Stirling Range NP. All of the Karri Forest including the eastern population of Karri in the Porongurups.

Little Woodswallow *Artamus minor* subspecies *minor* 13–15 cm

The smallest of the woodswallows, found in the northern parts of the GSW in the Mulga Region. Darker black-chocolate-brown than the even grey-brown Dusky Woodswallow. The whole body is black-brown with black-grey wings. Small white inside tip to the tail. Fine blue-grey bill. Can be found in open woodland but mostly woodland near rocky terrain, including steep rock faces or granite boulders. A gregarious woodswallow that will roost and loaf in a group mainly on cliff faces. During the day will perch on dead saplings or mulga and fly out hawking for insects. There are two subspecies: *minor* which is found in the GSW and *derbyi* found in the Kimberley and eastern northern Australia. **Nest:** The nest is normally placed on a rock ledge or in a crevice but occasionally in a broken off part of a tree or hollow. The nest is a small cup shape of twigs with fine grasses or twigs on the inner lining. Clutch size 2–3. **Similar species:** Dusky Woodswallow which is noticeably larger, is a lighter chocolate-grey-brown and has white in the outer wings. Rarely found in the same location except in the Mt Jackson region. **Status:** Uncommon and patchily distributed in the Mulga Region. **Where to find:** Walga Rock east of Cue. The 'Granites' north of Mt Magnet. Tallering Peak north of Mullewa. Wooleen Station. The base of the Kennedy Range (slightly north of this book's range).

Grey Butcherbird *Cracticus torquatus* subspecies *leucopteris* 27–30 cm

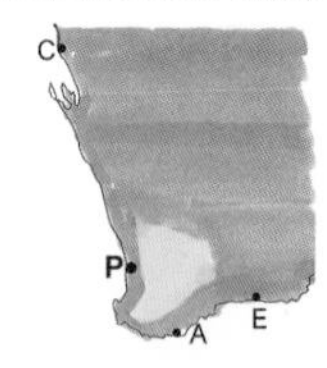

Found throughout the GSW even in many Perth suburbs. The Grey Butcherbird has a black head with white throat, grey back, black and white in the wings, all white underbody, black tail with white tip, white spot on lores. A massive bill for the size of the bird with a down curved black tip. Is a smaller bird than the Pied Butcherbird. Feeds on insects, lizards and small birds mainly young. Like all butcherbirds, has a strong and varied call that sounds like chuckling but is still melodious; is an accomplished mimic, although the author finds the western subspecies *leucopteris* mimics less than the east coast subspecies *torquatus*. Varied in its choice of habitat. Is the only butcherbird found in the wetter forests of the deep South West and much of the lower South West, although it avoids much of the central Darling Range. Found in the Wheatbelt. Transitional Woodland and Mulga Region. In the Mulga Region there is sharing or overlapping of territories but it is not totally understood how these habitats can support both Pied and Grey Butcherbirds with similar feeding requirements. The Grey Butcherbird is certainly more prevalent in the southern Mulga Regions and the Pied Butcherbird more so north. The Grey does frequent thicker stands of mulga in the south. There are five subspecies in Australia, in the Kimberley a bird known as the 'Silver-backed Butcherbird' is a distinct subspecies *argenteus*. The birds of the GSW *leucopteris* vary only subtly from the east coast birds. The Pilbara birds are lighter on the back than the South West birds and have a pure white underbody. **Nest:** Placed on a multiple fork 2–8 metres above ground or in lower shrubs or trees but requires dense outer foliage; the nest is constructed of loosely placed twigs but the inner lining is neatly woven grasses and fine twigs. Clutch size 3–4. **Similar species:** Pied Butcherbird, which is distinctly larger and has a black bib going down to the lower breast. Grey Butcherbird has all white throat and underbody, no bib. Pied has a black back not grey and its white collar extends completely around neck, the Grey Butcherbird's stops at the nape. Pied has an even more massive bill. Calls different. **Status:** Moderately common in lower South West. Common in parts of Perth. Uncommon in Wheatbelt. Moderately common in southern part of the Mulga. Uncommon further north. **Where to find:** Perth. Darling Range scarp. More common in southern coastal areas particularly in the Esperance region. Less common in the northern and eastern Wheatbelt than the Pied Butcherbird. Common on southern mulga stations and central mulga stations centred on Paynes Find, Yalgoo and Cue and Murchison Settlement.

Pied Butcherbird *Cracticus nigrogularis* subspecies *picatus* 28–32 cm

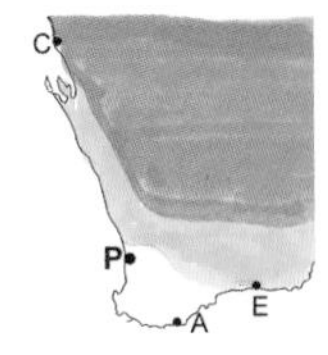

Found throughout the GSW but not the lower South West. A bird principally of semi-arid and arid regions of Western Australia. The sexes are almost alike. Both have black bib and head; white collar, black back and wing, with white in the wings. Black tail with white under-tail feathers near tip; white underbelly; massive bill. Female has slightly narrower white collar that is diffused with grey mottling but not always clear. The subspecies *picatus* found in most of Western Australia has slight differences to the east coast nominate race *nigrogularis.* Birds in the GSW have a wider white collar, longer bill, bib does not come as low and the clean marked break with white belly not diffused. There are small differences with the female which has a shorter tail and shorter tarsus. Feed on insects including beetles and grasshoppers. Some fruits, small reptiles, young birds. **Nest:** Large round twig nest with a deep centre placed in the fork of a tree, normally 5–12 metres high up in eucalypts but in mulga obviously lower down. Call is astounding and one American sound recordist said, it was one of the finest songsters in the avian world he had ever heard. A very rich melodious call, quite varied. Unlike the Grey Butcherbird's rapid staccato type call, the Pied Butcherbird's notes are long and slow. They will vary the song and bring in different elements. Pied Butcherbirds do not come down to the deeper South West preferring drier more open country. They are particularly common in the northern and central Wheatbelt and since land clearing have extended their range from the Mulga Region. Having groups of trees as in a roadside verge and then cleared open spaces to sight insects and other prey has been ideal for them. **Nest:** The nest is similar to the Grey Butcherbird's but tends to be higher and sometimes more exposed. Clutch size 3–4. **Similar species:** Refer to Grey Butcherbird notes. **Status:** Scarce in the lower South West including the southern Swan Coastal Plain and most of the southern coast. Moderately common in the inner Wheatbelt, getting more common the further east and north one goes. Uncommon in the eastern Transitional Woodland. Moderately common in the northern Transitional Woodland. Common throughout the Mulga Region. **Where to find:** North of Moore River. Wongan Hills. Kellerberrin. Merredin. Reserves near Hyden. Kalgoorlie. Wubin and all stations north of the Transitional Woodland line

Grey Currawong *Strepera versicolor* subspecies *plumbea* 44–57 cm

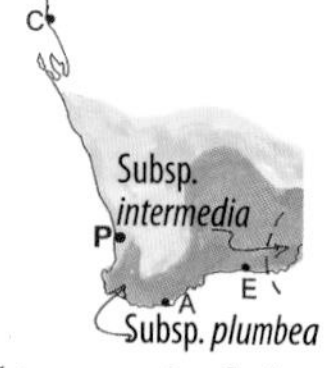

There are distinct variations in Grey Currawongs throughout Australia with six subspecies identified to date. In the GSW Region there is one subspecies *plumbea* that overlaps with *intermedia* on the southern belt of the Nullarbor. A very large crow-like bird but unrelated to the corvids. Grey Currawongs have a massive bill almost conical in shape. An all dark grey body and wings when at rest. Distinct yellow eye. White vent. In flight shows clear white bullseyes in wings and white vent and tip on under-tail. Even though all currawongs in the GSW are grouped under one subspecies *plumbea*, the author finds distinct variance in their grey colour, finding a clinal change from the lower south west birds being darker than those in the Transitional Woodland and getting lighter as one enters the mallee on the Nullarbor. The calls of birds in Jarrah Forest are distinctly different to birds east of Lake Cronin and also birds in the mallee in the Ongerup region, particularly the alarm calls. Grey Currawongs have varied feeding habits. They feed walking along in a Ground Cuckoo-shrike style, bobbing the head as they look for insects and spiders or small reptiles. They will cling to grasstree stems and pick out the many insects attracted to flowering grasstrees. They are a very successful hunter of small birds and the author has seen them pull a Striated Pardalote from a small nest hollow or take out the complete clutch of very young Common Bronzewing Pigeons. They will work through bush well after sunset, trying to flush out small roosting passerines. In a nesting territory, they can have a drastic effect on the bird population immediatly around a nesting site. **Nest:** Their nest is a bulky affair though not as big as a Raven's, about 5–10 metres high in eucalypt or other large tree, normally more concealed or less exposed than corvids nests. Clutch size mostly 3. **Similar species:** Could be confused with Australian Raven which has no white in the wings or tail, best seen in flight. Different bill shape and no yellow eye. **Status:** Moderately common in the Jarrah and Karri Forests. Moderately common in the southern Mallee Regions. Uncommon in the Wheatbelt mainly found on larger reserves. Common in the Transitional Woodland east of Hyden. Sporadic in the southern Mulga Region. Does not occur much further north than the Murchison River. **Where to find:** The Darling Range and scarp particularly on roadside verges of the Brookton and Albany Highways. Wandoo Conservation Park. Boyagin Rock Reserve. Dryandra Reserve. Stirling Range National Park. All the southern national parks from Leeuwin–Naturaliste in the west to Cape Arid in the east and north to Coolgardie and up to Mt Jackson.

Grey Currawong juvinile hybrid – *plumbea-intermedia*, found on Nullarbor.

Australian Magpie *Gymnorhina tibicen* subspecies *dorsalis* 37–43 cm

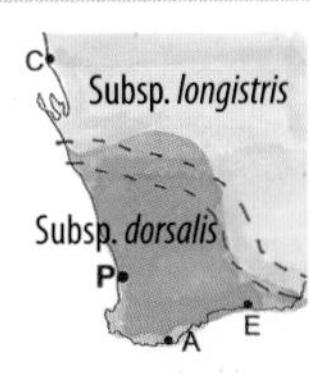

The Australian Magpie can be found throughout most of Australia and throughout the GSW, being most common in the South West. In the arid regions their distribution is fragmented and one may see a family group and then not another for a long way, sometimes as much as 20 to 40 km in remoter country. They prefer open areas with woodland to roost and nest in but feed almost entirely on the ground. Have adapted well to European settlement and are found throughout cities and towns. Magpies have a long stout bill with down curved hook at the end and long and strong legs with distinct pied plumage. There is great variation in patterning of plumage particularly the distribution of white on the back, and also in weight with a variance from 220 g to 350 g, which is a large disparity. Authorities identify 8 subspecies throughout Australia. Two can found in the GSW: *dorsalis* from the lower South West to the Murchison and then south east down to the edge of the Nullarbor, and above this line overlapping with the subspecies *longirostris* of the Pilbara. The South West birds are generally the largest of the subspecies and are likely to have a white back more than the 'black backed' form. As the species goes north and overlaps with *longirostris* there are more black backed magpies. The complexities of subspecies in Australia is compounded by the fact that there is partial migration of immature birds to other regions and in the South West immature birds go to northern areas. However the South West population is the most cut off from external influences and retains a higher degree of consistency, with males mostly white backed and on average larger than east coast birds. The average reader should not get bogged down with the complex taxonomy but it is interesting to see the changes from South West birds to Pilbara birds and Kimberley birds. Magpies are extremely territorial and will defend feeding areas aggressively. Family groups will sit together with head and bill pointing skyward, giving their combined carolling calls asserting territory with the same technique as Kookaburras. The family relationships and their complex behaviours are interesting, like submissive displays where one member will hold its head down fully extended while fluttering wings and a dominant bird will stand over and lightly peck at the neck or rear of head. Many such behaviours with magpies have been well studied. The Australian Magpie has a varied song which is linked to the social territorial group. They call well into the night during the breeding season, less so it seems in an urban environment. **Nest:** The nest is slightly neater than a Grey Currawong's but is a similar broad twig nest neatly lined with fine grasses and plant material. Often built quite high, from 8–15 metres. Clutch size 3–4. **Similar species:** None. **Status:** Very common now in urban environments. Common throughout the South West both in the Wheatbelt and the open forested regions. Less so in the denser forested areas of the Darling Range and Karri Forest. Moderately common to uncommon in the Mulga Region. **Where to find:** Throughout the GSW.

Western Bowerbird *Chlamydera guttata* subspecies *guttata* 27 cm

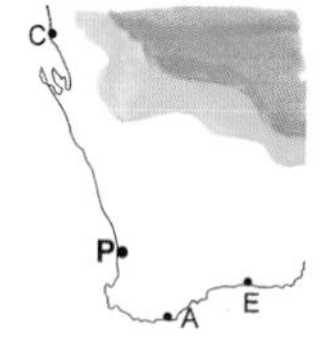

A stocky bowerbird of both central Western Australia and central Australia found in a variety of habitats, particularly stony country where the Rock Fig (*Ficus platypoda*) grows. It does however feed on a variety of fruits and other figs like Sandpaper Fig (*Ficus opposita*) in the northern range, the fruits of Sandalwood (*Sorghum spicatum*) and Northern Sandalwood (*Santalum lanceolatum*), Quandong (*Santalum acuminatum*) in the southern range. Has adapted to feeding around homesteads where there are fruiting trees and permanent water. The male's bower is normally built under an acacia tree with an umbrella covering, the bower being placed near the trunk of the acacia. This occurs in typical open mulga country. They also can be found away from rocky areas along creek lines that have thick riparian vegetation and will have their bowers in the dense vegetation where vines or dense shrubs are compacted together. One would never walk in these areas normally but their hissing, scalding and mimicry of other birds gives their bower's location away. Other typical locations particularly for the subspecies *carteri* can be in narrow gullies on the side of hills. As is well known, the male plays no part in the nest building and raising of young. His energies are entirely concentrated on maintaining a successful display bower. He is polygamous and will mate with any female that is attracted to the bower and will mate in or adjacent to the bower. The female locates the bower by hearing the male's contact calls that are made at the top of a nearby tree. It goes through its repertoire of chuckles, hissing and mimicry calls. Once the male sees that a female is attracted, he will descend from the tree and start a sideways hopping dance, near the bower and will try and lead the female into the bower. He will perform calling in the centre of the bower with his pink nape display plumes fully extended and the female may inspect the bower. If the female is impressed with the bower, she will allow the male to mate and in the breeding season the male maintains the bower, attending it most periods of the day and bringing new additions of white objects such as land snail shells, bits of white china, white quartz and small bleached bones. In addition, there will be some green objects, never as many as the white ones but nevertheless most bowers will have some. In the central Mulga Region they are normally non-ripened Sandalwood or Quandong fruit that have not turned purple and will last several weeks in a green state. The centre of the bower is an immaculate structure so finely woven with twigs that the passage of a bird moving through the bower is not hindered. Bowerbirds are unmistakable in flight being the only stocky orange-brown coloured bird to fly in the central semi-arid regions. Their flight is a long undulating flight only a few metres above the canopy of trees or ground. There are two subspecies of

Western Bowerbird: *guttata* found in central Australia and central Western Australia and an outlying population in the Cape Range near Exmouth, subspecies *carteri*. There are complex variations in tarsus and wing size but in the field Cape Range birds are darker, their plumage is richer orange-brown and particularly the underbody is darker. **Nest:** The female builds the nest and raises the young alone. The nest is an untidy affair of twigs in a shallow cup shape built normally in a three way fork in acacias or eucalypts almost always away from the male's bower area. Clutch size mostly 2 can be 3. **Similar species:** None. **Status:** Locally moderately common in the Mulga Region. Overall, uncommon in the Mulga Region. **Where to find:** Not far into the Mulga Belt just south east of Paynes Find on Pindabunna and Pullargaroo Stations and north of Kalgoorlie. Moderately common in the Mt Magnet, Meekatharra and Wiluna region and further north and east out of the range of the GSW.

Australian Raven *Corvus coronoides* subspecies *perplexus* 46–53 cm

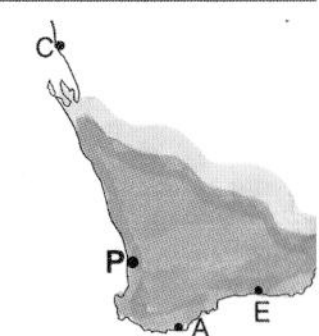

Most non birdwatchers think there is just one corvid and that they are all crows. There are 5 corvids in Australia; 3 occurr in Western Australia: two crows, the Torresian Crow (*Corvus oru*) and Little Crow (*Corvus bennetti*), and one raven, the Australian Raven (*Corvus coronoides*). In the GSW, the range of the Australian Raven extends as far as the Wooramel River and south east through Kalgoorlie down to the base of the Nullarbor at Eyre and Eucla. One of the largest corvids, it is found throughout the South West. It least favours the dense forested areas although it does occur in them, and is more common in the Wheatbelt, the Swan Coastal Plain and the open woodlands of the Transitional Woodland and parts of the southern Mulga Region. Basically a carrion eater scavenging on anything, being primarily an opportunistic feeder. Works in parties and family groups. Identifying corvids is not always easy but the Australian Raven is one of the easiest to identify in the field, as it has long throat hackles that are visible most of the time particularly when calling as illustratted below. Calls are the primary way birdwatchers differentiate one species of corvid from another. The Australian Raven has a few short loud calls finishing with a long extended call that reduces in volume 'aaahk, aaahk, aaahk .....aaaaaaah'. Calls vary and are complex withina family group. Sometimes it means food is available. Sometimes it is just a contact call, a single 'aaark'. Often a warning call. There are two subspecies of Australian Raven with only one in Western Australia *perplexus,* which has slightly shorter hackles although still long compared with other corvids and slightly smaller than the east coast subspecies *coronoides*. **Nest:** The nest is bulky and loosely constructed, lined with finer twigs or grasses and also sometimes wool or plant down is wedged into the fine twig lining. The nest is placed normally well above 8 metres. Clutch size 4–5. **Similar species:** Torresian Crow and to a lesser degree Little Crow. Even though some authorities say Torresian Crow looks the same size as the Australian Raven, the

raven certainly looks a bulkier corvid particularly around the head. If not extended the hackles hang from the throat giving the neck line a thicker appearance whereas the Torresian has only slight hackles that definitely do not extend from the throat to any great length. Also the bill is fractionally bigger and bulkier on the raven. It is not a diagnostic feature but the raven occurs mostly from the Transitional Woodland south west and the Torresian Crow rarely enters the South West Region, less so than even the Little Crow. The Torresian's call is different from the raven's, it gives a short faster call 'ark ark ark ark' sometimes slightly extended at the end but never as long or low pitched as the raven. It also a peculiar low toned gurgling call difficult to put into words. The Little Crow is easier to differentiate as they are distinctly smaller and the bill is shorter, slimmer and more pointed. Has no hackles at all and the jizz of a Little Crow is of a sleek smooth corvid with proportionally longer looking legs and less feathering on the thighs. In full sunlight has a distinct sheen. Its call has similarities to Torresian but is lower and mellower sounding 'naark, naark……naark, naark'. **Status:** Common in the Wheatbelt and Swan Coastal Plain. Uncommon in the lower south Jarrah Forest and Karri Forest. **Where to find:** Perth and other large towns. Throughout the Wheatbelt. Roadside verges particularly on the Albany Highway through the Jarrah Forest.

Torresian Crow *Corvus orru* subspecies *cecilae* 46–51 cm

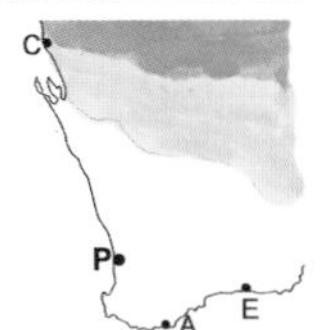

A corvid of the drier regions of central Western Australia and the Kimberley and other states. Does not come down to the South West and rarely comes past the line from Shark Bay south east to Paynes Find, Southern Cross and east through to Norseman then north to Zanthus and through the Great Victoria Desert to central Australia. Its range virtually extends where Australian Raven does not occur. Does not favour the very open arid areas of the desert. Found more around watered areas or along river and creek systems. Will come around station properties scavenging for food. More omnivorous than the Australian Raven taking fruits as well as carrion or small, live prey. Less flocking than Little Crow. The Torresian's call is different from the ravens, it gives a short faster call 'ark ark ark ark' sometimes slightly extended at the end but never as long or low pitched like the raven's. **Nest:** Nests singly not in groups, as does Little Crow. The nest is similar to that of the Australian Raven and placed normally higher than 6 metres. Clutch size 4–5. **Similar species:** Australian Raven and Little Crow, refer to notes on Australian Raven. **Status:** Common in the mid to northern region of Western Australia not so common in the southern Mulga Region. Uncommon in the northern Transitional Woodland. **Where to find:** Carnarvon region, Gascoyne River. Mt Magnet and north. Kalgoorlie and north.

Little Crow *Corvus bennetti* 44–48 cm

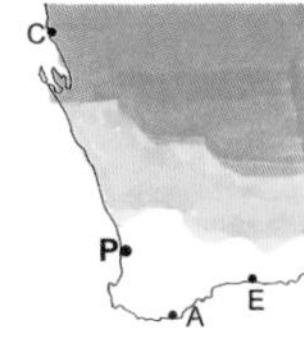

The smallest of the corvids. A sleek smooth plumaged crow often found in large flocks that can fly high in spiralling flights, calling constantly and often performing aerodynamic displays in all directions. They do come into the northern and eastern Wheatbelt in summer and are often overlooked by birdwatchers presuming them to be ravens. They come further south than the Torresian Crow which makes it easier to split from Australian Raven, as Torresian looks similar to Australian Raven. The Little Crow is more prevalent in the open mulga away from water than the Torresian Crow. Also more likely to inhabit sand dune desert areas than Torresian Crow. Will often nest in small colonies. Found alongside outback roads feeding off road kills and when Wedge-tailed Eagles feed on carcasses will still come and try and take the meat, being a very agile corvid. Will shuffle wings when alighting. Its call has similarities to Torresian but is a slower more mellow 'naark, naark……naark, naark'. **Nest:** A smaller nest than the other two corvids and also can be lined with earth matted with the fine grass lining. The Little Crow's nest can be much lower and sometimes in denser mulga is only 4–6 metres off the ground. Clutch size 3–4. **Similar species:** Torresian Crow and Australian Raven, refer to notes on Australian Raven. **Status.** Common throughout the Mulga Region and desert regions. Uncommon in the Wheatbelt in summer. **Where to find:** Any station property north of Paynes Find. Kalgoorlie and Carnarvon.

Horsefield's Bushlark *Mirafra javanica* subspecies *woodwardi* 12–15 cm

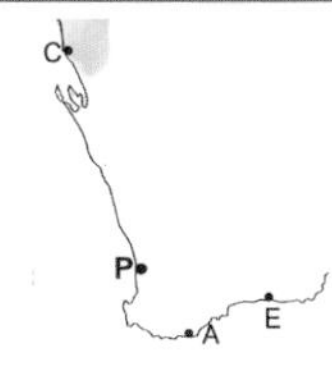

A short tailed stocky lark with a finch-like bill. Has a short crest when raised. Easily identified in flight by short triangular wings and short tail distinguishing it from the Australian Pipit and the songlarks, all having longer tails and wings. A bird of the semi-tropical and tropical north found from as far south as Cobra Station and north across the grass plains south of the Pilbara and east to Lake Gregory. Has a preference for short grassed plains, some spinifex plains and occasionally samphire flats but mainly grassed country, particularly on black soil plains. Being a seed eater, it must always be not too far from water. The subspecies *woodwardi* which is the only subspecies within the range of the GSW, is one of the lightest fawn coloured birds of the species. There is great variance within the *javanica* subspecies throughout Australia and much of this is related to the soils where they feed; obviously survival from raptors is increased by blending in with the soil colour as there are often no shrubs to retreat to. **Nest:** The nest is a well concealed, deep cup placed alongside grasses, often having a partial hood of grasses. The inner lining is fine woven grasses. Clutch size 3–4. **Similar species:** None really, possibly Australian Pipit which is a slightly longer bird with longer tail and longer legs and stands more upright. Outer white tail feathers are more prominent on the pipit, breast more streaked. **Status:** Common on grass plains north Carnarvon. **Where to find:** Comes as far south as the Carnarvon region on the open grass plains but mainly north of the Gascoyne River, becoming more common the further north one goes.

Zebra Finch *Taeniopygia guttata* subspecies *castanotis* 9–11 cm

A small finch found throughout most of the semi-arid and arid regions of Australia. They do come into the northern Wheatbelt, particularly north of Beacon and Bonnie Rock mainly in the summer. In the mulga they become more common the further north and north east one travels. They are a common sight at cattle and sheep troughs gathering often in hundreds particularly after the breeding season. They are a highly nomadic species travelling to regions where the winter or summer rains have been heavy. The sexes are different. The male has a large orange patch on the lores, the female just grey lores. The male flanks are orange with white spots, the female has no colour on the flanks just the same underbody fawn. The male has a grey throat and upper breast with fine grey-black barring and at the base of the chest a diffused black band. Zebra Finches must come to water and rarely are more than 10 km away from a water point. The author once found a rock hole in the desert. Looking into the hollow he could see no water at the bottom, but suddenly out of

a small crack no more than 10 cm wide a few birds flew out, such is the need and ability to find water. They feed almost entirely on the ground sometimes in the company of Southern Whiteface. **Nest:** The breeding habits of Zebra Finches are well known mainly from captive birds, but in the wild they breed in loose colonies making a ball nest. There will often be 2 or 3 nests in one thick acacia bush such as Kurara (*Acacia tetragonophylla*). Nest locations can vary, obviously most nests will be in dense bushes but it's not unusual to see them in the base of larger raptors' nests such as a Black-breasted Buzzard's or a Wedge-tailed Eagle's nest. One station owner told the author that he had one days break from using his plane and came back a day later and they were building a nest in the engine intake grill, such is the opportunistic nature of these birds. They can breed at any time of year and will starting mating within 24 hrs after heavy rains, although rain is not the only key factor; grass conditions and state and abundance of available seed are crucial. They also build roosting ball nests, which are untidier than true breeding nests. Clutch size 4–5. **Similar species:** None. **Status:** Very common in the Mulga Region. Uncommon in the northern Wheatbelt. **Where to find:** Throughout the Mulga Region, more prevalent north of Mt Magnet.

Star Finch *Neochmia ruficauda* subspecies *subclarescens* 11–12 cm

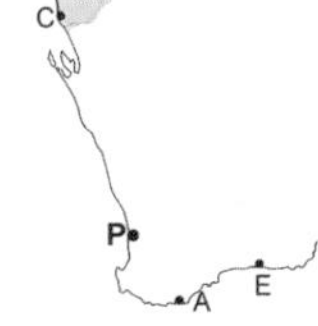

An uncommon finch in the northern part of the GSW. Requires areas with lush rank grass which restricts its distribution, so in this region is confined to areas near Carnarvon and a few locations up to Rocky Pool, tending to be a summer visitor from the Pilbara in good seasons. A flocking finch rarely seen alone. The male has a large facial red disc and bill with white spotting over the lores. Rear of head, upperbody and wings olive-green. Breast and flanks green with extensive white spotting. Belly and vent pale yellow. Tail dark cinnamon-brown with rump having white spots. Female very similar but facial red disc smaller and upperbody a duller olive-green. Underbody less contrasting green with white spots. When native grasses are lush and long, will cling to a stem dropping it to ground and then run bill along the stem taking the seed. In drier conditions will feed from ground. There are three subspecies in Australia, *subclarescens* found in the Pilbara, Kimberley and Gulf of Carpentaria, *clarescens* in the Cape York region and *ruficauda* in fragmented populations in northern Queensland. **Nest:** Nests in low thick shrubs rather than tall grasses, mostly near water. The nest is an oval shape ball with a side entrance, woven into the branches of a dense bush or located in thick tall grasses. The inner nest is made with fine grasses and lined with feathers. Clutch size 4–5. **Similar species:** None. **Status:** Uncommon in Carnarvon and lower

Gascoyne River region. More common north of the region in the Pilbara, like Millstream or Opthalmia Dam near Newman and even more so in the Kimberley like the Kununurra area. **Nest:** Often a suspended nest from a hanging shrub, often exposed. **Where to find:** On the edge of Carnarvon in the cultivated areas and a few pools along the lower Gascoyne but not common and transitory.

Red-browed Finch *Neochimia temporalis* 10–13 cm Introduced

An introduced finch from the east coast, found in a few creeks on the Darling Range scarp surviving in riparian vegetation. A finch with a distinct red supercilium stripe and dark olive back. Dark grey head and underbody. Bright red rump and upper tail, very distinct in flight. Black lower tail, red bill. The bird on the east coast is mainly found in lush vegetation and in the west it survives in the few wetter creek lines close to Perth on the Darling scarp. **Nest:** The nest is a bottle shape, turned on its side with a drooping entrance hole. In the Darling Range mostly placed in thicker bushes like banksias and dryandras. Clutch size 4–6. **Similar species:** None but could be confused with the endemic Red-eared Firetail which has barring on underbody, not plain grey. Has no red supercilium stripe. Head and back is brown not olive-green. **Status:** Scarce in the Darling Range. **Where to find:** Piesse Brook. Helena Valley. Bickley Brook.

Red-eared Firetail *Stagonopleura oculata* 11–13 cm

Endemic to Western Australia

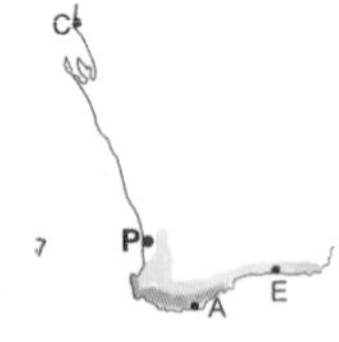

Found only in the wetter lower South West wherever there is lush thicker vegetation. Mainly found along creeks and rivers in riparian vegetation. Common in peppermint groves (*Agonis flexuosa*), also in coastal heath. The sexes are almost identical in the field, having small red patch on the ear coverts, small black area on the lores and a bright red bill. Chest and throat have faint light and dark brown barring. Belly bold black and white barring. Red rump and upper tail and black middle and end tail. Call is easily imitated, having a downward and then upward fine high pitched whistle 'wheeee..... wheeee ... wheeee'. Feeds mostly on the ground. Its range extends from the Helena Valley in the northern part of the Darling Range east to Wandoo Conservation Park on Qualen Road, Darkin, south to Cape Naturaliste and all along the southern coast to Cape Le Grand. Found on offshore islands in the Recherche like Woody Island. Inland to the Stirling Range and middle Fitzgerald NP. **Nest:** Typical finch ball nest placed in various locations, mostly above 3–4 metres up in low tree often peppermint trees.

The author found one on the side of East Mt Barren wedged into the side of a Royal Hakea, not a typical location. The nest is a dense ball of loose grasses with a side entrance tunnel. The inside is neatly lined with grasses and often with feathers or plant down; normally placed in the outer foliage of a drooping eucalypt or peppermint tree. Clutch size 4–6. **Similar species:** None. Refer to notes on Red-browed Finch. **Status:** Locally common in South West. **Where to find:** Wungong Gorge. Upper Bickley Brook. Ellis Brook. Along the southern coast from Cape Naturaliste to Cape Le Grand. Common between Walpole and Albany.

Painted Finch *Emblema pictum* 10–12 cm

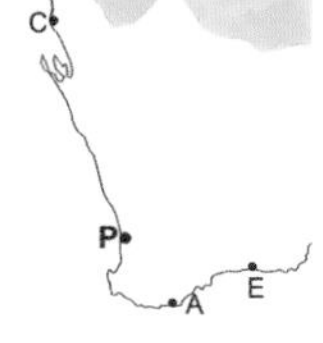

A bird of the northern parts of Western Australia but occasionally can be irruptive and come down to the Gascoyne and Murchison catchments, particularly when the Pilbara region has experienced drought and more rain has fallen in the Gascoyne region. Frequents rocky habitats with spinifex (*Triodia*) and other grasses, normally never great distances from water. The male has a red facial patch from the forehead down to the upper throat. Brown upperbody and most of the head. The underbody is black with bold white spotting. Bright red rump and upper tail. Bi-coloured bill with lower mandible red. The female is very similar

but the red facial patch is not as large. The white spots on the underbody are longer and cover more of the black underbody, appearing more like barring than just white spots. It has a plaintive, chirping call often given in flight. **Nest:** The nest is a ball shape of woven dry grasses almost invariably placed in spinifex either within the spinifex clump or wedged at the base on the ground below overhanging spikes of the spinifex. Clutch size 3–5. **Similar species:** None. **Status:** Common in the Pilbara and Kimberley but scarce in the northern part of the GSW. **Where to find:** Occasionally in the middle Gascoyne region centred on Glenburgh Station also north west of Meekatharra.

Chestnut-breasted Manikin *Lonchura castaneothorax subspecies castaneothorax* 12-13 cm

Introduced

Introduced to the Perth region in the early 1970s. Found naturally in the Kimberley, Northern territory and all the way down the east coast to the state of Victoria. A bird that frequents reed beds, long native grasses particularly the various canegrasses (sorghum) species. Always found in groups feeding on grass seeds often hanging on the side of long grasses and its own weight dropping the stems to the ground, then it will feed off the seed heads. There are four subspecies in the world with only one in Australia. Nest: In long grasses where it will weave its bottle shaped nest between grass stems. Normally uses flat bladed grasses. Clutch size: 4–5. **Similar species:** None in the South West. **Status:** Scarce in the South West. **Where to find:** Previous sightings were at Herdsman Lake.

Australasian Pipit *Anthus novaeseelandiae* subspecies *australis* 13–18 cm

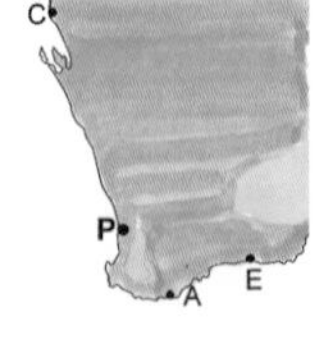

A very common pipit, found throughout much of Australia and all of the GSW although does not frequent the heavily forested areas of the Darling Range and the southern Karri Forests. Its preferred habitat is open spaces often quite bare, sometimes stony; wherever there are short grassed or bare soils in the Mulga Region, roadside verges, claypans, eroded areas near creeks, open areas in samphire, open bare areas in fields. Its bobbing tail is a feature of this small bird whenever it alights. Has a relatively long tail with a similar jizz to northern hemisphere wagtails but the tail is not as long and it does not wag its tail constantly like wagtails do. Feeds entirely on the ground with a typical run and pick technique. In flight white outer tail feathers are the main feature to quickly identify it from songlarks, and more extensive white than Singing Bushlark. There are thought to be eight subspecies in Australia but this is open to debate. Only two in the GSW: *australis* basically north and east of the Transitional Woodland line and *bilbali* in the South West, both extremely similar with only small differences. Bergman's law applies with southern birds being slightly larger getting smaller in a clinal change the further north one goes. **Nest:** A small flat cup shape nest is built at the base of grasses or against fallen timber with loose litter. The inner lining is woven fine grasses. Clutch size normally 3. **Similar species:** Singing Bushlark which has shorter tail, less white in the outer tail feathers and a more finch-like bill, not long and slender. Not as upright or as long legged. Has more chestnut in wings. Stockier jizz. **Status:** Common throughout the GSW except the heavily forested regions. **Where to find:** Anywhere there is open ground and grassed areas, including playing fields in towns.

Yellow Wagtail *Motacilla flava* subspecies *tschutschensis* 17 cm Vagrant

C
P
A
E

A rare bird to the GSW but has been seen in Carnarvon and Perth. A species with a large number of subspecies, various authorities identifying 13–22 subspecies. Their range extends through Europe, Russia, the Far East. Siberia and Alaska. Migrates to the southern hemisphere between October and March. The subspecies *tschtschensis* migrates from eastern Siberia and western Alaska down to China and Indonesia but can fly on down to Australia. Other subspecies have migrated to Australia. Often found in northern towns wherever there are well watered grassed areas. Yellow Wagtails have a grey upperbody and bright yellow underbody in breeding plumage. The non-breeding plumage is mostly seen in Australia, the yellow underbody is more diffused and paler. Has a white supercilium stripe. Long grey-black legs. Very long dark grey tail with white in the outer tail feathers. **Similar species:** Grey Wagtail which has a distinct black throat in the breeding season but moults to white in non-breeding. Yellow Wagtail always has yellow throat. Supercilium stripe not as long. Citrine Wagtail has all yellow head even in non-breeding plumage. **Status:** Rare in the GSW. Scarce in the Pilbara. Uncommon in a few locations in the Kimberley. **Where to find:** Have to go to Port Hedland for a chance and almost guaranteed in Broome during mid summer months.

Mistletoebird *Diccaeum hirundinaceum* 9–11 cm

A small bird similar in shape to pardalotes. The male very distinctive with a bright red throat. Blue-black upperbody with a slight metallic sheen. Underbody off white with unusual feature of a black central band running from breast to vent. Red vent and undertail. Stout small bill. Female has plain grey-brown head and upperbody, lacks the blue-black back. Has pinkish vent and under tail. Vertical band on belly is dark grey-black and underbody diffused grey-white. Found in a variety of forested areas including open woodlands and mulga but always where there are trees that are parasitised by mistletoe. Where there are extensive stands of mistletoe the higher the probability of Mistletoebirds being present. They range throughout the GSW but are scarce in the thicker Jarrah Forest and Karri Forest. Their primary food is mistletoe fruit but they eat other fruits and also insects. In adaptation to feeding on such a high percentage of small fruits the Mistletoebird's digestive system has evolved into a unusual structure. They possess a rudimentary gizzard and a simple digestive tract with no enlargements and a long intestine, so berries pass from the oesophagus straight to the intestines. The berries pass through the body in as short a time as 4 minutes. They have the well known habit of defecating on branches, the seed being stuck to the branch by a sticky coating surrounding the seed. The bird is the primary transporter of mistletoe seed to other host trees. There are four subspecies of Mistletoebird throughout Australasia but only one in Australia. **Nest:** Their nest is unusual in as much as it is pouch shaped with a long oval entrance. It is a soft nest made from spiders webbing and fine grasses, the outside always is woven with either insect larvae sacs or plant down. Placed in the outer foliage of a eucalypt or acacia, often well hidden. Clutch size 3–4. **Similar species:** None. **Status:** Uncommon to moderately common throughout range. **Where to find:** Particularly prevalent in the inner Wheatbelt in Wandoo and York Gum Woodland. Moderately common in the Mulga Region.

Above: Female

White-backed Swallow *Cheramoeca leucosternus* 13–15 cm

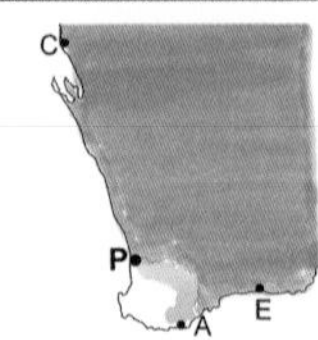

A solitary swallow that does not flock like other swallows, only flying with the immediate family. Has distinct patterning on the body, with a white crown, black eye band running from lores through the eye and around the nape. Triangular white patch on the back. White throat and armpits. Long tail. A fast flyer. Found primarily in semi-arid and arid regions near sand banks where it nests. Is a sedentary swallow so will remain in areas that afford a good nesting site and abundant food. One location due east of Hyden has been used for the last 20 years. Found throughout the GSW, except areas within the lower South West roughly from Perth south east around the Jarrah Forest down to Albany. If approaching a nest locality the swallows will normally fly very high and sometimes out of sight, mostly though will remain at least 200–300 metres high watching their territory. Adults and dependent young leave the nest together one after the other, flying high while making a high pitched chirp contact call; will circle for a while and then leave for feeding areas sometimes over heath or tree tops. They come back to rest during the day and then return to feed often not until just after the sun has set. **Nest:** A long tunnel excavated in a sand or clay bank with twigs at the base of a small nest chamber. Clutch size 4–5. **Similar species:** Can not be confused with any other swallow. **Status:** Uncommon throughout range in the GSW, a little more common out of the range in the desert regions. **Where to find:** Just north of Perth. Lancelin. Jurien. Hill River. Odd gravel pits in the Wheatbelt. On the Hyden-Norseman road. Even sand banks within the Transitional Woodland. In the Mulga Region.

Barn Swallow *Hirundo rustica* 15–18 cm   Vagrant

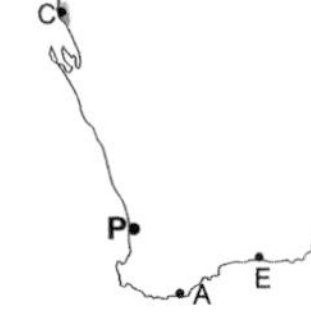

A rare vagrant to the GSW, has been seen in Carnarvon. Far more prevalent in the Kimberley in Broome and Derby. Breeds throughout the northern hemisphere. It is a regular visitor to northern Australia but never in huge numbers although flocks of 200 plus have been sighted in Broome. Often perches on telegraph wires particularly in Derby. **Similar species:** Very similar to the resident Australian Welcome Swallow but has longer tail streamers and a distinct black band at the base of the orange-chestnut throat. Underparts a pure white whereas Welcome Swallow has a slight greyish off white appearance. At rest say on wires, Barn Swallow shows longer tail streamers. **Status:** Rare in the GSW. Locally common in parts of the Kimberley between November and March.

Welcome Swallow *Hirundo neoxena* subspecies *carteri* 14–16 cm

A very common swallow found throughout the GSW although its numbers diminish from the Pilbara and the GSW towards the desert regions. Sexes alike in the field. Has an orange-chestnut forehead and throat with black lores. Black-blue back with glossy sheen in full sunlight. Tail passes wing tips when at rest. Found in a variety of habitats, mostly where there are open areas with woodland adjacent and often over water and tree canopies. Requires reasonable insect populations in flight which the semi-arid and arid zones do not have. Often around islands and coastal waters. In the southern Mulga Region around dams and troughs. Apparently was restricted to the coastal regions when Europeans first settled these shores but with land clearing spread to Kalgoorlie and further north. There are two subspecies in Australia *neoxena* on the east coast and *carteri* in the South West. One cannot split them in the field but the South West birds have a fractionally shorter tail and slightly longer bill. **Nest:** Usually placed on a rock ledge often with a cover above nest. Since European settlement, has taken advantage of additional nesting sites particularly in towns under garage roofs or under eaves, particularly in the Mulga Region where nests sites are not so plentiful. If you are near a body of water, you can park a vehicle for few hours and birds will begin to investigate the interior of the car as a possible nesting site almost oblivious of your presence. Their nest is a compact cup shaped nest, preferably on a horizontal surface. Consists of mud pellets mixed with grasses to make a dense hard nest. Clutch size 3–5. **Similar species:** Refer to Barn Swallow. **Status:** Common throughout the South West, becoming less common the further north and north east one goes. Uncommon in the Jarrah Forest and Karri Forest.

Tree Martin *Hirundo nigricans* subspecies *neglecta* 12 cm

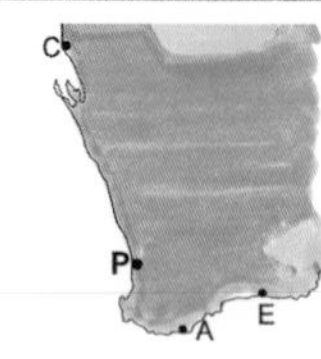

Found throughout the GSW wherever there are eucalypts. In the breeding season will form small groups within a woodland, nesting not far from each other and feeding often in groups. The South West birds are partially migratory, moving north to the Pilbara and semi-arid regions of Western Australia. After the breeding season, they form larger groups and will disperse north mid summer to end of summer. Some birds do however remain in the South West. They are very common in Karri Forest and Wandoo Forest. There are two subspecies in Australia, *nigricans* which breeds in Tasmania and migrates in late summer along the east coast with some birds flying to New Guinea and *neglecta* which breeds in all parts of southern Australia and moves north in late summer. **Nest:** They nest in tree hollows in both live and dead branches. Eggs are laid either on loose existing timber debris or leaves, twigs or grasses within the hollow. Prefer horizontal entrances on branches if available. Clutch size 4. **Similar species:** Fairy Martin, which has an orange-chestnut crown not black-blue. Does not nest in trees but makes a mud nest in caves or in culverts. **Status:** Common throughout the South West particularly in the heavier forested regions. **Where to find:** Darling Range. Karri Forest and much of the Wheatbelt and Transitional Woodland.

Fairy Martin *Hirundo ariel* 12 cm

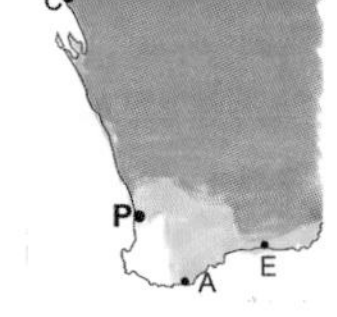

Found throughout the range of the GSW, except the heavily forested South West corner. Not as common in the South West as the Mulga Region and even more common the further north one travels with the Pilbara and Kimberley having the greatest numbers; since European settlement with the introduction of culverts and bridges, the population has increased throughout its range. Fairy Martins are mostly found near water, and in the Mulga Region when good winter rains have fallen they become increasingly active in spring, particularly if there is plenty of surface water, as they require water to mix with earth to make their mud nests. Many of the earth nests found in caves can be many years old and the remoter the country the more caves are used, as culverts are few and far between. Fairy Martins have an orange-chestnut crown, black-blue back, black wings, white rump and white underbody and throat. The throat is faintly streaked with fine pale brown markings. In flight shows a short square tail with a shallow wedge shape. Feeds in flight on insects but will come to

ground to take insects but not as much as Tree Martins. **Nest:** A bottle shaped structure with the neck of the bottle lying horizontal which is the entrance tube. The nest cavity in the bulbous part of the bottle shape is lined with grasses. Fairy Martins nest communally, in fact throughout their whole life they remain in a communal group. Clutch size 3–5. **Similar species:** Tree Martins which have a black-blue crown not orange-chestnut colour. Have a small orange-chestnut patch on the forehead just above the bill. Have the same jizz and white rump as the Fairy Martin so it is important to check the colouring of the head. In flight Fairy Martins make more of a buzzing twittering call than Tree Martins. **Status:** Not common in the South West and the Southern Mulga Regions. Moderately common when there is sufficient surface water in the Gascoyne River catchment and northern Goldfields. **Where to find:** Can be common on the Carnarvon floodplains. Throughout the Mulga Region in areas that have had good winter rains.

Australian Reed Warbler *Acrocephalus australis* subspecies *gouldi* 16 cm

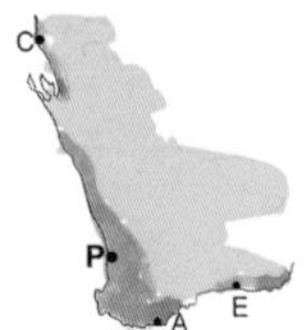

A medium sized reed warbler, found in fragmented populations wherever there are reasonable stands of reed beds. The majority of birds in the GSW region can be found in wetlands south west of a line from the Murchison River in the north to Bremer Bay in the south. Mainly sedentary in Western Australia but there is certainly movement to drier regions, establishing territory in new reed beds formed from either bores or new sewerage works. Their call is very strong and lets one know they are resident. They can exist in the smallest patch of reed beds as is often the case in the Mulga Region where excess water from bores forms only small wetlands. There are two subspecies in Australia, *australis* in northern and eastern Australia and *gouldi* in the South West and Pilbara region. The difference is related to wing size and bill length but so marginal it is not easily seen in the field. **Nest:** They build a deep cup shaped nest, woven between two or three reed stems mostly over water. Clutch size mostly 3. **Similar species:** Oriental Reed Warbler, which has not yet been recorded in the GSW. It is a slightly bigger bird with a larger bill and faint fine black streaking on the side of the throat. Call very similar but can be distinguished as it is a far more grating rougher call, not as soft as Australian Reed Warbler's also not quite as fast. This bird can be overlooked and if found in this region would most probably be in the Carnarvon region reed beds. Little Grassbird is much smaller, with rufous crown and streaking on the breast. Call is totally different. Tawny Grassbird not found in this region. **Status:** Locally common throughout the South West wetlands. **Where to find:** In Perth: Herdsman Lake. Lake Monger. Lake Gwelup. Bibra Lake. Other areas: Benger Swamp near Harvey. Lake Seppings, Albany. Found on most large freshwater lakes with reeds in the South West.

Little Grassbird *Megalurus gramineus* subspecies *thomasi* 12–15 cm

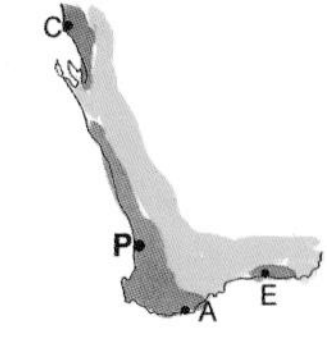

A similar range in the GSW to that of the Australian Reed Warbler, both requiring reed bed habitats. Little Grassbird is a small reed dwelling warbler with a fine down curved bill. Has a fine white supercilium stripe, dark rufous crown, faint black streaking on the breast, bold dark brown mottling on the back. Relatively long tail for its size. Call is mournful soft whistle, the first note extended, then three rapid notes and final extended note 'weeee... wee, wee, wee...weeeeee'. Calls constantly in the breeding season but very little out of breeding. Will occupy even smaller bodies of reeds than Australian Reed Warbler, often being found in outback dams with reeds. It will also inhabit thicker samphire around estuaries such as at Peel Inlet. There are three subspecies in Australia: *gramineus* from Tasmania, *goulburni* from eastern Australia and up to the Kimberley and *thomasi* found in the GSW as far as Shark Bay. **Nest:** Similar to Australian Reed Warbler but smaller entrance that is more concealed, the nest chamber is lined with feathers. Sometimes uses old reedwarblers' nests. Not only nests in reeds but also melaleuca and samphire shrubs. Clutch size 3–4. **Similar species:** Tawny Grassbird not found in this region. **Status:** Common in all wetlands with reed beds. **Where to find:** In Perth. Eric Singleton Sanctuary, Bayswater. Herdsman Lake. Alfred Cove. Bibra Lake. Peel Inlet. Most wetlands in South West. Many bores throughout Mulga Region like at Cobra Station. In town wetlands at Carnarvon.

Photo Michael Morcombe

Rufous Songlark *Cincloramphus mathewsi* 19–20 cm

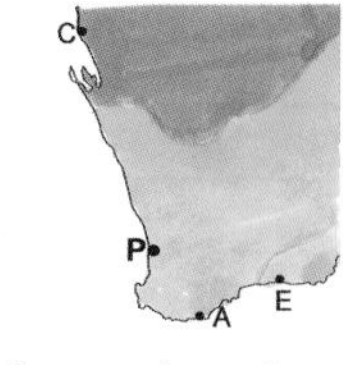

Movements of Rufous Songlark within the GSW are dependent on weather conditions. If the Mulga Region is experiencing bad droughts more birds will enter the South West, for example Dryandra Woodland NR will in some years have breeding birds and other years no birds. In the South West birds arrive in early spring and leave in early summer, however numbers are greatest in the Mulga Region particularly in areas where good rains have fallen. They prefer open woodland with long grasses. Have a preference for creeks and river systems in the Mulga Region where grasses and ephemeral plants are at their peak in growth. Their call is in some ways similar to Brown Songlark but much softer and more musical. In the breeding season, the male calls from a perch and then will fly into the sky but not as high as a Brown Songlark's uttering its call as it ascends at a low angle and then descending into the grasses. The Rufous Songlark is a plain fawn coloured songlark with a white supercilium stripe, slight flecking on the breast and a distinct chestnut rump. The sexes are very similar but the female is slightly smaller. **Nest:** The nest is an open cup structure placed on the ground either within a grassed area or at the base of a larger clump of grass with dry grasses leading from the top making it well camouflaged. Clutch size 3–4. **Similar species:** Brown Songlark female. The female looks very similar to both sexes of the Rufous Songlark but lacks the chestnut rump. The streaking on the back is stronger, more bold but is not an easy diagnostic feature to pick. Australian Pipit is smaller and has a more upright stance and has white in the outer tail feathers and no chestnut rump. **Status:** Uncommon to moderately common in open woodland in the South West including parts of the Wheatbelt. Not found in heavy forested areas of the South West. Can be very common in areas of the Mulga Region. **Where to find:** Most Wandoo reserves in the Wheatbelt in spring, early summer in good seasons. Found in grassed areas of the Transitional Woodland. Any station in the Mulga Region.

Brown Songlark *Cincloramphus cruralis* 19–25 cm

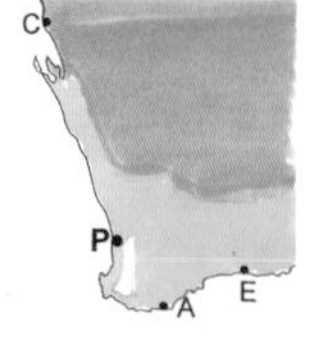

Found throughout the GSW in areas of open treeless grasslands, farming areas, sparsely wooded areas and samphire flats. Does not enter the heavily forested parts of the South West and rarely occurs in open woodland such as Wandoo, Salmon Gum or York Gum unless adjacent to large open areas. The male is far larger than the female, one of the largest variances between the sexes of any Australian bird. The male weighs on average 70 g, the female just 33 g, less than half the weight. In breeding, the male develops a very dark brown plumage mainly on the underbody. In non-breeding is still darker than the female but the throat lightens to a patchy off white with dark brown flecking and the breast lightens. Immature males have similar colouring to the female but are still twice the size. The female is a lighter fawn coloured bird with darker streaking on the upperbody and proportionally shorter tail. In the breeding season the males fly almost vertically, while calling as they ascend

in skylark fashion, then they drop with wings held out extended almost in a 'parachute' drop, gliding to the ground. They will also call from the top of the tallest shrubs, with tail cocked. The call is a metallic grating discordant call 'pitchuweedeewe….pitchuweedeewe….. pitchuweedeewe'. **Nest:** On the ground under clumps of grass. In samphire or low bushes. Sometimes semi-colonially in samphire in good years. Clutch size 2–4. **Similar species:** The female is very similar to the Rufous Songlark but lacks the rufous rump and the bill is thicker and the upperbody a slightly lighter fawn colouring. **Status:** Common locally in good seasons in the Mulga Region. Moderately common in good seasons in the outer Wheatbelt. **Where to find:** Samphire flats in the Wheatbelt. Hummock grasslands, samphire and claypans in the Mulga Region.

Yellow White-eye *Zosterops luteus* subspecies *balstoni* 9.5–13 cm

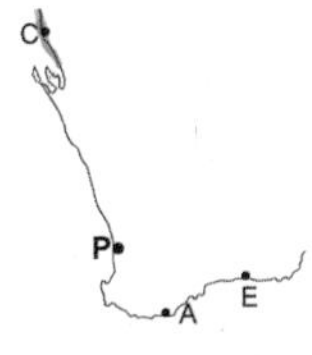

Mostly found in mangroves. In the GSW region from Long Point in the south to Lake Macleod in the north of the region. A small White-eye with an all yellow underbody. Lime-green head and upperbody, fine bill, distinct white eye ring. Small yellow streaks on the lores. An active feeder moving along the coastline within its territory. Feeds on insects as well as nectar and fruit. Does not travel far from the coast except in a few localities in the Pilbara where they have been sighted as far inland as Millstream. Normally in ones and twos but occasionally groups of up to ten birds work through the mangroves together mainly out of the breeding season. There are two subspecies at present: *luteus* from coastal north Queensland to northern Kimberley, and *balstoni* from west Kimberley to Long Point and Peron Point in the Shark Bay region. **Nest:** Small cup nest placed in fork of mangrove 2–3 metres high. The nest is made of grasses and bound together with spiders webbing. Clutch size 2–3. **Similar species:** Silvereye, which has a grey-white underbody with faint buff flanks but no yellow. No yellow patch on lores. Has grey-green mantle not lime-green. Territories can overlap. **Status:** Common in all the mangroves from Long Point to New Beach and north to Carnarvon and Lake MacLeod. **Where to find:** New Beach. In Carnarvon, Mangrove Point. Oyster Bay, Babbage Island and Miaboolia Beach.

Silvereye *Zosterops lateralis* subspecies *chloronotus* 11–13 cm

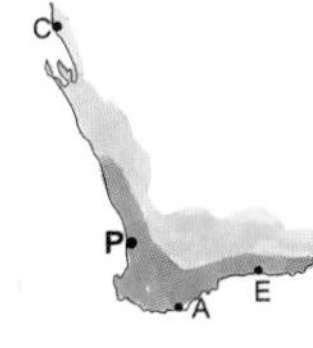

A common bird throughout much of the GSW. There is a marked movement of Silvereye in the late summer and through winter along the coast moving north, then returning to breed in late spring. They range as far north as Coral Bay and then not far from the coast until Moora and then across to Kalgoorlie and down to the Eucla coast. Silvereye are extremely common in the lower South West Region and along the southern coast with large numbers in the Esperance region. Sexes are alike. The South West subspecies *chloronotus* has an olive-green mantle not a grey mantle, shorter wings and tarsus than the east coast nominate subspecies *lateralis*. **Nest:** A neat woven cup nest made from fine grasses and bound with spiders webbing. The base of the nest has a layer of feathers or dry grasses, placed in the centre of a low shrub. Clutch size 2–4. **Similar species:** Besides Yellow White-eye discussed under that specie, the only other small greenish coloured bird it could possibly be confused with is the Weebill which has an olive-brown rather than olive-green back. Yellow underbody not grey. Bill far smaller and thicker. **Status:** Very common in the lower South West. Uncommon inland away from the coast. **Where to find:** Throughout the South West.

The following are additional introduced or uncommon to rare resident birds or rare vagrants that may be seen in the GSW that are not illustrated in this publication. This covers the vast majority of land and shorebirds that are possible to see in the GSW.

Mallard *Anas platyrhynchos* 55–70 cm — Introduced

An introduced species from Europe, native to Europe, Central Asia and North America. Introduced species are always a concern particularly as this species is related to the Pacific Black Duck which is endemic to Australia, and interbreeding does occur. It was introduced in the 1860s to the east coast and then finally here in 1912 and is still resident on some Perth wetlands. **Similar species:** Female Pacific Black Duck. **Status:** Uncommon.

Australian Little Bittern *Lxobrychus minutes* subspecies *dubius* 25–36 cm — Vagrant

A very small Bittern, the male having a black crown, chestnut-orange face and nape, black back, rump and tail feathers. When at rest shows cream-brown wings but in flight the primary feathers show black. Has a distinct dark brown lateral band running from the throat down to the lower belly. The female lacks the black back, rump and tail feathers, instead has a mottled brown and pale cream back. Found in dense reed beds. **Similar species:** Yellow Bittern which is an extremely rare vagrant only sighted in tropical Australia and unlikely to be found in the South West. Male Yellow Bittern lacks the Black back instead has a chestnut-orange back. **Status:** A scarce to rare species in the South West. Still not established whether they are a winter spring visitor as the only sightings have been during this period of the year. **Where to find:** Nests have been located at Lake Jandabup in the past. Sighted at Carine Swamp. Wetlands due west of Frankland, especially Kulinilup Lake. Also previous sightings in the Moore River region north of Perth.

Black Bittern *Lxobrychus flavicollis* subspecies *australis* 56–64 cm

A medium sized, dark bittern with a prominent yellow-cream stripe running from the lower jaw done the side of the neck to the shoulder. Also has finer stripes on the throat and breast. Often seen at rest, perched high in paperbark or riverine eucalypts. Tends to frequent the larger rivers of the lower South West including the Blackwood, Donnelly, Frankland, Warren and Shannon Rivers. Has been found nesting on small freshwater lakes surrounded by dense stands of paperbark, particularly on the Swan Coastal Plain south of Mandurah. There are three subspecies in the world with one in Australia**. Similar species:** None. **Status:** Scarce in the South West relatively common in the Kimberley. Often missed as hunts predawn and dusk a lot and well hidden when resting high in tall riverside trees. May be under recorded in the South West. **Where to find:** All rivers mentioned above.

Australian Bittern *Botaurus poiciloptilus* 65–75 cm

The largest of all bitterns found in Australia. A secretive species rarely sighted and more often heard than seen. Its deep booming call uttered in the breeding season can be heard several hundred meters away. It calls mainly at dusk and dawn. Requires dense permanent reed beds. Authorities are quite rightly concerned for the status of Australian Bittern. At Benger Swamp in the early 1980s in one bird count alone, eight Australian Bittern were sighted. Recent surveys sighted no bittern there, which is a concern as there have been few sightings in recent years. **Similar species:** None. **Status:** Scarce and its population could possibly be threatened in the South West. **Where to find:** In the Perth region, has been sighted at Herdsman Lake, Lake Jandabup and Lake Thompson. In the lower South West at Lake Muir, Kulinilup Lake. Lake Angove and Lake Pleasant View.

SNIPE: Latham's Snipe *Gallinago hardwickii* 28–30 cm; Pin-tailed Snipe *Gallinago stenura* 25–27 cm; Swinhoe's Snipe Gallinago megala 27-29 cm; Painted Snipe *Rostratula benghalensis* 23-26 cm

All vagrants to the GSW

There are 4 species of Snipe that have occurred in Western Australia and are possible to be found in the GSW, Latham's, Pin-tailed and Australian Painted Snipe have been recorded in the GSW and there is the possibility of Swinhoe's occurring here.

Latham's, Pin-tailed and Swinhoe's are all of the same genus *Galinago*. Australian Painted Snipe is totally unrelated being of the genus *Rostratula.* Snipe are generally very shy and skulking birds who are well camouflaged with their brown streaked plumage except the Australian Snipe, which is far more colourful. Splitting the genus *Galinago* is no an easy task and although having seen them throughout Australia at varying times and at least 10 times in the South West, the author still has trouble identifying these species such is their cryptic nature of *Galinago* snipe. Some ornithologists can tell the differences in flight and even call when taking off but this requires many sightings of these rare species, however, Latham's if seen well is easier to identify as the toes in flight do not pass the tail. In both Swinhoe's and Pin-tailed the toes pass the tail tip slightly more so in the Pin-tailed. Latham's is the largest of the three species 29–33 cm, but the difficulty is compounded by the fact that females of all species are larger. The main way to identify the species correctly is having a bird in the hand. Latham's has the least quantity of tail feathers of 18. The tail feathers pass well beyond the wing tips at rest. Pin-tailed 25–27 cm is closer in size to Swinhoe's 27–29 cm. The wing tips at rest almost meet the tip of the tail in the Pin-tailed and they have 24-28 tail feathers. Swinhoe's wings when at rest stop well before the tail tip similar to Latham's. **Status:** All 3 species are rare in the GSW with Swinhoe's having not been recorded. **Where to find:** In Perth; Kogolup Lake. Jandabup Lake. Neerabup Lake. Possible in any small wetland, not with dense reed beds but mostly lakes with tall wet grassed margins. In the South West any wetland with sufficient wet grassed margins with little human disturbance.

Australian Painted Snipe 23–26 cm

A very attractive species and easily identified from the *Galinago* species. It is a smaller bird 23-26 cm. The nape on the female is a rich deep chestnut-red brighter bleeding into a dark black head and throat. The male has a grey-brown head and neck with fawn lateral streaks running down the throat. Strong barring on the back of both sexes. There is a white-eye stripe extending past the eye in both sexes. A distinct white bar breaks the deep chestnut-red breast from a grey. **Status:** Rare in the GSW. **Where to find:** Has been sighted in several wetlands mainly on the Swan Coastal Plain both south and north of Perth. Has been sighted in Carnarvon. Was apparently, more common on the Swan Coastal Plain in the early 1900s.

Ruff *Philomachus pugnax* 26–32 cm — Vagrant

The species name that is used is the name given to the male bird and the female is called a Reeve. The name Ruff is used because the male in breeding develops the most distinct plumage of any wader having a set of plumes that emanate from the ear coverts and neck that forms a ruff around the head and neck. These plumes develop shortly before the displaying period in the breeding season. The colours of the individual males vary greatly some having black crown feathers others pure white. Ruff in non-breeding plumage is still a very distinct looking shorebird having a bulky body, perhaps the deepest set body of any wader with a long neck and disproportionate small head size to body size. Slightly decurved bill and medium length legs. Will feed on mudflats but has a preference for freshwater to brackish lakes and pools. Often one of the first waders to take flight when approached being generally wary, will stand upright and stretch neck when alert and nervous and will generally take flight when you approach. There are no subspecies the bird being monotypic. **Similar species:** In Australia none. **Status:** Scarce in the GSW. **Where to find:** Most years at least 5–10 sightings from different wetlands in the GSW are made each year with Lake MacLarty being one of the best locations to see this bird.

Red-necked Phalarope *Phalaropus lobatus* 18–19 cm — Vagrant

A small headed wader, with a fine bill. Feeds on both saline and fresh water but in the South West Region found mainly on saline waters, Has for many years been sighted on Rottnest Island in late spring through to Autumn but less so in the 2004 on. Has the characteristic habit of swimming in circles one way and then the other picking at aquatic invertebrates from the surface of the water while constantly bobbing its head. It will feed on lake margins but most of its feeding is done while swimming. They rarely venture on land to feed and do so just to loaf. It breeds in the high Arctic in marshes in northern Europe, Russia and North America. **Similar species:** Grey Phalarope. Chances of getting Grey Phalarope in the GSW is fairly remote and far less so than Red-necked Phalarope which itself, is very scarce. In non-breeding plumage they are similar but the Grey is a larger bird with a shorter and thicker neck and its back is more even grey less scalloped. In breeding unmistakable. The Red-necked Phalarope has a chestnut band running from the eye down to the side of the neck stopping on the upper breast. The female chestnut band is broader than the male and passes around the chest. The Grey Phalarope has complete orange-chestnut neck and underbody both for the male and the female. **Status:** Rare in the GSW. **Where to find:** One or two birds have been seen fairly regularly on Rottenest Island in past years but in recent years far less so. Largest numbers recorded out of this region have been at Leslie Salt Works in Port Hedland.

Oriental Plover *Charadrius veredus* 21–25 cm — Vagrant

Breeds in remote grass plains of Mongolia and northern China. Almost all the worlds' population migrates to Australia in our summer. Has a preference for inland grass plains but congregates sometimes in thousands on the northwest beaches. Rarely comes down to the GSW and the author's most southerly sightings of this bird were on the Nullarbor Plain after severe inland dust storms. A tall plover having very long yellow-cream legs. In non-breeding plumage has a distinct white supercilium stripe and dark crown, beige neck and darker back with an all white underbody. In breeding plumage the neck and breast turn a chestnut-orange colour with a strong black margin forming at the base of the chestnut-orange on the breast, which contrasts with the white underbody. Has an unusually fine long bill for a plover. **Similar species:** None really, the nearest would be a Large Sand Plover which is smaller, shorter neck shorter and far more robust bill with shorter legs. Head colouring different. Large Sand Plover has black facial patch running through eye. **Status:** Scarce in the GSW very common in areas in the Kimberley and the rest of northern Australia. **Where to find:** No specific areas in the GSW, only chance sightings mostly inland.

Kelp Gull *Larus dominicanus dominicanus* 49–62 cm

Unlike the Pacific Gull, which is endemic to Australia, the Kelp Gull can be found on the coastlines of the Antarctic, the sub Antarctic islands, southern Africa and southern South America as far north as Peru. Over the last 60 years the Australian population of Kelp Gull has been expanding on the east coast and its range is still increasing, but in WA it is still very uncommon with rare sightings on the west coast and several sightings on the south coast. Distinctive features include: smaller than Pacific, smaller head, smaller less massive bill, red-orange on lower bill, complete white tail, nostril fine and elongated, small white tips on the outer primaries. There are two subspecies in the world, *vetula* in South Africa and *dominicanus* in Australasia**. Nest:** Nest site and clutch size is the same as that for Pacific Gull. **Status:** Vagrant, scarce. **Where to find**: Best chances on south coast between Bremer Bay and Cape Arid.

Lesser Crested Tern *Sterna bengalensis* subspecies *torresii* 38–42 cm

There are two subspecies in the world *torresii* visiting Australia's shores. A tern of tropical and subtropical waters common in the northern parts of Australia, easily seen in Broome. Does not pass the Shark Bay region and even then scarce in that area, greater chance in Carnarvon. One of the two shaggy crested terns of Australia the other being the Crested Tern which is common in the GSW. **Similar species:** Crested Tern which is a larger tern, bulkier in the body and thicker neck. Lesser Crested looks slimmer. The main features to look for is that Crested has a yellow bill and the Lesser Crested has an orange bill. In breeding plumage the crests on both species are pure black with no white streaking on the forehead and crests are more extensive at the rear. The important feature is that the black crest on the Lesser touches the base of the bill on the forehead but with Crested there is a white gap splitting the black crest from the yellow bill on the forehead. **Status:** Uncommon in the Carnarvon area, scarce in the Shark Bay area and rare further south. **Where to find:** Best north of the region from Exmouth north. Relatively common in Broome.

Common Tern *Sterna hirundo* subspecies *longipennis* 32–37 cm Vagrant

There are 3 subspecies in the world and any one may come to these shores. Common Tern is certainly a common tern in the northern hemisphere but in the GSW is scarce. It is far more common on the east coast of Australia and large numbers have been sighted in the Broome region in excess of 400 birds but those numbers are exceptional. In the GSW it has been sighted several times and the author has seen it in Mandurah. The problem with identifying the Common Tern is that it is very similar to the Arctic Tern which also breeds in the Northern Hemisphere and like the Common Tern it comes to Australian waters but less so than the Common Tern. **Similar species:** There are a few differences but all slight. The main feature is that the Arctic's tail passes the wings at rest whereas the Common is the same length. The Common is slightly larger, bulkier bird. The Arctic's bill is finer and shorter and legs are shorter. Its flight is slower and more graceful than the Common. **Status:** Rare in the GSW. **Where to find:** Can turn up anywhere like at the Eye Bird observatory beaches or any inlet but chance sighting only. Greater chance north of this region.

Arctic Tern *Sterna pardisaea* 28–35 cm Vagrant

Is monotypic and as mentioned under Common Tern, extremely rare in the GSW seen mostly after storms. Far less chances of seeing this species than Common Tern. Breeds in the far north of the Northern Hemisphere migrating in their winter to Antarctic waters. **Similar species:** Refer Common tern. **Status:** Rare. **Where to find:** Lower South West and southern coastline.

Common Redshank *Tringa tetanus* 27–29 cm

Vagrant

Certainly common in the Northern Hemisphere where it breeds but not here in Australia. Rare in the GSW with sightings on Rottnest and on some inland lake systems far more common in the far northwest particularly in the Broome region. An unmistakable medium sized wader with its long orange-red legs. Has an orange base to the bill with a black tip. In non-breeding plumage has similarities to Common Greenshank but has more streaking on the breast. In breeding plumage scapulars on the back become much darker brown and the throat and underbody become heavily streaked. Larger than a Marsh Sandpiper but smaller than a Common Greenshank. There are 6 subspecies in the world and it is not established yet what subspecies occur in Australia. **Similar species:** The closest is the Spotted Redshank which is even rarer in Australia than the Common Redshank so chances of seeing this species in the GSW is fairly remote. The Spotted is very similar being a slightly larger bird 29–31 with a slightly longer neck and head looks smaller in proportion to body. The bill is much longer than the Common Redshank on the Spotted it is 57 mm on the Common it is 43 mm a marked difference. In non-breeding plumage it is very difficult to split the birds and bill size, neck length and body size are better feature to split than plumage colour. The supercilium stripe is more pronounced on the Spotted and has a whiter underbody. In breeding plumage there is no mistaking the two, with the Common having an overall brown colouring with heavy brown-black markings. The Spotted has a complete black head, neck and underbody with distinct white edges to the scapular feathers on the back contrasting with black-brown centres. **Status:** Extremely rare in the GSW. **Where to find:** Best chance out of this region, very good chances in winter in the Broome region in the Kimberley.

Common Starling *Sturnus vulgaris* 21 cm

Introduced (NSW) Vagrant (WA)

Introduced to eastern Australia from Europe, the Common Starling has now spread to much of Australia including NSW, Victoria, South Australia, Tasmania and Queensland. Over the last twenty years or so, small flocks have been entering across the eastern border of Western Australia. A multicoloured bird with a metallic tinge to its plumage. Highly gregarious, flocking in huge numbers when flying to roosting sites. Has preference for urban environments but also has spread to farming areas. A pugnacious bird forcing many birds from their nesting sites particularly parrots. In fact once starlings have nested in a tree hollow other native birds will generally not return to the nest site, such is the odour left by these birds. This species is a major problem in the eastern states and is commonly seen feeding in fields, has a preference for urban environments with open grassed areas or cultivated fields nearbye. They are a major pest to orchardists damaging fruit. Birds have been expanding into Western Australia for many years now and birds are eradicated when sighted by the agricultural authorities. The author has seen first hand small flocks flying past Nullarbor Roadhouse just before the Western Australian border flying west towards WA. They are a problem in the Esperance region at this very time.

NOTE TO THE READER: Anyone sightings these birds in Western Australia should report these sightings to the Department of Agriculture and Food at their nearest regional office. They have an internet site: www.agric.wa.gov.au and a free call number 1800 084 881. Many people in Western Australia still have no idea what a major problem these birds can be so do phone in any sightings, you will be doing both farmers and birds a big favour.

Photo from donation collection Birds Australia – photographer unknown.

GLOSSARY

Arboreal: dwelling in trees.

Axillaries (axillars): the feathers at the base of the wing where the wing connects with the body. Example: Grey Plover in flight is identified from Golden Plover by these feathers.

Carpal: the region of the wing where it bends (anatomically at the wrist).

Cheek: the area on the side of the head, technically the 'jaw'.

Cline: a gradual change in the plumage or size of a species over its range.

Colonial: relates to species that nest or roost in groups colonially. Example: Banded Stilt.

Cosmopolitan: in this context a species found throughout much of the world.

Crepuscular: species that are active at twilight. Example: Letterwing Kite.

Decurved: a bill that is downward curving. Example: Eurasian Curlew.

Diurnal: active by day.

Dorsal: feathers on the upperbody.

Eclipse plumage: the dull plumage of the male followingthe breeding period showing some breeding colours. Example: All male waders particularly those from the Arctic that over -winter in Australia go through this stage; also male Fairy-wrens.

Endemic: species that are restricted in distribution within a country or region. Example: Western Spinebill is restricted to south Western Australia.

Family: the taxonomic order above genus, containing one or more genera.

Flight feathers: The longest wing feathers consisting of primaries and secondaries.

Gape flange: soft skin extending from the mouth often yellow as seen in young birds but occasionally is part of an adult bird's plumage as in Purple-gaped Honeyeaters.

Hackles: extended throat feathers.

Host: the species that incubates the eggs of a parasitic bird (typically the eggs of cuckoos) and raises the young of the parasitic species, mostly at the detriment of their own offspring.

Invertebrate: an animal lacking a spinal column or backbone such as molluscs, insects and worms.

Iridescence: the metallic or shiny effect seen when looking at certain species, feathers like the Shining Bronze Cuckoo. Feather colouring is created by two main pigments 'melanin' which produces black or dark brown colouring or carotenoids that produce red, orange and yellow feathers. Also contained in feathers is a protein known as 'keratin' and the translucent keratin reflects certain colours particularly the blues, greens and violets typically seen on the wings of bronzewing pigeons.

Jizz: a word to decribe the overall all shape of bird. It is extreemly important when one has little time to see a species and needs to identify it by shape and size alone.

Lore: (pl. lores; adj. loral) the area on the head between the bill and the eye. Sometimes it can be bare skin as in Great Cormorant but mostly feathered, typically seen in the female fairy-wrens.

Mandible: the lower part of the bill sometimes called lower mandible although we tend to use the plural to describe both upper and lower portions of the bill.

Monotypic: having only one type of species in a genus.

Morph: a colour variation in certain species such as Brown Falcon, is not consistent and has no taxonomic standing.

Moult: the occurrence when species shed their old feathers and replace them with new. This occurs with many birds and some like swans cannot fly during this period until they have developed new feathers.

Nocturnal: active during the night.

Palaearctic region: the biogeographical region in the northern hemisphere that includes North America and Eurasia south to the Himalayas.

Passerine: pertains to the largest Order of birds the Passeriformes, the 'perching birds'.

Pelagic: the term referring to the 'open seas' so pelagic birds are those that frequent the high seas most of their lives.

Plumage: refers to all the feathers on a bird and is also used to describe the colour changes that a species may go through when in moult or ageing.

Primaries: the largest outer wing feathers.

Raptor: refers to birds that have powerful claws and sharp talons used in tearing flesh from its prey. Mostly refers to the Falconiformes, the hawks and their relatives, but also includes the owls.

Secondaries: the wing feathers between the primaries and the body, which are attached to the ulna.

Secondary coverts: the feathers that cover both the primaries and secondaries consisting of the greater, median and lesser coverts.

Species: a single bird or other animal that collectively breeds within its own group and isolated from other groups.

Subspecies: a geographic population of a species that has developed marked differences either in plumage or size from the nominate race and retains their differing characteristics when breeding, however, when one population of subspecies overlaps with another they will interbreed producing intermediate characteristics known as hybrids.

Supercilium: a lateral area above the eye that often looks like an eyebrow, known as a superciliary stripe; is common in many birds including several honeyeaters and babblers.

Tarsus: a term that loosely describes the leg of bird although it truly applies to the lower limb of the leg.

Taxonomy: (adj. taxonomic) a scientific hierarchical classification of all plants and animals in terms of their relationship to each other.

Underbody: a loose term to describe all parts of a bird from the chin to the undertail coverts.

Upperbody: a loose term to describe all those parts of the upperbody but does not normally include the head or tail.

Vagrant: a species that is irregular or rare to a geographical area.

Vertebrate: all those animals that have a vertebral column, known as a 'backbone animal'.

Wattle: a fleshy appendage that hangs from the head or neck and is usually unfeathered bare skin, often brightly coloured as in the Red Wattlebird.

Glossary of terms used in the book to describe various vegetation habitats

Karri Forest: The tall Karri (*Eucalyptus diversicolor*) forests of the deep south west.

Jarrah–Marri Forest: The predominant eucalypts Jarrah (*Eucalyptus marginata*) and Marri (*Corymbia calophylla*) that form a forest band from north of Perth all the way to the south coast.

Wandoo Woodland: Refers to the beautiful white and grey barked Wandoo tree (*Eucalyptus wandoo*) that once was far more extensive in range than the Jarrah Forest but now has mostly been cleared for the Wheatbelt, hence the decline in several species particularly the western form of the Crested Shrike-tit (*leucogaster)* whose primary habitat was the Wandoo Woodland.

Salmon Gum Woodland: The extensive open woodlands that start in the eastern Wheatbelt, mostly remaining in remnant reserves. Past the Vermin Fence they occur as a natural woodland as far as Balladonia in the east. There are over 100 eucalypts within this belt but Salmon Gum (*Eucalyptus salmonophloia*) is one of the predominant trees characteristic of that region.

Banksia Woodland: Open woodlands where banksias are the dominant taller tree, normally with an understorey of shrub-heath.

Melaleuca Thickets: Dense stands of tea tree thickets normally to 1.4 m high. One of the favoured habitats of the Southern Scrub-Robin and the Shy Heathwren.

Mulga Woodland: Refers to one of the predominant acacias in the region, known as Mulga (*Acacia aneura*). The mulga is a vast vegetation zone that stretches right across from the west coast to the central parts of the eastern states. There is however a multitude of acacia species that grow in the zone.

Riparian: Refers to the denser vegetation that grows along stream and river systems.

Mangroves: Refer to the coastal mangrove forests that hug the mid west coastline. They are far more extensive further north and in the Kimberley with the variety of mangrove species becoming more diverse the further north one goes.

Mallee Woodland: Refers to the multi-branched eucalypt known as Mallee. It has the ability to always re-sprout after fire unlike larger eucalypts that may be killed by fire. Mallees are generally but not always multi-stemmed. Mallees grow a lignotuber, commonly known as a mallee root. It is in fact a basic trunk; the branches grow from the top of the tuber through the surface of the soil and the roots grow from the sides and base of the lignotuber. So when a fire comes through the mallee, only the exposed branches are burnt and the lignotuber, being a submerged trunk, survives and re-sprouts.

Kwongan Heath: Is a flora rich body of shrubs often no higher than 80 cm. These heaths can cover extensive areas as in the Fitzgerald River National Park. The Stirling Range National Park. Dunn Rock Nature Reserve. Tarrin Rock Nature Reserve and Lesueur National Park.

Scrub-Heath: Similar to Kwongan Heath but often has taller shrubs to 2 m.

Mallee–Heath: Predominately heath mostly to 1 m high but with scatterings of various mallee species throughout.

Samphire: Predominately samphires of the chenopod family. Succulent plants that can grow on high saline soils often on the edge of lake systems.

List of Latin names for some of the Eucalypts used in this book

Black morrel	*E. melanoxylon*
Coolabah	*E. victrex*
Jarrah	*E. maginata*
Karri	*E. diversicolor*
Marri	*Corymbia calophylla*
(All blood woods are now under the genus *Corymbia*)	
Merrit	*E. flocktoniae*
Powderbark Wandoo	*E. accedens*
Salmon gum	*E. salmonophloia*
Swamp yate	*E. occidentalis*
Tuart	*E. terminalis*
Wandoo	*E. wandoo*
Yate	*E. cornuta*
Tingle (yellow)	*E. guilfoylei*

READERS CHECKLIST

Possible land and shorebirds seen in the Greater South West

Does not include pelagic and extremely rare vagrants. Names based on Christidis and Boles nomenclature 2008. Birds highlighted in red are endemic to Western Australia. Birds highlighted in blue are introduced species. There are only two endemic species to Western Australia found outside the GSW and they are the Black Grasswren and the newly established Kimberley Honeyeater which was formerly grouped with the Northern Territory White-lined Honeyeater but has now been split as a distinct species.

	DATE	WHERE SEEN
Asian Dowitcher		
Australasian Bittern		
Australasian Darter		
Australasian Gannet		
Australasian Grebe		
Australasian Pipit		
Australasian Shoveler		
Australian Bustard		
Australian Hobby		
Australian Little Bittern		
Australian Magpie		
Australian Owlet-nightjar		
Australian Painted Snipe		
Australian Pelican		
Australian Pied Oystercatcher		
Australian Pratincole		
Australian Raven		
Australian Reed-warbler		
Australian Ringneck		
Australian Shelduck		
Australian Spotted Crake		
Australian White Ibis		
Australian Wood Duck		
Baillon's Crake		
Banded Lapwing		
Banded Stilt		
Banded Whiteface		
Barking Owl		
Barn Swallow		
Bar-tailed Godwit		
Baudin's Black-Cockatoo E		
Black Bittern		

Black Falcon		
Black Honeyeater		
Black Kite		
Black Swan		
Black-breasted Buzzard		
Black-eared Cuckoo		
Black-faced Cormorant		
Black-faced Cuckoo-shrike		
Black-faced Woodswallow		
Black-fronted Dotterel		
Black-shouldered Kite		
Black-tailed Godwit		
Black-tailed Native-hen		
Black-tailed Treecreeper		
Black-winged Stilt		
Blue-billed Duck		
Blue-breasted Fairy-wren		
Blue-winged Kookaburra		
Bourke's Parrot		
Brahminy Kite		
Bridled Tern		
Broad-billed Sandpiper		
Brown Booby		
Brown Falcon		
Brown Goshawk		
Brown Honeyeater		
Brown Quail		
Brown Songlark		
Brown-headed Honeyeater		
Brush Bronzewing		
Budgerigar		
Buff-banded Rail		
Bush Stone-curlew		
Cape Barren Goose		
Carnaby's Black-Cockatoo E		
Caspian Tern		
Cattle Egret		
Chestnut Quail-thrush		
Chestnut Teal		
Chestnut-breasted Quail-thrush		
Chestnut-rumped Thornbill		

Chiming Wedgebill		
Cockatiel		
Collared Sparrowhawk		
Common Bronzewing		
Common Greenshank		
Common Noddy		
Common Redshank		
Common Sandpiper		
Common Starling I		
Common tern		
Crested Bellbird		
Crested Pigeon		
Crested Shrike-tit		
Crested Tern		
Crimson Chat		
Curlew Sandpiper		
Diamond Dove		
Dusky Gerygone E		
Dusky Moorhen		
Dusky Woodswallow		
Eastern Barn Owl		
Eastern Curlew		
Eastern Great Egret		
Eastern Osprey		
Eastern Reef Egret		
Eastern Yellow Wagtail		
Elegant Parrot		
Emu		
Eurasian Coot		
Fairy Martin		
Fairy Tern		
Fan-tailed Cuckoo		
Flock Bronzewing		
Fork-tailed Swift		
Freckled Duck		
Galah		
Gilbert's Whistler		
Glossy Ibis		
Golden Whistler		
Great Cormorant		
Great Crested Grebe		

Great Knot		
Greater Sand Plover		
Grey Butcherbird		
Grey Currawong		
Grey Falcon		
Grey Fantail		
Grey Honeyeater		
Grey Plover		
Grey Shrike-thrush		
Grey Teal		
Grey-crowned Babbler		
Grey-fronted Honeyeater		
Grey-headed Honeyeater		
Grey-tailed Tattler		
Ground Cuckoo-shrike		
Ground Parrot		
Gull-billed Tern		
Hardhead		
Hoary-headed Grebe		
Hooded Plover		
Hooded Robin		
Horsfield's Bronze-Cuckoo		
Horsfield's Bushlark		
Inland Dotterel		
Inland Thornbill		
Jacky Winter		
Kelp Gull		
Latham's Snipe		
Laughing Dove I		
Laughing Kookaburra I		
Lesser Crested Tern		
Lesser Noddy		
Lesser Sand Plover		
Letter-winged Kite		
Little Black Cormorant		
Little Button-quail		
Little Corella		
Little Crow		
Little Curlew		
Little Eagle		
Little Egret		

Little Grassbird		
Little Penguin		
Little Pied Cormorant		
Little Tern		
Little Woodswallow		
Long-billed Corella		
Long-toed Stint		
Magpie Goose		
Magpie-lark		
Major Mitchell's Cockatoo		
Malleefowl		
Mangrove Grey Fantail		
Marsh Sandpiper		
Masked Lapwing		
Masked Owl		
Masked Woodswallow		
Mistletoebird		
Mulga Parrot		
Musk Duck		
Mute Swan I		
Nankeen Kestrel		
Nankeen Night-Heron		
New Holland Honeyeater		
Noisy Scrub-bird E		
Northern Mallard I		
Orange Chat		
Oriental Plover		
Oriental Pratincole		
Pacific Black Duck		
Pacific Golden Plover		
Pacific Gull		
Painted Button-quail		
Painted Finch		
Pallid Cuckoo		
Peaceful Dove		
Pectoral Sandpiper		
Peregrine Falcon		
Pied Butcherbird		
Pied Cormorant		
Pied Honeyeater		
Pink-eared Duck		

Pin-tailed Snipe		
Plumed Whistling-Duck		
Purple Swamphen		
Purple-crowned Lorikeet		
Purple-gaped Honeyeater		
Rainbow Bee-eater		
Rainbow Lorikeet		
Red Knot		
Red Wattlebird		
Red-browed Finch I		
Red-browed Pardalote		
Red-capped Parrot E		
Red-capped Plover		
Red-capped Robin		
Red-eared Firetail E		
Red-kneed Dotterel		
Red-necked Avocet		
Red-necked Stint		
Red-tailed Black-Cockatoo		
Red-tailed Tropicbird		
Redthroat		
Red-winged Fairy-wren E		
Regent Parrot		
Restless Flycatcher		
Rock Dove I		
Rock Parrot		
Roseate Tern		
Royal Spoonbill		
Ruddy Turnstone		
Ruff		
Rufous Fieldwren		
Rufous Songlark		
Rufous Treecreeper		
Rufous Whistler		
Sacred Kingfisher		
Sanderling		
Scarlet Robin		
Scarlet-chested Parrot		
Sharp-tailed Sandpiper		
Shining Bronze-Cuckoo		
Shy Heathwren		

Silver Gull		
Silvereye		
Singing Honeyeater		
Slaty-backed Thornbill		
Slender-billed Thornbill		
Sooty Oystercatcher		
Sooty Tern		
Southern Boobook		
Southern Emu-wren		
Southern Scrub-robin		
Southern Whiteface		
Spinifex Pigeon		
Spiny-cheeked Honeyeater		
Splendid Fairy-wren		
Spotless Crake		
Spotted Dove I		
Spotted Harrier		
Spotted Nightjar		
Spotted Pardalote		
Square-tailed Kite		
Star Finch		
Straw-necked Ibis		
Striated Heron		
Stubble Quail		
Swamp Harrier		
Swinhoe's Snipe		
Tawny Frogmouth		
Tawny Grassbird		
Tawny-crowned Honeyeater		
Terek Sandpiper		
Thick-billed Grasswren		
Torresian Crow		
Tree Martin		
Varied Sittella		
Variegated Fairy-wren		
Wandering Whistling-Duck		
Wedge-tailed Eagle		
Weebill		
Welcome Swallow		
Western Bowerbird		
Western Bristlebird E		

Western Corella E		
Western Gerygone		
Western Rosella E		
Western Spinebill E		
Western Thornbill E		
Western Wattlebird E		
Western Whipbird		
Western Yellow Robin		
Whimbrel		
Whiskered Tern		
Whistling Kite		
White-backed Swallow		
White-bellied Sea-Eagle		
White-breasted Robin E		
White-breasted Whistler		
White-breasted Woodswallow		
White-browed Babbler		
White-browed Crake		
White-browed Scrubwren		
White-browed Treecreeper		
White-browed Woodswallow		
White-cheeked Honeyeater		
White-eared Honeyeater		
White-faced Heron		
White-fronted Chat		
White-fronted Honeyeater		
White-naped Honeyeater		
White-necked Heron		
White-plumed Honeyeater		
White-winged Black Tern		
White-winged Fairy-wren		
White-winged Triller		
Willie Wagtail		
Wood Sandpiper		
Yellow White-eye		
Yellow-billed Spoonbill		
Yellow-plumed Honeyeater		
Yellow-rumped Thornbill		
Yellow-throated Miner		
Zebra Finch		

INDEX – Latin

INDEX – Common

Selected references

Barrett, G. et al. 2003, *The New Atlas of Australian Birds*, Birds Australia.

Beruldsen, G. 2003, *Australian Birds their Nests and Eggs,* G. Beruldsen, Kenmore Hills, Qld.

Brooker, M. I. H. & Kleinig, D. A. 2001, *Field Guide to the Eucalypts, Volume 2,* Bloomings Books.

Christidis. L. and Boles.W . E. 2008, *Systematics and Taxonomy of Australian Birds,* CSIRO.

Geering, A., Agnew, L. and Harding, S. 2007, *Shorebirds of Australia.* CSIRO.

Hayman, R., Marchant, J. and Prater, T. 1986, *Shorebirds. An identification guide to the waders of the world* Croom Helm.

Higgins, P. J. et al. 1990–2006 *Handbook of Australian New Zealand and Antarctic Birds Volumes 1 to 7,* Oxford University Press, Australia.

Jaensch, R., Vervest, R. and Hewish, M. J. 1988, *Waterbirds in Nature Reserves of South Western Australia 1981-1985,* Report No. 30, Royal Australasian Ornithologists Union.

Johnstone, R. E. and Storr, G. M. contributor Darnell, J. C. Volume 1. 1988, Volume 2. 2004, *Handbook of Western Australian Birds Vol. 1 & 2,* Western Australian Museum.

Morcombe, M. 2004 *Field Guide to Australian Birds*, Steve Parish Publishing.

North, A. J. *Nests and Eggs of Australia*, 1984, Oxford University Press, Melbourne.

Pizzey, G. and Knight, F. 1997, *Field Guide to the Birds of Australia*, Harper Collins.

Robson, C. 2002, *A Field Guide to the Birds of South-East Asia*, New Holland, United Kingdom.

Birding organizations in Western Australia

There is only one organization in Western Australia that concentrates purely on birds and that is the WA branch of Birds Australia which has its head office in Melbourne.

The WA office is located in the grounds of Bold Park. The address is as follows:

Birds Australia Western Australia
Peregrine House, 167 Perry Lakes Drive, Floreat WA 6014
Telephone (08) 93837749 Facsimile (08) 93878412
Email: mail@birdswa.com.au

The Birds Australia WA branch holds many birdwatching excursions. It also has regular talks held in the lecture hall close to the Perry Lakes Drive office. All members of the public are more than welcome.

The Birds Australia WA chapter also publishes a quarterly newsletter highlighting meetings, sightings and various activities or reports on conservation or birds.

Acknowledgements

The writing of this book between February and May 2008 was based mostly on personal experience but perhaps the main acknowledgments must go to two sources of reference. Firstly, the phenomenal series of HANZAB (Handbook of Australian New Zealand and Antarctic Birds) produced by Birds Australia. The senior editors and coordinators as well as the countless contributors have made this one of the benchmarks of Australasian ornithology. Without that reference much of the material pertaining to subspecies could not have been written and the author appreciates the painstaking task of assembling such a wealth of information.

Secondly, reference was made to the works of the ornithologist Ron Johnstone of the Western Australian Museum. Ron has done so much to pioneer research and understanding of Western Australian ornithology while at the same time always willing to help amateurs like myself in the past and I gratefully acknowledge the large body of works you have contributed to this state.

For this publication I have chosen not to trouble or seek information from any authorities regarding information on certain species, intending the book to stand own its own merits although I am sure some bird authorities will find fault in this approach, such is the world of birding. However, I must thank Leslie and Michael Brooker and also the wonderful ornithologists Ian and Eleanor Rowley, for assisting me with information on Variegated Fairy-wren and its distribution and relationship with Blue-breasted Fairy-wren. Also to the young researcher Jessica van der Waag for checking my notes on Malleefowl, thank you and all the best with your future studies, you have worked so hard on Kelly's precious bush block near Ongerup backed up by the Denning's.

Thanks to Ian Standring for your useful feedback and I am sorry I could not meet all of the suggested changes owing to the imminent 'burn out' factor and wanting to 'put the book to bed', but I really appreciate your advice and help Ian.

Thanks to Philip and Kathy Pain of Eagles Heritage Wildlife Centre in Margaret River, for allowing me the privilege of quiet photographic time with some of the precious raptors in your unique collection in the deep south west. You both work hard for little reward but give so much pleasure to so many visitors and residents of this state.

To June Hutchinson for painstakingly wading through and editing my draft copies of the text, it is never an easy task with Simon's writings. I appreciate it so much June but more so the gentle manner in which you tackle my works. For early help on text and advice from Diana Davies, I thank you. Also my good friend Pura Mohsenzadeh for checking the first few pages. Its important to note that there will be textual errors in this book but they are totally the responsibility of the author.

To friends Colin and Linda Andrews for your moral support, also to Sue Templeton and many other friends; their support was greatly appreciated.

For the images in this book other than the author's, the following contributors are gratefully acknowledged:

Graeme Chapman for supplying images from his collection, one of Australia's foremost bird photographers.

Michael Morcombe for supplying an image from his vast collection. Michael has produced a staggering quantity of books. For your support and friendship over the years, Irene and Michael, I thank you.

Adrian Boyle, for your image, thank you. You have years on me, Adrian, and your enthusiasm will take you far.

Alan Collins for his image of Pectoral Sandpiper.

Brett Barrett for the photograph of the rare Ground Parrot, kindly supplied by Brenda and Stephen Newbey.

To Leanne Quince, Graphics Above, for the biggest task of all, structuring Simon's concepts and designs into a presentable publication, thank you, Leanne, yet again.

Since giving up running birding tours, which certainly took its toll on my health for various reasons, I have become a little more reclusive in my activities and do not get involved as much in the social birding world as much as I could, preferring to seek solitude in the bush photographing this wonderful land and its nature. I have however been a member of Birds Australia since 1975. Over those years I have witnessed the many hard working amateur bird watchers who have given so much of their time and effort and in a small way I wish to thank them. We know that a few seek kudos by establishing themselves in positions of status, no more so than the birding world but it's the unsung heroes that the author wishes to recognise and mention.

In particular, to Bryce and Gail Wells for all the hard years of working tirelessly on both the Eyre and Broome Bird Observatories for little financial reward. Bryce, though you often say to me 'you're a gentlemen and a scholar', we know who the true gentlemen is. Your work promoting bird watching with young people is so needed in these challenging times for the youth of today.

To the late Alan Jones who not only in his teaching capacity but later in retirement did much to foster birding with the young and obtain many grants for Birds Australia, ably assisted by his supportive partner Rose. Western Australian birding will miss you.

To Perry and Alma de Rebeira who have worked for years with novice bird banders teaching them the skills of mist-netting and banding. To Liz Walker who has worked tirelessly in recent years for Birds Australia WA and also to the many other volunteers that assist with the running the Western Australian branch. To Shapelle McNee who I know so well and has done so much, to foster and improve research on some of our rarest Western Australian birds and is the last person in the world to seek status. We all love you dearly, Shapelle. To Rod Smith for all the years of hard work not only in the banding world but also in the running of Eyre Bird Observatory with George and Pam Agar. Also, likewise, all the volunteers at Eyre and Broome Bird Observatories.

To Frank O'Connor who has done much to assist the novice birdwatcher and help me on various tours, you're a good man Frank and wish malice to none. You will crack the big WA total soon I'm sure.

John Darnell has contributed greatly to the WA Museums records on wader movements within this state and few can match his vast knowledge on shore and pelagic birds a truly dedicated birdwatcher.

To John Lawson and Lisa Richards, caretakers in the Dryandra Woodland Reserve who have made my many visits to my bush retreat such a pleasure, as I am sure you have for so many.

There are of course some highly qualified ornithologists who have done more than their share in bettering the understanding of ornithology. As a very young man in the mid 70s I was privileged to accompany the late Dom Serventy on a few birding trips. He not only had a great wealth of knowledge but also was another true gentleman a man of a different era and definitely a true scholar who did so much to pioneer the early work in ornithology for this state. In the 1980s Roger Jaensch not only did extensive research into waterbirds and other groups of birds but gave so much back to all the amateurs within the society guiding and assisting people often thrice his age, we do not forget all the tireless work you did Roger even though it was so many years ago and it has been rarely matched to this day. Also the same for Doug Watkins.

Alan Burbidge is a another fine ornithologist who has not only contributed much to the knowledge of Western Australian ornithology but like Ron Johnstone has always given freely of his knowledge to me, I thank you Alan.

To anyone I have overlooked I sincerely apologies and wish you all many years of enjoyable birdwatching.